NATHALIE SARRAUTE

Nathalie Sarraute

A LIFE BETWEEN

Ann Jefferson

PRINCETON UNIVERSITY PRESS

PRINCETON & OXFORD

Requests for permission to reproduce material from this work
should be sent to permissions@press.princeton.edu

Published by Princeton University Press
41 William Street, Princeton, New Jersey 08540
6 Oxford Street, Woodstock, Oxfordshire OX20 1TR

press.princeton.edu

Library of Congress Cataloging-in-Publication Data

Names: Jefferson, Ann, author.
Title: Nathalie Sarraute : a life between / Ann Jefferson.
Description: Princeton : Princeton University Press, [2020] | Includes
bibliographical references and index.
Identifiers: LCCN 2019051178 (print) | LCCN 2019051179 (ebook) |
ISBN 9780691197876 (hardcover ; acid-free paper) | ISBN 9780691201924 (ebook)
Subjects: LCSH: Sarraute, Nathalie. | Poets, French—20th
century—Biography. | Women poets, French—20th century—Biography.
Classification: LCC PQ2637.A783 Z719 2020 (print) | LCC PQ2637.A783
(ebook) | DDC 843/.914—dc23
LC record available at https://lccn.loc.gov/2019051178
LC ebook record available at https://lccn.loc.gov/2019051179

British Library Cataloging-in-Publication Data is available

Editorial: Ben Tate and Charlie Allen
Production Editorial: Ellen Foos
Jacket Design: Leslie Flis
Production: Jacqueline Poirier
Publicity: Alyssa Sanford and Katie Lewis
Copyeditor: Joseph Dahm

Jacket photograph ©Isolde Ohlbaum

This book has been composed in Miller

Printed on acid-free paper. ∞

Printed in the United States of America

10 9 8 7 6 5 4 3 2 1

CONTENTS

Illustrations · ix
Preface · xi
Acknowledgements · xvii

BETWEEN WORLDS, 1900–21

CHAPTER 1. Russian Childhoods, 1900–05   3

CHAPTER 2. Between Petersburg and Paris, 1905–11   17

CHAPTER 3. Schooldays, 1912–18   32

CHAPTER 4. England, 1919–21   44

CHAPTER 5. Berlin, 1921–22   59

CHAPTER 6. Pierre Janet's Patient, 1922   67

TENTATIVE BEGINNINGS, 1922–44

CHAPTER 7. Independence, 1922–25   79

CHAPTER 8. Raymond   88

CHAPTER 9. Coming of Age with Modernism, 1923–27   95

CHAPTER 10. Marriage and Motherhood, 1925–33   102

CHAPTER 11. The First Tropism, 1932–34   112

CHAPTER 12. A Pause, 1935–37   119

CHAPTER 13. Publication, 1938–39   131

CHAPTER 14. Jewish by Decree, 1939–42   142

CHAPTER 15. In Hiding, 1942–44   156

AMBIVALENT ALLEGIANCES, 1944–58

CHAPTER 16. Saint-Germain-des-Prés, 1944–47   173

CHAPTER 17. The Elephant's Child, 1947–49   185

CHAPTER 18. New Horizons, 1949–53   196

CHAPTER 19. A Gallimard Author, 1953–56   211

CHAPTER 20. The Nouveau Roman, 1956–59   218

GOLDEN FRUITS, 1959–70

CHAPTER 21. "One of the Great Novelists of Our Time,"
             1959–62   235

CHAPTER 22. Nathalie Abroad, 1959–64   245

CHAPTER 23. A Reading Public, 1963–66   259

CHAPTER 24. Friendships   269

CHAPTER 25. "The Heroine of Post-Stalin Russia,"
             1960–67   283

CHAPTER 26. Radio Plays, 1962–72   296

CHAPTER 27. The Writing Life, 1964–68   304

CHAPTER 28. Revolution and May 68   311

CHAPTER 29. Israel, 1969   318

ON HER OWN TERMS, 1970–99

CHAPTER 30. The End and Afterlife of the Nouveau
        Roman, 1971–82   329

CHAPTER 31. Plays on Stage, 1972–88   343

CHAPTER 32. A Life and a Death, 1983–89   352

CHAPTER 33. The Last Decade, 1990–99   363

Notes · 381
Bibliography · 413
Index · 417

ILLUSTRATIONS

1. 29/12 Ulitsa Pushkina, Ivanovo, October 2017. (Author's photo) — 4

2. Ivanovo-Voznesensk, view of the manufacturing district, early twentieth century. (http://pavel -subbotin.livejournal.com/14373.htm) — 6

3. Natacha with her father in Moscow, 1904 or 1905. (Sarraute Family Collection) — 15

4. Polina and Kolya, 1909. (Sarraute Family Collection) — 21

5. Aftermath of the Fonarny expropriation, October 1906. (K. Bulla) (http://foto-history.livejournal .com/2315965.html?thread=34799549) — 23

6. Vera Tcherniak. (Sarraute Family Collection) — 26

7. Natacha and Lili, around 1911. (Sarraute Family Collection) — 29

8. Identity book issued to Nathalie Tcherniak, 1919. (Sarraute Family Papers) — 49

9. Cherwell Hall, summer 1921. Nathalie bottom left, Lena second from left in the back row, Miss Talbot centre of middle row. (Sarraute Family Collection) — 56

10. Nathalie, Assia Minor, Lena Liber, and "Eva," 1922. (Sarraute Family Collection) — 82

11. Raymond Sarraute, 1930s. (Sarraute Family Collection) — 89

12. Nathalie with Claude, 1927. (Sarraute Family Collection) — 106

13. Nathalie, Claude, Anne, and Dominique, summer 1933. (Sarraute Family Collection) — 110

14. Red Square, Moscow, 1935. (Sarraute Family Collection) — 122

15. The gardener's house, Janvry, June 2016. The house next door is the former bakery. (Author's photo) — 158

16. Identity card issued in the name of Nicole Sauvage. (Fonds Nathalie Sarraute, Bibliothèque nationale de France) — 162

17. Chérence, April 2011. (Author's photo) — 200

18. Nathalie with Maria Jolas in Chérence, 1960s. (Sarraute Family Collection) — 202

19. Dominique Aury, Jean Paulhan, and Marcel Arland in Paulhan's office at Gallimard, 1953. © D.R. Coll. J. Paulhan / Paris. — 215

20. With Robbe-Grillet, 1963. (Sarraute Family Collection). — 221

21. The Nouveau Roman photo. © Mario Dondero / Ed. Minuit / Leemage. — 225

22. Mary McCarthy interviewed by Jean-François Revel, *New York Times*, 16 May 1971. © Bruno Barbey, Magnum Photos. — 274

23. With Monique Wittig, Chérence. © Sande Zeig. — 279

24. Occupation of the Hôtel de Massa, 21 May 1968. Nathalie third from the left. © René Pari, *Le Figaro*. — 314

25. With Jean Ricardou, Nouveau Roman Colloquium, Cerisy-la-Salle, July 1971. © Archives Pontigny-Cerisy. — 333

26. *Isma*, directed by Claude Régy. With Pascale de Boysson, Gérard Depardieu, and Dominique Blanchar, 1973. © Archives Nicolas Treatt. — 345

27. Nathalie in the 1980s. © Daniel Psenny. — 370

"I ALWAYS SAY that I don't have a biography. Biography is nothing." "I don't think you can write a valid biography of anyone." "Biographies are always wrong."[1] Nathalie Sarraute's condemnation of biography was unambiguous, and the verdict on this one has been declared in advance: "I'm very glad to know that I won't be reading it," she remarked. "I'm sure that everything will be wrong."[2] The prospective biographer has been warned.

This hostility towards biography was shared by many others of a literary generation who heard Roland Barthes announce "the death of the author," and who had grown up under the tutelage of Proust, "against Sainte-Beuve" and the practice of reading literature through the lens of the author's life. Nathalie Sarraute herself was categorical: "Explaining the work through the life seems totally aberrant to me."[3] Biography was in any case bound to be a falsification because for her, as the poet Rimbaud reputedly said, "life is elsewhere." It certainly wasn't in the bird's-eye view of the biographer, who will condense a lifetime into a few hundred pages, and cannot hope to do justice to the feeling of life as it is lived from moment to moment: "Life is made up of changing, fluid moments, constant flux, differently coloured moments, and what I experienced fifteen minutes ago is different from what I'm experiencing now or will experience this evening."[4]

A related problem is the tendency of biography to reduce its subject down to a single identity, ignoring the fact that "a human being is so complex that, sometimes, when I think about someone, first one aspect appears, and then another and then it all disintegrates. There's no overall picture."[5] Having grown up in France as the daughter of émigré Russian Jews, Nathalie Sarraute knew only too well how labels that fix an identity—whether foreign, Jewish, or female—can be used to segregate and exclude. For all these reasons, biography was bound to appear as a negation of her own experience and the convictions that underpinned her writing.

She was always adamant that, while her writing was true to her own inward psychological experience—where life is lived from moment to moment and where no individual can be reduced to a single identity—she never portrayed the external events of her life in her work. "There are hardly any scenes in my books that are taken directly from my own experience," she would say, a point she sometimes repeated in even starker terms: "I never drew on my own life, except for fleeting sensations, but nothing continuous."[6] Until the eve of her eighty-third birthday, when she published *Childhood*, this is largely true.

But if the life is not in the work, the work was most definitely in a life about which she once said, "Ultimately, I've only ever lived for an *idée fixe*" and "the only real adventures were books."[7] There were in fact other adventures, but the chronological perspective of biography is particularly well suited to an author for whom writing was a constantly renewed search for something that she never quite captured. This sense is encapsulated in her oft-repeated formulation "the achievement is in the pursuit," which she almost certainly invented and misattributed to the nineteenth-century English poet Robert Browning. Or as she said in her own words, "I write in order to try and portray something that eludes me."[8] This intangible something was the psychological reality whose exploration she made her own: the semiconscious, involuntary reactions that underlie all human exchange, and to which she gave the name "tropisms." By pausing to pay attention to these reactions, which are barely registered in everyday life, she reveals an internal underworld of frequently violent dramas of attraction and repulsion, of fear and what—in a phrase borrowed from Katherine Mansfield—she called the "terrible desire to establish contact."[9] Her work tracks these unseen dramas in a variety of contexts and external circumstances, some of which were indeed based on her own lived experience, but were never portrayed or acknowledged as such.

Born in tsarist Russia a few months into the twentieth century, she died in Paris less than three months before its end, and she was affected by some of that century's major historical events—the First World War, the Russian Revolution, the Second World War, and the German Occupation of France—as well as by the social transformations that had such an impact on the lives of women. She was cosmopolitan in outlook, spoke four languages, and maintained close connections with England, Germany, the United States, and Russia. And while carving out a path of her own, she was also associated with some of the foremost cultural figures and literary movements in twentieth-century France, from Sartre and *Les Temps modernes* to Robbe-Grillet and the Nouveau Roman. But despite having links with many worlds, she was never fully part of any. Always at odds or to one side, her self-chosen place was invariably *between* rather than within.

Much the same can be said of the material available to her biographer, where she remains elusive. She didn't keep a diary, and there is very little personal correspondence. She donated her manuscripts to the Bibliothèque nationale, but did so with a forty-year embargo on the grounds that "the formless things I write for myself are entirely personal," and that as a result "readers would just come up with misleading interpretations."[10] These manuscripts will not be available until 2036. Her engagement diaries from the 1950s onwards provide a record of the many people she knew and frequented, and some of these friends and acquaintances subsequently published memoirs where she is recalled. Such correspondence as there is (some two dozen boxes also bequeathed to the Bibliothèque nationale) mostly concerns her professional activities and dates from the second half of her life when her belated literary career finally began to take off. Letters were in any case not her natural medium. "It's as if letters required another language, a language I don't possess," she explained; and she confessed to one of her correspondents that "it's difficult to appear sincere in a letter. Everything immediately becomes frozen in conventional formulae."[11]

Her natural medium was the spoken word, in face-to-face exchange or on the telephone, that quintessentially twentieth-century means of communication. There are consequently only a few surviving traces of a lifetime's talk, for which the term "conversation" might suggest something too formal. But she was an adept at the interview, a practice that has been an integral part of literary culture since the mid-twentieth century. Those she gave for newspapers, literary journals, radio, and television provide an invaluable if not always entirely consistent record of autobiographical information and comment. She claimed—with some justification—that she had an excellent memory.

In what follows I have had recourse to all of this material. I have also drawn on *Childhood* and the eighteen-page biographical "Chronology," which she contributed to her *Complete Works*. A lightning visit in 2014 to her weekend house just before it was sold gave me the chance to glance through the contents of her library there, and I have generously been given access to papers that remained with the Sarraute family. Interviews of my own with a number of her surviving friends, acquaintances, and family members have been a further invaluable resource.

And I have my own memories, which go back to the start of my time as a graduate student in the early 1970s when, awestruck, I visited her at her home in Paris and was quite unprepared for the warmth and informality of her welcome. I had first discovered her work in 1969, when more than half of it remained to be written, and I was immediately and enduringly drawn to it. I attended talks she gave in London and in Oxford, where I would sometimes accompany her on visits to the places she had known as a student at the university. From the late 1980s we met regularly during the preparation of her *Complete Works*, for which I edited some of the texts. But I claim no special privilege for these memories. It never occurred to me—nor, I suspect, to her—that I might one day find myself writing the story of her life. Thanks to this acquaintance I came to know her as "Nathalie," but always referred to her in an academic context as "Nathalie Sarraute" or even just "Sarraute." For the purposes of the biography she will, however, be "Nathalie" in order to mark the difference between the life and the work, and not to imply any presumption of intimacy.

Her views about biography were in fact more nuanced than many of her pronouncements would suggest. She had her own interest in the lives of writers: George Painter's biography of Proust was on her bedside table where I saw it in her weekend house twelve years after her death; Virginia Moore's life of Emily Brontë was just one of several literary biographies in her library; and she herself professed great enthusiasm for Dostoevsky's correspondence, which she persuaded her publisher Gallimard to bring out in a French translation.

"I couldn't tear myself away from it," she once admitted in an interview, explaining that "you're glad to discover what was happening and to find out about a whole society, a whole milieu, a whole period, and Dostoevsky's responses as seen by his friends and his brother." She nevertheless insists that for all this fascination, "the real Dostoevsky is elsewhere, in his work."[12] The life has its place, so long as it doesn't become a substitute for the work.

Indeed, there would appear to be a law of cultural inevitability whereby the "work"—whether that of Dostoevsky, Proust, or even Nathalie Sarraute—will sooner or later find itself complemented by the "life": a companion piece drawn into being by the gravitational pull of the writing, enhancing it through the addition of a further dimension, and giving it a context rather than imposing an interpretation. A decade and more on from her death, it seemed to me that the time had come to submit to this pull and that to continue to deny this to Nathalie would be to do her a greater disservice than the one she was once so sure that this biography would be.

ACKNOWLEDGEMENTS

THIS LIFE OF NATHALIE SARRAUTE—a slightly revised and up-dated version of the French translation that has already appeared in France—owes its existence to her daughter, Dominique Sarraute, who convinced me to write it, while leaving me free to do so as best I thought. Our conversations over the past seven years have pro-vided friendship, encouragement, and information in equal mea-sure. My debt to her is incalculable.

Nathalie Vierny gave me access to papers remaining in the Sar-raute family, which have continued to be an invaluable resource, and Antoine Vierny lent me the key to no. 12 rue de l'Église in Chérence, where I was able to look through Nathalie Sarraute's library. Olivier Wagner of the Bibliothèque nationale, who took over the responsi-bility for the Sarraute archive from Guillaume Fau, has been an unfailing support: his knowledge of the archive, his understanding, and his responsiveness to my numerous requests have gone well beyond the requirements of mere professionalism.

I am immeasurably indebted to Daniel Lee, who directed me to a number of historical sources, unearthed documents, and made sense of unfamiliar catalogues. I am equally indebted to Evgenia Molkova, who has been an essential and extraordinarily generous guide to Ivanovo-Voznesensk, past and present. I thank them both for their reading of the relevant chapters. Irina Zorina helped me revive my rusty Russian and opened windows on a Russian literary past, supplemented for the Soviet period by Barbara Heldt and Gerry Smith, who kindly read the chapter on the Soviet Union. Arnaud Rykner, who knows more than anyone else about Nathalie Sarraute's theatre, answered queries and read the chapters on the plays. Claire Boniface has been an indefatigable, self-appointed lit-erary *nark* for all things Sarraute-related: several of her finds have found their way into the book. I thank her and Brigitte Loir for an illuminating evening spent with their reading group, *Voix au chapitre*.

Georges Lomné introduced me to the Gilbert Gadoffre Archive at the Université Paris-Est Créteil Val de Marne; Armande Ponge equipped me with a tailor-made archive of documentation about the relations between Nathalie Sarraute and her father Francis Ponge; Hélène Catsiapis and the Association amicale des anciennes et anciens élèves du Lycée Fénelon welcomed me to one of their weekly gatherings and passed on a treasure trove of information; Lucile Roussier accompanied me in my exploration of Janvry; and Olga Danilova spent a precious afternoon Googling Russian websites with me.

I have been constantly touched by the kindness of strangers who have responded unstintingly to enquiries. Among these are Caroline Barrera, Philippe Delvit, Peggy Frankston, Pierre Moulinier, Natalia Tikhonov-Sigrist, Mme Torrione-Vouilloz of the Archives administratives et patrimoniales de l'Université de Genève, the archivists of the Lilly Library, Bloomington, St Anne's and St Hilda's Colleges, Oxford, and the William Alwyn Archive at the Cambridge University Music Department.

I am also grateful to the staff of the Bibliothèque nationale de France; the Inathèque; the Taylorian Library in Oxford; the Beinecke Rare Book and Manuscript Library at Yale University; the Ivanovo State Archive; the Archives nationales de France; the Archives de la ville de Paris; the IMEC in Caen; the Archives du Mémorial de la Shoah, Paris; the Institut d'histoire du temps présent (IHTP-CNRS); and the Bibliothèque Jacques Doucet.

Much enlightenment and a great deal of pleasure came from interviews with the late Annie Angremy, Fernando Arrabal, François-Marie Banier, Jean-Damien Barbin, Tom Bishop, the late Jean Blot, Paule du Bouchet, the late Michel Butor, the late John Calder, Hélène Cixous, Hélène Comay, Marie Darrieussecq, Max Dorra, Jean-Pierre Faye, Françoise Guyon, Betsy Jolas, James Knowlson, Arno Mayer, Nicole Minor, Géralde Nakam, the late Georges Raillard, Claude Sarraute, Nora Scott, Philippe Sollers, Jean-Yves Tadié, Olivier Tcherniak, and Nathalie Vierny.

David Bellos, Françoise Benassis, Marietta Chudakova, Serge Gavronsky, Stéphane Gumpper, Adam Guy, Emmanuelle Jacquot, Jean-Louis Jeannelle, Alice Kaplan, Catriona Kelly, Jack Klempay, Christian Limousin, William McMorran, Valerie Minogue, Michel

Sarraute, Florent Serina, Alexis Tadié, and Sande Zeig have been the source of invaluable information and documents of various kinds. Leo Shtutin produced illuminating summaries and analyses of the novels by Nathalie Sarraute's mother when they defeated my own limited competence in Russian. My French translators Pierre-Emmanuel Dauzat and Aude de Saint-Loup were a constant source of editorial wisdom, Ellen Foos steered the volume through production with unfailing goodwill and professionalism, while Ben Tate and Mary Leroy provided encouragement from a very early stage.

The book has been further nourished by conversations with Didier Alexandre, Françoise Asso, Sheila Bell, Sylvie Cadinot, Rolande Causse, Anne Fuchs, Monique Gosselin, Carrie Landfried, Hermione Lee, Ève Morisi, Michel Murat, Philippe Roussin, Tiphaine Samoyault, Anne Simonin, Susan Suleiman, Céline Surprenant, Alexandr Taganov, Pierre Verdrager, Martine Boyer-Weinmann, and Martha Zuber.

I am grateful to a number of institutions which have made the writing of this book possible: the British Academy for a BA/Leverhulme Small Research Grant; the Faculty of Modern Languages, Oxford for travel funds; the Fondation Maison des Sciences de l'Homme for a six-week invitation in the summer of 2014; the Eugene Ludwig Fund at New College, Oxford for a contribution towards translation costs; and the Institute of Advanced Studies in Paris where I held a fellowship in 2016 with the financial support of the French State, programme "Investissements d'avenir" managed by the Agence Nationale de la Recherche. The working conditions, the conviviality, the intellectual stimulus, and the beauty of the surroundings in the Hôtel de Lauzun on the Île Saint-Louis have all left a real if intangible mark.

Rainier Rocchi shared his unparalleled knowledge of the Sarraute bibliography, offered constant encouragement, and meticulously read the entire book in draft. The text has benefitted hugely from Elisabeth Ladenson's editorial energies and her salutory reminders of the needs of readers. Michael Holland has lived with the project throughout its duration; his support, knowledge, library resources, and editorial expertise are woven into the fabric of the entire text.

In sum, I have been blessed with the greatest support. I thank every person I have listed here—many of whom are owed thanks under several headings—and ask forgiveness from any I have failed to name.

Note: References to Nathalie Sarraute's works are to the published editions listed in the bibliography. Where English translations of cited works exist, references are to these. Occasional modifications to the translations in quoted extracts are signalled by an asterisk attached to the page reference. All other translations are my own.

Between Worlds, 1900–21

CHAPTER ONE

Russian Childhoods, 1900–05

ON A LATE OCTOBER MORNING in 1990 Nathalie Sarraute returned to the house at no. 29/12 Ulitsa Pushkina in the Soviet industrial town of Ivanovo, where she had been born ninety years
earlier. Throughout her life she had retained the memory of a long,
single-storey wooden building with intricately carved window surrounds of the kind found all over Russia, and a few examples of
which still exist in Ivanovo. This "immutable image" is vividly recalled in *Childhood* as a fairy-tale vision that encapsulated the Russia she had left behind forever at the age of eight.[1] But the house
Nathalie found on that cold October morning was not at all as she
had for so long remembered it: in reality, it was a solid, stone-built,
two-storey dwelling, which had fallen into serious disrepair. The
paint was peeling, the stucco was crumbling, the roof had been
patched up with corrugated iron, and steel panels were propped
along the front to keep out rain and melting snow. Nathalie was
photographed beneath the wooden archway that led to the now neglected grounds, but she didn't venture inside, as the house had
long since been turned into *kommunalki*, the one-room apartments
introduced under Stalin in the 1930s. It was a homecoming of sorts,
but not the one she had for so long imagined.

Much else had also changed. The child born as Natalia Ilyinichna
Tcherniak to Ilya Evseevich Tcherniak and his wife Polina Osipovna

FIGURE 1. 29/12 Ulitsa Pushkina, Ivanovo, October 2017. (Author's photo)

on 5 July 1900 in Ivanovo-Voznesensk had long since acquired a French name and French nationality. The Julian calendar used in tsarist Russia had been replaced by the Gregorian calendar, bringing her birthdate forward to 18 July; under the Soviets Ivanovo had dropped the Voznesensk component of its hyphenate; and the streets on whose corner the house stood had both been renamed. Just over a year later, in December 1991, the Soviet Union itself would collapse, almost seven decades after its foundation.

In 1900 the house on what was then Mikhailovskaya Ulitsa had been one of two brand-new dwellings, converted from a pair of disused textile-printing workshops by the widow of a local industrialist, and rented out as living accommodation. The Tcherniak family occupied the first floor in the larger of the two, and it was here that Natacha (as she was always known) spent the first two years of her life.[2] But impermanence was written into her childhood from the start, and in 1902 her parents separated. Polina left Ivanovo with Natacha, while Ilya stayed behind. No longer requiring family accommodation, he gave up the lease on the apartment and subsequently took lodgings at two other addresses on streets whose names have also changed.[3] And so, despite its solidity as an edifice, the house where Natacha was born had no lasting place in her life except as the false memory of a childhood home that had never existed.

Documentary evidence of her birth has proved equally insubstantial. The file in the Ivanovo Regional State Archive recording births and deaths at the turn of the century contains no trace of Natalia Ilyinichna Tcherniak. Nor is there any record of her elder sister, Elena, who, according to Nathalie herself, died probably in Ivanovo-Voznesensk, almost certainly in 1899, and very likely at the age of three. However, the Tcherniaks were Jewish, and under the tsarist regime, births, marriages, and deaths were documented in church registers. In 1900, at a time when there were fewer than two hundred Jews out of a total population of fifty-four thousand, Ivanovo-Voznesensk had no synagogue and no rabbi to register the death and the birth of the Tcherniaks' small daughters.[4] There was thus no administrative structure through which the very existence of Natalia Tcherniak could be given official acknowledgement. This absence established a pattern that would recur throughout her long life, where the world didn't always seem willing to accommodate her and where recognition would all too often appear wanting.

Ivanovo-Voznesensk was an unlikely place for the Tcherniaks to have settled. They had had no previous connection with the city until Ilya moved there in 1900 to set up a small dye-manufacturing business. Known as "the Manchester of Russia" for its textile production, Ivanovo had grown from modest flax-weaving origins in the early eighteenth century to become the centre of Russia's largest industry, incorporating the neighbouring suburb of Voznesensk as production expanded. By the end of the nineteenth century, imported cottons had replaced locally grown flax, while weaving and fabric printing had been mechanised and were carried out in large factories, which employed ever-increasing numbers of workers. Technical experts were required for some of the processes, including the production of the mineral dyes used in the printed calicos for which Ivanovo was renowned. As a qualified chemical engineer, Ilya Tcherniak had been encouraged to move to the city by one Vassiliy Lavrentievitch Mokeev, who lent him the money to set up a chemical dye business of his own.[5]

FIGURE 2. Ivanovo-Voznesensk, view of the manufacturing district, early twentieth century. (http://pavel-subbotin.livejournal.com/14373.html)

He was born Israël Evseevich Tcherniak on 13 November 1869 in Monastyrshchina, a small urban settlement on the bank of the River Vikhra in what is now the Smolensk Oblast.[6] Home to a sizeable population of Jews—including the Hebrew-language novelist Peretz Smolenskin—Monastyrshchina was in the Pale of Settlement, the vast swathe of western Russia, present-day Poland, and Ukraine to which Russian Jewry had been confined since the end of the eighteenth century. Israël was one of several siblings, and his father was a guild merchant, which gave him the right to trade. He dealt in timber and was almost certainly affluent enough to have his sons educated at one of the local schools for Jewish children.[7] However, strict quotas in higher education drove Jews abroad, and in 1892 Israël (as he still styled himself) became a student at the University of Geneva. After taking courses in botany and mineralogy, he graduated in chemistry in 1896 and, inspired by Carl Vogt, the much-revered professor of geology and zoology, obtained a doctorate in physical sciences a few months later.[8] The Geneva address on his university file is 21 rue de la Roseraie.

This is also the address given for Polina Osipovna Chatounov-skaia, who had joined the university in 1893, taking an eclectic mix of courses in political economy, history of civilisation, general history, archaeology, and linguistics. She dropped out in the winter semester of 1895–96 without taking a degree.[9] Polina had been born Khina Perl in 1867 in Ukraine and was later known to her family as Paula.[10] Nathalie herself claimed that her mother was born in what was then Elizavetgrad (subsequently renamed Kirovograd and then Kropyvnytskyi) in central Ukraine, that she was orphaned young and was brought up by her elder brother who became a famous mathematician. This was undoubtedly Samuil Osipovich Shatunovsky, whose biographical record indicates that he was born in March 1859 in Znamenka on the Dnieper River into a large family of poor Jewish artisans, although in later life Polina claimed that she descended from Russian aristocracy.[11] In any case, Samuil, who studied in Saint Petersburg and later taught at the University of Odessa, was perhaps not the ideal parent substitute for the unabashed narcissist that Nathalie always made her mother out to have been.[12]

Ilya and Polina both exemplify the transition that took place in the last decades of the nineteenth century amongst educated Russian Jews. Whereas their parents were mostly religiously observant and Yiddish-speaking, for this younger, cosmopolitan generation, Jewishness was essentially a cultural rather than a religious category, from which there emerged a new Jewish intelligentsia who sought assimilation, education, and new ideas. They Russified their Jewish first names—Ilya for Israël, Polina for Khina Perl—and were not observant. Their languages were Russian with supplementary French, and there is no evidence that, as adults, either of Natacha's parents ever spoke Yiddish. For them, being Jewish was a fact to be neither concealed nor advertised, and they considered it bad manners to mention ethnicity at all. However, the world in which they lived proved less respectful of this courtesy.

No. 21 rue de la Roseraie in Geneva may have been a boarding house for Russian students, which would explain how Ilya and Polina met. Geneva attracted a large number of young Jews debarred from studying in Russia, who formed their own émigré society. Exposed to new ideas, many became politicised and acquired revolutionary aspirations in response to the increasingly harsh anti-Semitic regulations introduced by Alexander III after the assassination of Alexander II in 1881.[13] Although neither of them seems ever to have been involved in political activism, Ilya and Polina both had Socialist Revolutionary sympathies, and Ilya was a party member.[14] The Socialist Revolutionaries were eventually eclipsed by Lenin's Social Democrats, from whom they differed in their belief that revolution would be brought about by the peasants rather than by Russia's small urban proletariat and that the intelligentsia (many of whom were in exile) would lead the political awakening of the country's destitute peasantry.[15]

The abrupt end to Polina's studies, which coincided with the completion of Ilya's degree course, suggests that the couple got married at this time. The hypothesis has a certain plausibility given that Natacha's elder sister supposedly died at the age of three in 1899. Elena—known as Liolia—would therefore have been born in 1896, and this may well have been the reason why Polina failed to complete her studies.[16] According to Nathalie's later accounts of her parents' early life, Ilya abandoned an academic career in order to be able to provide for his wife. The arrival of a child would have made this an even more pressing requirement. But exactly what became of the Tcherniak couple during the following three years is a mystery. It's possible that they headed for Ukraine, from where Polina's family originated, and where another brother, Grigory Shatunovsky, a lawyer, figures in the 1895 business directory for the town of Kamyanets-Podilskyi in western Ukraine.[17] Documents in the Ivanovo archives allude to a diploma that Ilya had gained at the St Vladimir Imperial University in Kiev, and these further qualifications would certainly explain how he had obtained sufficient expertise to go into business manufacturing mineral dyes.

The Tcherniaks first surface in the annals of Ivanovo during the year 1898–99 in association with the local Temperance Society. They may have seen membership of the socially enlightened society as a means of being accepted as Jews: one of the most prominent charitable figures in Ivanovo-Voznesensk was a Jew by the name of M. M. Jakub, who taught at the technical school, ran a library, and had considerable influence on the cultural life of the town.[18] But being Jewish, Ilya nevertheless required authorisation to reside and conduct business outside the Pale of Settlement, and on 28 April 1900 he was granted official permission to settle in Ivanovo-Voznesensk. A certificate dated 10 June 1900 confirmed that he had "acquired possession of an establishment for the preparation of mineral colours."[19] The little factory—a wooden building located close to the Sokovsky Bridge on the River Uvod in the centre of Ivanovo-Voznesensk—initially had just three employees. In *Childhood* Nathalie later recalled visiting her father's place of work and having to negotiate a muddy courtyard, avoiding puddles of all colours before reaching the interior with its beaten-earth floor, its chemical reek, and the laboratory benches where Ilya, dressed in a white coat, was absorbed in scrutinising test tubes clamped to wooden rods. His energetic and scrupulously professional devotion to work comes through in all Nathalie's memories of her father. An active figure in the Ivanovo-Voznesensk branch of the Russian Technical Society, he evidently succeeded in acquiring some social status as well as making a success of his business.[20]

Polina's experience of Ivanovo-Voznesensk was very different from that of her husband. She was no doubt grieving for Liolia, who had died of scarlet fever the previous year, but while Ilya was establishing his colourant factory, she was pregnant with Natalia. In the absence of reliable information about the date of Liolia's death, it's impossible to know whether Natacha was conceived as a substitute for the dead girl or as her younger sister. But either way, her first years were lived in the shadow of the baby with the beaded cap and the startled gaze who looked like Polina, and whom Natacha knew only from a photograph kept by her father. Growing up in the wake of a dead sibling, she was always aware of death hovering on the periphery of her childhood.

She was cared for by a nursemaid, leaving Polina with time on her hands in the cultural backwater of Ivanovo-Voznesensk, where she was almost certainly better educated than the wives of the other industrialists, who may also have been reluctant to mix with Jews—even assimilated and cosmopolitan Jews like the Tcherniaks. Cultural life in the town was mostly geared to the working population, which had the benefit of two circuses, eight "electric theatres" providing entertainment in the form of proto-cinematic moving images, and three conventional theatres, one of which was occasionally

visited by theatrical troupes from Moscow. All this offered slim
pickings for a cultivated woman who, like Flaubert's fictional Madame Bovary, found herself bored by provincial life and no doubt
longed for real drama and perhaps a real lover who would carry her
off to a more exciting world. Flaubert's heroine suggests itself as a
more appropriate analogy than the similarly frustrated three sisters
in Chekhov's 1901 play of that name, as records from the municipal
police files indicate that Natacha had originally been called
Emma.[21] This was an unusual first name for a French woman, let
alone for the daughter of Russian Jews, and in naming the child
after Emma Bovary, Polina was acting entirely in the spirit of the
extravagantly literary gestures Flaubert ascribes to his fictional
protagonist.

Having literary ambitions of her own, she was evidently not content with gestures. A little over two years after the Tcherniaks' arrival in Ivanovo-Voznesensk, she announced that the marriage was
over and that she would be going abroad. The divorce that later
followed was a rare occurrence at the time, and Ilya saw to the necessary administrative procedures. The first of these was the belated
certification of Natacha's birth as the prerequisite for equipping her
with a passport. On 5 April 1902 he applied to the municipal police
department requesting a document to present to the rabbi of
Nizhny-Novgorod and Vladimir confirming that a daughter, Natalia, had been born to himself and his wife on 5 July 1900. He included witness statements from two doctors and a midwife, who
had attended the birth. It was only when Ilya collected the documents on 25 April 1902, almost two years after her birth, that Natalia Ilyinichna Tcherniak finally acquired official certification of her
existence. Polina applied to the Police Department on 4 May for
permission to travel abroad with her young daughter, accompanied
by a nursemaid from one of the neighbouring villages. She gave ill
health rather than marital breakdown as her reason for leaving the
country, but strangely includes her original Jewish first name (Khina
Perl) in the document, and even more bizarrely describes Ilya as a
dentist. Ilya added a note to say that he had no objection to his wife
and daughter going abroad. Authorisation was granted by the end
of May, and Polina departed taking Natacha with her.

Polina never returned, and although Natacha came back to Ivanovo on subsequent occasions to visit her father, she was too young to have retained any memories of the first two years of her life. As far as memory was concerned, those years were a blank to be conjured into existence through hearsay and wishful thinking. She had left nothing solid behind and had put down no roots. Her parents had separated, and it was several decades before she saw them together again. At the last minute, further splits had emerged as they hesitated between Russian and Jewish versions of their names, and a fancifully literary alternative to Natacha's own name had appeared in the police files, along with a strange redefining of her father's profession. Fiction and inconsistency presided over her departure for a different country and a different kind of childhood.

There's no record of the journey that took Polina, Natacha, and the nursemaid to Europe. But they must have travelled on the overnight train that still takes passengers from Ivanovo to Moscow. From there they would have embarked on one of the long railway journeys with which Natacha would later become familiar as she shuttled between divorced parents, France and Russia. Polina's first destination was Geneva, which required a change in Berlin, and before that, as for all trains leaving Russia for Western Europe, a change of gauge at the Prussian border. In later years, Nathalie would recall the waiting room at the border station in an image that recurs elsewhere in her work as one of bleak desolation. The journey to Geneva would have taken at least three days, or more if it involved an overnight stay in Berlin.

Polina's reasons for going to Geneva, the place where she had studied at university and met the husband she was now divorcing, remain obscure. But she didn't stay for long, Geneva being in the words of Joseph Conrad "the respectable and passionless abode of democratic liberty, the serious-minded town of dreary hotels, tendering the same indifferent, hospitality to tourists of all nations and to international conspirators of every shade."[22] Although she had allegedly been expelled from school for distributing revolutionary literature, Polina was not much interested in conspiracy, and soon left for Paris, a more exciting destination, where she settled with a new husband, Nikolai Petrovich Boretzky-Bergfeld.

The man whom Natacha always knew as Kolya was a writer and historian. Born in May 1880 in Tiflis, he was thirteen years younger than Polina and is known as the author of three authoritative histories, one of Hungary, one of Rumania, and one titled *The Colonial History of Western European Countries*. They were published in quick succession in Russia between 1908 and 1910, and the histories of Hungary and Western Europe are sufficiently well regarded to have been republished in 2013 and 2015. There's no indication that Kolya ever studied in Geneva, but perhaps there were other reasons for the couple to meet there. The speed of their relocation to Paris certainly suggests that they had known each other previously and had perhaps been conducting their relationship by correspondence during the three years that Polina spent in Ivanovo-Voznesensk. At any rate, unlike Emma Bovary, she had found the lover who would provide her with an escape from her marriage and open the way to a new life in Europe's most culturally vibrant capital. Kolya was first and foremost a human passport to a cosmopolitan cultural world and the opportunity for Polina to establish herself as a writer, both of which had been so frustratingly lacking in industrial Ivanovo.

On their arrival in Paris, Polina and Kolya took accommodation in the fifth arrondissement on the rue Berthollet, just off the rue Claude-Bernard, before moving to a small, sparsely furnished apartment around the corner at no. 3 rue Flatters. In one of the interviews she later gave to a Russian journalist, Nathalie mentions that her mother placed her in a "pension" for a while, perhaps because the Russian nursemaid, about whom nothing further is known, had returned home.[23] This stay, however brief, must have been a brutal immersion into a foreign language and an even more brutal separation from Polina. The neighbourhood was home to a Russian émigré community, many of them driven out of Russia for their political views. There was a Russian library close by on the Avenue des Gobelins run by a poetry-loving Menshevik, who supplied readers with Russian-language newspapers. A Socialist Revolutionary canteen served Russian food not far away on the rue de la Glacière, and a nonpartisan restaurant in the rue Pascal was known for its *bitochki* and indifferent borsch. But it was discussion rather than food that drew the émigrés together, until the talk turned to politics, when rival allegiances would drive them apart again.[24]

The Russians were not the only new arrivals in an increasingly cosmopolitan Paris. Picasso had come from Spain in 1900, as had the German painter Paula Modersohn-Becker. Her friend the sculptor Clara Westhoff had recently married Rainer Maria Rilke, who lived in the same neighbourhood as Natacha's recombined family. Newcomers to Paris were struck by the speed of the traffic, the height of the double-decker horse-drawn trams, the endless clanging of the bells on the omnibuses, the bawling newspaper sellers, and the sheer size and bustle of the crowds in the streets. Many of them also remarked on the hats worn by the Parisians, especially the huge feathered concoctions favoured by the most fashionable women.[25] The city was a world away from Ivanovo-Voznesensk.

The Russian émigré community was a largely adult one, and the little apartment in the rue Flatters was no exception. Natacha was cared for by a French nursemaid with whom she must have spoken French, but whose habit of dousing her hair in vinegar to treat migraine did not encourage intimacy. Evenings were spent in adult company as Polina, Kolya, and their Russian friends talked into the night, until someone carried Natacha off to bed. Except for the ghostly presence of her dead sister, Natacha had no experience of other children, and her first and only contact with girls and boys of her own age was at the École Maternelle in the rue des Feuillantines. Situated at the upper end of the rue Claude-Bernard, it was a very different place from the former convent on the same street where Victor Hugo and his siblings had played a century earlier, and which he recalled in poems that generations of French children learned by heart in primary school.

At the age of three Natacha found herself plunged into an unfamiliar French-speaking institution, which she later compared to a children's penal colony whose inmates, wearing clogs and black pinafores, spent their days marching single-file round a bare courtyard.[26] Since the neighbourhood was largely working class—as the mention of clogs indicates—her companions almost certainly belonged to a world that was socially, culturally, and linguistically very different to her own. Middle-class children of that age would normally be kept at home to learn their first rudiments from their mothers or a nursemaid. Offering noncompulsory education to children between the ages of two and six, and attended by only 25 percent of the child population, nursery schools existed in practice to provide daycare for working parents. For Polina, this was no doubt its main purpose. Children were introduced to reading and writing at the age of five, and it was here that Natacha first encountered written French.[27] She later dated her real initiation into the French language to this experience.

Her life was lived between several alternating worlds—Paris and Russia, mother and father, and two versions of childhood. With Polina and Kolya, childhood took the form of premature access to adult life, which mostly meant that Polina would be absorbed in her writing, while Natacha's demands for attention would be met with a "you can see very well that I'm busy."[28] With Ilya, by contrast, she was allowed to be a child. Having lost one daughter to scarlet fever, he was evidently determined not to lose a second to divorce. He travelled to Paris to visit her, or had her join him for holidays in Switzerland, and sometimes arranged for her to come either to Ivanovo-Voznesensk or to Moscow where he now had an apartment. It was Ilya, and not Polina, who taught her to count and to recite the days of the week, who invented pet names for her—Tashok, Tashotshek, and Pigalitza (little sparrow)—sang lullabies when she couldn't sleep, bought her a coat in which she looked as pretty as a picture, and would kneel down to help her put on a new pair of gloves.[29] One way of describing all this is to say, as she later did, that she was horribly spoiled by her father, but, in contrast to Polina's distracted indifference, his attentions exhibit devoted paternal concern for his young daughter.

The childhood photographs of Natacha are almost all taken at her father's instigation, their cardboard mounts stamped with the names of professional photographers in Moscow and Ivanovo. However, the photograph where Ilya appears in profile and Natacha is dressed in frilled white and stands, legs akimbo, on a Turkish rug amongst potted plants and occasional tables was taken not, as Nathalie claimed, in the family home in Ivanovo, but by a Moscow photographer, in Ilya's apartment, or even in the photographer's own studio, where something off camera has evidently startled them both. The idea that Ilya had remained in Ivanovo as the guardian of her childhood home was another illusion.

FIGURE 3. Natacha with her father in Moscow, 1904 or 1905. (Sarraute Family Collection)

Nathalie's account of her early years in *Childhood* balances French and Russian versions of this time with idealised images of each: the Jardin du Luxembourg for Paris, and for Russia an idyllic summer spent with her Shatunovsky cousins in Kamianets-Podilskyi. The scenes in the Luxemburg Gardens are decked out with the features that appear in so many other literary accounts of Parisian childhood, with the model boats in the pond, the hoops, the statues of the kings and queens of France, the Punch and Judy show, and the merry-go-round, which is the subject of a poem of that name by Rilke.[30] The holiday with Uncle Grisha's family in Kamianets-Podilskyi, with its images of fond parents, family meals, outings in a horse-drawn carriage, games with cousins, loyal family retainers, and a kind-hearted coachman, is bathed in an atmosphere that recalls Tolstoy's evocation of his own early years in the first of his three autobiographical volumes, also called *Childhood*.

As remembered in Nathalie's *Childhood*, both scenes—the Luxemburg Gardens and the Russian country house—are portrayed with an awareness of their stereotypical character, derived from literary models that were almost too good to have been true. They are glimpses of a life that Natacha never quite had, but which she had been granted "on loan," as if to offset more complex and unstable realities, holding out the promise of a childhood to which she remained—as she later said a certain kind of writer always was—"morbidly attached."[31]

CHAPTER TWO

Between Petersburg and Paris, 1905–11

LIFE CHANGED AGAIN WHEN, in late 1905, Polina and Kolya returned to Russia, and, after a summer spent with Ilya, Natacha
joined them in Saint Petersburg. They occupied an apartment at no.
8 Ulitsa Bolshaya Grebietskaya (later renamed Ulitsa Pionierskaya)
in an up-and-coming new neighbourhood on the so-called Petro-
grad Side. On the northern bank of the River Neva, the area was
very different in character from the gloomy and slightly sinister
Saint Petersburg familiar from Gogol and Dostoevsky. The architecture was modern and stylish, and no. 8, while not the grandest
building on the street, was lavishly appointed with stucco mould-
ings, a spacious entrance hall, a lift, and a uniformed doorman.
(The building has since lost some of its stucco, and the ground floor
houses a slightly garish beauty parlour.) The Boretzky-Bergfeld fortunes had improved, no doubt because, with his three histories in
the offing, Kolya was able to live more comfortably from his pen. A
nursemaid, Gasha, was hired to take care of Natacha.

The couple had, however, returned to Russia at a time of dramatically increased political unrest, triggered in January 1905 by
Bloody Sunday, when a crowd of unarmed petitioners demonstrat-
ing outside the Winter Palace was fired upon by the Imperial Guard.
The result was a massacre. Strikes and further violence ensued,
as revolutionary groups saw a chance to press for further change.

Left-wing terrorists embarked on a programme of assassination of government officials. Right-wing extremists, many of whom blamed Jews for the recent revolutionary initiatives, responded by instigating a new wave of pogroms, in which the ultra-nationalist and xenophobic Black Hundreds played a key role.

Ilya was directly affected by the political repercussions in Ivanovo-Voznesensk. A strike amongst local textile workers in May 1905 led to the creation of the first Russian Soviet, which set out demands for reforms, such as an eight-hour working day, safer conditions on the factory floor, paid sick leave, and health and education provisions. When these demands were not met, a general strike was called, and on 3 July the tsarist authorities retaliated, opening fire on an outdoor meeting and indiscriminately killing dozens of workers. The general strike was eventually called off following concessions made by the employers, but disruption returned in the autumn, when pogroms targeted homes and business of several Jews. Ilya wasn't harmed, but he was vulnerable as he had joined a small Jewish prayer group and was a member of the board, which included some of those whose homes were wrecked in the attacks.[1] This is the only trace of any active religious affiliation on his part, and his reasons for joining the group were almost certainly social. However, it made him a potential target for the anti-Semitism that he had first encountered on his arrival in Ivanovo-Voznesenk, when one of his workers had objected to taking orders from "a Yid."[2] Concluding that it was no longer safe for them to remain in Ivanovo, several Jews left the town for good, and Ilya may well have retreated to the security of his apartment in Moscow.

Meanwhile, Kolya and Polina were making the most of being back on home territory and soon established themselves in the capital's literary and cultural world. Visitors to the apartment in the Ulitsa Bolshaya Grebietskaya included the writer and journalist Vladimir Korolenko, editor of the influential monthly journal *Russkoe Bogatstvo* (Russian Wealth). Considered "the most attractive representative of idealist radicalism in Russian literature," Korolenko was a social critic and revolutionary, who at the time was heading a campaign against military law and capital punishment.[3] His journal had previously been associated with the Narodniki (forebears of the Socialist Revolutionaries), but in the first decade of the twentieth century it was allied primarily with the Popular Socialists, a dissident wing of the party. Although Polina's interests were literary rather than political, it was thanks to Korolenko that she was able to publish some of the work whose creation absorbed her for so many hours of Natacha's childhood.

Despite this absorption, Polina's output was far smaller than Nathalie later suggested. She published just two novels and submitted a few short stories to literary competitions, using the masculine pseudonym of N. Vikhrovsky, whose choice Nathalie attributed to its root in the word *vikhr'* (whirlwind), but which may also have been suggested by the name of the river in Ilya's hometown, the Vikhra.[4] Her first novel, *Ikh Zhizn* (Their Life) was serialised in 1918 in *Russkoe Bogatstvo*, but when the journal ceased publication towards the end of the year because of the Civil War, the unpublished chapters were lost.

In a letter of 1918 to the literary critic Arkady Gornfeld, Korolenko acknowledged Gornfeld's negative opinion of *Ikh Zhizn*, but goes on to say that he considers Polina's novel worth publishing since, for him, her writing has "a certain original truth."[5] This was a generous view, and one more easily maintained in 1918 than a century later when there is little appetite for Polina's artificially quaint literary manner. Set in a village at an unspecified date, and somewhat lacking in narrative focus, the novel offers an unremittingly dismal picture of provincial life through a disconnected array of characters. Strangely, given the period in which it was written and the political allegiance of the journal in which it appeared, there is no attempt to provide any social analysis of these bleak circumstances. At the same time, the focus on individual fate is not supported by any developed sense of psychology. With no solid narrative core and no central protagonist around which to organise the material, the novel's lack of coherence is no doubt due to its piecemeal composition over an extended period.

Undaunted by the curtailment of the publication of *Ikh Zhizn*, and convinced that she was "a great genius," Polina carried on writing.[6] Her second novel, *Vremya* (Time), appeared in 1932, when it was brought out by an émigré publisher in Berlin. It maintains the literary idiom of the first novel, but with an added hint of autobiography. Like *Ikh Zhizn*, it's set in a nonspecific small provincial town, but being an overnight train ride away from Moscow, it recalls Ivanvovo-Voznesensk. The characters are predominantly artisans, like Polina's father, although there is no reference to any of them being Jewish. One is a watchmaker, but time, which gives the novel its title, is generally stagnant and, as in *Ikh Zhizn*, life is squalid. Not surprisingly, several of the characters long for Moscow, as do the characters in Chekhov's *Three Sisters* and much as Polina herself must have done in Ivanovo-Voznesensk. No mention is made of external political events, but unlike the previous novel, *Vremya* makes some attempt to advance a social statement about the lives of people in the provinces, and particularly the lives of women.

It also attempts a slightly greater degree of psychological realism, but there is little subtlety to the portrayal of the largely stereotypical characters, and with its contrivedly folksy style, the novel remains a conventional and anachronistic affair. Polina's generic protagonists and her tendency to lapse into melodrama are the obverse of the literary principles that in the future would underpin the writing of her daughter.[7] However, in speaking more favourably about Polina's talent than the results might appear to warrant, Nathalie later attributed her own literary aspirations to a gift which, despite their differences, she considered she had inherited from her mother.[8]

Natacha's relations with Kolya—who never attempted to adopt the role of father—were warm and affectionate, but an episode recalled in *Childhood* defines Natacha as a "foreign body" when, as she tries to join a mock tussle between Kolya and Polina, Polina rebuffs her with the words "Husband and wife are on the same team."[9] Linked by their common interest in books and writers, the couple shared a world to which Natacha did not fully belong. Human relations were literary relations, and happy families were literary families—as they were in the version of the card game Natacha sometimes played in the evenings with her nursemaid and the other servants, where "Happy Families" consisted not of parents and children but of the works of a given author: *Anna Karenina*, *The Kreutzer Sonata*, and so on for Tolstoy, *Fathers and Sons*, *Sketches from a Hunter's Album*, and so on for Turgenev.

Kolya and Polina were always reading, and Natacha joined them in this activity, becoming a voracious reader in her turn. Books were places where a solitary child could go in search of a substitute fam-

FIGURE 4. Polina and Kolya, 1909. (Sarraute Family Collection)

ily, and they introduced her to worlds she could share with other children who continued to be absent from her own life. Some grew up in happy families, like the heroine of Mme de Ségur's *Misfortunes of Sophy*, whose endearing misdeeds were usually forgiven by her understanding mother. (A hugely successful author of children's books, Mme de Ségur was an early example of a Russian-born writer who found a place in French literature.) Many of the books also depict less than perfect family lives, like that of the young hero of Hector Malot's *Nobody's Child*, who is launched into a precarious existence when he is sold by the drunken husband of his foster mother.

Reading had its necessary complement in writing, and it was in the Russian language that Natacha first mastered penmanship. After briefly attending school in Saint Petersburg, she continued her education in a more haphazard way with a private tutor at home. (Ilya had objected to the school's pedagogical methods.) Nathalie's large, confident handwriting, quite unlike the script taught in French schools, was formed in her Petersburg years, where, in emulation of both Kolya and Polina, she also put it to creative use. The result—as later recounted by the adult Nathalie in an interview with a journalist and again in *Childhood*—was in Polina's literary manner. But her juvenile literary ambitions were aborted when the family friend she remembered as Korolenko advised her to learn to spell before trying to write stories.[10] In all, books provided a complex strategy for dealing with home life, offering both a means of becoming part of the not-quite family constituted by the Boretzky-Bergfeld household and an escape from it into an alternative world.

However, external events intruded into Natacha's life with what proved to be lasting, if not immediately obvious, repercussions. In mid-October 1906, a few months after her arrival in Saint Petersburg, a group of revolutionaries carried out an armed raid on a carriage transporting state funds. It was one of the most daring and spectacular of the many terrorist attacks, which in the month of October alone numbered 121, along with 362 so-called "expropriations." As the carriage rounded the corner at the intersection of Fonarny Pereulok with the Ekaterinsky Canal (now Griboedov Canal), a bomb was thrown, setting off a violent explosion; the carriage was surrounded by a group of well-dressed young revolutionaries, and several bags of money were seized before the mounted guard escorting the carriage opened fire, killing four of the attackers. Some of the bystanders were injured in the ensuing shootout, and in all 366,000 of the 600,000 roubles in the carriage were stolen. The authorities, who were now cracking down on all

FIGURE 5. Aftermath of the Fonarny expropriation, October 1906. (K. Bulla)
(http://foto-history.livejournal.com/2315965.html?thread=34799549)

forms of revolutionary activity, immediately rounded up eleven
suspects, eight of whom were summarily executed on the night of
31 October.[11]

The Tcherniak family were drawn into the affair when the police
suspected Yakov Tcherniak—Ilya's youngest brother whom Natacha
knew as Uncle Yasha—of having participated in the attack, or at the
very least of having helped prepare the bomb. Like Ilya, Yakov had
studied chemistry in Geneva, where he gained a doctorate and came
under the influence of exiled Socialist Revolutionaries. On returning
to Russia, his political views had hardened, and he joined the dissident Maximalists, a quasi-anarchist group who broke away from
the Socialist Revolutionary Party with a more impatient approach
to the revolution, supporting both excessive terror and a strategy of
"expropriation" to fund their political activities. Yakov's knowledge
of chemistry would certainly have been useful for the creation of
explosives, and it's possible that he did indeed help to make the

bomb used in the Fonarny raid. He may also have had a part in the bomb used a few months earlier in an assassination attempt against the interior minister, Stolypin, which killed twenty-eight people and injured several others, including two of Stolypin's children. But at the time of the Fonarny attack, Yakov was in Paris and had been abroad for several weeks.[12]

Lured to Stockholm by a telegram purporting to come from a Maximalist associate but which may in fact have been sent by the Russian secret police, Yakov was arrested on arrival and imprisoned in response to Russia's demand for his extradition. Ilya intervened on behalf of his younger brother, hired a lawyer, and enlisted the help of Sweden's sole Socialist deputy, Karl Branting, who ran a press campaign protesting against the extradition order. Other European socialist groups joined in the protest, and, throughout the month of February, under the auspices of the socialist leader Jean Jaurès, the French socialist newspaper *L'Humanité* reported on the Tcherniak case, beginning with the letter sent by Jaurès to the Swedish foreign minister, which roundly condemned the demand for Yakov's extradition.

The Swedish newspaper *Sozialdemokraten* also published a carefully worded letter from Ilya Tcherniak accusing the Swedish chief of police of anti-Semitism for having claimed that Russian revolutionary extremists were all Jews. While acknowledging that years of oppression had led many Jews in Russia to take an active part in the campaign for freedom, and that his brother had participated in the 1905 revolution in Russia, he also claims that, at the time, everyone in Russia was to a greater or less extent a revolutionary. He categorically denies that his brother had any part in the Fonarny raid. The letter was republished in French in the March number of *La Tribune russe*, the Paris-based monthly journal of the Socialist Revolutionary party, which carried a whole dossier devoted to Yakov Tcherniak.

When the Russian police failed to provide written evidence to support the extradition order, the Swedish government climbed down and released Yakov who by now had lost weight and grown a large beard. He boarded a steamer in Göteborg under a false name and set sail for Antwerp, where Ilya had arranged to meet him. However, when the ship arrived on the morning of 13 February 1906

Yakov was found dead, having succumbed to noxious gases whose source was never identified. Three other passengers also died, and there was a strong suspicion that the Okhrana, the tsarist secret police, was responsible. Representatives from socialist parties across Europe gathered a few days later for a funeral that attracted several thousand mourners and lasted for several hours. The ceremony was attended by a Russian rabbi at the request of Yakov's grief-stricken parents who were too frail to make the journey.

Nathalie often told the story of her Uncle Yasha's association with the Fonarny raid and its aftermath, mentioning that an unsent postcard addressed to her had been found on his body. She also emphasised the amount of publicity the case received and seemed proud of the unprecedented recognition that had been granted to a member of the Tcherniak family by such well-known figures as Jean Jaurès, Karl Branting, or even, as she would have it, the king of Sweden. But death had once again come close, this time through a fond uncle, whom Natacha remembered from his visits to the rue Flatters, and whose physical resemblance to her father only fed her constant terror that Ilya might die. In later years she described death as an "obsessive fear" which she had had "since always—since early childhood." And, she adds, "I never stop thinking about death. The least happiness is contaminated and destroyed by the thought."[13]

As a result of this episode, it was impossible for Ilya to return to Russia, and he settled in France, trading the status of Jew in Ivanovo for that of Russian émigré in Paris. The move had consequences that would eventually determine the course of the life of his daughter. But for the time being, Natacha's annual visits to her father continued as before, except that the direction of travel was now reversed as she made the two-day journey from Saint Petersburg to Paris on the luxurious *Nord Express* with its embossed leather-lined compartments, its blue upholstery, and the silver dining service in the restaurant car. These details were later recalled by Vladimir Nabokov who regularly took the train with his family in the same years, and with just one year's age difference, the two future writers may have passed each other in the corridor or glimpsed each other across the aisle in the well-appointed dining car.[14]

Ilya was obliged to start afresh, and the Établissementss Tcherniak opened in 1910 in Vanves, just outside the Paris city limits. By

FIGURE 6. Vera Tcherniak. (Sarraute Family Collection)

1924 it had fourteen employees, who included one Russian, one Pole, a Belgian foreman, two French secretaries, a Belgian concierge, and eight workers on the factory floor, of whom four were French, one Belgian, and three Czech. This was probably a more cosmopolitan workforce than most other local businesses, and with Ilya's dedication, it flourished. During the First World War the little factory supplied dyes to two companies working for the Ministry of Defence, and eventually established a reputation for its reds, one of which is officially known as "Tcherniak Red."[15]

In addition to rebuilding his professional life, Ilya had also acquired a new personal life, and in January 1909 he married Vera Sheremetievskaya. Born in Moscow on 26 September 1885 (old style), she was sixteen years his junior. They had met in Moscow, but as Vera wasn't Jewish, permission to marry in Russia could be granted only on condition that Ilya convert to Christianity. He refused to claim beliefs that he did not sincerely hold, and it seems that he and Vera had been living as a married couple for some time before their union became official, since accounts of Yakov's funeral refer to Ilya and his "wife."[16] The move to France obliged Vera to spend the rest of her life in exile, and although her grandfather, an officer by the name of Charles Feue de la Martinière, had been French, she herself never fully mastered the language.

After a brief stay in the rue du Loing, the couple set up home in the rue Marguerin around the corner in the fourteenth arrondisse-ment, where the Tcherniaks inhabited a world of largely Russian-speaking émigrés. Many of these were political refugees, such as Vladimir Lvovich Burtsev, editor of several periodicals, and V. N. Agafonoff, leader of the Socialist Revolutionaries in Paris and au-thor of a book about the foreign activities of the Okhrana. Between 1909 and 1913, Lenin and his wife Krupskaya lived in the nearby rue Marie-Rose. Nathalie often mentioned that her father played chess with both Lenin and Trotsky in the Café du Lion at Denfert-Rochereau, where Russian émigrés would congregate, and where Lenin held political meetings. During the First World War, Ilya sub-scribed to the Paris-based Russian political newspaper *Nashe Slovo*, co-edited by Trotsky and described by Trotsky's biographer as being along with Lenin's *Social Democrat* "the laboratory of the revolu-tion."[17] In *Childhood*, Nathalie recalls others whose names do not appear in the history books, but who had also lived for their political beliefs and very often paid heavily for them. She describes these melancholy exiled revolutionaries in glowing terms as "extraordi-nary human beings, . . . heroes who faced the most terrible dangers without flinching, who stood up to the Tsar's police, threw bombs" and who, even at the point of death were ready to cry, "Long live Revolution! Long live Liberty!"[18]

In early 1909, Polina sent Natacha to join her father a few months ahead of her usual summer stay, ostensibly because Kolya needed to travel abroad for his research. Polina was responding very fast to Ilya's recent marriage. There may also have been a hint of malice in wishing Natacha on the new couple just as they were setting up home and, although Polina would not necessarily have been aware of this, when Vera was pregnant with the couple's first child. There was no sense that this would be a permanent arrangement, but

Nathalie's memory of the journey from Saint Petersburg is fraught with retrospective anguish at parting from her mother who left her in Berlin. This was the moment when, as Nathalie later said, her childhood was "definitively broken," and she made the last tearful leg of the journey to Paris accompanied by a family friend, given the honorific title of "uncle."[19]

It wasn't the first time Natacha had met Vera whom she recalled from a previous visit to her father, when he was lodging in the rue Boissonade. The street was a double cul-de-sac between the boulevard du Montparnasse and the boulevard Raspail, and housed a floating cosmopolitan population, including several painters, and a number of Russians. Its bohemian character is captured in Natacha's memory of dancing with a young woman dressed in men's clothes, who was not yet her father's second wife.[20] However, the Vera of the rue Marguerin was a very different quantity, and Nathalie almost always referred to her not as her *belle-mère* (stepmother) but as her *marâtre*, the French word for stepmothers of the wicked variety. It didn't help that, unlike Polina who prided herself on her looks, Vera was physically unprepossessing, with thin lips and protruding lower teeth. When Lili was born in August, Vera's neurotic devotion to her own child and Natacha's summary expulsion from her bedroom in favour of the new baby made it very clear to her that, as Vera was soon to say, this was not her home.[21]

Lili, whose real name was Hélène in a strange resurrection of Ilya and Polina's first-born daughter, was by all accounts a sickly and difficult child, whose screams and tantrums dominated the household. Natacha never established a close relationship with her younger half sister—as the studio photograph of the two girls (probably taken around 1911) eloquently suggests. It cannot have been easy for Vera to have become both stepmother and mother in a short space of time, especially while Ilya was absorbed in setting up his new business. But she seems to have made no effort to hide her reluctance to accommodate her husband's child, and when Polina failed to send for her after the summer, Natacha found herself between two homes, in neither of which she felt she had a place.

This situation became starker some eighteen months after Natacha's arrival in Paris, when Polina forced a decision by refusing to come in person to take her back to Saint Petersburg. Ilya wasn't

FIGURE 7. Natacha and Lili, around 1911. (Sarraute Family Collection)

willing to return Natacha himself unless she specifically wished it, thus confronting her with a painful choice. She chose to stay, but at the cost of having appeared to reject the mother whom she nonetheless missed sorely. This much is evident from the message she wrote on the back of a studio photograph that Polina and Ilya sent from Kerch in Crimea for Natacha's ninth birthday. Natacha writes (in Russian), "The photo is so dear to my heart [and] all my life as I look at the photo I will think that there is a person who loves me and it's Mama."[22] However, another photograph of the couple a year or two later has a message from Natacha to her mother alone. Writing in both French and Russian, she thanks Polina for "a first and perhaps even last portrait," and signs "Nathalie Tcherniack, Paris," as if to assert a French identity and indicate that there was now a geographical, linguistic, and emotional distance between them. The distance was confirmed when, in 1911, Polina curtailed her only visit to Natacha in Paris, declaring that Ilya had turned her daughter into a "monster of egotism."[23] Natacha was once again made responsible for her mother's rejection.

An escape from family tensions was provided by school. Natacha was initially sent to a small private establishment run by Les demoiselles Brébant, where she relearned the basics of written French before joining the local primary school in the rue d'Alésia. It helped that Russian "Natalia" translated so easily into a recognisably French "Nathalie." In any case, it was a matter of principle for the French schools of the Third Republic that no child should be treated as a "foreign body," and that differences of race, class, nationality, or religion were invisible in a system designed to educate the nation's future citizens. This was a world in which Natacha thrived, and she soon excelled, earning the affection and interest of her teachers. School also provided a private channel of communication with Ilya who, in the absence of a son, was only too happy to encourage his daughter's academic ambitions. Natacha and he would discuss her homework, and she would give him the results to read before submitting them to her teachers whose good opinion mattered to her. Russian remained the language of home, but she learned to write in French and took considerable pleasure in her mastery of the language.

French was also the language of most of the books that she read, and they became another refuge from the emotional tensions of home, while offering a sympathetic portrayal of the lives of orphans and unwanted stepchildren. Stepparents abound in the literature of the nineteenth century. *David Copperfield*—often mentioned in *Childhood* in conjunction with Hector Malot's *Nobody's Child*— tells the story of a boy with a cruel stepfather, who knew what it was like to lose a family home but was nonetheless parented by a series of maternal and paternal substitutes. Families are forcibly separated in Harriet Beecher Stowe's *Uncle Toms' Cabin*—another favourite of Natacha's—but in this case parental love is undimmed by adversity. She wept most over the death of Uncle Tom himself, perhaps because, as Ilya had once been, he was separated from his own children. Her greatest devotion was to Mark Twain's *The Prince and the Pauper*, where Edward, the son of Henry VIII, and Tom Canty, the unloved son of a beggar and thief, exchange places, each a foreign body in an alien world where neither is recognised for who he really is.

French authors considered suitable reading for children, such as Pierre Loti and René Boylesve, provided Natacha with examples of written style, which she successfully emulated in her French compositions, while *Rocambole*, Ponson du Terrail's multivolume adventure novel, offered simple, straightforward escape. When Vera's mother came to stay with her daughter for several months, she introduced Natacha to classics of both French and Russian literature which they read together. Educated at the Smolny Institute for Noble Maidens in Saint Petersburg, "Babushka" spoke perfect French, and for the duration of her stay in the Tcherniak household, she became the grandmother that Natacha had never had, sharing a love of literature that Lili never acquired.

Babushka's return to Moscow was a great loss, and from then on Natacha's links with Russia were mainly in the form of the postcards she received from Polina, and occasionally Kolya. Alongside requests that Natacha write more often, there are frequent references to Polina's headaches, and on one occasion to a cricked neck that prevented her from holding a pen. They both continued to write as if to a much younger child, describing an outing to a waterfall or the sighting of a large and very ancient carp.[24] But as the years passed, the Natacha they were writing to was less and less the child they still imagined her to be, and this misperception only compounded the distance already separating mother and daughter.

CHAPTER THREE

Schooldays, 1912–18

CHILDHOOD ENDS IN 1912 when, at the start of the autumn term, Natacha—who must now become Nathalie—takes the tram to her new school, the Lycée Fénelon. The first lycée for girls in Paris, the school had been founded just three decades previously, following the Loi Camille-Sée of December 1880, which established state secondary education for girls. The school's original head, Mlle Cécile Provost, was still in post, overseeing a project that was in many ways a pioneering venture, implementing an ambition that had been discussed and debated for more than two centuries. However, girls' education was still conceived in terms very different to that of boys. Its aim was not to provide pupils with the knowledge for which they undoubtedly had the aptitude, but to equip them for marriage and motherhood. Their curriculum would not include the "dead languages" (Latin and Greek); philosophy, the pinnacle of the French education system, would be taught in a reduced form as *morale* (ethics); and science would be kept to an elementary minimum. Instead, pupils would concentrate on French, literature, modern languages, and history, supplemented by the "occupations of their sex," such as needlework, hygiene, and singing. Moreover, the number of years devoted to the secondary education of girls would be limited.

In practice, this meant that most girls left with the *Certificat d'études secondaires* (secondary education certificate) after only three years, or after five, with the *Diplôme de fin d'études secondaires* (secondary education final diploma). Relatively few stayed on for the *baccalauréat*, which was taken after six years, with separate syllabuses for girls and boys. Although some changes were made to the original educational programme, introducing Latin and philosophy (but not Greek), it was not until 1924 that there was a single *baccalauréat* for both sexes. Academic aspirations were pitched accordingly, and when Nathalie sat the exam in 1918, she was one of forty-one in the school (less than half the original intake for the year), of whom only twenty-seven passed. With the introduction of compulsory primary education in 1882, teaching had become available as a career for women, where the majority became primary school teachers. A career in secondary education was reserved for those who passed the highly competitive entrance exam to the École normale supérieure. Only a very few girls took this exam, and those who won a place—as Simone Weil and Simone de Beauvoir did a few years later—joined the all-female École normale supérieure located on the outskirts of Paris in Sèvres where they studied for the necessary qualification known as the *agrégation*.

Discipline in the school was strict. When male teachers came to take some of the higher classes, a *surveillante* (supervisor) would be present, knitting imperturbably for the duration of the lesson. Nathalie was very conscious of the differences between the education she was receiving and the experience on offer at the boys' lycées. She later described this dual system as "a monstrous segregation," and it induced in her a keen sense of competition with her invisible male coevals.[1] The Lycée Fénelon eventually became coed in 1979, and Nathalie's grandson Nicolas Revel was a pupil.

There was also a certain amount of self-imposed social segregation. Fees were relatively high, and the majority of the girls came from well-to-do Parisian families who moved in different social circles from the Tcherniaks. Nathalie recalled other girls saying that they couldn't invite her home "because my mother doesn't know your mother."[2] The exception was Assia Minor, daughter of a leading Socialist Revolutionary activist, who became a close friend. After *Childhood* was published, one of Nathalie's former classmates wrote to congratulate her on the book, but regretted that there hadn't been more about the Lycée Fénelon of which her memories were fonder than those of Nathalie, whom she recalled as having had the "detachment of a slightly sad child."[3]

Reports for individual students from these years have not survived, but the annual prize lists record Nathalie's success across a range of disciplines. In July 1914, she was awarded second prizes in French language, literature, and arithmetic, with *accessits* in history, "diction," and needlework. She received a commendation for German, her name appeared on the "roll of honour," and she shared the "excellence" prize with one Claire Billard. There are similar results in the following years, with additional success in maths, physics and chemistry (a single subject), as well as hygiene in 1915.[4] The name of Assia Minor, Nathalie's rival in academic success, appears in the school's annual prize lists only slightly less frequently and slightly less illustriously than hers. These prizes mattered to Nathalie Tcherniack, as she styled herself, with an emphatic *-ck*, and she continued to set great store by her academic achievements.

They were once again a way of obtaining the interest and affection of her teachers, and three in particular stand out. The first was Mme Guillaumin, who taught French in Nathalie's third year at the lycée. Nathalie kept her French schoolwork from this year, during which pupils studied Molière and Corneille, and wrote free compositions on a variety of subjects, including one where pupils were instructed to recount their memories after discovering a trunk of discarded toys in an attic. Nathalie often mentioned her pleasure in writing these compositions, which she describes as still being in the style of the minor late nineteenth-century writers René Boylesve or Pierre Loti. She mostly received marks of seven or eight out of ten (nine on one occasion), along with comments that praise her intelligence, and occasionally encourage greater precision of detail and expression. In one remark—recalled with amusement years later— the teacher points out that when the Spanish ambassador enters the room of Louis XV's chief minister the Duc de Choiseul, it's an error to write that the door creaks open, because "a minister's door does not creak."[5]

Mme Guillaumin encouraged her pupil's literary talents, and Nathalie later claimed that her teacher thought so well of her school compositions that she read them aloud to her husband, who turned out to be the late impressionist painter Armand Guillaumin. He painted several portraits of his wife, often reading—as in the case of one dated 1914, the year in which she taught Nathalie. Mme Guillaumin was different from most of the other teachers at Fénelon, many of whom had been at the school since its inception, never married, and were now getting on in years. She is remembered in a comically exaggerated scene in the 1968 novel *Between Life and Death* as the teacher tiptoeing away from the budding writer, whose future success she is confidently predicting. But the joke is not so much on the teacher as on the aspiring novelist. From the perspective of the adult writer, Nathalie's dutiful school compositions were a false start, and the pleasure she took in producing them an equally erroneous foretaste of writing that was eventually experienced in a very different mode.

Two years later, in 1916–17, when Nathalie was preparing the *baccalauréat* in Latin and languages, she had two other teachers who played a similar role in encouraging her, M. Georgin for Latin and M. Béthou for French. The women teachers at Fénelon were mostly insufficiently qualified to teach at *baccalauréat* level, and male teachers were brought in from prestigious boys' lycées, such as Henri IV and Louis le Grand to take these classes. Five years younger than Nathalie, Sartre remembered M. Georgin from his time at Henri IV as an excellent teacher, and Nathalie later described being taught by him as having been "a real event in my life and my education."[6] She appreciated the intellectual freedom opened up by these male teachers with whom it was possible to have "real conversations," and who were not fixated on the niceties of written presentation that preoccupied their female colleagues. She was almost always guaranteed to be top of M. Georgin's class, and on the one occasion when another girl received a better mark, she tore up her work after school and threw it into the pond in the Luxemburg Gardens, furious with herself for having slipped from being in first place where she could be guaranteed to be "beyond comparison."[7] Unlike home, where the impossible Lili was always unfairly preferred to Nathalie, school held out the chance of being in a class of her own, the recipient of the affection and esteem of teachers who made her feel that she deserved them.

M. Béthou seems to have been an equally excellent teacher, and the written work in French literature that Nathalie kept from her year with him provides a record of detailed and penetrating study of French authors from both the seventeenth century (Molière again,

La Rochefoucauld, La Fontaine) and the nineteenth (Gautier, Hugo, Lamartine, George Sand). The essays address such topics as the oral style of the authorial voice in the text (La Fontaine), the writer's sympathy for the poor and neglected (Hugo, Lamartine, George Sand), the limited ability of the public to judge true merit in works of literature (Molière's *Misanthrope*), and the possibility of writing anything new in literature.[8] An essay on Montaigne's return to his château in 1581 lends him a reflection on his constant observation of his own inconstancy of judgement and action. Two women writers feature on the syllabus, but without reference to their sex: George Sand and Mme de Lafayette, whose imagined thoughts on the death of her friend La Rochefoucauld are the subject of another essay. These were all issues that would be germane to Nathalie's own writing in later life, but what emerges most obviously from the schoolwork of the sixteen-year-old student is her close attention to the texts, a capacity for subtle critical analysis, and a sense of real engagement with literary writing. In later interviews she recalled that M. Béthou had opened her eyes to such new ways of approaching literature that she had written her compositions just for him, wanting to make them perfect and handing them in only at the very last moment, which sometimes meant delivering them in person to the concierge at his home address in the fifteenth arrondissement.

In the same year she also studied philosophy. These lessons compared unfavourably with those in Latin and French, and the teacher—one of the women on the Fénelon staff—had simply dictated the standard philosophy textbook to the class.[9] This was Paul Janet's *Traité élémentaire de philosophie à l'usage des classes* (Elementary treatise on philosophy for schools), first published in 1879, and subsequently republished in revised editions. Janet—uncle of his more famous psychiatrist nephew Pierre Janet—had been appointed professor of philosophy at the Sorbonne in 1864, but by 1917, when Henri Bergson was the best-known representative of French philosophy, Janet and his book must have seemed very out of date to intellectually curious students. However, his treatise laid the groundwork for a conception of psychology that would form the basis for Nathalie's own writing, long after name of Paul Janet had ceased to have currency. Although she always steered clear of any association with philosophy—for which she claimed a lack of both interest and aptitude—her study of the subject in her last year of secondary school is more directly linked to her subsequent writing than her study of French literature and her French compositions.

In fact, it's quite astonishing in the light of her later writing to read the opening paragraph of a philosophy assignment dated 30 October 1917 and headed "On the Nature and Function of Subconscious Psychological States":

> The term subconscious is given to states that escape the full consciousness of the subject. These states are so to speak "below" consciousness, in half-lit regions where we do not perceive them distinctly. In our "field of consciousness," they occupy the obscure margins surrounding the well-lit centre, where our feelings are indistinctly active, our memories, our inclinations, the motives for our actions, our efforts—of which we are not aware or which we do not properly understand. An act, a thought, a feeling, "which are the effect of these obscure forces and whose roots lie well beyond our own individual natures," will emerge suddenly to consciousness and lead us to search for the causes behind them and cast light on these obscure states.[10]

Nathalie's literary writing is nothing less than her own attempt to explore these "obscure states" and to examine what the essay describes as the "subterranean life of the mind." In fact, this paragraph written by the seventeen-year-old schoolgirl reads uncannily like the definition of the tropism in the 1964 preface to *The Age of Suspicion*, where, half a century later, she speaks of "these movements, of which we are hardly cognizant [and which] slip through us on the frontiers of consciousness in the form of undefinable, extremely rapid sensations." Like the subconscious states of the philosophy essay, "they hide behind our gestures, beneath the words we speak and the feelings we manifest, . . . they develop and pass through us very rapidly in the form of frequently very intense, brief sensations, without our perceiving clearly what they are."[11]

The rest of the school essay veers off to discuss various forms of automatism, a major philosophical interest in the latter part of the nineteenth century, and it concludes with a rather pious assertion of the value of full consciousness, which "raises man to the rank of superior being, and makes him the crown of creation." This was not a view to which Nathalie would later subscribe, but the nod to

Cartesian tradition aside, her thinking remained powerfully marked by the philosophical outlook of the preceding decades, which presupposed an unbroken continuum of body and mind, where "at one extremity . . . everything is unconscious and purely physiological and at the other everything is conscious and purely psychological."[12] These are the words of the philosopher Théodule Ribot (he is cited in Nathalie's essay) in whose pre-Freudian conception of subconscious existence, psychological phenomena are transmitted through "sensation." This became a key term in Nathalie's own conceptual lexicon. Although this way of thinking soon fell out of use, the philosophy she learned at school provided her with a language for conceptualising an inner life which—as she says in the same 1964 preface—she had been aware of since childhood, and which she would go on to explore for literary rather than philosophical purposes.

Meanwhile, from the start of Nathalie's third year at Fénelon, the First World War had been unfolding in the background. In the summer of 1914, Polina arranged to holiday in France with Nathalie, and took rooms for them in the seaside resort of Saint-Georges-de-Didonne, south of La Rochelle on the Atlantic coast. Nathalie joined her mother for what was only their second reunion since 1909, and the rift from the previous visit was apparently healed. The house, which overlooked a large orchard, was charming, and Polina was delighted with everything she saw: the sea, the pine trees, and the flowers. Mother and daughter shared jokes, acting out a scene from a play performed by a touring theatre company, where a character melodramatically declares, "My house is not a mousetrap!"[13] All this was abruptly curtailed with the outbreak of the First World War. Orders for general mobilisation were issued on 2 August, and the following day Germany declared war on both France and Russia. Polina was immediately desperate to leave. A return to Russia through Germany now being impossible, she departed for Marseille from where she could reach Saint Petersburg via Constantinople. Her fear of being stranded in France and her evident joy at the prospect of returning to Russia and seeing Kolya were felt by Nathalie as a further repetition of her original abandonment. She did not see her mother again until 1921, the ensuing years of war and revolution having made the intervening separation definitive.

In the light of this episode, the French composition about the trunk of forgotten toys written two months later reads with a new resonance. When the narrator of the composition comes across her long-discarded doll, she takes it in her arms, filled with "remorse for having abandoned the child I once cherished so much."[14] The doll's hair is half unstuck, it has lost an eye, which is now rolling around in an empty skull, its nose is flattened, the colour has faded from its cheeks, and its muslin dress has been reduced to rags. None of this is implied in the subject prescribed by Mme Guillaumin, which simply asks for an account of the memories brought back by the rediscovered toys. Nathalie's composition ends with the reflection that what lies ahead is life "with its real sorrows, its possibly all-too rare joys," destined to become "more and more complicated without ever turning back." Mme Guillaumin's approval—the composition earned a mark of eight—was perhaps some compensation for the loss obliquely evoked in the assignment. There was another, even more oblique compensation in the form of Russian literature and its picture of Russian life, as Nathalie discovered Tolstoy's *War and Peace*, followed two years later by Dostoevsky's *Crime and Punishment*. Through their pages she acquired an imaginary link with the country to which Polina had returned. She read both authors in Russian, and their emotional impact was so powerful that rather than engage in classroom discussion about Tolstoy, she simply refused to acknowledge having read him.[15]

With the war, teachers and pupils at the school shared a common anxiety. As Ilya still had Russian nationality, he was not called up, but many girls had fathers or brothers at the front. One new pupil turned out to be the daughter of the writer Charles Péguy, who had just been killed in the Battle of the Marne. Nathalie had strong patriotic feelings for France, encapsulated in the reproduction of Antoine-Jean Gros's portrait of a dashingly heroic Napoleon at the Pont d'Arcole, which hung on her bedroom wall. And on a school visit to the Musée du Luxembourg, she was entranced by Edouard Detaille's grand history painting, *The Dream*, where a sleeping army shares a single dream of military glory. The lycée made its own modest contribution to the war effort, as girls were encouraged to knit or crochet scarves, gloves, and socks during recreation, or to hoe potato fields in the southern suburbs of Paris on Thursdays when there were no lessons. In 1917, a Braille workshop was set up in one of the classrooms to provide reading matter for soldiers who had lost their sight.

On 23 March 1918, a Saturday and the last day of the spring term, the war suddenly came closer with the arrival of Big Bertha. The huge long-range gun was deployed in the last stages of the war to fire shells on Paris, where it killed over two hundred fifty people and wounded some six hundred others. When the sirens started around nine o'clock in the morning the girls were herded into the school's cellars, where they spent the rest of the day, and more shells were fired during the night.[16] After this, like several other parents at the school, Ilya decided that Paris was not safe for his daughter, and he made plans for Nathalie to finish her studies out of harm's way. This may have been convenient for other reasons, since there was now a new addition to the family in the form of a half brother, Jacques, born in December 1917 and named after Ilya's dead brother Yakov.

Nathalie spent the summer term in Montpellier where she prepared for her *baccalauréat* and was accompanied by a Miss Rogers, who was perhaps Lili's English governess at the time. Ilya arranged private philosophy tuition with Edmond Cramaussel, who taught the subject at the boys' lycée and was the author of a book on Schleiermacher's religious philosophy—not a topic likely to have interested his new pupil. In June she sat the *baccalauréat* exams and passed, but not surprisingly under the circumstances, without any commendation. In later years she rarely spoke about this period of her life, during which she was doubly bereft: away from her family (though this had its advantages) and without the presence of her closest friend Assia Minor, who had returned to Russia with her family in August 1917.

While the war continued in Europe, revolution had finally arrived in Russia in February 1917, offering a chance for political émigrés to resume lives that they had previously been forced to abandon. It was an opportunity that, unlike the Tcherniaks, the Minors had immediately taken up. Osip Minor was one of the organisers of the Socialist Revolutionary party. He had twice been arrested and imprisoned in Russia while the family lived in exile in Paris. Ilya kept an eye on the children in the absence of their father and was regarded by them as "a great guy who improves on acquaintance."[17]

Assia was the youngest, and she and her three older brothers—Choura (Alexandre), Ilouche, and Léon—were "like a second family" to Nathalie who was in the habit of spending a good deal of time with them.[18] The Minors' apartment had been a haven, and in the letters Assia wrote to Nathalie from Moscow she recalls their long homework sessions in the family dining room. All this had now vanished. Assia's affection for her friend is palpable: each letter begins "My adored darling," she wishes Nathalie were with her to share her despair when things go badly, and she includes pen portraits of her landlady and the landlady's children, which suggest that she and Nathalie had a common, quasi-novelistic interest in human beings and their qualities.

The brothers write with evident, if slightly teasing affection, and Choura provides a vivid character sketch of Nathalie in response to her comment that she doesn't attract interest from other people. She attributes imaginary faults to herself, says Choura, physical and personal failings which she then exaggerates, making life unnecessarily miserable for herself. People who know Nathalie find, like the class-mate at Fénelon, that she has an aura of sadness that one would not normally expect in someone of her age, but also many qualities. Her apparent coldness is actually just shyness. In one of her letters, Assia remarks that both she and Nathalie had always been old beyond their years. And Léon, who seems to be a little in love with her from a distance of several thousand miles and at least two years, writes in 1919 of the small, dark-haired girl with disturbing brown eyes, who must now be a woman, and he alludes with fraternal rivalry to the crush that Nathalie once had on his older brother Ilouche.[19]

Following his release from prison after the February Revolution of 1917 Osip Minor had been appointed mayor of Moscow and president of the city Duma (parliament). Assia was studying botany at Moscow University while Choura continued his medical studies. Léon was a trainee army officer (a "junker") living in barracks and Ilouche was in the Caucasus, where he attended political meetings and proved to have a talent for political oratory. These French-speaking, French-educated children were now making a life for themselves in Russia, and Léon writes later to say that he feels more at home in Russia than in France, and that he sees his future there.

In early November 1917 the Moscow Duma was dismissed after the Bolsheviks took over, and Osip Minor was removed from his post. Assia expresses indignation to Nathalie, outraged that her father, who had given his whole life to the Socialist Revolutionary cause, had been branded a counterrevolutionary traitor. With civil war breaking out and their lives now in danger, both Choura and Assia write to Nathalie mentioning the noise of cannon fire in the background, bodies lying in the street outside, and the absence of anything left to eat other than a few potatoes and a small amount of black bread. They were afraid of having their throats cut by the Bolsheviks who had also taken over Léon's barracks, where the family feared for his safety. Nathalie's friends were not just absent, but living in a different world from which they might never return. In fact, both Ilouche and Léon subsequently perished, and Choura only narrowly escaped a firing squad.[20]

By spring 1919 the Minor children and their mother were in Odessa, which had been reclaimed from the Reds in August 1918. The children had abandoned their studies and were earning their keep by giving French lessons. Although life was hard, it was at this point that Léon envisaged a continuing future in Russia and urged Nathalie to join them. With her knowledge of Russian, he says, she would be "like a fish in water." He also advises her to equip herself with the means of earning a living: "We live in a century of revolutions and you know yourself what happens to wealth under those circumstances. The person who has a profession is saved. The ignoramus is thrown out onto the streets."[21] Polina was also in Odessa, where her mathematician brother Samuil Shatunovsky still taught at the university. The Minor family saw her occasionally, and Léon mentions that she jokes with them about the home that isn't a mousetrap. Assia adds a postscript in Russian to one of her letters (apart from the odd Russian word or name, they are otherwise all in French) to say that Polina writes to Nathalie often and hopes to see her soon in Odessa. If Polina's letters got through, Nathalie does not seem to have kept them, and she certainly never made the journey to Odessa. She did, however, keep several letters from each of the Minor children, whose stay in the city came to an end when it once again fell to the Reds in February 1920.[22]

It's hard to know how seriously Nathalie might have taken the prospect of returning to Russia and acquiring a Russian identity. The Russian world she knew from her family's social circle in Paris was a largely émigré, Socialist Revolutionary one, whose raison d'être had now been swept away by the Bolshevik Revolution. The émigrés about to arrive in Paris were the White Russians for whom experience of the tsarist regime had been very different to that of the Minors or the Tcherniaks. Besides which, it was ten years since Nathalie had left Saint Petersburg to live with her father in Paris, and by 1919, her thoughts were not with Russia, but England, and— perhaps keeping Léon's advice in mind about the importance of having a career—she was studying English at the Sorbonne.

CHAPTER FOUR

England, 1919–21

THANKS TO *David Copperfield* and *The Prince and the Pauper*, England was always part of Nathalie's mental geography, but it acquired a new reality with the arrival of the nannies hired by Vera to teach Lili. It was from them that Nathalie learned English. Having spoken German with a Swiss nursemaid as a child, she had opted for German at Fénelon where the German teacher, Mme de Saint-Étienne, had an excellent reputation and used the so-called "direct method" promoted by Sartre's grandfather, Karl Schweitzer.[1] But English was considered a sign of distinction, and it was a cachet that Vera was keen to reserve for Lili, redressing the unfair advantage that she saw Nathalie as having had, since she already spoke three languages and excelled at school, whereas Lili did not. The English nannies had instructions to speak English only to Lili, and were reprimanded if they were seen or heard talking to Nathalie. This prohibition was the surest way of inciting an extracurricular passion for the forbidden language.

She was also drawn to the young women employed by Vera. It didn't take them long to grasp the underlying dynamic of the Tcherniak household, and to realise that they "occupied the 'hottest seat,' the most dangerous position in the house [because] they were in charge of Lili." If Lili complained, Vera invariably took Lili's part against the nanny. This turned the nannies into Nathalie's secret allies, and one of them, a Miss Philips, whom she met years later pushing a pram in the Bois de Boulogne, claimed that she still had nightmares about Nathalie's stepmother. None of them stayed for long, which is no doubt why Nathalie talks about them in the plural. But they were a plural who were emblems of a single type: "ingenuous young English girls," daughters of clergymen or schoolteachers, raised in idyllic rural surrounds, and who had stories of "'real' childhoods . . . lived in insouciance, in security, under the firm, benevolent guidance of united, fair and calm parents."[2] Everything, in other words, that Nathalie's own childhood was not. The nannies conjured up a world for which she felt longing and affection, without ever having experienced it herself. On evenings when Ilya and Vera were out, and with no one to prevent her from doing so, Nathalie would slip into the nanny's room to talk English, learn nursery rhymes, read English children's books, and hear about this other place. Everything about it charmed her, but it was off-limits, and could be glimpsed only in secret.

In her first critical article, written in 1947, Nathalie presents herself in the guise of Rudyard Kipling's Elephant's Child from the *Just-So Stories*, which she may well have discovered during her evenings with the English nannies. The Elephant's Child is routinely spanked by every member of his family for asking unpopular questions, but he gets his revenge through the inadvertent acquisition of a trunk, and eventually "nobody spanked anybody any more." England was a place where wrongs—especially family wrongs—were righted, and justice prevailed. The benevolent families that Nathalie ascribed to the English nannies embodied the values she discovered in the English books she read as a child. Her love affair with England and the English language was not easily extinguished, and she eventually persuaded Ilya to allow her to learn the language by more official means. As a result, she had private lessons with an *assistante* from the English department at the Sorbonne, who came to the house three times a week. The term she spent with Miss Rogers revising for the *baccalauréat* in Montpellier was also a perfect opportunity for Nathalie to improve her English. And so, in October 1918, she enrolled at the Sorbonne to study for a degree in the subject.

If England was a dream that Nathalie nurtured as an idealised "elsewhere," the study of English at the Sorbonne was a disappointment, which brought that elsewhere no closer. She was appalled that so few of the professors made any attempt to speak the language, she rarely attended classes, and she found the place altogether "stern" and isolating.[3] Two-thirds of all the students enrolled at the Sorbonne studied *lettres* (humanities), and women had full access to university education where their numbers increased steadily from 22 percent in 1906 to 41 percent by the 1930s.[4] But unlike the teachers at Fénelon, the professors—all men—were remote authorities, and students did not mingle outside class.

This did not, however, prevent Nathalie from establishing a keen rivalry with a young man from the prestigious, all-male École normale supérieure in the rue d'Ulm, and she later recalled her determination to get better marks than the unfortunately named M. Bœuf. The teacher encouraged this rivalry by constantly comparing them, and for Nathalie, "the worst misfortune which [she] could suffer was to receive a grade lower than his!"[5] She was pitting herself against a student who had had the benefit of the sort of lycée education she had been denied at Fénelon. He would have been through the notoriously demanding and academically ambitious *classes préparatoires* (such as those in the Lycées Henri IV or Louis le Grand), which trained students for the competitive entrance exams for the *grandes écoles*.

The social aspect of university life that Nathalie missed at the Sorbonne was a central part of the experience of the young men at the all-male École Normale in the rue d'Ulm, an institution through which many of the literary and intellectual figures of the twentieth century passed, encouraged by their teachers and making lifelong friends. It was these relationships that endowed the school's alumni with a sense that they already had a purchase on the cultural and intellectual world to which many of them aspired. Aside from the fact that women did not have access to this world—the École normale supérieure in Sèvres on the outskirts of Paris had none of the social and cultural advantages of the rue d'Ulm—university education itself was less well considered than that of the *grandes écoles*, where gaining a degree was incidental to the principal goal of passing the competitive *agrégation* examination.

Although Nathalie was dismissive of the English teaching she found at the Sorbonne, the department had some distinguished professors, notably Emile Legouis, who was appointed to the chair of English in 1919, and his younger colleague Louis Cazamian, who later succeeded him. Nathalie recalls only Cazamian speaking English and having a decent accent, but both men wrote in English as well as French. Between them, they covered the entire history of English literature from its beginnings to what was then almost the present day, and their jointly authored *History of English Literature* published in 1921 (and later translated into English) became the standard reference work for many decades.

Cazamian had a particular interest in Victorian fiction, but closer still to Nathalie's own concerns was his study of what he called "literary psychology," the subject of a book he published in 1920, and which would have been the topic of his lectures during the years that Nathalie was at the Sorbonne. It's very likely that through these lectures she became acquainted with the poetry of Robert Browning, to whom she later attributed the fictitious quotation "The achievement is in the pursuit." In his *History of English Literature* Cazamian describes Browning's work as one of the richest and most penetrating studies in psychology in English, and he singles out Browning's use of monologue as a means of revealing the inner life of his characters. Commenting on *The Ring and the Book,* Cazamian stresses in particular "the relativity of perceptions, the distinct and interfering waves which the shock of a single event sends surging through various minds."[6] These were precisely the issues that interested the adult writer that Nathalie later became.

English literature more generally made a vital contribution to the development of her literary sensibility, and she continued to read English authors (in English) long after she had left the Sorbonne. As she once commented in an interview, "I don't think I would have written the way I did if I hadn't always read the English. They were part of the world I lived in."[7] When it comes to the novel, the English—*les Anglais*—include a fair number of *Anglaises* in the feminine, since women were far better represented in the English literary tradition than they were in France. Nathalie never specifically mentions Jane Austen, George Eliot, or Mrs Gaskell, but she refers frequently to the Brontës—and especially to Emily—whose work she almost certainly encountered while at university. Very soon the name of Virginia Woolf would be added to this pantheon of English women writers.

Nathalie's enthusiasm for the English language and English literature nevertheless continued to be frustrated by the forms in which she encountered them at the Sorbonne. Unlike the assignments for the teachers who mattered to her at Fénelon, she never kept any of the compositions she wrote as part of her degree course, and she seems to have decided to be done with the experience as quickly as possible. She sat her final exams a year early in 1920, after just two (rather than the usual three) years of study, evidently indifferent to the grade she was likely to obtain. The result—recorded on the "Certificate of Aptitude" for the Degree in Modern Foreign Languages and Literatures awarded on 5 July 1920 to Nathalie Tcherniack (*sic*) and signed, amongst others, by Professors Legouis and Cazamian—was a mere *passable*, the lowest of the four available classifications. The exams included translation in and out of the language, a further translation from Latin, grammatical commentary on a selection of literary extracts, and a French composition on a modern French text, the exercise in which Nathalie scored the most respectable of what were otherwise mediocre marks. She took German in order to meet the requirement for a subsidiary language, and there is no sign of any test of oral proficiency in either language.[8]

She had already taken steps to acquire this proficiency when, after her first year at the Sorbonne, she made her first visit to England, and spent two and a half months with the Gregory family in Harrow-on-the-Hill, on the outskirts of London. It's not clear how the connection with the Gregorys was made, but it was possibly through Miss Rogers, who had been Nathalie's companion in Montpellier. Everything about the England she discovered in the summer of 1919 confirmed the idealised image that had long since taken root in her mind, and of which there was so little trace at the Sorbonne. Harrow-on-the-Hill was an ancient parish with some fine domestic architecture, exemplified no doubt by Douglas Lodge on London Road, the home of the Gregory family. Most probably a large Victorian villa like its neighbours, Douglas Lodge seems not to have survived, several of the larger houses having been demolished to be replaced by apartment blocks in what remains a well-to-do neighbourhood. The 1911 census records that the house had ten rooms, and that its occupants were Joseph Gregory, a retired naval captain aged sixty, his wife Constance, fourteen years his junior, his daughter Sheelah, born in Dublin in 1901 (and so one year younger than

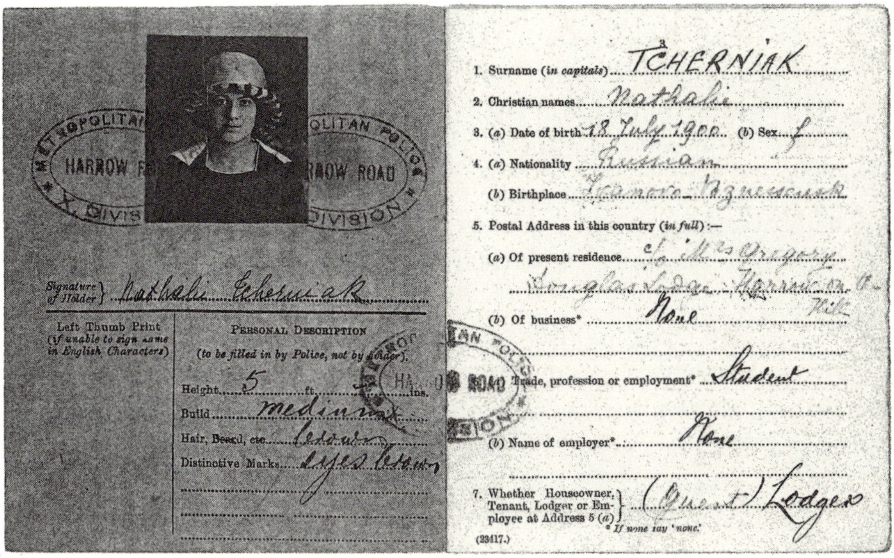
METROPOLITAN POLICE HARROW ROAD X DIVISION

Signature of Holder } Nathalie Tcherniak

Left Thumb Print (if unable to sign name in English Characters)

PERSONAL DESCRIPTION (to be filled in by Police, not by holder).

Height 5 ft. ins.

Build medium

Hair, Beard, etc. brown

Distinctive Marks eyes brown

1. Surname (in capitals) TCHERNIAK

2. Christian names Nathalie

3. (a) Date of birth 18 July 1900 (b) Sex f

4. (a) Nationality Russian

(b) Birthplace

5. Postal Address in this country (in full):—

(a) Of present residence c/o Mrs Gregory

(b) Of business* None

6. (a) Trade, profession or employment* Student

(b) Name of employer* None

7. Whether Houseowner, Tenant, Lodger or Employee at Address 5 (a) } (Guest) Lodger

* If none say 'none.'

(23417.)

FIGURE 8. Identity book issued to Nathalie Tcherniak, 1919. (Sarraute Family Papers)

Nathalie), an Irish cook, and a local housemaid. An older son, Brian O'Terrall, was not registered as an occupant, and by 1919 he had he already followed his father into the Merchant Navy. Nathalie later recalled a large garden with lawns, flowerbeds, and the family dogs.

The Identity Book issued to Nathalie Tcherniak states that she arrived in England on 3 July 1919, having travelled from Boulogne to Folkestone. As an "alien," less than a year after the end of the war, she had to register any change of residence with the local police station or Alien Registration Office, and the document duly records that at the end of August she spent twelve days—presumably holidaying with the Gregory family—on the coast in Southsea, Portsmouth, where Captain Gregory would have had naval connections. She finally returned to Paris on 15 September. Her nationality is given as Russian. She has a Russian passport, issued in Paris in May of the same year, no doubt acquired in anticipation of the trip to England, as this was the first time she had left France since arriving from Saint Petersburg ten years previously. She is described as being exactly five feet tall, which is quite small, especially by English standards, of medium build, with brown hair and brown eyes. (In later years Nathalie enjoyed pointing out that the appropriate translation of the French word *petite* in her case would be "short" rather than "petite" in the English sense.) Her employment is registered as "student," and she is described as being a "guest" at the Gregorys' address. In the photograph she is wearing a pale cloche hat with a striped brim and a dress with a faintly naval-looking white collar. There is a quietly determined set to the chin, and she stares with steady confidence at the camera. The likeness is confirmed by two official stamps applied at the Harrow Road branch of the Metropolitan Police.

Two and a half months of total immersion in the English language must have allowed her to make considerable strides in speaking and, above all, to make firsthand acquaintance with an English way of life. The enchantment that England had exerted from afar when she listened to the English nannies talk of home was not dispelled by the reality. The formal courtesy of social relations came as a welcome alternative to the emotional volatility of the Tcherniak household, and Nathalie always ascribed to the English an avoidance of all "personal remarks," an expression that she occasionally had cause to invoke in later life. She was delighted when, in response to a polite enquiry about her journey, she was advised that it was better not to say that she had been terribly seasick on the Channel crossing, and to reply instead, "I'm afraid I'm not a good sailor."[9] She saw in the formulation not just an amusing euphemism, but a respect for the feelings of others that she always viewed as characteristically English. At any rate, it was a turn of phrase that she would never have learned from her teachers at the Sorbonne.

She doesn't seem to have formed a particularly close bond with Sheelah, but she admired her good looks and blonde colouring, which (though Sheelah may well have been Irish) Nathalie always held up as an English ideal and contrasted with her own physical appearance. She played tennis and attended a cricket match at Lords cricket ground, an occasion of which there is no like in France. Mrs Gregory took her on a visit to family friends in Bedford Square in Bloomsbury, which would come back to her when she read Virginia Woolf's *Mrs Dalloway* a few years later.

Traces of this English interlude can be found in her first book, *Tropisms*. In no. 15 a young woman is verbally assaulted by an old family friend as he repeats English names—Shakespeare, Dickens,

Thackeray, Dover—and demonstrates his command of a correctly pronounced "th." No. 18 is set in England itself—on the outskirts of London—where an old lady with white hair and pink cheeks sits by a wisteria-framed French window looking out onto a rain-drenched lawn. "She sits there, very stiff, very dignified, quite sure of herself and of others, firmly settled in her little universe. She knows that in a few minutes the bell will ring for tea."[10] Tea will be prepared by Ada the cook who meanwhile is peeling vegetables in the kitchen and shares the same unshakeable certainties as her employers. Whether or not Ada "really" existed, the scene has all the elements of equanimity, domestic peace, and horticultural charm that Nathalie persisted throughout her life in seeing in her romanticised image of England and the English. It was a necessary counterweight to everywhere else. And that included the Sorbonne where she resumed her studies at the start of the new academic year.

One reason for her wish to be done with study at the Sorbonne may well have been the reappearance of Polina in her life. While Polina had been in Odessa, Kolya had been fighting with the White Russian army. He was evacuated between December 1919 and March 1920, and by May 1920 was in Yugoslavia.[11] He and Polina subsequently managed to reach Budapest, but Hungary was in political turmoil, having lost a substantial part of its former territory after the First World War. The country that Kolya knew so well no longer existed, and the couple made plans to move to Paris, where they joined the influx of their fellow countrymen, who found asylum in France and were exemplified by the White Russian aristocrats down on their luck or the bourgeois businessmen trying to make good, who people the novels of Joseph Kessel and Irène Némirovsky.

In the information she provided for the Chronology in the *Complete Works* Nathalie records that she went to fetch Polina and Kolya from Budapest in 1920, but she included no details about precise dates and practicalities. Given both the political instability in Eastern Europe and the restrictions placed on the lives of young women at the time, it seems unlikely that she made the journey on her own. It's possible that Ilya felt some responsibility for his former wife and her second husband, and that Nathalie went with him to act as a buffer in their relations. Alternatively, a common acquaintance such as the "uncle" who accompanied her from Berlin to Paris in 1909 may have agreed to go to the couple's rescue, taking Nathalie with him. However it came about, this was the first time that mother and daughter had met since the summer of 1914 when the outbreak of war forced Polina to curtail her holiday in Saint-Georges-de-Didonne. The politics of postrevolutionary Bolshevik Russia and postwar Hungary had brought Polina back to a Paris she knew from the first years of the century, but for Nathalie the presence of her resolutely disunited parents in the city no doubt made life complicated. Renewed escape to England was an obvious solution, and in 1920 she embarked on a course of study at the University of Oxford.

She arrived on 4 October 1920, accompanied by her father. They stayed at the Randolph Hotel, an imposing piece of Victorian Gothic architecture in the centre of town, which had been built in the 1860s for the incipient tourist trade and was two decades older than any of the newly founded women's colleges. The first of these had opened just four decades previously, and women's access to the university was still very limited. Nathalie was to join the Society of Home Students, which subsequently became St Anne's College, the fifth of the five women's colleges. Its original purpose was to provide university tuition for young women living in or around Oxford, but it had expanded to cater to students from overseas, who in the years following the end of the war numbered about one quarter of the society's total.[12] Nathalie was one of these. To please her father she planned to study chemistry, although it's likely that her chief reasons for being in Oxford were to improve her English and to get away from home.

The College Register records her qualifications (the *baccalauréat* in Latin and languages), previous education (Lycée Fénelon and the Sorbonne), date and place of birth, parents' place of birth, home address (5 rue Nouvelle-Stanislas, Paris), and father's occupation ("manufacturer"). It also records that references had been supplied by Mrs Gregory of Harrow-on-the-Hill and Professor Vinogradoff, a family friend who had recommended Home Students, since the society's vice-principal was a former student of his.[13] Vinogradoff, a medieval historian who had previously held a chair at Moscow University, had political views that were on the same spectrum as those of the Tcherniaks, and he could equally well have been part of their émigré community in Paris. He had left Russia in 1901 and published a book arguing for constitutional change and deploring the condition of Jews in Russia as "a scandal."[14] Since 1903, he had held the chair of jurisprudence in Oxford, where his lectures—which Nathalie attended—were delivered in a heavy Russian accent and mostly went over the heads of his students.[15] He must have been a curious reminder of home.

Unlike the other colleges, Home Students had no buildings of its own, and its affairs were administered from the private residence of its principal, Mrs Johnson. She was seventy-four years old and soon to retire. In a portrait that bears some resemblance to the old lady in the *Tropisms* text, an American student, who arrived at the same time as Nathalie, recalled her as "a charming, pink-cheeked lady," who nevertheless had something quite formidable about her.[16] She greeted each new arrival with questions about her journey, enquired whether she had enough warm clothes, and then devised an individual course of study tailored to the student's particular interests. She also arranged accommodation for each of her charges, and most lodged with private families in the town. Nathalie, however, was assigned to Cherwell Hall, a teacher-training college under the principalship of Miss Talbot, known by the students as "Miss Tall-but-thin." She immediately threw herself into student life. The personal attention from both principal and tutors along with the camaraderie amongst students were quite new to her, as were the semirural surrounds. She had a bedroom overlooking the River Cherwell, was enchanted by the lawns and the garden outside, and ate in the communal dining hall where meals were preceded by the inevitable grace, "For what we are about to receive, may the Lord make us truly thankful."

The unfamiliarity of college life was offset by the presence of another Russian émigré, Lena Liber, who enrolled at Home Students at the same time. It's not clear whether the two girls had known each other previously or whether they met in Oxford. The College Register records that "Helen" Liber was born in January 1900 in Rogachov, Russia, had graduated in 1918 from Travnikov's Gymnasium in Moscow, and had studied at the Faculty of Medicine in Paris. Her father's name and occupation are given as Moses Liber, Director of Paley & Liber Co. Ltd., London, and his home address is also in London. Lena's home address is in Paris. In other words, she had lived between three worlds—Russia, England, and Paris—a mixed allegiance with which Nathalie was also acquainted. Lena became her closest friend, and the friendship lasted until Lena's death in 1961.

Nathalie loved everything about Oxford, starting with the food, which included porridge, kippers, custard, and buns from a nearby bakery. In later years she would ask her English friends to bring a tin of Bird's Eye custard powder when they came to Paris. Even the extremely strict rules seemed amusingly harmless. The sexes were rigorously segregated. Male and female students sat separately at lectures and were forbidden to speak to each other in the street, where the bowler-hatted university police, known as Bulldogs, enforced university regulations. One girl was actually expelled for climbing out of the library window at night to meet a student from one of the men's colleges, an exploit that Nathalie and the other students regarded as heroic.[17]

Nor does she seem to have experienced her status as a foreigner to be grounds for any sense of exclusion. She was nonetheless obliged to register with the Aliens Department at Oxford police station, which she did on 10 November. She was nicknamed "the Indian girl" by the other students on account of her dark complexion, and after mentioning that she was Jewish, she was persuaded by Miss Johnson to attend the synagogue, which she did just once. Her positive appreciation of British decorum redeemed everything. On one occasion, when she met Mrs Johnson in the street and tried to hand her a message which she was on her way to deliver, Nathalie took it in good part to be pulled up short by the upright college principal, who instructed her to "put it in my pigeon hole." She was quite right, said Nathalie, remembering the incident nearly eighty years later. "It's terribly bad manners to accost people in the street like that."[18]

She also loved the physical activities that were part of student life. She walked over Magdalen Bridge to attend lectures in the Examination Schools in the High Street or to study in the Radcliffe Camera library, and bicycled to tutorials on the other side of town. She played hockey, and when the summer came she played tennis and learned to row. She also discovered a talent for punting, was promoted to "captain," and supervised the Boat Club's rigorous swimming test, which required girls to complete two lengths of the pool fully clothed before they were allowed to venture out on the flat-bottomed college punt. She kept a handcrafted theatre programme for *Scenes from Cranford*, adapted from Mrs Gaskell's novel and performed by an all-female cast on 26 May 1921. (Drama was also strictly segregated.) And she lists the name of every student on the back of a group photograph taken outside Cherwell Hall in the summer term.[19]

Although her essays (three of which she kept) suggest that she wrote English with less ease than French, Nathalie's linguistic competence was more than adequate for both social and academic purposes. Having begun by studying chemistry, she then switched to history, a change Ilya was perhaps persuaded to accept thanks to Vinogradoff's reputation as a historian. In the summer she studied the Early Middle Ages with Miss Lees, one of the three tutors who taught history in the Society of Home Students. She read Gibbon's *Decline and Fall* and wrote essays on Charlemagne, the breakup of the Holy Roman Empire, and the Viking invasion of Europe, which Miss Lees judged to be "very good."[20] She writes her name sometimes as Tcherniak and sometimes as Tcherniack.

The lifelong glow that Oxford retained in Nathalie's memory may have been enhanced by the euphoria created by the transformation of the status of women in the university, when their demand for full membership was finally granted in 1920. Women had been permitted to sit for university exams since 1892–93, but the university's statutes prevented them from being awarded the degrees to which their academic achievements had in principle entitled them. A ceremony on 14 October included the first women to receive a degree in the university's six-hundred-year history. This change also meant that from October 1920 the ceremonial enrolment into the university known as "matriculation" included women students, for whom a new soft cap was designed in place of the allegedly unbecoming mortarboard worn by the men. As a participant, Nathalie must have witnessed the excitement generated by this historic change of statute.

The first woman to receive an honorary degree from the university was the fifty-three-year-old Queen Mary, who was awarded an

FIGURE 9. Cherwell Hall, summer 1921. Nathalie bottom left, Lena second from left in the back row, Miss Talbot centre of middle row. (Sarraute Family Collection)

honorary doctorate of law on 11 March 1921 in the university's ceremonial building. The royal party was welcomed at Lady Margaret Hall, where the fellows and students of the all-female college gathered in the gardens along with those of the Society of Home Students. Nathalie was present, and the event was the start of her lifelong passion for the British royal family, whom she chose to fantasise as perfect beings exempt from the doubts and vacillations of the tropism, and whose fortunes she later followed closely in the popular press, especially in the case of the future Queen Mother, who was just two weeks younger than herself.

The prominence given to the education of women through the university's awarding of degrees was part of broader changes in the position of women in British society. Two years previously, in 1918, the right to vote had been granted to women over the age of thirty who met minimum property qualifications, and a further act of Parliament in the same year allowed women to be elected as MPs. France, where women did not obtain the vote until 1944, must have seemed very retrograde by comparison.

The year in Oxford was one of the happiest of Nathalie's life, and she wanted to stay on. Her plan was to continue her studies in history and to contribute to the cost by giving private lessons. She had already started offering tuition in French, reading Balzac's *Eugénie Grandet* with one of her pupils. When Ilya refused to approve the plan—whether because the fees were prohibitive or because, as Nathalie sometimes claimed, he did not wish to see his daughter become a bluestocking—she was distraught to find herself back in Paris. In later years she consoled herself with the example of a Russian émigré acquaintance, Eugène Vinaver, who came to Oxford the following year to study for a postgraduate degree, and ended up making a career in England as professor of French in the northern industrial city of Manchester. "My father saved me from Manchester," she later said.[21]

Life in England—an England of decorum and afternoon tea, punting and custard—never felt like exile. To be a foreigner in a foreign country was very different from being treated as a foreigner at home, whether as the barely tolerated stepdaughter in the family or as the girl whose mother didn't know the mothers of the other girls at school. Rules in England never appeared designed for exclusion but were a kind of game you could play by complying and excelling in activities as varied as swimming tests, punting, or history essays. But by the end of June 1921 she was once again back home in Paris.

CHAPTER FIVE

Berlin, 1921–22

NATHALIE'S RESPONSE to the stresses of family life was to go abroad again. If a return to Oxford was ruled out, the alternative was to improve her command of German by studying in Berlin. However, as she later somewhat cryptically commented, it wasn't at all the same, and proved to be "a period of emotional disarray."[1] She spent several months of the academic year 1921–22 as a student at the Friedrich Wilhelm University (later renamed Humboldt University), where she attended lectures by Werner Sombart, but beyond also mentioning that she read Thomas Mann's *Tonio Kröger*, she volunteered very little about this time.

She kept a certificate dated 12 May 1922 testifying to her enrolment as a student in the Philosophy (Humanities) Faculty at the university. Her name is given as if transliterated directly from the Russian—"Natalia Tscherniack"—and her nationality as "Russa" (the certificate is in Latin).[2] Defined as a Russian national—which, legally speaking, she was—she looked in official terms no different from the increasing numbers of mostly Jewish students who, since the 1880s, had come from Russia in pursuit of the higher education that the *numerus clausus* denied them at home. And she almost certainly found herself in Russian émigré circles, since the family connections with the city were Russian. The "uncle" who had accompanied her from Berlin to Paris in 1909 was a Russian friend of both parents, and in a postcard sent to Natacha from Saint Petersburg in November 1910, Kolya mentions visiting his cousin Lev in Berlin and asks Natacha whether she remembers him.[3]

The emotional tenor of Berlin in Nathalie's memory cannot have good. It was a place of painful separation, where she had effectively been abandoned by her mother in 1909. The German language was another matter. It was in German that she had once defied her Swiss-German nursemaid's prohibition, "Nein, das tusst du nicht" (No, don't do that), with a "Doch, Ich werde es tun" (Yes, I will), slashing a silk-upholstered sofa with a pair of scissors in the act of rebellion whose echo launches the writing of *Childhood* over seven decades later. As a child, one of Natacha's favourite books was the German *Max und Moritz*, whose rhymes she knew by heart (though whether in German or in French she doesn't say), and she also loved Dr Heinrich Hoffmann's *Struwwelpeter*. Having acquired a good accent at school thanks to Mme de Saint-Étienne's devotion to the direct method, and having continued the study of the language at the Sorbonne, Nathalie was linguistically, if not socially or emotionally, equipped for her stay in Berlin.

Moreover, the Germany that had been France's enemy during the First World War no longer existed. The reign of the kaisers was over, the country had had its own revolution, and although the Spartakists had been brutally suppressed and its leaders, Karl Liebknecht and Rosa Luxemburg, slaughtered, the country now had a Social-Democrat government under Friedrich Ebert. Since the turn of the century Germany had also been a magnet for Russian socialist and liberal exiles who looked to the German socialist movement for support. This tradition continued after the October Revolution, and a good number of the Russians who came to Berlin at this time were the Socialist Revolutionaries, who found the new German political regime more congenial than the Bolshevik one back home. Between 1919 and 1923 Germany saw the arrival of large numbers of Russians, and in 1921–22 Berlin alone was home to between two hundred and fifty and three hundred thousand émigrés.[4]

One can only speculate about where Nathalie lived during her time in Berlin. Did she stay with Kolya's cousin Lev? Or did she take lodgings in one of the many boarding houses where Russian émigrés found refuge? In his novel *The Gift*, Nabokov conjures up the atmosphere of one such place, which the hero, a young Russian poet born on almost the same day as Nathalie, makes his temporary home. Nabokov's fictional poet was not the only literary immigrant, and in his preface to the English translation of the novel, Nabokov comments on the "tremendous outflow of intellectuals" who formed "a prominent part of the general exodus from Soviet Russia in the first years of the Bolshevist Revolution."[5] These émigré Russians congregated in the southwestern suburbs of Berlin, where local Berliners jokingly referred to Charlottenburg as "Charlottengrad" and renamed the Kurfürstendamm the "Nöpski Prospeckt." Russian could be heard in the street, Russian shops were opening up, and balalaikas played in restaurants that served Russian food.

Nabokov himself was studying French and Russian at Cambridge University, but returned at the end of each term to join his family who had been living in Berlin since August 1920. In September 1921, they moved to Wilmersdorf, which Nabokov's biographer describes as "the cultural hub of the whole emigration."[6] The area became home to the writers who were part of this "outflow" of Russian intelligentsia, many of whom were still young. The journalist and historian Ilya Ehrenburg arrived in Berlin in the autumn of 1921. He took lodgings in the Pension Krampe in the Trautenau Strasse, which occupied the fourth and fifth floors of a large building and was reached by a grand marble staircase with chandeliers and a nude statue bearing an electric lamp. These details are recorded by the young Russian writer Nina Berberova, who arrived in Berlin in June 1922 with her husband, the poet Vladislav Khodasevich, whom Nabokov later described as "the greatest Russian poet that the twentieth century has yet produced."[7] The occupant of the room next to theirs was the poet Andrei Bely.

It is tempting to assume that Nathalie was also living in this area, but wherever she was, life in Berlin would have had its hardships. There was both political and economic instability: Ebert's social-democratic government was precarious, and Ehrenburg recalls the pervasive sense of imminent revolution. The reparations required from Germany by the Treaty of Versailles had crippled the economy, and the value of the deutschmark was plunging. Apartments were cold and food was short. There were intermittent strikes and signs of political extremism. In March 1922, while Nathalie was still in Berlin, Nabokov's father was assassinated by extreme rightists as he tried to protect the leader of the Russian Constitutional Democratic party, who was delivering a lecture in Berlin's Philharmonia Hall.

In June of the same year—but presumably after Nathalie had left—
Walter Rathenau, the Jewish foreign minister, was assassinated on
the way to his ministry. Between 1919 and 1922 there were over three
hundred political murders in Germany, and anti-Semitism was on
the rise. Ilya Ehrenburg remembered being called a "dirty Pole" and
seeing a chalked slogan threatening "Death to the Jews!"[8]

The Russian cultural hub that was Berlin in the first years of the
decade was a draw even for writers who had remained in Soviet
Russia. Visitors included the Russian formalist Viktor Shklovsky,
the poets Mayakovsky and Yesenin, Lily Brik and Osip Brik, as well
as Lily Brik's younger sister, Elsa Triolet, who was living in Paris
after marrying a Frenchman. Several Russian publishers set up in
Berlin, and Polina's novel *Vremya* was later published by one of
these new émigré publishing houses. Russian literary life was based
mostly in the cafés, such as the Leon on Nollendorfplatz and the
Landgraf café on the Kurfürstendamm, which hosted regular readings, lectures, and discussions. Berberova was a regular at the literary gatherings in the Leon on Nollendorfplatz, while Ehrenburg
frequented the House of Arts whose Friday gatherings at the Landgraf café also drew Aleksei Tolstoy, Aleksei Remizov, Mayakovsky,
Yesenin, Tsvetaeva, Bely, and Boris Pasternak. Most of the literary
émigrés stayed in Berlin for only a short time, and soon moved on
to other destinations. Berberova lived in Paris for twenty-five years
before eventually settling in the United States, and Nabokov took
US citizenship after leaving Germany in 1937. Ehrenburg had already spent several years in Paris, which he continued to visit after
returning to Moscow in 1923. Pasternak also returned to the Soviet
Union, as did Bely, Aleksei Tolstoy, Shklovsky, and Tsvetaeva, all of
whom had been in Berlin in the early 1920s.

In sum, the year that Nathalie spent in Berlin coincided with the
start of the brief period between 1921 and 1923 when the city became the literary capital of the Russian intelligentsia. Several of its
exponents were writers of her own age who had already embarked
on a literary career, but having reached adulthood in Russia, they
remained Russian writers, even when they later wrote in an adop-
tive language—English for Nabokov and French for Berberova and
Triolet. Had she stayed in Saint Petersburg, grown up, and been
educated there, Nathalie might have become one of them. But there

is nothing to suggest that she took any interest in the Russian literary life of Berlin in the early 1920s, or made any attempt to join it.

Instead, she pursued a programme of immersion in the German language and German culture, attending lectures at the university given by Werner Sombart. A well-known professor of sociology, Sombart is barely remembered now, but at the time he had a reputation equal to that of Max Weber, his friend, rival, and colleague, whose *Protestant Ethic and the Spirit of Capitalism* (1920) was matched by his own study of *The Jews and Economic Life* (1915). If Nathalie knew about this book—and perhaps through Kolya she did—she may well have been curious, since she was herself the daughter of a Jewish manufacturer. But in any case Sombart, who by 1921 was in his late fifties, had become something of an academic celebrity. He cultivated the image of a "super-intellectual scholar, politician, expert and lover" and was much in demand as a lecturer, speaking on topics such as the shortcomings of modernity, culture and the individual, and the future of the Jews.[9]

His lectures at the university attracted large numbers. In the autumn semester of 1921, Nathalie would have been one of 681 students who enrolled for his course on "The Theory and History of the Proletarian Movement." Sombart was using these lectures to develop an extensive critique of Marxism and revise his earlier ideas which had earned him a reputation as "the red professor." He remained loyal to a Marxian notion of class struggle, but condemned what he called "proletarian socialism." In its place, he advocated a return to a social order based on the old associations of church, town, village, clan, family, and vocation. As part of this ideal, he became increasingly preoccupied with questions of race, and in due course his beliefs would lead to support for Hitler's national socialism and a conception of the sociologist's role as "superior handmaiden" to the political system. How much of this was evident to Sombart's audience in the early 1920s is hard to say, but Nathalie must have appreciated his view that sociology should not be a narrow science of materialism but part of the humanities. And regardless of their content, his lectures could be enjoyed as sheer performance, since, in the words of one his former students, Sombart incarnated "a new type of the combination of the man of the world and artist."[10] Nathalie never said what she thought of Sombart or his lectures, but on the rare occasions when she alluded to her time in Berlin, she always mentioned that she had attended them.

Did she also know that Sombart had spent time in Paris in the early years of the century when he had a brief affair with the German painter Paula Modersohn-Becker, who painted portraits of both him and Rainer Maria Rilke in 1906? This is pure speculation, but the connection with Sombart might have intrigued Nathalie when she discovered Rilke's *Notebooks of Malte Laurids Brigge* soon after her return to Paris. The volume had been published in 1910, and when she read it—in the original, thanks to her recent immersion in the German language—it made an enormous impression on her.

However, this was later. The literary experience that marked her stay in Berlin was her discovery of Thomas Mann's 1905 novella *Tonio Kröger*, which she came across by chance in a bookshop one day. Reading it gave her a first intimation of the possibility that she might herself write. She expresses this rather strangely when she says, "I had the impression that it was me who was writing it." This sense of recognising herself in Thomas Mann's novella was first and foremost the revelation of a kindred sensibility. "It was so much me, my way of feeling things," but a way of feeling things that she had never seen expressed by anyone else, and which she describes as "a painful split between the trompe-l'oeil vision of the world offered by society and my own experience, which wasn't part of anything known or accepted."[11] She expands on this elsewhere by saying, "I felt very close to Tonio Kröger, the nostalgia, and the feeling of being outside, at once attracted and repulsed by people who are 'comfortable in their own skin.'"[12]

Mann's novella tells the story of a young man with passionate literary and artistic interests, who feels both alienated from and drawn to the bourgeois world of the German town where he grows up. Right from the start Kröger acknowledges that "he was isolated, [and] did not belong among decent normal people." With an equally ambivalent commitment to art and writing, he finds himself "between two worlds . . . at home in neither [which] makes things a little difficult for [him]." The experience of being between different worlds and at home in none had long been Nathalie's. And as the character sketch in Choura Minor's letter from this time suggests, her response to this feeling was not unlike that of Kröger, who is characterised as being inclined to "a morbid instability and a lack of confidence."[13]

There were other, more specific similarities. Kröger's father is a businessman, as was Ilya Tcherniak, and his mother is described, like Polina, as beautiful, but someone to whom "nothing really mattered" and who, after the death of Kröger's father, departs with a new husband to "far-off blue skies."[14] Aside from family circumstance, Kröger is almost as cosmopolitan as Nathalie. And after leaving his hometown and saying goodbye to the house where he was born, he travels through Europe and befriends a Russian artist, Lisabeta Ivanovna, with whom he discusses Russian literature and the artistic vocation in a conversation that forms the central episode of Mann's text.

The question of a literary vocation had not yet taken clear shape for Nathalie. Her own accounts of its emergence vary. Sometimes she claims not to have considered writing for many years; at other times she suggests that the desire to write had long been present, but that she had found "neither subject matter nor form that belonged to me and motivated me to write."[15] If *Tonio Kröger* was a revelation, it was because she saw for the first time that her own sensibility could be material for literature. Thomas Mann, writing in German, was a much more convincing model than the young Russians who met every week in the literary cafés of émigré Berlin. Many of these were poets, and Nathalie was never drawn to poetic form. As a novella, *Tonio Kröger* represented a type of prose writing that was distinct from the novel, a genre which, even after she began writing, she could, for a long time, not imagine adopting. Short forms also have obvious appeal to a language student who might be daunted by length, and for whom the challenge of a foreign language necessarily slows the pace of reading. In Nathalie's case the slower pace no doubt made her particularly sensitive to "something in the rhythm, in the sentences" of Mann's prose that gave her the sense that she was writing the book herself.[16]

It was this encounter with a novella written in German by a German author that revealed to Nathalie that she did after all have something specific to her—her own sensibility—which had the as yet obscure potential to take form in writing that might ultimately be her own. The books that prepared the way to this future weren't confined to a single language or a single literary tradition. Between them, Dostoevsky's Russian, Thomas Mann's German, the English of Virginia Woolf, and the French of Proust (the last two of whom Nathalie was yet to discover) formed a literary landscape within which the Russian-born, quadrilingual French writer would eventually establish a place of her own.

CHAPTER SIX

Pierre Janet's Patient, 1922

WHEN NATHALIE RETURNED from Berlin in June 1922 she reentered family life after almost two years living away from home. The household revolved around the two younger children, Lili who was now twelve and Jacques, four. Nathalie herself would soon be turning twenty-two. Despite her degree in English from the Sorbonne, her year of history in Oxford, her introduction to sociology in Berlin, and her mastery of foreign languages, it was no clearer than it had been when she left for Germany what she might do with her life. Teaching had no appeal, and she needed to make a decision about a career.

The home atmosphere in the rue Nouvelle-Stanislas (now rue Péguy), just off the Boulevard du Montparnasse, was not good, and Nathalie became the conduit for the tensions that were no doubt exacerbated by her renewed presence in the family. The narrator of *Portrait of an Unknown Man* describes himself as a "conducting rod" for all the currents in the surrounding human atmosphere, and it's hard not to assume that Nathalie is writing from her own experience.[1] In any case, it must have become clear at some point that she was in a state of some distress, as the emotional disarray she experienced in Berlin worsened on home territory. Unlike Polina, who resented the time spent at Natacha's bedside during her childhood illnesses, Ilya had always been attentive to his daughter's medical

[67]

needs. When she had become ill one summer after a botched diph-theria inoculation, he had rushed her by taxi from Meudon to Paris and arranged an emergency appointment with a top paediatrician. It was almost certainly he who now arranged for her to be seen by France's top clinical psychologist, Pierre Janet.

In later years Nathalie spoke to very few people about this epi-sode, but in the course of one of the conversations I had with her in the 1990s, she mentioned it—unprompted—to me. The two things that she said were, first, that she had merely been the visible symp-tom of what would now be called a dysfunctional family and, sec-ond, that as Janet escorted her to the door at the end of each session, he would place his hand on her breast. Inappropriate as this was, Janet may have justified the gesture to himself on clinical grounds, since he believed in "excitement" as a treatment for a certain type of patient.[2] However, as told by the adult Nathalie nearly seventy years later, it encapsulated her unqualified scorn for the psychiatric pro-fession in general and for Janet in particular. She didn't say when she had been his patient: there are no records in her own papers, and none in the Janet archive because, for reasons of confidentiality, he requested that all his five thousand files of patients' notes be destroyed after his death. But given the circumstantial evidence, it seems most likely that she saw Janet on her return from Berlin in the summer of 1922.

Despite her dismissive account of the episode, Janet's role in Na-thalie's subsequent development as a writer was decisive, and he haunts her early writings: as the professor lecturing at the Collège de France in *Tropisms* no. 12, as the "specialist" to whom the narra-tor is sent by his parents in *Portrait of an Unknown Man*, and very briefly in his own right when, in 1947, she cites examples from his *De l'angoisse à l'extase* (From anguish to ecstasy) in her essay "From Dostoievski to Kafka." Nathalie's library in her house in Chérence contained several volumes by Janet, and his influence is perceptible in both her ideas and her lexicon. But he was equally important as the foil against whom she eventually established herself as a writer. The experience which made her a patient and which clinical psy-chology defined as a pathology was ultimately recast as a universal reality and a subject worthy of literary exploration.

Nephew of Paul Janet whose philosophy textbook Nathalie had studied at school, Pierre Janet was the leading figure in French clinical psychology in the early years of the twentieth century. He was at the height of his reputation the 1920s following the publication of his three-volume *Médications psychologiques* in 1919 (translated as *Pyschological Healing*). Thanks partly to the dominance of Janet himself and to the French psychological tradition more generally, Freudian psychoanalysis was slow to become established in France. French translations of Freud began to appear only in 1921, French psychoanalysts were still few and far between, and many of the founders of the Société psychanalytique de Paris, created in 1926, came from abroad. These included the Polish-born Eugénie Sokolnicka, negatively portrayed by Andre Gide in 1925 as the therapeutically, conceptually, and morally inept Madame Sophroniska in his novel *The Counterfeiters*. In the *Surrealist Manifesto*, published the previous year, André Breton advanced a more positive view of psychoanalysis, particularly as represented by Freud's *Interpretation of Dreams*. But it was not until the late 1920s that the first French writers underwent Freudian analysis when both Georges Bataille and Michel Leiris signed up with Adrien Borel. There was also active hostility towards Freud, not least on the part of Janet himself. As early as 1913, he challenged Freud's claim to originality and asserted that well before Freud, he, Janet, had discovered the cathartic cure for neuroses. He disputed Freud's symbolic interpretation of dreams and his sexual theory of the origins of neuroses, and, because of its exclusive focus on the mind—as distinct from his own broader psychophysical notion of "conduct"—he dismissed psychoanalysis in general as metaphysical.[3]

In later years, Nathalie herself was vehement in her denunciation of psychoanalysis. In this she echoed some of Janet's own views, but her objections also allowed her to avoid any mention of his name, which, in any case, would by then have meant very little. His star waned dramatically in the 1930s, and his death in 1947 went almost unnoticed. When asked in an interview whether she had ever had an analysis, Nathalie replied, "Never, never, never. I never went near it," and somewhat provocatively, she adds, "Most of the people I knew who were psycho-analysed were much madder after than they were before." She repeatedly criticises psychoanalysis on the grounds of its reductiveness. For Freudians, she says, "everything is very simplified and sexual, and a human being is reduced to sexual drives."[4] As well as vehement in her critique, she could also be rather flippant, suggesting a somewhat limited engagement with Freudian thought: "It's not because I use the word 'carrot' in a sentence that I'm thinking about the phallus . . . it drives you crazy," she once said.[5]

She was always suspicious of the modishness of psychoanalysis whose fortunes were revived by Jacques Lacan in the 1960s and 1970s. A Russian friend, Léon Chertok, who was in analysis with Lacan in the early 1950s, recalls her being equally dismissive of Lacan himself: "How she loathed Lacan! I was very good friends with her at the time. We were two slightly bohemian friends, Russian Jews. . . . I'd often meet her at the 'Petit Saint-Benoît' restaurant after my session. And she would always greet me with a 'Sooo? . . .' And she'd immediately start to tell me terrible things about Lacan, orgies, frightful stories. . . . All this undoubtedly contributed to my negative transference!"[6]

More specifically, and somewhat more seriously, she objected to the psychoanalytic notion of the unconscious, on the grounds that "the unconscious is above all else the thing I know nothing about."[7] Her domain was the *sub*conscious, which, unlike the *un*conscious, is ultimately accessible. (She inherited the term *subconscious* from the French psychological tradition, and the concept is central to Janet's work.) She also feared the creative inhibition that she felt Freudian analysis would have entailed, and she claims on more than one occasion that "psycho-analysis would have prevented me from writing. It would have forced me so see things that I didn't spontaneously see, but that I am told are seen by Freud and his followers."[8] She was spared this eventuality by having received treatment too early to encounter its Freudian manifestation. She nevertheless had Janet's so-called psychological analysis to reckon with.

Since 1902, he had occupied the chair of experimental psychology at the Collège de France, where his lectures drew colleagues from abroad as well as the general public for whom lectures at the Collège were primarily intended. His early work was on hysteria and automatism (the subject of Nathalie's philosophy essay at the Lycée Fénelon), and he saw himself as continuing the French psychological tradition inaugurated by Théodule Ribot. It was Pierre Janet's own study of automatism that led him to coin the term "subconscious." Another coinage, "psychasthenia," gained currency after the publication in 1903 of his influential study, *Les Obsessions et la psychasthénie* (Obsessions and psychasthenia), and he used it in preference to the more common "neurasthenia" to refer to states characterised by worry, anxiety, and obsessions. The word appears in Nathalie's first novel, *Portrait of an Unknown Man*, and it seems more than likely that she was personally familiar with the condition itself.

If Ilya had any perspicacity about the nature of his daughter's distress, Janet's area of expertise made him the obvious choice. Nathalie would have seen him at his home, a spacious apartment at 54 rue de Varenne in the elegant seventh arrondissement, where he received private patients in the afternoons. Although neither she nor any other patient ever left a record of their treatment with him, the writer Raymond Roussel later included Janet's own account of his case as a chapter in his *How I Wrote Certain of My Books*. Roussel reproduces the report verbatim from Janet's *De l'angoisse à l'extase* where he is referred to by the pseudonym "Martial" and described as having suffered "a curious crisis" at the age of nineteen which left him with an unshakeable "sensation of universal glory"— not a condition to which Nathalie was prone.[9]

Janet's work is richly illustrated with examples from his case notes, and his patients are portrayed and quoted at length under pseudonyms, such as Roussel's "Martial" and the mystically minded Madeleine in *De l'angoisse à l'extase*, or, more commonly, with abbreviations of the kind that Nathalie satirises in *Portrait of an Unknown Man* where the narrator refers to "one of those psychiatric handbooks in which the patient is decked out for convenience's sake with an occasionally rather ridiculous name, such as Octave or Jules. Or simply Oct. M. aged 35."[10] However, there is no trace of any "Nat. F. aged 22" in Janet's work, and none of the cases he describes matches the profile that Nathalie would have had at the time.

Janet himself, born in 1859, was now sixty-three. Physically he was on the short side, with penetrating dark eyes and a neat, well-groomed beard. The description of the professor at the Collège de France in *Tropisms* no. 12 is an unflattering but recognisable portrait: "With his sharp, mischievous little eyes, his ready-tied cravate and his square-trimmed beard, he looked enormously like the gentleman in the advertisements who, with one finger in the air, smilingly recommends Saponite, the best of soap-powders."[11] Saponite was much used between the wars, and there was indeed an advertisement for the detergent that matches this description.[12] Physical appearance aside, Janet's skills as a psychotherapist were widely recognised. As the range of therapies discussed in *Les Médications psychologiques* suggests, he had an eclectic and undogmatic approach to technique, and he set great store by getting to know his patients. In principle, he was just the sort of avuncular figure that Nathalie was usually drawn to, but her depiction of him is harsh, and the attentions of the specialist in *Portrait of an Unknown Man* come across as little more than a thinly disguised exercise in psychological classification.

It's impossible to know how long Nathalie's treatment lasted. It may have been quite brief, and its practical outcome largely positive, since it seems more than likely that Janet recommended that Nathalie move out of the family home to put some distance between herself and the source of her problems. In *La Médecine psychologique* (Psychological medicine), written at around the time Nathalie was his patient, he claims that many nervous conditions are caused by the social environment in which the patient lives and that the patient's "psychological ruin" can often be attributed to the "everyday social relations with family members, friends, and people close to him." He refers to "mal-adjustments in the family," and in the case of an unmarried adult child, he advises separating the patient from the home environment, especially when this environment contains "an individual suffering from neuropathy and capable of becoming aboulic, authoritarian or teasing, touchy or persecutory."[13] Vera was very probably a match for this profile, and, as an unmarried adult daughter still living in the family home where she would normally have been expected to stay until marriage, Nathalie certainly fits the bill for Janet's practical recommendation. Ilya was no doubt persuaded to accept the idea, since, by October 1922, she was sharing an apartment with her friend Lena Liber.

Despite his intervention, Nathalie cannot be said to have been definitively cured by Janet. She remained prone to anxiety and obsession throughout her life. In conversation with the literary critic Francine Mallet for a TV film in 1976, she acknowledges that *angoisse*—a word that can mean both "anxiety" and "anguish," and is often best translated as "angst"—has been present in all her work from *Tropisms* onwards, and that it's a feeling she knows well. In her case, she says, it's a response to mortality and the prospect of extinction, and it's something so powerful that she can deal with it only by displacing her worries onto relatively trivial preoccupations: "It's as if, perhaps for good reason, I can't bear to face things—serious things—directly. And so the anxiety gets focussed on small things. An object I've lost, and can't find . . . a letter I've mislaid, things like that, which aren't that important, but at the time I feel angst." When Mallet comments that Nathalie's fictional narrators seem to experience a similar angst, Nathalie concurs, spelling out the detail of their experience: "They're also very anxious because they have the impression that they're marginal, that they're blamed by other people, and regarded as if they were a dead person."[14] But, she adds, in everyday life no one pauses to pay attention to this kind of response.

It's not too fanciful to assume that when Nathalie visited Janet, she presented with a version of these anxiety-induced impressions. She was also—again on her own admission—prone to obsession. Experiences described in her writing are often quite compulsive: chewing fingernails, eating peanuts, scratching an itch. Natacha in *Childhood* is subject to "ideas" which take hold of her and which she cannot control. The characters in her novels relate to the world obsessively, and such obsessions—ideas that persist in the patient's mind in a recurrent and distressing manner—are the stuff of Janetian psychasthenia, and are extensively described in *Obsessions et la psychasthénie*.

It's no surprise that Janet seems to have got under Nathalie's skin, and her preoccupation with him evidently continued well beyond the therapeutic episode. The description of the professor at the Collège de France in *Tropisms* strongly suggests that she attended some of his lectures during the 1920s, joining the audience that crammed into the dingy, airless lecture room and endured its backless benches. She might not have been particularly interested in the course Janet gave in 1922–23 on "The Evolution of Memory and the Notion of Time." But the following series, "Affective Social Feelings, Love and Hate," could well have brought her to the Collège, as might the course for the year 1925–26, "The Stages of

Psychological Evolution and the Role of Strength and Weakness in Mental Functioning," and, above all, "Interior Thought and Its Disturbances," which was Janet's topic for 1926–27. As the quotations, vocabulary, and allusions in her books indicate, she read a good deal of Janet's published work. The two volumes of *De l'angoisse à l'extase*, which she owned and which she quotes from directly, were published in 1926 and 1928, respectively. She also owned a copy of the fascicule publication of the lectures on "Interior Thought and Its Disturbances," published in 1927.[15]

Twenty years later she was still wrestling with Janet's influence in *Portrait of an Unknown Man*, at a time when her life was in danger under the Occupation and, in principle, she had far more pressing concerns. Although the novel's narrator is a middle-aged man, he, like Nathalie, is sent to the specialist by his parents for treatment of an anxiety that goes back to his childhood. In describing the specialist's method, he paraphrases some of the cases in Janet's *De l'angoisse à l'extase*, but without mentioning either its title or its author. However, the contents of the psychiatric treatise he consults are clearly those of this two-volume study, and he borrows Janet's clinical language wholesale: "neuropath," "ambivalence," "rumination," "psychasthenic," and the "mind shrinkage" discussed in the book. He even cites the term *mal-mal*, used by one of Janet's female patients to refer to the feeling of emptiness to which she is subject, and which the narrator himself admits to having experienced.

Given her manifest antipathy, one may wonder what it was about Janet that preoccupied her for so long. One very basic explanation is that, as she insists in her 1947 essay on Dostoevsky and Kafka, the domain of the writer she eventually became is psychology. The psychologist and the novelist share an interest in the inner life, and for both Janet and Nathalie that inner life extends beyond the conscious mind into the obscure regions of the subconscious. Janet's conception of the subconscious, positioned at the lower end of a continuum of consciousness, was derived from the French psychological tradition exemplified by his philosopher uncle Paul Janet, which Nathalie had already encountered. It prefigured her own conception of the semiconscious psychological life that lies behind the visible surface of human exchange and which she later called tropisms.

Similarly, his dynamic conception of the mind, where consciousness is understood as a form of activity rather than a static entity, paves the way for her conception of these tropisms as movement. And although the word "tropism" itself is not part of Janet's lexicon, its biological associations chime with his view of the continuity between the physiological and the psychological elements of existence. These are very broad similarities, but there is enough common ground to explain why Nathalie might have had reason to engage with the ideas she encountered as Janet's patient. Equally, the differences would explain her exasperated desire to work out for herself why his worldview could not be adopted as her own.

This has to do in part with his lack of interest in literature and artistic matters. The professor at the Collège de France in *Tropisms* takes sadistic pleasure in reducing writers (Proust and Rimbaud) to a series of pathological "cases." He is also portrayed as having a dismissive and supercilious attitude towards his patients, although this would be unfair to Janet who gives generous space in his books to his patients' stories. Nevertheless, the underlying principle of his practice as a clinical psychologist was that the minds of patients are quite unlike the minds of their doctors.

This is profoundly at odds with Nathalie's conviction that the psychology of the tropism is universally shared. She refuses the distinction between the normal and the abnormal mind, and she ended up writing from the very angst that initially led her to Janet's consulting room. As she says in the interview with Francine Mallet, her writing is driven by "the angst produced by things that can't be named, things without form, things that others haven't got hold of, classified, pigeon-holed, then thoroughly labelled, and completely stripped of their angst-producing character."[16] But as she also says in another interview, while it may be *angoissant* to write, it's even more *angoissant* not to write.[17] Writing was a solution that Nathalie eventually found to angst, but this was not until a decade later. The solution she opted for in the autumn of 1922 was a degree in law, and she enrolled at the Faculté de Droit.

Tentative Beginnings, 1922–44

CHAPTER SEVEN

Independence, 1922–25

THE DECISION TO STUDY LAW was a "last resort."[1] After returning from Russia, Assia Minor had enrolled as a law student at the
Faculté de Droit, and the combination of camaraderie and competition dating from their Fénelon days may have induced Nathalie to
follow her friend's example. But she also had good personal reasons
for choosing law. The family atmosphere she was so keen to escape
had given her a powerful sense of natural justice, added to which
she enjoyed argument. She and Ilya had always had lively discussions, and she describes him as someone "who could get worked up
about ideas." Since she too felt strongly about the issues that touched
her, their discussions were often heated: "We would have violent
arguments for all sorts of reasons. I think it was always over differences of opinion." One of their fiercest arguments was about Proust,
when Nathalie's enthusiasm was dismissed by her father for whom
Proust was "that homosexual snob" and a "pretentious modernist,"
at which she left the house in rage.[2] Even without argument, she
enjoyed talking, and she imagined that a degree in law might give
her scope to exercise this talent in the courtroom: "I thought that
the law would suit me, not because I liked law . . . but because I
liked to discuss, to debate, to speak my mind."[3] It was a career as an
avocat that she envisaged, rather than that of a *notaire*, an option
that in any case remained closed to women until 1948.

The acquisition of a law degree was not Nathalie's only aim. Law
was a path to independence which she sought by other means, not
least by living away from home. The apartment she shared with

Lena Liber was located over a café at 58 Boulevard Raspail, on the intersection with the rue du Cherche-Midi in the sixth arrondissement. This is the address given throughout Nathalie's degree course on her student record card.[4] From the Boulevard Raspail, it was a twenty-minute walk through the Luxembourg Gardens to the Faculté de Droit on the Place du Panthéon. The family home in the rue Nouvelle-Stanislas was just ten minutes away in the other direction, which meant that she was able to maintain contact with her family while preserving her autonomy.

For the first time in her life she was part of a social circle of like-minded people of her own age and background, young women, mostly with Russian-Jewish origins, who, like her, were French-educated and French-speaking and preparing to embark on professional careers in postwar France. She later claimed that there were assumptions about sexual equality in Russian émigré circles that made it a matter of course for women to obtain professional qualifications and pursue an independent career. But if this was the case, it applied to these first-generation émigré daughters rather more than to their mothers. Although Polina was a writer, she relied on Kolya for financial provision, while Vera never undertook professional work. Positive examples of professionally independent women in Nathalie's childhood were rare: Assia's mother had her bookshop, and in *Childhood* Nathalie recalls Mme Pereverzev, a dentist and the mother of her friend Micha, who would emerge from her consulting room in the family home, a dental instrument in her hand, to ask the children to make less noise. There had been women teachers at the Lycée Fénelon and Home Students in Oxford, but at the Sorbonne and the Faculty of Law the professors were all men.

Women of the younger generation were belatedly beginning to enter the legal profession. This had been possible only since 1900, and they had yet to become fully established within it. The first case defended in court by a woman dated only from 1907.[5] The Law Faculty in Paris had been the last of the faculties at the Sorbonne to accept women students, and in 1905 they constituted only 1 percent of those studying law. By virtue of their sex, women were considered to be constitutively unsuited to jurisprudence. "Women are all intuition," one professor of law had declared, adding, "They can often see the correct solution but without being able to trace their reasoning and explain it [because] what the female mind lacks is the capacity for nuanced legal reasoning."[6] There was also a fear that when they discovered more about the law they would start demanding the equality inscribed in the French constitution. For Nathalie there was a further problem, namely that, as a result of recent legislation, which ratified a long-standing convention, she would be unable to practise at the bar without having French nationality.

Women were accepted in greater numbers to study medicine and pharmacy. Lena Liber had resumed her medical studies at the Faculté de Médecine; two of Nathalie's other friends, Nadia Wilter and Sonia Dobkovitch, were also studying medicine; and Fernande Elosu, a politically radical acquaintance and a frequent visitor to the apartment in the Boulevard Raspail, was studying pharmacy.[7] Nadia's sister Nora was one of the first women to study engineering, and another Russian friend, Mania Lézine, took the *agrégation* and taught English in one of the Paris lycées. (Mania was a few years younger than Nathalie and the daughter of a friend of Vera's.)[8] They belonged to a new generation of young women, for whom the world of the 1920s was very different from the one their mothers had known before the First World War. This was partly an effect of the war itself when, in the absence of sufficient menfolk, women had taken over traditionally male jobs, and wives had single-handedly assumed family responsibilities. But as the title of Victor Margueritte's best-selling 1922 novel, *La Garçonne* (*Bachelor Girl*), suggests, it also transformed women themselves, prompting the reactionary writer Drieu la Rochelle to lament that civilisation "no longer has sexes."

This was a characteristic conservative response to the new phenomenon of the "modern woman" who, in the words of the editor of the literary weekly *L'illustration*, was "freer in her behaviour than women before the war . . . she dances without a corset, she swims in a maillot. . . . Above all she has a taste or desire for independence, or rather . . . she is absolutely determined to be independent."[9] She had shortened her skirts and cut her hair while seeking entry into the workplace and obtaining qualifications for professions that had long been the preserve of bourgeois men. In 1923 a journalist remarked that "a woman doctor, lawyer, engineer, painter, sculptor or composer is no longer a phenomenon. It is scarcely an exception to

FIGURE 10. Nathalie, Assia Minor, Lena Liber, and
"Eva," 1922. (Sarraute Family Collection)

the rule."[10] Nathalie and her friends were perfect examples of these modern women with their professional ambitions and their irrepressible desire for independence.

A photograph from 1922, which Nathalie kept and later had copied and enlarged, shows Nathalie, Assia, Lena, and someone named on the back as Eva striding down a country road on the edge of a forest in high summer. Four more of the group are following behind, and all of them appear to be attired for a special occasion. Their dresses are loose-fitting, their skirts are mostly calf length, and Lena's hemline stops at the knee. Presumably none of them is constrained by a corset. Assia and Nathalie both have short hair, and Nathalie is wearing a headband across her forehead in the flapper style of the decade. The fact that she had copies made of the photograph suggests that it had special significance for her, perhaps as a record of friendships, many of which were for life, but also as an image of the freedom and independence that she always treasured.

It was in this spirit that in November 1922 she embarked on the three-year course that would lead to a degree in law. However, the reality of legal study proved not at all to her taste, and, as she later said, "it became clear that law bored me very much."[11] Worse still, she found it hard, with civil, commercial, and financial law being particularly forbidding. She persevered, passed the first- and second-year examinations, and scraped through her finals on a resit in October 1925, after initially failing in July because of her poor performance in commercial law. She may have been distracted by her marriage in July of that year to Raymond Sarraute, a fellow law student, whom she met in 1923 (about whom more in the next chapter). After graduating she immediately enrolled for a doctorate in law, which she doesn't seem to have taken very seriously, and which she soon abandoned. Instead, she embarked on what proved to be a desultory career as an *avocat*.

By the time she graduated, the obstacle of her Russian nationality had been removed, as she succeeded in obtaining French nationality in February 1925. At that time naturalisation was far from being a foregone conclusion, since it was rarely granted to foreign-born women who were neither wives nor dependent daughters. Most women who acquired French nationality did so in conjunction with an application made by a husband or a father. Nathalie submitted her application in October 1924, presenting herself as a student at the Faculty of Law, spelling her name "Tcherniack" as her father did, and giving her address as that of the parental home (5 rue Nouvelle-Stanislas), in order to maximise the association with the application made simultaneously by Ilya for himself and his dependents (Vera, Lili, and Jacques).

The initial independent assessment recorded in December by the Paris Prefect of Police was unfavourable. His letter draws attention to Nathalie's having spent a year in Oxford and studied in Berlin, as if to suggest that her loyalties did not lie entirely with France. He concludes that there are no grounds for granting the request of "Mlle Nathalie Tcherniak," and he recommends that her application be adjourned. However, a handwritten note, appended in the margin of the letter and dated 24 February 1925, records the decision to grant her French nationality on payment of the standard fee of 1,276 francs.[12] The Prefect's response to Ilya's application is considerably more positive, and the request was approved. Had Nathalie waited until she was married, an application from the spouse of a French national would almost certainly have been accepted, but she evidently preferred to find a solution in her own right.

Even with the requisite French nationality, her career as an *avocat* never took her further than intern status. She never showed any professional ambition, and despite having been nominally a member of the bar between 1926 and 1940, she had, on her own admission, done almost nothing.[13] She was mostly sent to La Santé prison, where she took on cases that were randomly assigned to her, and she worked for a time in the chambers of one Maître Dulud. She later claimed that she had earned so little from her efforts as an *avocat* that the proceeds would not have covered the professional license fee, except that as a result of an administrative oversight she was never asked to pay it.[14] Although her talent was for talk, she found the language used in court at the time "unbearably grandiloquent and sentimental."[15] (Grandiloquence was invariably a fault in her eyes.)

The anecdotes she would relate about her experiences were comic vignettes in which she gave herself the role of professional incompetent. On one occasion she found herself closeted with a huge defendant who went by the name of Bubu-les-yeux-tatoués (Bubu-tattoo-eyes), and she was so terrified that she instantly begged to be let out. In another story she had just finished successfully defending a case of theft when she discovered that her handbag was missing, and protested. On being asked by the judge what she thought had happened, she pointed to the defendant she had just reprieved, claiming, "He must have taken it!" She then found the handbag, which she had simply mislaid.[16]

There is very little trace of Nathalie's legal career in her novels. The name "Dulud" appears once in *Between Life and Death*—but it is simply one name in a list of several—and, as with so many of her other experiences, her time as a lawyer is never directly represented as part of the narrative content of her work. The occasional image conjures up the courtroom: Alain Guimier in *The Planetarium* (1959) appears briefly in his father's eyes as a shifty delinquent in the dock, and in *Do You Hear Them?* (1972), the central character—an art lover—is cross-examined in an imaginary court hearing where it is established, somewhat ludicrously, that his children "despised art" and had wilfully rejected all the cultural opportunities he had offered them. He is instructed by the imaginary judge to raise his hand, take the oath, and confine himself to the facts in answering questions; but the whole scene—like so many in Nathalie's work—is written in a mode of comic exaggeration whose sole function is to provide an analogy, not to depict any supposed reality. These are episodes with stock characters, which anyone could have invented on the basis of courtroom scenes from films or books, such as Kafka's *Trial* or Camus's *The Stranger*, both of which Nathalie had read.

In her own estimation, the main benefit she derived from her pursuit of a legal career was her discovery of the spoken language, which came via the exercise known as the *conférence du stage*. This is an annual oratory contest for aspiring *avocats*, with a history going back to the Ancien Régime. Organised by the twelve winners from the previous year, known as "secretaries," it's held in the imposing Bibliothèque des Avocats on an upper floor of the Palais de Justice. Competitors are given a topic, which usually has both legal and social implications, and is related to decisions recently taken in the higher courts. There are three rounds, and the fifteen-minute speeches are a test of rhetorical skill, where, as well as exhibiting a command of legal knowledge, candidates must also demonstrate an ability to persuade and to entertain their audience. Success in the contest is often prelude to a distinguished career.

Encouraged by Raymond who had got through to the second round of the lecture competition in 1928, Nathalie decided to try her hand in the 1929–30 competition. Presenting herself on 17 January 1930, she found the exercise far more congenial than day-to-day legal practice. As she later explained in an interview,

> I couldn't bear the way lawyers spoke in the Assizes. I had to deliver several speeches for the *conférence du stage*, and in writing them, I adopted a language close to the audience, and very different from the style of an academic speech for the defence. For me, speaking for the defence

meant speaking to people. I liked persuading people, but doing so directly, and avoiding high-falutin' language. Without being presumptuous, I can tell you my lectures made quite an impact. More than anything, communicating orally in public rescued me from the pernickety style of academic writing. It was a real step forward. A little as if, in its own way, the bar had given me back the use of speech. In its way, or rather in mine. . . .[17]

The Use of Speech was the title of a collection of short texts that Nathalie wrote years later and published in 1980, but the absorption of speech into the written language is a feature of all her work.

Although her talks for the first round of the competition were a success, she was eliminated in the second round when the topics didn't inspire her. Not having any serious professional ambition, she was not unduly disappointed; but she was evidently not aware that being Jewish, foreign-born, and female she had stood very little chance of success in the first place. In addition to the suspicion in which women were held by the legal profession, there was a widespread assumption amongst lawyers that there were too many Jews in the Palais de Justice, and no desire amongst the lawyers adjudicating the competition to give them any encouragement by selecting them as "secretaries."[18] Even without the obstacles of these prejudices, Nathalie's lack of interest in the law confirmed the misogynistic stereotype of the intuitive woman with no capacity for legal reasoning. But, regardless of these handicaps, the *conférence du stage* had been the means of liberating her from the formality of the written French she learned at school, and revealing her aptitude for the kind of language that would in due course make it possible for her to write.

There was another, very different sphere in which she found a kind of independence and sought equal footing with men. She had always enjoyed sport—tennis, swimming, and the punting she mastered as a student in Oxford—and in the 1920s she took up mountaineering, an enthusiasm she shared with Lena. A photo she selected for inclusion in the first book-length study of her work in 1965 shows the two of them with crampons, goggles, and poles, standing at the summit of Mont Blanc with five other similarly equipped figures, and all seven attached to each other by ropes knotted around the waist.[19] Nathalie gives the date as 1923, and identifies two of the figures as students from England, and two more as guides. She and Lena are the only women in the group, and there is scant evidence of others making it to the summit at this time. It was no small undertaking. Even the easiest of the routes takes climbers across snow, ice, and a glacier, and requires twelve hours of solid exertion at high altitude. If Nathalie offered the photo to the authors of the monograph, it was no doubt because she saw the climb as an achievement that proved her the equal of the men standing beside her.

The following summer she and Lena went to La Bérarde, a centre for mountaineering in the Massif des Écrins in the Rhône Alps. They stayed at the Hôtel Tairraz, in a small hamlet dwarfed by mountains whose slopes rise steeply on all sides. Photographs kept by Nathalie show two unidentified figures amid the snow, one of them straddling a small crevasse, perhaps on the so-called tormented glacier of La Pilatte. Another shows a man astride a rock on the Cornes de Pié Bérarde. This trip seems to have been Nathalie's last mountaineering escapade, since there's no record of any others. Like her experience of the law, it survives in her work in the form of occasional images: a character briefly sees himself in his mind's eye cut off by a crevasse, and in an equally incidental allusion there is mention of the mountain hut at the l'Aiguille du Goûter, from where Nathalie's group very probably set out on their climb to the summit of Mont Blanc.[20]

Raymond Sarraute did not share Nathalie's passion for mountaineering. In a postcard he sent in July from Winteregg in Switzerland where he was on holiday, he professes his respectful admiration for Nathalie's extraordinary feats, news of which had already reached him, most likely communicated by Lena. He uses the formal *vous* form—as would have been normal at the time—but the tone is playful, and suggests a certain intimacy, since, in addition to commiserating about the bad weather which had also prevented him from playing tennis, he says that he hopes that "the blues" have not got the better of her and that she is more interested in climbing than in "psycho-pathology."[21] By the following summer, Raymond and Nathalie were married, and holidays thereafter would be spent in the Mediterranean sun rather than among Alpine snows.

CHAPTER EIGHT

Raymond

NATHALIE AND RAYMOND FIRST MET in 1923 when he asked to borrow her lecture notes to catch up after being ill. She was twenty-three and he twenty-one. They married eighteen months later, immediately after sitting for their final exams. Unlike Nathalie, Raymond enjoyed legal study, his father was a lawyer, and he himself went on to become an *avocat* at the court of appeal, specialising in commercial law (Nathalie's bugbear), with occasional sidesteps into other spheres. He also had a keen interest in literature, and this was the ground on which he and Nathalie shared a deep and lifelong understanding. Having spent two years in a sanatorium with suspected tuberculosis, he had had plenty of time to read. He also had a strong visual sense, and a visual culture that was much more developed than Nathalie's. When he visited her at no. 58 Boulevard Raspail, he was taken aback to see her own artistic taste exemplified by the reproduction of Gros's unashamedly romantic Bonaparte au Pont d'Arcole, which she had brought with her from home.[1]

They would meet after classes, and talk for hours as they walked in the Luxemburg Gardens, Nathalie on the way home to the Boulevard Raspail and Raymond to the nearby rue du Regard where he lived with his father. "From the moment I met Raymond, I just talked and talked and talked . . . about all the things I had never talked to anyone about before," she recalled. This talk evidently included the "psychopathology" mentioned by Raymond in his post-

SOCIÉTÉ NATIONALE DES
CHEMINS DE FER FRANÇAIS
ET RÉSEAUX ALGÉRIENS

CARTE DE SURCLASSEMENT N° 12056
Valable du 1ᵉʳ Octobre 1938 au 30 Septembre 1939
(Nom et prénoms).
Délivrée à M *Sarraute Raymond*
Officier de Réserve inscrit à l'École de Perfectionnement de
l'intendance
à *Paris*
demeurant à *Paris |16|*
12 Avenue
Pierre | de Serbie
Signature
du Titulaire

Le Fonctionnaire délégué
de la Société Nationale des Chemins de fer français.

Voir Observations essentielles
au verso

FIGURE 11. Raymond Sarraute, 1930s. (Sarraute Family Collection)

card of 1924, but more than anything else, and "with a sort of rapture," literature. As she later said, "He played a huge part in my literary education," he introduced her to contemporary writing, and he licensed her passionate preoccupation with all things literary.[2] The start to her own writing was still some way off and its means not obvious at a time when she was still anticipating a career in law, but the meeting with Raymond was a turning point, and he remained her closest literary ally until his death in 1985.

He was tall, blond, and handsome, with a gentle smile that was noted by many of those who met him. If Nathalie was attracted by his looks, she would always stress the disparity between the two of them on this score, claiming, "I've never understood how this archangel married such an ugly wretch!" But her incredulity was also a form of defiance. Almost as a matter of principle, she refused to cultivate her own attractiveness, as if to say to the world, "I'll be ugly and you'll love me, and you'll love me truly, for myself and not for my beauty."[3] What Raymond thought of Nathalie's physical appearance is not known—in fact she dressed fashionably in the 1920s—but she found in him someone willing to respond to her implicit demand, and who would love her "truly, for herself." Apart from her teenage flirtations with Assia's brothers, she does not seem to have had a close relationship with a man before meeting Raymond, and there was none afterwards. What she found in him was primarily a soul mate. The bond between them was based on the fact that, as she told the actress Isabelle Huppert, "we developed at more or less the same time and we had very similar tastes and sensibilities."[4] Raymond was the one person in her life by whom she felt understood.

He was born on 10 October 1902 in the fourteenth arrondissement. His birth certificate records that his parents—Joseph Sarraute and Livcha Lourié—lived at 93 Boulevard Port-Royal, not far from the rue Flatters where the two-year-old Natacha had recently arrived with Polina and Kolya. Joseph was twenty-eight and a lawyer, Livcha thirty-three and a doctor, and they had married in 1898. Livcha died in 1908, when Raymond was only six, an event which in Nathalie's estimation had left him from an early age with a strong sense of detachment, and "an extraordinarily strong sort of sense of the emptiness and the basic futility of existence."[5] This was also perhaps the basis for the integrity that she admired in him along with a total absence of any personal ambition.

On the face of it, their family backgrounds could not have been more dissimilar. The Sarrautes were conservative Catholics from Carcassonne in southwestern France (Raymond's Uncle Léon was a priest and one of his aunts was a nun), whereas the Tcherniaks

were metropolitan, Socialist Revolutionary, Russian-Jewish émigrés. However, Joseph Sarraute had broken with family tradition
and was active in socialist groups in the 1890s and early 1900s. He
had also broken with tradition by marrying a Russian Jew.

Joseph was a striking figure who remained closely involved in his
son's life. He was handsome and energetic and, according to his
granddaughter Claude Sarraute, had a reputation as a ladies' man.[6]
He was a friend of the then French president, Alexandre Millerand,
onetime socialist, under whom he previously served in the Ministry
of Commerce, Industry, Posts and Telegraphs. Remembered by colleagues as "absent-minded and brilliant," he was also "a very cultivated man."[7] Nathalie, who got to know him well, described him as
"a jurist with a passion for his profession and an intellectual with a
passion for philosophy," adding that Raymond took after his father
in "this ferocity and this diversity of interests."[8]

Joseph had turned his back on his rentier heritage after being
radicalised as a student in Toulouse, where he graduated from the
Faculté de Droit in 1894. He then moved to Paris, where he wrote a
thesis on the length of the working day—the issue that galvanised
the strikers in Ivanovo-Vosnesensk in 1905—and was active in journalism. Two influential articles in *La Revue socialiste* in 1900, later
published in book form as *Socialisme d'opposition, socialisme de
gouvernement et lutte de classe* (Socialism in opposition, socialist
government and class struggle), earned him a reputation as the
theorist behind the reformist socialism of Jean Jaurès. With a Jewish wife, he was particularly alert to any form of anti-Semitism, and
the support of both Jaurès and Millerand for Dreyfus may well have
weighed in the shift of his political allegiance from more radical to
reformist socialism. Having connections with Russian socialists
through Livcha and his friend Charles Rappoport, Joseph would
also have been aware of the Socialist Revolutionary émigré groups,
and the French socialist support for Yakov Tcherniak would not
have escaped his notice in 1907. Despite the apparent differences in
their backgrounds, Raymond and Nathalie did, after all, belong to
overlapping worlds.

On a more personal note, they had similar family situations,
since—albeit for different reasons—they were both motherless, and
each was close to a supportive father. It was Joseph Sarraute who

had raised Raymond and his sister Véra after their mother died. Thanks to her early death, her Russian-Jewish origins, and the paucity of information about her, Livcha was a mysterious and somewhat exotic figure in the Sarraute family annals. Nathalie's accounts always stressed her beauty, which had allegedly cast a spell over Lenin, whom Livcha was said to have known through a friendship with Lenin's wife Krupskaya, and at whose feet Nathalie claimed Raymond had played as a child. Except that sometimes the family narrative replaced Krupskaya with Rosa Luxemburg. There is little likelihood that Livcha knew either woman, since the Lenins didn't arrive in Paris until after her death in 1908. She was born in Kozlovichi in Belarus on 22 June 1869 (the date given on her doctoral thesis), and so was almost five years older than her husband, or six if you believe the birthdate of 1868 given on her student record card at the Faculty of Medicine in Paris. Her family lived in Kiev, where her father was a lawyer—and where Ilya Tcherniak later studied. She herself had been unable to study at the city's St Vladimir University, which closed its doors to female students in 1888. And as an imperial edict of 1882 had also debarred women from studying medicine in Russia, she had been obliged to seek alternative solutions abroad.

France was one of the few countries where women had access to medical study. It's not clear where Livcha began her studies, but in 1893 she transferred to Toulouse for her final year. The university was not a prime destination for foreign students at the time, and since its Faculty of Medicine had only recently acquired full faculty status, Livcha's move to Toulouse is likely to have been for personal reasons. Her student record at the Faculty of Medicine in Paris, where she went on to do her doctorate, gives an address for 1893 at 7 rue de l'Estrapade, in Paris, with a Mme Sarraute named as her "guardian."[9] This Mme Sarraute was almost certainly Joseph's mother, as Claude Sarraute mentions that Raymond Sarraute *père* lived in Paris for a while.[10] With so little to go on, it is tempting to speculate—in the colourful vein of Nathalie's later anecdotes—that Livcha had met Joseph in Paris, and that it was love that took her to Toulouse. At any rate, with or without love, she graduated there in 1894, and moved with Joseph to Paris in 1895 to continue her medical studies. She received her doctorate in 1899 at the Faculty of

Medicine in Paris, one of only nineteen women to do so. Her thesis examined the influence of rest on the duration of pregnancy and argued for improved working conditions for pregnant women. Livcha was herself pregnant at the time, and on 22 July 1898 she gave birth to a daughter, Véra, who later followed her mother into a career in medicine.

Livcha is one of the few women doctors listed in the Bottin-Didot directory of 1901, where she has an entry under the name "Dr Mme Sarraute" and a professional address at 2 Place de la Nation. There's no entry for her in the following year, when a second pregnancy and the ensuing birth of Raymond no doubt curtailed her professional activities. Apparently undeterred, and presumably accompanied by her two children, she then practised as the local doctor in the tiny village of Souancé-au-Perche between Chartres and Le Mans until, in 1904, she handed her practice over to her Russian friend Sophie Oguse, wife of Joseph's friend Charles Rappoport.[11] By 1906 the family home had moved to Passy, where the air was said to be clearer than in the city and which had a long-standing reputation for its health benefits.[12] Livcha was very probably suffering from the tuberculosis that would kill her two years later, and with which Raymond was later wrongly diagnosed. Joseph had meanwhile diverted his energies from politics and journalism to his career as an *avocat*, and after Livcha died he never remarried.

This history left its mark on Raymond, who inherited from both parents a strong sense of social justice, and his air of gentle reticence was belied by his passionate opposition to all manifestations of anti-Semitism and his equally passionate defence of immigrants, causes to which he later lent his legal expertise. His commitment to republican values also made him a lifelong loyal member of the Freemasons. In the 1940s and 1950s he published four books—two on the legal situation of the Jews in France, one on the status of immigrants in France, and one on intellectual property in the cinema. And he was liked and respected by everyone who met him. He had also witnessed in his parents the value that they both ascribed to a professional career. His mother's professional independence was unusual for the time, but it was a model that Nathalie was geared to emulate. Nevertheless, when she married Raymond in 1925, she took his surname—as was common at the time—and never again used her father's name. The Russian-born Natalia Tcherniak became an entirely French-sounding Nathalie Sarraute. Like her family and her Russian émigré friends, Raymond always called her Natacha, but unlike them he had never learned his mother's language, and never subsequently did so.

CHAPTER NINE

Coming of Age with Modernism, 1923–27

THE MEETING WITH RAYMOND launched Nathalie into a renewed engagement with literature. She took out a subscription to the *Nouvelle revue française* whose January 1923 number was given over to an homage to Proust who had died the previous year. The monthly publication covered theatre, art exhibitions, film, and literature, both French and foreign, including Joyce's *Ulysses* and Dostoevsky's *Eternal Husband* (a favourite of Nathalie's), Dada, and Surrealism. Its pages were required reading for anyone with cultural interests, and Nathalie's library in her house in Chérence contained a yellowing run of the journal starting in 1923. One number has her friend Assia's name on the cover. But did either of the two young women register as remarkable that the *NRF* was written almost exclusively by men about books that were also only slightly less exclusively by men?

Raymond introduced Nathalie to a number of works by Gide that she had not previously read. His *Fruits of the Earth*, from 1897, had already fired up a young generation of readers with its rallying cry of "Families, I hate you!" and Nathalie had "adored" the book in her teens. Born in 1869, Gide belonged to her parents' generation, but in the 1920s he embodied the new spirit of the postwar era. His defence of homosexuality in *Corydon* was published in 1924, and established his reputation as an opponent of conventional morality.

He also represented a challenge to a certain literary conservatism, and in an interview to mark his centenary in 1969, Nathalie recalled that Gide "taught us to look at things in a different way." He confirmed her view that Jarry's *Ubu roi* was "a great play," wrote about Dada "with penetration," and attacked conservative literary critics like Emile Faguet. In sum, "he was a man on the alert, struggling constantly to liberate himself, and to disregard all prohibitions. His presence and his words were a great support for us. His taste mattered for us."[1] (The "us" presumably refers both to the younger generation in general and to Raymond and Nathalie in particular.)

She later dismissed Gide's novels as "artificial" and "cold-blooded," claiming a little bizarrely that their style made her think of jam.[2] What interested her more were his critical essays and reflections, several of which appeared in the *NRF*. His study of Dostoevsky, published in 1923, championed the Russian novelist in psychological terms to which Nathalie must have warmed at a point when she was seeking an alternative to Janet's version of psychopathology. But it was Gide's *Paludes* that spoke most directly to her. Written in 1895, it's a strange, generically indeterminate text, part dialogue, part self-commentary in the slightly satirical idiom adopted by its narrator, whose aesthetic principles prevent him from composing a traditional novel, and who is writing—or rather not writing—a book called "Paludes." Gide's *Paludes* demands the active participation of its reader, and it still strikes a curiously modern note. As with Thomas Mann's *Tonio Kröger*, it was a book Nathalie felt she could have written herself.[3]

Raymond also introduced her to the novels of François Mauriac. By no means an avant-garde figure in the manner of Gide, Mauriac was nonetheless acquiring a reputation for his portrayal of family tensions in novels such as *A Kiss for the Leper* (1922) or *The Desert of Love* (1925), which Nathalie read several times, and in which she said she found revealing insights into her own father.[4] She regarded Mauriac as the French novelist whose novels most resembled the great Russians, and her library in Chérence contained almost all of his work, including his critical essay on fiction, *Le Romancier et ses personnages* (The novelist and his characters), published in 1933. Her own novels would later take family life as fertile ground for exploring the psychological volatility of human interaction.

   Proust, however, was the major discovery of these years, and for once it was one that she didn't owe to Raymond. Her accounts of exactly when—and what—she first read are slightly inconsistent. On some occasions she says it was in 1923, and on others, 1924, sometimes mentioning *Swann's Way*, and at other times *In the Shadow of Young Girls in Flower*. But since she also mentions that her reading of Proust took place in Chamonix during the summer she climbed Mont Blanc, this would make 1923—the year after his death—the more likely date. It would also suggest that the photo of the summit of Mont Blanc, when Nathalie and her friend Lena were themselves "young girls in flower," was an oblique memento of what in retrospect proved to have been a crucial moment for her future writing career. As she later said, "[Proust] gave me a sense of discovering a new world," and it was a discovery that gave her the unprecedented impulse to "write an article to talk about him."[5] She never wrote the article and never hinted at its projected content, but *Remembrance of Things Past* was a revelation: "If I'd never read Proust, first, with that world of feelings—admittedly analysed—but seen through a microscope, a whole universe opening up which we could feel but had never seen in literature . . . , I would never have written what I did."[6] She then read the remaining volumes, the last one of which was published (posthumously) in 1927, and she reread him repeatedly throughout her life.

   She never took much interest in poetry, and it was thanks to Raymond that she read Mallarmé. Like Gide, Mallarmé was a highly self-reflexive writer and the author of important essays on poetry from which Nathalie later quoted in her own critical essays. It was also thanks to Raymond that she read Victor Segalen, who had recently died prematurely at the age of forty-one, and Apollinaire, who at the age of thirty-eight had been a victim of the 1918 flu epidemic. Had it not been for their untimely deaths both poets would still have been active in the 1920s. Neither had lasting appeal for Nathalie, and her tastes in poetry remained chiefly confined to Baudelaire and Rimbaud. But an example was set by all four writers—Apollinaire, Segalen, Baudelaire, and Rimbaud—since, by breaking out of the formal structure of verse and developing various types of free verse and prose poetry, they each found ways of putting prose to new poetic use.

It was the prose writing of the German poet Rainer Maria Rilke, *The Notebooks of Malte Laurids Brigge*, that made one of the deepest impressions on Nathalie in the 1920s. She read it in 1926, possibly in the French translation published that year, but more likely in the 1910 German original. The first part of the book describes the narrator's life in exile in Paris at the turn of the century, as he wanders the streets and neighbourhoods where Natacha lived with Polina and Kolya during the same years. She would have recognised both the places and the slightly alienated exile mood of Rilke's evocations, and perhaps imagined having passed him in the rue Saint-Jacques or outside the Val-de-Grâce hospital on the Boulevard Port-Royal, both of which are mentioned by Rilke's fictional Malte. The generic indeterminacy of *The Notebooks*—based on the fragmentary form of the *kleine Prosa* (short prose) that was a feature of modern German literature—would have suggested new literary possibilities at a point when Nathalie was convinced that the novel had reached an impasse as a literary genre.

In 1927 she read Virginia Woolf's *Mrs Dalloway*, which had been published two years previously. She also read Woolf's essay "Modern Fiction" in *The Common Reader*, published in 1925. In words that Nathalie quoted in a critical essay of 1954, Woolf writes that for the moderns literary interest lies "in the dark places of psychology," where "the emphasis is upon something hitherto ignored [so that] a different outline of form becomes necessary, difficult for us to grasp, incomprehensible to our predecessors."[7] This novelty in both psychological content and literary form must have been a revelation to Nathalie as she read *Mrs Dalloway*, which she considered a masterpiece, and whose own dark places include psychopathology in the form of extreme insanity and a psychiatrist who has no insight into the mind of his unhappy patient. Given her own recent experience of psychotherapy, and at a point when she was almost certainly attending Janet's lectures on "Interior Thought and Its Disturbances" at the Collège de France, Woolf's remarks were timely. The French translation of Woolf's novel didn't appear until 1929, and Nathalie almost certainly came across the English original in Sylvia Beach's English-language bookshop, Shakespeare and Company, at no. 12 rue de l'Odéon in the sixth arrondissement. She subscribed to the shop's lending library, whose records reveal that between May and July 1926 she borrowed Poe's *Tales* and Conrad's *Lord Jim*, the latter perhaps prompted by the *NRF* special number on Conrad which came out after his death in 1924.[8]

This abundance of literary example and future influence also included Joyce's *Ulysses*, whose use of interior monologue and unprecedented access to mental life Nathalie regularly mentioned in later interviews—perhaps a little dutifully—as having been an essential part of her literary formation. The English original had been published in Paris by Sylvia Beach in 1922, and as a subscriber to the *NRF* Nathalie would have come across an article by Valery Larbaud the French champion of Joyce's work in the January 1925 number of the journal. The book was a landmark for her, but not an inspiration of the kind that Proust, Rilke, and Woolf had been. She had an even cooler relation to Surrealism, whose first manifesto appeared in 1924. As she said in reply to a questionnaire in 1963, "I followed their manifestoes and writings with interest, no doubt, but without feeling involved." The movement's antiestablishment posture was in the spirit of the times, but she was put off by Breton's defence of psychoanalysis.[9] And although his scepticism with regard to the novel matched her own, by citing Dostoevsky's *Crime and Punishment* as an illustration of the genre's unacceptable realism, Breton would nonetheless not have endeared himself to her.

Culled from interviews given by the established novelist half a century and more after her first encounter with their writing, this roll call of names reads as a retrospective means of situating her work in the mainstream of European modernism and establishing her own literary legacy. But in the 1920s, long before they entered any consecrated history of Modernism, each book represented a new discovery to be discussed—rapturously—with Raymond. Poised between law and literature, reading and writing, France, Germany, and England, the novel and some other as yet unspecified form, she was exhilarated by the pervasive atmosphere of innovation:

> I had the impression that a new world was opening up, carried by new forms, and that it was impossible, after these revolutionary works, to write as one had written before. It was also impossible to imitate them.

Their strength came from the novelty of their discoveries. Certain poets, moreover, like André Breton and Max Jacob, were claiming that the novel was no longer an art.

It also seemed to me, that apart from those great revolutionaries of the first quarter of the century, the novels that did meet with success were not very worthwhile.

However, if Nathalie was to write, it was not clear what form that writing might take: "I did not like *Bella* [1926] by Jean Giraudoux or *Les Enfants terribles* [*The Holy Terrors*, 1929] by Cocteau, that were so greatly acclaimed. One needed a certain amount of courage to dare to criticize them. Thus I thought that despite the pleasures I had drawn from my 'French compositions' and the boredom that legal work instilled within me, nothing could incite me to write."[10] This note of wariness about books that attract general acclaim is sounded in many of the later writings, but here it positions her once more between her sense of participating in a new cultural era and an equally strong sense of needing to keep her distance from any diktats that might issue from it. Her alliance with Raymond was insurance against finding herself enrolled into any such cultural consensus. Neither she as an individual nor the two of them as a couple were part of any literary circle, and they formed a little *cénacle* of their own.

This literary independence becomes a leitmotif in Nathalie's recollection of the plays they saw in this period. Recalling Georges Pitoëff's productions of Chekhov in 1922, when his company staged *The Seagull* and a revival of *Uncle Vanya* at the Comédie des Champs-Elysées, Nathalie contrasts her own enthusiasm with her parents' lack of appreciation for "the subtlety of the exchanges and the comedy of the repartees."[11] And when she and Raymond attended the Pitoëffs' production of Pirandello's *Six Characters in Search of an Author* at the same theatre in 1923, she claims that there was only a handful of people in the audience for a play which she describes as having been "an event" for her. The performance left the couple "in a state of total enthusiasm." And, she adds, "Coming out of the theatre after a play it was impossible for us not to think the same thing."[12] She relied on this sense of identical responses, which are almost always presented as going against the grain of family or public opinion.

Although they lived the *années folles* rather more soberly than many of their contemporaries, there were lighter moments in the couple's cultural activities. They were not part of the Jazz Age and didn't frequent the nightclubs and cabarets in Montmartre or Montparnasse where Michel Leiris, Georges Bataille, and others were drinking the nights away and discovering *l'art nègre* and black performers. But Nathalie had always been a moviegoer, having occasionally gone to the cinema with her father after school. She and Raymond continued this habit and in 1925 they saw Charlie Chaplin in *The Gold Rush*, which Nathalie later recalled in her novel *Martereau*. Allusions to Fritz Lang's first talkie, *M* (1931), and to Josef von Sternberg's *Blue Angel* (1930) found their way into other novels. In a letter of 1928 to Nathalie, Raymond mentions that he plans to go and see *Siren of the Tropics* starring Josephine Baker, and elsewhere he alludes to having dropped in at the music hall as if this were something he regularly did.[13] They saw Fritz Lang's *Metropolis* in 1927, and Nathalie fainted from terror when the robot appeared.[14] She maintained a lifelong interest in film, but always as a spectator. Unlike others of the Nouveau Roman generation, she was never tempted to write for the medium.

In many ways the 1920s—a decade of Europe-wide artistic experimentation, questioning, and creation—were the years of Nathalie's most decisive literary formation. Its influence remained with her throughout her creative life, even when, for the rest of the literary world, the decade had become a distant memory.

CHAPTER TEN

Marriage and Motherhood, 1925–33

NATHALIE AND RAYMOND were married at the Mairie of the sixth arrondissement on 28 July 1925, a few days after Nathalie's twenty-fifth birthday. Raymond was still only twenty-two. It was a low-key affair, which took place at ten thirty on a Tuesday morning with Ilya and a medical student by the name of Marie Lataste acting as witnesses.[1] The age difference between Nathalie and Raymond does not appear to have been an issue in their relations, but for public consumption Nathalie later shaved two years off her birthdate to disguise her seniority. She even lied quite brazenly about it when the editor of a German biographical dictionary asked for clarification of discrepant information on the subject.[2] The absence of a French birth certificate allowed a certain latitude with regard to such facts.

Marriage—which Nathalie claimed she undertook to please her father, who would not have countenanced any other arrangement— allowed her a definitive escape from home and ultimately saved her from having to make a career in a profession for which she had no inclination. It was a partnership of equals, and unlike many other women writers of her generation, she had a husband who encouraged rather than objected to her desire to write. The marriage lasted until Raymond's death in 1985. Jean Blot, a Russian-born French diplomat and writer who knew the couple well, recalls that "their relationship, their love for each other, which survived many heartbreaks and dramas, and never lost its intensity from their early days in the Faculté de droit right up to the grave, was a moving sight. [Raymond] was the silent father-figure, but his protective presence was dominant."[3] In the modern spirit of the postwar times, Nathalie and Raymond agreed that for the sake of any future children they would start by remaining faithful to each other, but that thereafter they would be free to pursue other relationships. Claude Sarraute intimates that Raymond took advantage of this agreement, but that Nathalie, who was always wary of the disruption that physical passion would bring, did not.[4] Her ideal was a sort of fusion that transcended sexual difference, and there is certainly little eroticism in her writing, where the body operates primarily as a kind of seismograph for the tropism.

The couple began married life in an apartment at no. 16 rue Lacretelle, just off the rue de Vaugirard in the fifteenth arrondissement. Nathalie immediately had to revise for her resits, and they then embarked on their respective legal careers, Nathalie toiling as a law intern while Raymond worked alongside his father in the rue du Regard. The principle of equality that underpinned the marriage led Nathalie to make demands for independence in the shape of the heroine of David Garnett's 1922 novel *Lady into Fox*. She owned a copy of the 1925 edition and was probably aware of the French translation, which was published in 1924 and reviewed in the *NRF*. Son of Constance Garnett, the English translator of Tolstoy, Dostoevsky, and Chekhov, David Garnett was a member of the Bloomsbury Group and later married Virginia Woolf's niece Angelica Bell. The Bloomsbury connection would have been enough to interest Nathalie, but the book's allegorical narrative evidently struck a chord with her.

It tells the story of a young married couple whose life is disrupted when, for unexplained reasons, the wife begins to turn into a fox. Although horrified by her new condition (she eats raw meat and rabbit fur), the husband responds to her continuing need for his affection by trying to keep her safe. But her vulpine nature takes over, and she escapes into the wild. Even when she has a litter of cubs with another fox, the husband remains as devoted as ever, visiting her in the woods, and making no attempt to tame her. "Yet," says the narrator, "this all proceeded one may say from a passion, and a true conjugal fidelity, that it would be hard to find matched in this world."[5] The fox-wife is eventually tracked down by the hunt, and when she seeks refuge in the garden of the marital home her husband is unable to save her as she is ripped to death by the hounds. It's a tale of conjugal devotion that depends on the husband's acceptance of his wife's aberrance and her need for freedom, and the book's message is commemorated in the pet names that Nathalie and Raymond use in their letters to each other: Nathalie becomes an ungendered and partly Anglophone "Petit Fox" (Little Fox), while Raymond is a protective "Chien Loup" (Wolf Hound), often abbreviated to "C.L." Nathalie frequently signs off as "Ton Fox."

Prior to the entry of "Fox" and "Chien Loup" into their exchanges, the couple had alternative pet names for each other, which date from early in their marriage when they use a single, invented, unisex, and faintly Russian-sounding "douziki." Raymond signs off as "Ton Douziki qui t'aime Tout" (Your Douziki who loves you Totally), the abbreviation of which—D. Q. T. T.—is used in some of his later letters. Nathalie—never a great correspondent—is less extravagant, but, like both Alain and Gisèle in *The Planetarium* written thirty years later, she found in marriage an experience of fusion and happiness that nothing else matched. (Alain also finds that his wife looks like a little fox cub.) This fusion is expressed in a shared private language with words like "raca," which seems to mean "mean and angry," and expressions like "having a monkey's skin" to mean something like an extreme version of "the blues," a condition which both Nathalie and Raymond periodically complain of.

There were times when Raymond asserted his own demands, spending evenings with his father to discuss metaphysics and religion, topics on which he felt closer to Joseph than to anyone else, since, as he reminds Nathalie, she "doesn't have the same concerns as her douziki."[6] She herself mentions that Raymond "had an extreme and intransigent side to him . . . [being] very passionate in his opinions." And—like any couple—they were capable of fierce disagreements; Claude Sarraute remembers a protracted argument about Chaplin's *Monsieur Verdoux* where neither side would budge, and Nathalie recalled that there were issues, including politics, on which, although they were broadly in agreement, she and he occasionally had intractably divergent views.[7]

Towards the end of 1926, after less than eighteen months of marriage, Nathalie became pregnant. There's no knowing whether the pregnancy was intended or accidental, or something between the two. Contraception was not as widely practised in France as in other Western countries, and French natalist policies had led to legislation in 1920 prohibiting the promotion of birth control and the distribution or sale of female contraceptives, such as vaginal sponges, douches, pessaries, and cervical caps. Abortion had long been a crime in French law, but after even more punitive antiabortion legislation was passed in 1923, procuring an abortion carried a prison sentence. Condoms, rarely used by married couples, were regarded primarily as protection against sexually transmitted diseases. Many couples had recourse to the inherently unreliable rhythm method, but the most commonly practised form of birth control—even after the introduction of the pill in the 1960s—remained the equally unreliable *coitus interruptus*.[8]

With Nathalie's legal career less than fully launched, the timing of this pregnancy was less than optimal, especially as it coincided with Raymond's eighteen-month-long military service. He was stationed in the barracks in the Château de Vincennes on the outskirts of Paris, from where he was able to make weekend visits home. Towards the end of her pregnancy Nathalie moved back to live with Lena in the Boulevard Raspail, and Claude was born on 24 July 1927, a few days after Nathalie's twenty-seventh birthday.[9] Family photos show her holding Claude on her lap, shoulders hunched and barely smiling. Dressed in a coat with an expensive fur collar, she looks as though she has just arrived or is about to leave. The baby was cared for by a nursemaid since, as Nathalie often explained, bourgeois women of her generation invariably employed someone to look after their children. It was almost certainly at this point that the family moved to the rue d'Assas in the sixth arrondissement, close to the Luxemburg Gardens, Nathalie's old stamping ground.

Raymond wrote regularly from Vincennes, but Nathalie reacted badly to his absence. His (undated) letters try to reassure her of his love, and he promises to try to be "the kind of douziki you like." He

FIGURE 12. Nathalie with Claude, 1927. (Sarraute Family Collection)

worries about her health, urges her to try and sleep during the day because she looks tired, and hopes that she will not allow herself to become prey to her "ideas." He advises her to use work to take her mind off negative thoughts and suggests that she learn a new set of topics in law, such as wills and probate, assuring her that "I think you'll soon get interested and you'll have the impression that you're learning things you will need to know, which is a very encouraging feeling."[10]

Both young parents take evident pleasure in the baby, but they talk about her in a curiously objectifying comic language as "the monster-baby" and always in the masculine. In the only letter written by Nathalie to have survived from this time, she describes to Raymond an alarming episode where the baby choked and seemed to stop breathing. She begins disingenuously by saying, "Nothing much new since yesterday," but then continues,

> Yesterday evening immediately after I got back the monster-baby almost died. It had just eaten & all of a sudden it began to choke. It turned deep red, its head hung down on its chest and its eyes rolled upwards. It was unable to utter a sound. You can imagine how frightened we were, because babies very often choke to death. Blanche [presumably the nursemaid] turned it upside down and started tapping it on the back and all at once a stream of curdled milk shot out of its mouth and nostrils & it started to scream, much to our delight.

She goes on to say that the baby was now better, had gained a hundred grams, and was sleeping soundly "with a sated and satisfied look, and both its fat cheeks drooping onto the pillow. I'm going to photograph it in the sunlight so that later on it can admire its huge moon face." Nathalie herself was not doing as well, and she concludes her letter by saying, "I feel sad & tired [she uses the masculine form]. I've decided tonight to start working—otherwise I feel too low."[11] She signs off as "Le Dou-zi-ki-ke-tuém-tou" (The douziki you love totally), using the masculine at a time when pregnancy and motherhood defined her incontrovertibly as female, and also making Raymond the one who loves, while she is the one who is loved.

Despite apparently following Raymond's advice about the salutary effects of legal study, Nathalie's state of mind did not improve, and she succumbed to what appears to have been postnatal depression. This was no doubt exacerbated by Kolya's death in 1927. She lost his benevolent, avuncular presence in her life, and now that Polina was on her own, this placed a burden of responsibility on Nathalie. Unlike the "monster-baby," she was neither sleeping nor eating. She lost weight and—very likely at Ilya's instigation—she entered the Clinique Val-Mont in Glion, near Montreux in Switzerland, where she spent several weeks during February and March 1928.

Val-Mont was the creation of Henri-Auguste Widmer, who had trained in psychiatry under Charcot and was particularly interested in the dietary aspect of mental illness. He was also an art lover, and over the course of his career he amassed a sizeable collection of paintings and sculpture. Built in 1905 the clinic catered for digestive, nutritional, and nervous conditions, and treatment took the form of a strict dietary regime, electrotherapy (not to be confused with electroconvulsive therapy), hydrotherapy, and heliotherapy. Thanks to its spectacular setting above Lake Geneva, and its combination of progressive treatments, Swiss hostelry, and artistic décor, Val-Mont had built up a reputation amongst a cultivated European bourgeoisie in the early years of the century. Proust had twice been on the point of spending time there, and Rilke was a frequent visitor between 1923 and his death in December 1926. The painters Renoir and Degas also figure in the clinic's annals.[12] Nathalie was one of the last patients under Widmer's directorship before he retired in 1928 and handed over to a successor. She may have been aware of Rilke's recent presence, but apparently found no one during her own stay with whom she felt any affinity.

She never talked about this episode, and evidence about her condition and her stay comes almost entirely from private correspondence. Postnatal depression was still poorly understood at the time, and her treatment consisted of diet and bed rest. The letters she received from Raymond, Lena, Nadia Wilter (now du Bouchet), and her father repeatedly urge her to gain weight. Raymond insists that she follow the regime prescribed for her, however unpalatable, and Lena—who was medically trained—reminds Nathalie that she needs to gain a minimum of five kilograms before she can return to Paris. Raymond regrets that she still "feels low" and that her fellow inmates have not proved more interesting. His letters provide regular updates on the "monster-baby" in the couple's shared idiom.

Ilya, Lena, and Nadia all write to Nathalie in Russian, whether because they considered it the language most likely to touch her in her current state, or as a means of maintaining privacy in the clinic. Ilya is clearly concerned about Nathalie's state of mind, reassures her that she shouldn't worry about money (he was no doubt footing the bill), insists that her health should be her sole priority. He reassures her that she has "a wonderful husband" who loves her a great deal, a delightful daughter who is developing well and will be a source of great happiness to her, and finally, that once she has regained her health, she will have "a marvellous career."[13] (He presumably had a legal career in mind.) Lena advises her not to spend her time criticising the clinic, but to take advantage of the good things it offers. She is adamant that to concentrate on getting better is not selfish, and instructs Nathalie to take herself in hand by telling herself that everything is fine. There doesn't seem to have been any significant psychotherapeutic treatment at Val-Mont, and Nathalie's correspondents all write as if it were up to her to find a way back to a more positive outlook. She was treated by one Dr Brûlé, whose name she uses in her 1963 novel, *The Golden Fruits*, and left in mid-March, evidently without being entirely cured: a note from one of the doctors in the clinic forwards a prescription to her and expresses the hope that the pleasure of being in her own home will allow her to recover her "moral equilibrium," her appetite, and the kilos she still lacks. Despite the end of Raymond's military service recovery was slow, and Nathalie's health remained fragile: ten years later she was once again advised to leave the city for fresh air and rest, and to take medication prescribed by her doctor.[14] The couple's two careers nevertheless resumed, Raymond made his unsuccessful attempt at the *conférence du stage* in the autumn of 1928, and encouraged Nathalie to try her hand the following year.

In early 1930 she became pregnant again, and shortly after Anne was born in October of that year the family moved to no. 12 square Henry Paté, a recently constructed development built around a private square in the Auteuil neighbourhood of the sixteenth arrondissement. Nadia du Bouchet lived in the same building with her husband Victor and their two young children, André and Hélène. Nadia was working as a doctor and was the family's main breadwinner. Nathalie was one of the few people to visit the du Bouchet apartment on the floor immediately above the Sarrautes', and the children of the two families saw a good deal of each other. Hélène du Bouchet remembers Nathalie setting out for work every morning wearing professional attire and carrying a briefcase, "before she became herself." She also remembers being spellbound by Nathalie's stories, which usually involved dissecting people with equal measures of sharpness and humour, reducing her audience to a mix of tears and laughter.[15]

Given Nathalie's diffidence about a legal career, the interruptions caused by the births of her two daughters were perhaps not entirely

FIGURE 13. Nathalie, Claude, Anne, and Dominique,
summer 1933. (Sarraute Family Collection)

unwelcome. But she was still in limbo, suspended between law, motherhood, and the literature that she continued to read but was not yet writing. She later told her friend the dress designer Sonia Rykiel that she didn't think she had a strong maternal instinct. But she involved herself extensively in her children's lives, albeit, as Claude recalls, and as she herself admitted in another interview, by treating each child as if she could be revised and corrected like a page of manuscript until she was as good as perfect.[16]

Nurture also took precedence over nature in Nathalie's conception of gender. After a third daughter, Dominique, was born on 25 February 1933, Nathalie found herself the mother of three girls. Like Simone de Beauvoir, she was convinced that femininity was both a learned phenomenon and a social disadvantage, and for this reason she gave two of her three daughters first names—Claude and Dominique—used for both boys and girls. At home, the girls enjoyed more feminine diminutives, Claudie and Domi. Anne was known in the family as Aniki, but Nathalie always used the masculine when talking to or about her children, referring to them as *les petits* (the little ones), addressing them as *mon petit*, or saying things like *t'es fou* (you're crazy) in place of the feminine *folle*.[17] When they reached primary-school age she made sure to send her daughters to mixed schools, where they sat alongside boys in class.

In later years, when speaking about her family responsibilities, Nathalie made light of these demands, since in addition to the nursemaid, there was a maid of all work. A job advertisement placed by Nathalie in *Le Figaro* of 13 December 1931 specified that the maid needed to be a good cook but would be assisted by a cleaner. Nathalie herself never cooked or did housework. She also never spoke Russian to her children and sought instead to provide them with the advantages of an English-speaking nanny. However, she proved to be less fortunate in her choices than Vera had been, when one day she overheard Claude praying (in English), "Please baby Jesus, make nanny's horse win." The nanny—who also drank—was immediately dismissed and subsequently replaced by a series of young German women.[18]

Nathalie's emotional attachment to her children ran deep, and throughout her life she remained in close and regular contact with all three daughters. As she later said, "They're like a piece of me. . . . My daughters are like my very life. You can't talk about love, those words don't enter into it, it's not covered by words like that. I don't know what it is. . . . It's just a part of me."[19] And as if to demonstrate the point, she included a photograph of herself with her children in the first monograph devoted to her work. She is smiling.

CHAPTER ELEVEN

The First Tropism, 1932–34

IN THE SPRING of 1932, Nathalie and Raymond took an Easter holiday in England, leaving the children behind as they usually did when vacationing abroad. (Holidays with the children were spent in France, often with Nathalie in sole charge while Raymond stayed in Paris to work.) There's no record of where they went, but wherever it was, the trip was unusually restorative, and Nathalie returned "feeling good." As she later remarked, "I don't know why England has this effect on me [but] when I came back I felt livelier."[1] It was in this frame of mind that she composed the first of the short texts that eventually became *Tropisms*. It was written straight off, without corrections, and although she would never again write as easily or as quickly, it marked the start of her literary career. She was thirty-one.

Unlike most other writers, she had no preexisting juvenilia, no abandoned manuscript stored away in a drawer. Since her school compositions the closest she had got to writing was in imagination when she read Thomas Mann's *Tonio Kröger* or Gide's *Paludes* and felt as if she had written them herself. But the previously unfocused desire to write had now found its object: "Suddenly I had a very strong impression of something . . . a sort of inner movement occurring as two people met—and I wrote it down, just like a first poem, without knowing exactly what it meant. I never dreamt it would turn into a book, but I was so interested in that kind of movement that I wrote down some other texts."[2] In what she described as "an invisible dramatic action between two people," an anonymous "he" is in thrall to an equally anonymous "her," trapped by the anxiety that "she" instils in "him," and desperate to avert the threat he feels emanating from her as some potentially explosive but unspecified psychic phenomenon. Another text (the second in the published volume) followed soon afterwards, with equally anonymous characters perceived from the vantage point of the mental world of a figure identified only as "he."

It was a tentative beginning, but a decisive corner had been turned. Nathalie gave up her desultory legal career, no doubt partly because of her third—unplanned and ill-timed—pregnancy. In fact, reluctant to resign herself to the birth of another child now that she had started writing, she resorted to various homespun remedies—wearing thick woollens, drinking vinegar, and skipping—in an attempt to terminate the pregnancy. None proved effective, and Dominique was born almost a year after the first tropism.[3]

There was little in the current literary environment to encourage Nathalie in the vein that she was making her own. Coincidentally and no doubt a little disconcertingly, Polina's second novel, *Vremya*, was published in 1932 with the émigré publisher Parabola in Berlin. Other émigré Russians (most of them, incidentally, also Jewish) were making a name for themselves in French. Joseph Kessel, who had moved to France as a child and was two years older than Nathalie, began writing novels in the early 1920s. *Le Steppe rouge* (The red steppe, 1922) is set in Bolshevik Russia, and *Les Rois aveugles* (The blind kings, 1925), portrays episodes from the Russian Revolution. *Nuits de princes* (Princes' nights,) written in 1927, describes émigré Russian life in Paris, and confirmed the stereotype of the Russian émigré aristocrat reduced to driving taxis for a living.

Irène Némirovsky, who was Nathalie's junior by three years and had arrived in Paris with her parents in 1919, met with overnight success in 1929 for her novel *David Golder*, which tells the story of a Russian-Jewish émigré financier, his disaffected wife, and their spoiled daughter. A stage adaptation of the novel followed in 1930, and a successful film version in 1931. Her novella, *The Ball*, was published in 1930, clinching Némirovsky's reputation as a rising literary star. She also had an active link with the Russian language, and *David Golder* appeared in Russian translation in 1930, while *The Ball* and another novella were published in Russian by Parabola, Polina's publisher, in 1931.

Elsa Triolet, Nathalie's senior by four years, had settled in France, but she was still writing in Russian and publishing in the Soviet Union. Nina Berberova, one year younger than Nathalie (but not Jewish), had moved to Paris in 1925 and, like Triolet, was also writing in Russian. In other words, at the time Nathalie was embarking on *Tropisms*, her Russian émigré contemporaries were still drawing on a Russian identity, frequently describing Russian and Russian-émigré worlds, and were still at least partially reliant on the Russian language. Nathalie's Russian identity, by contrast, would play no part in her literary one. In later years, although she would always mention to interviewers that she was born in Russia, she would insist—albeit with some exaggeration—that French was her first language. In this way, her Russianness insured her against any unwanted association with French literary groupings, while her rootedness in the French language served to mark her off from her Russian-born contemporaries.

It is striking that several of these Russian writers were women. French women had also been writing in greater numbers since the early 1920s, many of them publishing prolifically. However, the price they paid for this increased literary presence was marginalisation into a category of "women's writing"—mostly romances and autobiographical fiction—addressed to women readers. A history of women's writing in France published in 1929, and of which Nathalie owned a copy, asserted that women were capable only of personal forms of expression, such as letters, lyric poetry, and confessional novels, and that they had no capacity for either the objective detachment or the formal perfection that real literary writing demanded. The author—a man—concludes that they succeed only when their work was "guided by men."[4] This was not exactly encouragement for the would-be writer.

The names of many of the women writers from this time have largely been forgotten, and the only two to be taken seriously were the poet Anna de Noailles and Colette, both a generation older than Nathalie. Colette, the creator of Claudine, wrote mostly about girls and women, and had recently published two semiautobiographical works, *Break of Day* (1928) and *Sido* (1930), based on memories of her mother. She was always happy to flaunt her femininity, and in 1932 she even opened a beauty salon selling her own line of products. Nothing could have been more antipathetic to Nathalie, who never mentions Colette. This is despite the fact that she would have had reasons for doing so after Lena married Hervé Gauthier-Villars, a naval officer, who was the nephew of Colette's first husband, Henry Gauthier-Villars.

What all these writers—the Russians and the women—have in common is a willingness to draw directly on events in their own lives, and to do so largely by means of conventionally realist representation and equally conventional forms of narrative expression. For those who made a living from their pen, this literary mode was reinforced by the need to appeal to a broad readership. The modesty of Nathalie's literary beginnings meant that her writing did not have to sell, and she was able to rely on Raymond's support, both financial and emotional, while she pursued her experiment with the "tropisms" that did not yet bear the name.

In her essay *A Room of One's Own*, published in 1929, Virginia Woolf recommends financial autonomy as well as the eponymous room for any woman wanting to write according to her own lights, and she gives a figure of five hundred pounds per year—the equivalent of around thirty thousand pounds today—as the financial price of literary independence. By deciding to write, Nathalie was making herself dependent on Raymond's income, but since she was earning very little money as a lawyer, her decision to abandon her career did not have a significant impact on family finances. In any case, thanks to her father's colourant factory, the Établissements Tcherniak, which in 1929 had become a joint-stock company, Nathalie now had a small private income. The capital value of the company was estimated at two and a half million francs—the equivalent of around one million euros today—and in 1932 Nathalie and Lili each received a thousand shares. Jacques received the same number when he reached his majority in 1937.[5]

The room of her own was a different question. Nathalie never mentioned where her earliest *Tropisms* were written. For her, the place that mattered most was the one she found in the writing itself.

As she later said, "I was in an area that was all my own, that belonged to me. I felt at home there," and she often used territorial metaphors when speaking of her writing.[6] It was also a place free of sexual difference. She always insisted that the tropism itself is an ungendered phenomenon, and that the writing through which she pursued it was equally ungendered. As she told Sonia Rykiel, when she wrote, she was "neither man nor woman, nor cat nor dog." And, she adds, "I never think about myself as a woman, I create a mix [*je me mélange*], I refuse to talk about women's writing, to join movements that separate men and women, it against my opinions."[7] It was genderlessness rather than androgyny that she sought.

These remarks date from 1984, when women's writing—or *écriture féminine*—meant something rather different from what it did in the late 1920s and early 1930s, but throughout her life Nathalie remained adamant in her refusal of all female identity in writing. In other ways, especially in these years, she was happy to maintain a female identity in her dress, and it's a nice coincidence that the question of gender arises with Sonia Rykiel, who like Nathalie was Russian and also wrote novels, but was primarily a dress designer. In the late 1920s and early 1930s, Nathalie used to wear couturier outfits, sold off after being worn by models in fashion shows. She had the perfect figure for them, and Claude Sarraute recalls her mother wearing designs by Poiret, which she later lent to the narrator's aunt in her novel *Martereau*.[8]

Tropisms, written very slowly with numerous revisions over the course of the next six years, is a remarkably assured achievement for a first publication. Each of the nineteen texts focuses on a momentary impression experienced by an anonymous character, sometimes male, sometimes female, often in the context of family or domestic circumstance. There are some glancingly autobiographical references to the "simultaneously depleted and protected existence" of exiles who do not allow themselves to resurrect memories of childhood in a distant but unnamed city, to the streets and squares of the Paris of Nathalie's early years, to England, to a thinly disguised Pierre Janet in the Collège de France, to the lives of women between shopping and tea parties, to Van Gogh exhibitions, and to more earnest young women who have read *Ulysses* and *The Notebooks of Malte Laurids Brigge*.[9] But the autobiographical dimension isn't signalled as such and is tangential to a writing whose main focus is a mental space with which Nathalie was familiar from her own inner life.

The texts—none more than three or four pages long—are not chapters in a novel nor short stories, nor are they quite prose poems in the manner of the two poets Nathalie most admired, Baudelaire and Rimbaud. (It wasn't until later that she came across the work of Francis Ponge.) They are a kind of synthesis of the long gestation out of which they emerged, from her schoolwork in French and philosophy, her encounter with Janet, the examples of Thomas Mann and Gide, the explorations of Dostoevsky, Proust, Rilke, and Virginia Woolf, and the oratory contest for young lawyers. And they laid the ground for all Nathalie's future work through their subject matter, their image repertoire, their style, and above all their limited length. A short span suited her talents and her slow rate of composition.

Speaking of her writing method in an interview in 1972, she commented on this question of pace and explained that her writing was "an extremely slow process. . . . The difficulty comes from the elusive character of the tropisms and the lightning speed with which they pass through us. So it's important not to work too quickly, because, if I did, I might miss these movements, which the conscious mind tends in any case to refuse to register. But it's also important not to work too slowly, in case this shifting substance becomes congealed."[10] By 1972 she had long since reconciled herself to the conditions she had found to be necessary for her writing, but it was over the course of the composition of *Tropisms* that these habits were established.

She also set great store by the quality of her writing, which, for all that she now felt liberated from the constraints of written French style and had adopted many of the characteristics of the spoken idiom, still needed to be the fruit of "work." Her texts are carried by the sense of movement she sought to capture and can be read with ease, but they bear multiple rereadings and, like poetry, are best read slowly or even aloud, the way she herself heard them in her head. As she later explained, "It's a writing that I hear as I write. I have to hear the words by articulating them inwardly."[11] She always tested her work by reading it aloud to Raymond. He rarely commented, and it was enough for Nathalie to hear herself reading to him for her to know whether she was on the right track. His encouragement was essential, but it was not enough to sustain her initial impetus. And despite the sense that she had finally discovered a place of her own, she seems to have lost her way, and the writing came to a halt.

CHAPTER TWELVE

A Pause, 1935–37

WITH THIS SUSPENSION of her writing Nathalie found new energy, which she focused initially on external activities, and she became involved in campaigning for the rights of women. The feminism she repudiated in literature was a goal she was happy to pursue in the political arena, seeing in it the prospect of the equality and the erasure of sexual difference that she regarded as both a fundamental human reality and a basic human right. Her deeply held belief in the principle of equality found political expression at various points in her life through her association with causes to which she became ardently, if mostly only briefly, committed. In this case it was the right to vote. She never belonged to any political party, although she later said that in her late twenties she had "almost" joined the Communist Party. This was probably under the influence of Lena, who was a member and never lost her communist sympathies.[1]

Nathalie's political feminism in the 1930s was channelled through the Ligue française pour le droit des femmes (French league for the rights of women), whose president was one of France's first woman lawyers, Maria Vérone. Nathalie probably met Vérone through Joseph Sarraute, who would have known her as a colleague, a committed socialist, and a friend of Jean Jaurès's. The Ligue's goal was complete equality between the sexes, and its central demand was the right to vote. All other major European countries had long since granted this right: the Soviet Union in 1917, Germany and Great Britain (for women over thirty) in 1918, and the Netherlands in 1919.

Much of the Ligue's campaigning was done by women lawyers, who had experience of speaking in public. With her success in the oratory contest Nathalie was particularly well placed to participate, and in 1935 she spoke on a number of occasions alongside Maria Vérone herself.[2] She may well have been on the platform at one such event in the rue Serpente on 22 March 1935, advertised in *La Semaine de Paris*.

By the mid-1930s the issue had become urgent. The French Chamber of Deputies had voted several times in favour of female franchise, but on each occasion the bill had been blocked by the more conservative Senate. When the senators renewed their opposition in 1933, women's groups intensified their demands. At the same time, partly because of the economic crisis, there was growing hostility to the presence of women in the workplace, and in February 1935 the labour minister announced to the Chamber of Deputies that the place of a mother was in the home, not the factory. The right to work was central to Nathalie's conception of female independence, and the minister's view would have roused her to protest.

The Ligue also campaigned for the independence of married women, an issue that directly concerned Nathalie since, as a married woman, her rights were restricted by the "civil incapacity" set out in Article 215 of the Napoleonic Code. This required husbands to provide authorisation for such activities as opening a bank account, obtaining a passport, and even enrolling at university. Raymond would never have sought to exploit this legal imbalance, but for Nathalie a matter of principle was at stake. The law was eventually changed in 1938, but even then old habits died hard.

Nathalie's enthusiasm for the feminist cause quickly waned because, in her view, women themselves were not interested in equality. She claims that there were occasions when she and Maria Vérone had audiences of only a small handful, and she rather dismissively asserts that French women were too much under the thumb of their husbands and fathers to attend the Ligue's meetings.[3] More generally, she saw French women as excessively compliant with an image of femininity requiring them to capture a man through their powers of seduction and thereafter to devote themselves entirely to him. The glimpses of women's lives in *Tropisms* portray them as impov-

erished by their pursuit of sartorial perfection and by their willingness to remain confined within a female domain of "sentiments,
love, life."[4] Such gendering was consistently rejected by Nathalie,
whether in her personal life, her professional activities, her politics,
or her writing. The writing, however, was still on hold. She acquired
a reader's card for the Bibliothèque nationale, but there is no record
of how often or how extensively she used the library's resources.

In May 1935 she took a trip to the Soviet Union with her stepmother Vera. For what reason is not clear, but perhaps it was to
reconnect with family after years of absence. This was the first time
Nathalie had returned to her native Russia since she left as a child
in 1909, and Vera had last visited in 1912. They were there for just
ten days under the compulsory auspices of Intourist, the state tourist company created by Stalin in 1929, which had its own hotels and
restaurants and its own guides recruited from the NKVD, the Soviet
secret police.

Nathalie was initially exultant to be back on Russian soil, and in
a letter to Raymond she extols "the incomparable and ravishing
beauty" of the Kremlin beneath her hotel window, the air which is
exactly as she remembers it from her childhood, and the wooden
houses with carved windows like the one she believed she had been
born in in Ivanovo. Her impression of still being connected to it all
through every fibre of her being may seem surprising, she writes,
but, she goes on, "I now understand why I continually analyse everything in France and 'see' it at a distance—and how I suffer there
especially from the quality of the air. It's perhaps an advantage for
the sharpness of my vision there, because here I can't judge things
from the outside but immerse myself with ecstasy in something that,
more than I realised, must continually have nourished my imagination and determined my feelings since childhood."[5]

This sense of her own ineradicable Russianness was, however,
mixed with more negative features, and despite the familiarity of
the air and the wooden houses, the country the two women found
was in many ways very different from the one they knew previously.
It was no doubt thanks to Intourist that Nathalie joined a crowd
on Moscow's Red Square where banners from the recent May Day
parade hailed the "revolutionary strength of the international

FIGURE 14. Red Square, Moscow, 1935. (Sarraute Family Collection)

proletariat" alongside the faces of Lenin and Stalin. She kept several photos of the occasion, including one of herself in the crowd of Soviet citizens into which she seems to blend as much as if she had never left and had made her life there rather than in France. Except that where many of those around her are smiling, she stares at the camera with a blank expression that hints at an underlying dismay.

Her memories of the Moscow of her childhood, when she spent one Christmas with her father and was showered with presents, were of a large square under the snow that she always associated with her memories of Russia, but there was none in May 1935. She may also have recalled the letters sent by Assia describing revolution and civil war in 1917, but even for those who had known the city well, Moscow had changed beyond recognition. Its population had swelled to over three million and new buildings were going up everywhere. Gide, who famously visited the Soviet Union in June 1936, a year after

Nathalie's trip, mentions having been struck by the ugliness of the city, whose unlovely appearance had "an oppressive and depressing effect on one's spirits."[6]

Stalin was everywhere in the form of enormous portraits and posters proclaiming "Hurrah for the best friend of physical culture—our native, beloved Stalin," asserting that "[Russia] is growing and getting strong," and instructing the young to "thank comrade Stalin for a bright and happy childhood."[7] The Intourist guide assigned to Nathalie and Vera would have ensured that they saw the extravagantly appointed Moscow Metro, which had just opened, and visited the flagship Park of Rest and Culture, where, like Gide, they might have observed a large crowd enraptured by a recitation from Pushkin's *Eugene Onegin*. A long-standing Russophile and a confirmed antifascist, Gide went so far as to claim that he had seen the "parturition of the future."[8] If Nathalie shared his enthusiastic sense of encountering a classless society in a new Russia, where everyone had the same needs and was equal to everyone else, she may also have shared the impression of complete depersonalisation that he was alarmed to think was mistaken for progress in the Soviet Union, fostering a uniformity of opinion and an intellectual conformism of the kind Nathalie also abhorred.

Behind this mix of perceptions, there was a more threatening political reality, which as Russian speakers who still had family in Russia, Nathalie and Vera would have been more aware of than the non-Russian-speaking VIP Gide. Stalin's reign of terror had recently begun in earnest after the assassination of Kirov, first secretary of the Leningrad Regional Communist Party Committee, in December 1934. He was shot by a gunman—almost certainly at Stalin's behest—in the Smolny Institute, which once housed the "noble maidens" of whom Babushka, Vera's mother, had been one. Nathalie and Vera were able not only to converse with their Intourist guide and other—presumably carefully vetted—Soviet citizens, but also to meet up with family, the Sheremetievskys on Vera's part, and the Tcherniaks on Nathalie's.

Under Stalin's terror, even those who had been spared by the revolution and the civil war were prime targets. Aristocratic families and those with any remaining wealth or property were liable to be arrested and sent to a gulag, or at the very least, thanks to the new policy of "condensation," to have their apartments forcibly turned into *kommunalki*, with one family to each room, and with bathroom, lavatory, and kitchen shared between all occupants. This was the case in the house where Nathalie had been born in Ivanovo-Voznesensk. Denunciation was rife—indeed, it was officially encouraged as a citizen's duty—and Vera's family was reluctant to discuss their situation for fear of the consequences. The very presence of Nathalie and Vera would have been enough to create problems, since émigrés who had chosen not to return within the time limit they had been offered were now regarded as "enemies."[9]

Nathalie was able to meet her father's younger brother, whom she refers to as "Pierre." (In reality his name must have been Piotr.) But he was in poor health and eking out a miserable existence with his three daughters. Although official Soviet policy was opposed to anti-Semitism, Jews were disproportionately represented in the political show trials that began in the 1930s, and Stalin's hostility towards his (mostly Jewish) rivals, with Trotsky to the fore, was beginning to rub off onto Jews like the Tcherniaks. Nathalie's loyalties would in any case have lain with the man who used to play chess with her father in the Café du Lion on the Place Denfert-Rochereau. She may or may not have known Pierre and her cousins from her childhood, but she felt a close bond with her uncle whom she found affectionate and generous.[10] But the charmed life of her uncle Grisha's family in Kamianets-Podilskyi had long since vanished, and with it the source of one of the happiest memories of her childhood. She never saw her Uncle Pierre again. By the end of their stay both women were thoroughly shaken by what they had seen, and Nathalie was left with a chilling impression of fear. In the few comments she made in later life about this visit to the Soviet Union, she mentions that Vera's family had suffered badly under the revolution, when they had been terrorised and decimated.[11]

The trip left its mark, and in a letter to Sartre written over twenty years later in November 1956 after a subsequent visit to the Soviet Union, Nathalie took issue with the comment he made in an interview in *L'Express* following the Hungarian Uprising, when he claimed that the Russians had known nothing of the deportations that had ravaged the Soviet population. Underscoring her personal connection to individuals in the Soviet Union, Nathalie maintains that the disasters suffered by the Soviet people in the intervening years were already present in the 1930s, and that although Stalin was chiefly responsible, their causes were also endemic to the Russian character:

> I have just returned from a trip to the USSR during which everything I learned about the issue of deportations merely confirmed what I saw in 1935, and I wonder what imposters have taken advantage of the fact that you are not able to make direct contact with the population, and have misled you in your invariably considerable efforts at greater lucidity and integrity.
>
> How, in addition to so many lies, did they manage to add the one claiming that 13 to 15 million deportees—the figure quoted everywhere in the Soviet Union and reported even by Russian-born French communists (you will tell me that it is impossible to know the exact figures, which is true) in any case it's a huge figure—that these deportees, who each belonged to a larger social group (kolkhozes, factories, offices, universities, families clustered in a single location) could disappear without out anyone around them knowing! The entire population was aware of people sentenced without trial or on the basis of mere (and false) witness statements and of the forced labour camps in Siberia. As for the denunciations on which the system was based and which were rampant from top to bottom of the social scale, they kept the entire country in a state of mistrust and fear.

Her reference to denunciations may have been given extra force by her own experiences in France under the Occupation, but she attributes a unique compliance to the Russian people:

> What the people did not want to think was that the system was Stalin's work. For them, Stalin was like the Tsars of the past, the fond and much-loved father, whereas the bureaucracy and the police were the wicked step-mother whose evil doings the father was unaware of.
>
> I understand your affection for the Russian people. In my case they oblige me to feel what I most hate and always forbid myself to feel: unreciprocated sentiments (because they are anti-Semitic to the core).

Like you I admire them for their fine and rare qualities, but one has to recognise that these qualities coexist with a form of abjection that is also rarely found elsewhere. A propensity for toadying and denunciation, which I regard as being, above all, the effect of exceptional suggestibility and puerility, and a taste for submissiveness that borders on masochism, are all Russian characteristics (I say this with despair) that no regime to date has managed to alter and on which, sooner or later, all Russian regimes come to rely. The same goes for the fundamental latent anti-Semitism that Stalinism had no difficulty in reigniting with an energy it never had even under the Tsars and which the current regime has continued to maintain in a devious and inchoate way.

She concludes by spelling out her personal involvement in this situation, explaining that she wishes her letter to remain private because of potential consequences for family and friends in the Soviet Union: "I have left behind close relatives, many friends, and all of them, even the former deportees, are sincerely attached to the communist regime, proud of its magnificent conquests, but, despite this, I fear, if only because of the hospitality they offered me and the correspondence we have exchanged, that they are under serious threat today."[12]

When Gide published his *Return from the U.S.S.R.* in November 1936, Nathalie must have read his account in the light of her own recent visit. She must also have followed the ensuing debates in the French press, fuelled by the vindictive attack mounted against Gide in the communist newspaper *L'Humanité* by the pro-Soviet writer Romain Rolland. Gide's anxieties about the detrimental effects of Stalin's Soviet regime on literary creativity would have been of particular interest to her, informed as they were by his belief that the great artists of European society are "essentially non-conformist" and that they proceed by going "against the current."[13] This was precisely how she saw her own work, and Gide's remarks very likely suggested that had she remained in Russia, or gone back in 1919, as Léon Minor had encouraged her to, she would never have been the writer she had finally and only recently become.

It was to her writing that she then returned with renewed focus. Just as the trip to England had launched the first "tropism" in 1932, so the visit to the Soviet Union would seem to have relaunched the project thanks to her recent insight into the Russian origins of her own sensibility and the confirmation of her sense of viewing life in France "at a distance." However, equally if not more important was her acquaintance with the American Maria Jolas, who became her lifelong friend, translator, and close literary ally. Born into a well-to-do southern family in Kentucky, Maria had come to Paris in 1919 as a music student, and stayed on after marrying Eugene Jolas, a journalist, critic, poet, and translator. Nathalie became acquainted with her when she sent Claude, Anne, and Dominique to the École Bilingue, which Maria had founded in 1932 on the outskirts of Paris in Neuilly.

Nathalie's wish to equip her children with proficiency in the English language was the prime reason for this move, but the coed school's progressive pedagogy also offered a positive contrast to her memories of the nursery school in the rue des Feuillantines. Maria Jolas herself was "viscerally opposed to the rigours and unrelieved seriousness—no singing or dancing, no handwork or dramatics— nothing but lessons and more lessons" that characterised French schools at the time, and the École Bilingue was run on child-centred principles in an atmosphere of "gaiety and youth."[14] However, the liberal ethos lost its charm for the Sarraute children when Anne found drawing pins on the seat of her chair and no action was taken.[15] Nathalie eventually withdrew the three girls, but a friendship had been established with Maria and, through her, a connection with both French and Anglophone contemporary literature.

Maria and Eugene Jolas were at the heart of avant-garde, expatriate American literary life in Paris. In 1927 they had founded the experimental literary journal *transition*, which styled itself "An International Quarterly for Creative Experiment" and sought to make a virtue of its editors' situation midway between French and American culture. The Jolases spoke French as well as English, and Eugene's mother tongue was German. They were friends with Joyce, whose *Finnegans Wake* was serialised in *transition* under the title "Work in Progress." Some of Beckett's early work appeared in the journal, which also devoted a substantial amount of space to foreign (mostly European) writers in translation. A manifesto appeared in June 1929 under the title "The Revolution of the Word.

Proclamation," its signatories declaring themselves—in capitals—to be "TIRED OF THE SPECTACLE OF SHORT STORIES, NOVELS, POEMS AND PLAYS STILL UNDER THE HEGEMONY OF THE BANAL WORD, MONOTONOUS SYNTAX, STATIC PSYCHOLOGY, DESCRIPTIVE NATURALISM [*etc.*]."[16]

These views chimed broadly with Nathalie's own, although proclamation was not a mode of expression that she favoured, nor was the radical reinvention of language practised by the more extreme contributors a strategy that interested her. She first became acquainted with the journal when she bought or was given a number in 1937, and borrowed an unspecified number or numbers from Shakespeare and Company in 1938, the year in which it ceased publication.[17] And she would have found encouragement in *transition*'s modernist literary ethos, its position between English and French, its openness to different national literatures—and, no doubt, its equal openness to writing by women, who were far better represented in its pages than in the French literary press.

Nathalie's friendship with Maria subsequently became a central component of her life. Maria had an infectious energy and a good-natured directness in her dealings with others, which Nathalie often found wanting in her French acquaintances. The two Jolas children, Betsy and Tina, born in 1926 and 1929 respectively, were close in age to Claude and Anne Sarraute, and Nathalie's circle of women friends was drawn even closer when, in 1949, Tina Jolas married Nadia du Bouchet's son, André. He later became managing editor of the postwar reincarnation of *transition*, which acquired a capital "T" under the general editorship of the art critic Georges Duthuit.

Other literary figures were brought to the École Bilingue through connections with the journal. Georges Pelorson, a journalist, poet, and translator, was appointed the school's principal in 1936, the year in which Nathalie's children joined. Pelorson contributed prolifically to *transition* between 1932 and 1938. He was a friend of Beckett's, and it was through Pelorson that Raymond Queneau was hired by the École Bilingue, before being mobilised on the outbreak of war. In late 1937, Pelorson and Queneau were involved in the creation of yet another literary journal, *Volontés*. Purportedly founded by Eugene Jolas, it was actually Pelorson's project. The editorial committee included the American novelist Henry Miller, who was also a regular contributor, as was Queneau, and in August 1939 the journal published Aimé Césaire's *Notebook of a Return to My Native Land*, which became one of the founding texts of *négritude*. (After the war Pelorson changed his name to Belmont, "perhaps to cast oblivion on collaborationist activities," as Maria Jolas disingenuously remarked, tacitly referring to Pelorson's activities under the Vichy government where he was responsible for the creation of new youth policies.)[18]

Bolstered by her encounter with Maria Jolas, the École Bilingue, *transition*, and the glimpse they offered of an active modernist world, Nathalie had further encouragement to resume her abandoned "tropisms." She also acquired a place in which to do so when in October 1936 she rented a room at no. 120 rue de la Tombe-Issoire in the fourteenth arrondissement. With three young children, a maid, a cleaner, and a nanny, domestic arrangements in the apartment at no. 12 Square Henry Paté were not conducive to writing, and a rented room of her own—as recommended by Virginia Woolf—was an obvious solution. Nathalie may also have been motivated by the prospect of the change that took place the following year, when Raymond went into practice on his own after his father's retirement, and the family moved to a large apartment at no. 12 avenue Pierre 1^e de Serbie in the sixteenth arrondissement, where Raymond had his office. There was no question of him going into partnership with another lawyer, and Nathalie was adamant that she would not take on the social role of a lawyer's wife by entertaining legal colleagues and clients. But even with these restrictions, Raymond's professional activities were likely to create further distraction with the ringing of the telephone, or the comings and goings of clients and legal colleagues. All this made a place to write an essential requirement.

The room in the rue de la Tombe-Issoire was on the second floor, overlooked the courtyard, and was equipped with a kitchen.[19] The lease was drawn up in Raymond's name, as the civil incapacity of married women was still in force, and it's an irony that the room guaranteeing literary independence for a woman writer required the legal authorisation of her husband. A good half-hour's bus ride away from the square Henry Paté in Auteuil, the rue de la Tombe-Issoire was located in the heart of the neighbourhood that Nathalie knew from her years growing up in the rue Marguerin. Writing was always in some sense a return to childhood, and she completed several of the *Tropisms* in the rented room. But, as she later said in an interview, she began to feel like a caged animal, and writing there ultimately proved to be a source of angst.[20] She never repeated the experiment, but thanks to finally having a place of her own, writing became a regular part of her daily routine and, despite slow progress, she gradually amassed tangible results to show for it.

CHAPTER THIRTEEN

Publication, 1938–39

BY THE SUMMER of 1938 she had written nineteen short texts and decided upon a title for them—*Tropisms*—a word and a phenomenon with which her work would become permanently associated. As the writer Hector Bianciotti once said, "To say *tropism* is to name Nathalie Sarraute."[1] It even featured in a crossword puzzle in 1965 as the solution to a clue mentioning Nathalie Sarraute and the Nouveau Roman.[2] She herself always downplayed its significance, portraying her choice of the term as a spontaneous expedient. "The word was in the air at the time," she later explained. "[Tropisms] are the movements of plants or lower organisms which turn towards or away from the light, [and] the title suited me because it allowed me to indicate that the movements are instinctive, activated by an external trigger, such as the presence of another person or an object, and are not under conscious control."[3]

Although she later affected not to recall his usage, Gide had used the word in *The Vatican Cellars* of 1914 to describe reflex responses observed in the behaviourist animal experiments conducted by the character Anthime Armand-Dubois. And Paul Valéry, who subsequently became Nathalie's bête noire, used it in his *Notebooks* to refer to such things as his dislike of the smell of basil leaves or the cooing of turtledoves in the early morning. He provides a more formal gloss, which recalls the automatisms discussed by psychologists in the late nineteenth century when he writes, "Without our being aware of it, we are inhabited by tropisms and unconquerable repulsions, which have no reflective status, but a total hidden power."[4] The *Cahiers* were unpublished at the time Nathalie was writing *Tropisms*, but the term was indeed manifestly "in the air," and she made it her own as the hallmark of her literary vision.

She never learned to use a typewriter, and it was Raymond who typed—and retyped—her work. He continued to do so for the rest of his life in an unusual reversal of conventional gender roles. He also typed her professional correspondence, and no doubt advised her on the wording of the covering letter that accompanied the manuscript dispatched on 28 July 1938 to two journals, the *NRF* and *Europe*, as well as to three publishers, Gallimard, Bernard Grasset, and Denoël et Steele. The draft is in Raymond's hand.[5] Denoël replied by return on 29 July, instantly accepting the manuscript. Nathalie was away on holiday with the children, presumably not having imagined that things would move so fast, especially during the summer break, and Raymond telephoned with the news. In due course, the other editors turned the manuscript down. Recalling these events in later years, Nathalie always implied that Denoël's acceptance had come after a long and demoralising series of refusals from the other, more prestigious and longer established publishers. In reality, it preceded their rejections, and did so with a gratifying alacrity.

Jean Paulhan, the chief literary editor at Gallimard, wrote on 23 August to reject the manuscript, but much more positively than Nathalie ever gave him credit for. He ascribes the decision to Gallimard's editorial committee and indicates that he personally was appreciative of the book's qualities: "Our Committee has not taken the manuscript you kindly submitted, and I must return it to you. This is not without some regret. I liked its curious subtlety."[6] He had presumably already written in similar terms to turn down the manuscript for the *NRF*, since Raymond writes enthusiastically to Nathalie in July after speaking to her on the telephone:

> As I said a moment ago we couldn't have hoped for anything better than these replies. It's perfect that the NRF didn't take your manuscript and that it was Denoël who wrote. I wonder what he will say about it. It seems commercially impossible for him to publish Tropisms and I'm amazed. As you said it's possible that he wants to take the risk and is

looking for a new literary success as opposed to a commercial one, for the reputation of his publishing house![7]

It was undoubtedly much better for *Tropisms* to appear as a published volume rather than in a literary review. Although Raymond was perhaps overoptimistic about the book's likely success, he quite justifiably reads the publishers' responses as a clear endorsement of Nathalie's literary talent:

> The letters from Paulhan and Denoël prove . . . that it was neither incomprehensible, nor infantile, nor the imaginings of a lunatic. This is such a disconcerting change of perspective that I can't get used to it. . . . I think it will finally give you the confidence and the awareness of the importance of your work which you so lacked, and the courage to get back to it this year. . . . *You know* that what you are doing is very good, keep hold of that mindset—the only one that matters—whatever happens.

He concludes with advice not to get caught up in trying to evaluate Denoël's response by wondering, "did he admire it a little, a lot, or passionately?," but just to carry on working. He underlines the word "work."[8]

Gaston Gallimard wrote on 14 October confirming Paulhan's rejection, but inviting Nathalie to "keep us informed about your literary production, and in particular to submit a novel to us, if you have written one."[9] The reply from Grasset finally came in November. Signed by Grasset's managing editor, the comments were not entirely negative ("there are undoubtedly some qualities in these pages"), but the manuscript was refused on the grounds, first, that it was "a little hermetic for a general readership" and, second, that it was simply too short to be viable as a book.[10] Grasset were the publishers of Némirovsky's *David Golder* and the novels of Jean Giraudoux, which Nathalie could never bring herself to admire. The imprint had less prestige in her mind than Gallimard, which was home to the *NRF* and had published a number of authors whom she most definitely did admire, notably Proust and Gide.

Denoël was a rather different prospect, and his interest placed Nathalie amongst a number of new and independent-minded authors such as Céline, Antonin Artaud, Tristan Tzara, and Raymond

Queneau. Louis Aragon was another Denoël author, and Elsa Triolet's first French-language publication, *Bonsoir Thérèse* (Good evening, Thérèse), was added to his list in October 1938. Unlike Gaston Gallimard, Robert Denoël read all submissions himself, did not delegate to an editorial committee, and relied entirely on his own literary judgement. Belgian by birth, he had come to Paris in 1926 at the age of twenty-four, and in 1928 created the Éditions Denoël et Steele with capital supplied by an American, Bernard Steele, who was interested in contemporary French writing. Céline, whose growing anti-Semitism Denoël was prepared to weather, later paid him tribute when he wrote that while Denoël could sell you down the river when necessary, "he had one saving grace . . . his passion for literature . . . he really recognized good work, he had respect for writers."[11]

Nathalie always spoke very warmly about her first publisher, and she was clearly charmed by him. He shared her interest in English and Russian literature, and she was particularly pleased to discover that he too had a special fondness for Dostoevsky's *The Eternal Husband*. He introduced her to the work of Henry James, whose *Aspern Papers* (the tale of an unscrupulous biographer) she then borrowed from Shakespeare and Company. And it was through Denoël that she became acquainted with the work of Raymond Queneau when he gave her a copy of *Chêne et chien* (Oak and dog), a comic autobiographical novel in verse, passages from which she could still recall verbatim years later. She was "delighted to be published in the same series" as Queneau, whose vernacular idiom and satirical account of his psychoanalysis must both have appealed to her.[12]

She signed a contract with Denoël on 10 October 1938. Royalties were set at 15 percent, and although the covering letter stated that her husband's signature would not be required (civil incapacity having now been removed from the statute book), Raymond nevertheless took the precaution of granting marital authorisation for the publication of his wife's work.[13] *Tropisms* came out in February 1939 with a print run of 650. In consultation with Denoël, Nathalie drew up a list of recipients for the 150 complimentary copies. It includes Jean Paulhan and Gaston Gallimard, a number of novelists (among them Gide), and several poets, as well as critics and essayists.

The name that mattered most to her was that of Gide, to whom she had previously sent her manuscript in the hope of receiving comment, guidance, and, perhaps, patronage from the living writer with whom she felt the strongest affinity. She kept a draft of her undated letter to him, to which she apparently never received a reply:

Dear Monsieur Gide,

I am sending you herewith a manuscript, "Tropisms," and beg you to glance at it, just a few pages_and to let me have your opinion.

It's the only one_Rilke being dead_that would be infinitely precious to me.

I imagine that you do not read all the manuscripts sent to you. Perhaps you do not read any that you have not had prior notice of.

But I know no one who could recommend me to you. And I think it would be pointless, and in fact impossible, for me to add any explanation to these pages.

I shall therefore wait with little hope.

I beg you to believe in my total admiration

Natalie [*sic*] Sarraute[14]

When the book came out she sought to ensure that Gide would read it by asking his personal secretary to leave a copy in a place where he was likely to notice it.[15] (The secretary was Maurice Saillet, who worked in Adrienne Monnier's bookshop, La Maison des Amis des Livres, just across the street from Shakespeare and Company in the rue de l'Odéon, which Nathalie also frequented.) She then sent a further copy with a note, addressing Gide as "*Cher Maître*" and saying, "If this little book, written after years of waiting and effort, might be accepted by you as a most sincere homage to the teaching that emanates from your work and your life, if it could make you feel the depths of the admiration they inspire in me, this would be the highest and rarest reward for my efforts."[16] No response was ever forthcoming from the seventy-year-old writer whose *Paludes* had been a revelation that made her own writing possible.

In all, the book received three published reviews. The first, in the *Gazette de Liège*, by Victor Moremans, a Belgian critic and a personal friend of Denoël's, was positive and perceptive, and concluded by saying that the book was "a preliminary sample of a body of work whose acuity and depth will perhaps surprise us one day."[17] Two others followed, both appreciative and both by poets: Henri Hertz in *Europe* in August and Joë Bousquet in the *Cahiers du Sud* in January 1940.[18] Nathalie never mentioned these further reviews, perhaps because they were slow to appear, and no doubt also because she always downplayed what recognition she did receive.

The imminence and outbreak of war were more serious complications, and the timing of Nathalie's first book was, to say the least, unfortunate. The absence of a speedier and more fulsome response was also due to the book's generic indeterminacy and its literary style, which Grasset had described as "hermetic." But what counted most of all was Nathalie's lack of literary associates or patronage. As a woman, she hadn't acquired the sort of social and literary connections which for many men came as a matter of course from their lycée education or the friendships made at the grandes écoles. Nor did she have the kind of means of entry into the literary world that other women—such as Colette or Elsa Triolet—enjoyed through their husbands or lovers. (Triolet was now Aragon's mistress, and they married the following year.) Without male patronage her book stood little chance of making any impact.

She did, however, receive a few personal letters of appreciation from people who were not personal acquaintances, and these letters meant a great deal to her. Max Jacob, a poet and critic whose work included the prose-poem collection *The Dice Cup* (1917), wrote addressing her as "*Madame et Maître*" and declaring her to be "a profound poet."[19] His letter is almost a prose poem in its own right. Jacob, who was quarter of a century older than Nathalie, died in Drancy in 1944, and they never met. Charles Mauron, an English specialist and a familiar of the Bloomsbury group, wrote on 28 January. Having translated two of Virginia Woolf's novels into French and published a collection of his own prose poems in 1930, he was well placed to appreciate Nathalie's literary idiom, as his letter attests, "Either I'm mistaken, or you have a *great deal* of talent, real talent." He backs up his praise with a shrewd characterisation of her writing: "an alert and responsive sensibility, a disdain for bombast and pretence, an attraction and a repulsion towards reality, a splendid nose for the insidious and loathsome, and style."[20] The combination of praise and perceptiveness was great encouragement and went some way to compensate for the lack of public recognition. In later years, Nathalie always treasured the personal responses of readers, and remained sceptical and often not a little scornful of the views of critics.

A third personal response came from the thirty-four-year-old Jean-Paul Sartre, in an undated letter, where he writes, "I like your book very much." He goes on to say, "I feel directly touched by it, and I also find that everything you write has charm—and each time you have someone speak, it's natural and accurate."[21] This was the first contact between Nathalie and Sartre, with whom she would become closely involved in the following decade. Where Jacob and Mauron were prose poets, Sartre was a novelist, and had made a name for himself with *Nausea*, published exactly one year previously by Gallimard. His collection of short stories, *The Wall*, came out in the same month as *Tropisms*, although no one thought to compare the two collections. He was five years Nathalie's junior, but there is already a hint of his later editorial role when he enquires about her future writing plans. *Tropisms* had carried an announcement for her next book, to be called *The Planetarium*, which Sartre says he is impatient to read, and he continues, "I hope that it's a long novel. If not, I hope you will write one soon and I think it should be excellent." The book, which Nathalie had already embarked upon, was not a novel, but another collection of short texts in the same vein as *Tropisms*. It was never finished, and she kept the title in reserve for what would indeed be a novel—her third, published some twenty years later.

The fourth personal letter about *Tropisms* came from Georges Pelorson. Unlike Sartre, who speaks of "charm," Pelorson accurately pinpoints an element of something harsher in her writing when he describes the work as "one those little gashes whose tight edges will not be easily sealed." But, he adds with equal astuteness, "the sharp-edged tone of the book" is balanced by "that strange tenderness one finds in surgeons," and illuminated by a style whose mastery he compliments.[22] These observations coming from a literary journalist and editor would have acted as an incitement to continue on the same path, and not to follow Sartre's recommendation that Nathalie write a novel.

By June 1939 she had six new texts in a fit state for publication, and with Raymond's encouragement she offered the new material to the literary review *Mesures*, which was edited by the seemingly ubiquitous Jean Paulhan on behalf of its creator, Henry Church (another rich American literary patron). Paulhan replied on 2 July turning down the submission, but he once again offsets a negative editorial decision with a personal appreciation: "It's no, and I'm sorry about this. Speaking for myself, I liked these pages which our Committee criticised for being a little unclear, a little too slow and lacklustre."[23]

Nathalie may have chosen *Mesures* because it was published under the aegis of Adrienne Monnier's bookshop, where Gide's secretary Maurice Saillet worked. She knew Monnier slightly but later said that the older woman had never offered any help with publishing.[24] (Intriguingly, however, the list of names for review copies of *Tropisms* appears under the letterhead of Monnier's bookshop.) By 1939 Monnier no longer had an active role in the journal's affairs, and in any case, women were very sparsely represented in its pages. In a total of twenty-two issues between January 1935 and April 1940, with an average of a dozen contributions per number, *Mesures* published just five contributions by contemporary French women writers. These included Marguerite Yourcenar (who was in fact Belgian) and Dominique Rolin (also Belgian), who later became a friend of Nathalie's. Women were still almost invisible in the Parisian literary world of the 1930s, except as wives, secretaries, or translators (sometimes in combination), and only very rarely as original writers. An evening in Monnier's bookshop on 1 July 1937 showcasing contributions to *Mesures* assembled twelve writers mostly of Nathalie's generation. All were men.[25] At the time, this must have appeared unremarkable, but to twenty-first-century eyes it seems extraordinary, and goes a long way towards explaining the difficulties Nathalie encountered in finding an outlet for her work.

Raymond wrote to her in response to Paulhan's rejection, as she was once again on holiday with the children while he stayed in Paris for work. It's a letter of reassurance and encouragement, and it also reveals the degree of critical attention he brought to Nathalie's writing:

> I've just read and reread your Planetarium. It's extremely good . . . from start to finish. Sincere, serious, with an occasional sad humour, and it exudes personality and intelligence. There isn't a single word that needs changing, and nothing slow about it. When you have enough pieces to be published it will produce a terrific effect of atmosphere and contained emotion.
>
> The passages I found a little slow the other day . . . the beginning of "objects" and a part of the "look" didn't make that impression at all on a closer and "fresher" reading. In fact they're full of wit, melancholy and mordant by turns, and they should certainly be left as they as they are.

He says he has also reread parts of *Tropisms* which, by comparison with the new texts, strike him as somewhat lacking in cohesion. As a result, "the general feeling isn't sufficiently apparent for the aesthetic impression to be entirely satisfying." He continues with a dose of pragmatism, and claims not to be surprised by the response from *Mesures*:

> I think that for many readers the Planetarium will be a more appealing book, but there's no denying that it's more difficult and the reply from the *Mesures* editorial committee doesn't seem at all surprising to me and it corresponds to the opinion that quite a lot of people will have.
>
> Your manner isn't easy, but don't let that upset you. It's proof that it's not banal, and that it departs from the standard techniques, that it's sincere and refuses to kowtow to readers' tastes. It's proof that it will be harder for it to become established but that it will do so more surely, and will last.

And finally, as before, he advises her to work:

> Have courage my darling. *You must* work. It would be an appalling
> waste if you gave up now that you're on the right path.
>
> You must work and move your Planetarium on during the holidays.
> I know it's not easy but you just need a few[x] hours every day where you
> can concentrate. I think the crucial thing for you is not to lose the habit
> of thinking about your subject matter and thinking about it intensively
> however briefly. . . .
>
> [x]I say a few: one or two would be good if they're concentrated.[26]

Nathalie didn't need encouragement to work, and thanks to the
room in the rue de la Tombe-Issoire, she had acquired a regular
rhythm for writing, even if it was just for the two or three hours a
day suggested by Raymond.

Mesures was not the only option for publication. Nathalie's personal acquaintance with Georges Pelorson through the École Bilingue provided her with an alternative opening, and the six new
texts were accepted by *Volontés*, the monthly literary review he had
founded in December 1937, with Raymond Queneau as its chief literary editor. Queneau's essay "Technique du roman" (Technique in
the novel), arguing for more attention to language and greater formal rigour in French fiction, had appeared in the first number, and
must have found a sympathetic response from Nathalie. Although
women were no better represented in the pages of *Volontés* than in
the *NRF* or *Mesures*, personal contacts counted, and Nathalie was
already in exchange with Pelorson about the journal in March 1939.
In the letter to her about *Tropisms* he mentions that he has just re-
sent her issue no. 14 of *Volontés*, and he invites her to contribute to
a survey organised by the journal: "Do you think that spiritual guidance is an organic function of human collectivities?"[27] The question
clearly didn't interest her, and she doesn't feature in the results published in the June 1939 number.

The new texts were scheduled for the September issue. On 12
August Pelorson wrote to say that they were with the printer and
that he urgently needed a reminder of her title—presumably "The
Planetarium"—about which he had reservations: "I've retained my
previous impression, which was that it sounded a little foreign (foreign to my mind, of course)." And he asks, "Can you change it? I

think Queneau shared my view."[28] But, with or without an acceptable title from Nathalie, and despite having reached proof stage, the
number never appeared. When the review folded, Pelorson tried
without success to interest Jean Paulhan in Nathalie's material for
the *NRF*.[29] In any case, when France declared war on 3 September,
Pelorson and Queneau had already been called up. And so too had
Raymond. The protracted start to Nathalie's writing career, which
had already been interrupted once, was again on hold. This time
through no choice of her own.

ν

CHAPTER FOURTEEN

Jewish by Decree, 1939–42

THE OUTBREAK OF WAR was not unexpected. As early as April 1938, shortly after the Anschluss, Raymond had received provisional call-up papers. Writing to Nathalie in July, he reports that "the news is not so good," and hopes that Denoël will not let an impending war get in the way of publishing *Tropisms*.[1] When hostilities were finally declared in September of the following year, Nathalie was in Bayonne, staying with Suzanne Elosu, the doctor sister of Nathalie's friend Fernande Elsou. Their father was a Spanish anarchist émigré, and it was no doubt he who exasperated Nathalie by asserting that "all these threats were just for show" and that there was actually a secret agreement between Hitler and Churchill. For her, by contrast, "What was happening was terrifying."[2] She was right to be afraid, but for reasons whose full extent she could not yet know.

With Raymond gone, Nathalie was now responsible for the three children. She initially made arrangements to stay in Bayonne, where she rented an apartment and enrolled Claude in school. However, she soon abandoned this plan and returned to Paris, perhaps in order to provide assistance for Raymond's legal practice. Evidently still anxious about the children's safety, she sent them to live out of the way of potential harm, but close enough for her to see them on a regular basis. Nadia du Bouchet had been appointed director of a TB Preventorium in a recently constructed sanatorium complex in Dreux, some ninety kilometres to the west of Paris, and was living with her own children in the nearby village of Saint-Georges-Motel. Knowing that Nadia was close by, Nathalie rented a house at the other end of the same village for the three girls and their German nanny, Lieselotte Wolff. Lieselotte, known as Lilo, had charge of the children during the week, and Nathalie joined them at the week-ends, taking the train from Paris to Saint-Georges (where the station is now closed). The Jewish Lilo had sought what later proved to be only temporary refuge in France from Hitler's anti-Semitic policies and was treated as a member of the family.

With the rank of "administrative lieutenant," Raymond received a salary from the army. But as his legal affairs required attention, Joseph came out of retirement to cover in his absence with assistance from Nathalie, who found herself drawn back into professional activities she thought she had long since escaped. Although commercial law was a field for which she had neither inclination nor aptitude, her reentry into this world brought her close to her father-in-law and she worked alongside him throughout the phoney war to keep Raymond's practice operational.

She also found time to write, and once again did so at Raymond's insistence. In an undated letter from 1939, sent after seeing Nathalie in Paris and finding her in low spirits, he urges her to

> take heart, find yourself again, and make a real effort to extricate yourself from everything that's crowding in on you and causing you to suffer. I know it's difficult and almost ridiculous to tell you, but it makes me so sad to see how you're overwhelmed by so many things that shouldn't matter to you. The only thing that matters and that you should think about is your work. It's too much of a waste to let yourself be slowly destroyed by little things that amount to nothing in the end.[3]

Raymond's absence must have reminded her of the months when he was doing military service, and he writes with very similar concerns about her psychological well-being. But it's clear that her writing had provided her with solutions to emotional distress that she had not discovered ten years previously. There's no way of identifying the work she did in response to Raymond's urgings, but having given up the room in the rue de la Tombe-Issoire, it was at this time that she acquired what became a lifelong habit of writing in cafés. She was not alone in this, since—especially as the war drew on—fuel was in increasingly short supply, and many writers gravitated to cafés where they could rely on a communal stove to keep warm.

The phoney war was abruptly brought to an end on 10 May 1940, when the Germans began their attack on France. Dreux was in the path of Belgian and French refugees fleeing the Germans in the east, and on the night of 9–10 June the town suffered intensive bombing, which resulted in heavy casualties. Nathalie drove to fetch her children, and they left—with Lilo and Polina—for La Baule, a seaside resort in southern Brittany which she knew from a previous summer holiday, where they joined some fifty other Russian Jewish émigrés. Two million Parisians—mostly women, children, and the elderly—had also taken to the road in advance of the Germans' entry into the capital, which fell to German control on 14 June. The majority headed south rather than west, but Nathalie may have been encouraged to go to La Baule by her old friend Lena, whose husband would have known the naval base at nearby Saint-Nazaire.

The town had already felt the effects of these events with the arrival of over a thousand refugees from the North and East of France. Their numbers swelled significantly with the exodus from Paris, although most of the new arrivals left after the armistice was signed on 22 June. As she had been in La Baule the previous summer, Nathalie was perhaps well placed to obtain suitable accommodation, and she stayed on with the children for whom the resort offered strangely normal summer holiday conditions. They played on the vast beach and swam, although this was at a time when bodies from the British naval fleet, which had been bombed by the Germans in Saint-Nazaire, were being washed up in the bay.

The reality, of which the children were not fully aware, was perilous. This much is evident from a letter Nathalie wrote to Raymond from La Baule on 6 July:

> After your letter of June 28th, I received a card you sent from Vichy on
> the 17th and a letter sent from the Dordogne on the 23rd, the day before

you left for Albi. The letters all show how concerned you are to find out what's become of us and how sad you are—so understandably! . . .— about everything that's happened. We were within a whisker of leaving for Bayonne & moving on from there to somewhere else—if I hadn't used all my strength to resist my father. Then we thought of going to wait for the Germans in Rennes! which is a big city: there was a bombing raid there the next day which lasted for two hours and left 4,200 victims. Fortunately we didn't budge—and then on the 17th and 18th La Baule was completely emptied. I wrote to you every day and telegraphed twice. In the end, the day the post office was due to close & the Germans were expected the next day, I sent you a final telegram and a final military post-card (like an SOS from a sinking ship!) to tell you that we wouldn't move from here—that we're all together and haven't had any news from you since June *8th*! There was complete silence after that—until your letter of June 28th which I received on July 2nd, and which I answered.

Communication was unreliable, but Nathalie was able to reassure Raymond that the family were safe and well:

We're all well. Your father too. He was euphoric until yesterday, when he saw that the Commercial Court was operating in Paris. . . . Where do you think it's all going? I'm impatient to get your news. The *boubous* [this is the word Nathalie and Raymond used for their children] are well—swimming & playing—and, since unlike me they don't know a word of German they can't act as interpreters, or reply, or have anything to do with the soldiers. They're dying to be with you again. *Write*. Everyone sends their love.[4]

A PS provides news of Nathalie's half brother Jacques, who was in a prison camp in Angoulême, but would soon be demobbed. As in the letter recounting the near choking of the "monster-baby," the tone is oddly jaunty, given the life-and-death circumstances it recounts. The Germans reached La Baule on 23 June, when Nathalie witnessed the tanks rolling into the town, an experience which, like so many others, leaves its trace in her writing only as a brief image, providing an analogy for the imposition of intellectual orthodoxy in her novel *The Golden Fruits*. Dominique remembers being petted by one of the German soldiers and not liking it.[5]

The family eventually left on 19 August, permission having been granted by the Standortkommandatur in La Baule on 3 August for "Frau Sarraute" to return to Paris in the family car with her mother and her three children. Raymond, who was stationed in Albi, had been demobilised on 12 August.[6] But normal life, if it resumed at all, did not last for long. On 27 August 1940 the first of what became an avalanche of anti-Semitic measures was announced, with the abolition of the Loi Marchandeau, which had prohibited anti-Semitism in the press. On 27 September a German ordinance was introduced requiring Jews in the Occupied Zone to register, and on 3 October the Statut des Juifs introduced by the Vichy government changed the definition of Jewishness from religious to racial criteria. Anyone with more than two Jewish grandparents was deemed to be Jewish. Vichy legislation applied in the Occupied Zone, and Jews living in Paris were instructed to register at their local police station. Dates for doing so were allocated on an alphabetical basis, and those with surnames beginning with S or T were to register on 17 October. Not being ashamed of being Jewish, Ilya was determined to comply and Nathalie decided to accompany him. They returned from registering with their identity cards stamped in bureaucratic red capitals: the word *JUIF* for Ilya and *JUIVE* for Nathalie. This decision set the course of her life for the next four years.

Raymond had strongly advised against registration. Nathalie was not a Jewish first name; she had French nationality; and, despite the disadvantage of her foreign birth, Ivanovo-Voznesensk was outside the Pale of Settlement, and the name Voznesensk, etymologically derived from the word "resurrection," had helpfully Christian connotations. Added to which, friends assured her that although Tcherniak was a Jewish surname in Belarus, it was common among non-Jews in Ukraine. In other words, she could easily have passed herself off as not Jewish, but a combination of loyalty to her father and a native streak of defiance led her to take the riskier path. At that point, it was far from clear where this path might lead.

Her decision was also conditioned by the family's attitude towards their own Jewishness, which had simply never been mentioned. Claude Sarraute later recalled the occasion when at the age of around ten she discovered that she was Jewish. Complaining one day to her grandfather that school dinners were horrible, she explained that this was because the catering manager was a Jew. When Ilya asked her what she thought a Jew was, Claude was happy to sketch the anti-Semitic stereotype of an unwashed miser, complete with hooked nose and protruding ears, at which Ilya revealed to her that both he and she were Jewish. The revelation came as a shock, and it cost her friendships at the École Alsacienne, where she remembers the children being free with anti-Semitic insults.[7]

This was in the late 1930s. Anti-Semitism had been on the rise throughout the decade, fuelled by an influx of mostly poor Jewish refugees from Eastern Europe at a time of growing unemployment in France. The election of Léon Blum, France's first Jewish prime-minister (Président du Conseil), was greeted with open hostility, and in September 1938 there were demonstrations against Jews in Paris. None of this can have gone unnoticed by Nathalie. Her literary interests would also have made her aware of the anti-Semitism of writers such as Céline (whose *Journey to the End of the Night* she nonetheless regarded as containing "great tenderness and great humanity," having been written at a time when, in her view, "Céline ... was an anti-racist"), Robert Brasillach, and Jean Giraudoux, whose book of political essays, *Pleins pouvoirs* (Full powers), published in 1939, warned against "a continual infiltration of barbarians" coming from Central and Eastern Europe.[8] Under the Occupation, anti-Semitism proceeded apace by more official means. In September 1940, the so-called Liste Otto was drawn up at the instigation of the former German ambassador to France, Otto Abetz, itemising, albeit in a rather haphazard way, 1,060 books by authors deemed undesirable for a variety of reasons, including Jewishness. Revised and extended versions of the Liste appeared in 1942 and 1943, and the latter included a supplement naming 739 French Jewish authors whose books were also henceforth banned. *Tropisms* was not included in any version of the list, but having declared herself to be Jewish, Nathalie in any case had ruled out all chance of further publication.

Things were no better in the legal profession. In October 1940 the Paris bar association, the Conseil de l'Ordre des Avocats de

Paris, sent out a request to all Paris-based lawyers asking them to declare whether they had been French nationals at birth. Nathalie complied in a letter dated 22 October, adding gratuitously and, under the circumstances, with a certain insolence, that under the terms of the law of 3 October debarring Jews from running businesses, she had effectively already been prevented from practising as a lawyer. In December she received a formal-looking certificate (which she kept and is now in the archive at the Bibliothèque nationale) stating that since her father was a Russian national at her birth, her name could not remain on the Register of the Association of Barristers at the Paris Court of Appeal. She was one of the 203 lawyers who, by March 1941, had been removed from the bar in Paris. The criterion of paternal nationality was a thinly veiled attempt to purge the profession of Jews, while allowing potential exceptions for assimilated "Israelites" who had been established in France for several generations, and a number of whom were distinguished lawyers.[9]

Nathalie was not materially affected by her exclusion from the profession since she had already abandoned it of her own free will, but the gradual accumulation of these anti-Semitic measures was menacing. After the war, Raymond and his friend and colleague Paul Tager published the full extent of four years of anti-Semitic legislation, under the title *Les Juifs sous l'Occupation. Recueil des textes français et allemands 1940–1944* [Jews under the Occupation. A compendium of French and German texts 1940–1944]. The book runs to 192 pages, in double columns. In their forceful introduction the authors comment that these measures had their own horror because, aside from all the arrests and deportations that Jews suffered, the legal statutes had the effect of making them "a sort of separate, floating population, condemned to inactivity, a real foreign body, a dead weight in the country."[10] Nathalie already had experience of being regarded as a "foreign body" within her own family, but also as a woman in the legal profession, at the ballot box, and in the Parisian publishing world. The anti-Semitic ordinances now inscribed this status in law.

According to a revision of the terms of the Vichy Statut des Juifs (Statute on Jews), Raymond was now defined as Jewish, since in addition to having two Jewish grandparents through his mother, he was also married to a Jew. With the *numerus clausus* of 2 percent imposed on Jews in all liberal professions, his livelihood was under threat. The solution he and Nathalie devised was to take preemptive action by obtaining a divorce so that he no longer had a Jewish spouse. Divorce by mutual consent was not available in France at the time, and so they proceeded on the grounds of *injures graves* (serious verbal abuse), with Nathalie as the plaintiff.

This required evidence, and she provided it in the form of an offensive letter to herself, which she exploited her literary talents to compose in Raymond's name. Such letters were commonly used by couples as a means of procuring divorce in the absence of other solutions. The document—in which Raymond declared that with effect from August 1940 he refused to allow his wife into their home—has not survived, but it was so persuasive that her lawyer later claimed that even after discovering that the case was a fabrication, his view of Raymond had been permanently tainted.[11] When the divorce was pronounced on 29 January 1941 Nathalie was already deemed to be living with her father, from whose premises she would now be legally entitled to have Raymond removed, with police assistance if necessary.[12] As the innocent party, Nathalie was also entitled to alimony, but she announced with bravado that Raymond's behaviour had been so despicable that she wouldn't accept a single penny from him. And although she also told the court that she and the children would continue to live with her father, she promptly returned to the marital home in the Avenue Pierre 1er de Serbie, where life continued as before.

Except that this was now impossible. Many of Nathalie's close friends were leaving France. Maria Jolas and Nadia du Bouchet had both departed for the United States, and Assia Minor (now Assia Gavronsky) soon followed suit. Being Jewish, neither Nadia as a doctor nor Assia as a lawyer was able to practise. Nearer to home, Ilya's business was under threat from the new anti-Semitic economic measures, and he was making plans to go to Switzerland. He tried to persuade Nathalie to join him with the three children, but she preferred to stay in Paris with Raymond—another decision with what proved to be life-threatening consequences.

As a first move in the overall aim to eliminate Jewish influence from the national economy, the German ordinance of 18 October 1940 had required all Jewish businesses in the Occupied Zone to be registered and placed under trusteeship. This affected Ilya's Établissementss Tcherniak in Vanves, and on 31 December 1940 a substitute—"aryan"—managing director was appointed. A business acquaintance chosen by Ilya himself, he was a Belgian engineer by the name of Edgar Demarteau, who owned an optical instrument company in Paris. Another of Ilya's professional acquaintances, the managing director of another colourant business, was appointed "temporary administrator" in June 1941.[13] In this way, Ilya did everything he could to leave his factory in safe hands for the duration of his absence.

Over the course of the next two years, as the legislation designed to "Aryanise" the French economy was ratcheted up and came under the supervision of the Commissariat Général aux Questions Juives (General Commission for Jewish Affairs), Demarteau bought out all Jewish stakeholders in the Établissementss Tcherniak. These included Messieurs Woog and Vischniac, chemical engineers employed by the factory, an American by the name of Edgar Abel Chernack, who was almost certainly a Tcherniak relative (his father having emigrated to the United States, where he specialised in the manufacture of flexible tubing), and the three Tcherniak children, Nathalie, Lili, and Jacques. Woog and Vischniac could not be traced, but Lili—who had married and was now Madame Berenstein—was tracked down to her home in Lausanne. They are all referred to in the correspondence simply as "the Jew X" (*le juif Woog* or *la juive Berenstein*), and the value of the business and the corresponding shares was set conveniently low for the purchaser. This was on the grounds, first, that the success of the factory depended on Ilya Tcherniak's personal expertise, which he was no longer available to contribute and, second, that the raw materials for the colourants were in reduced supply.[14] Demarteau's role was nonetheless understood by all parties as being entirely well intentioned.

Nathalie and Raymond had both been fired up by De Gaulle's appeal of 18 June, when, as the Germans overran France, he had declared in a broadcast from London that "the cause of France is not lost," that "France does not stand alone," and that "she can make common cause with the British Empire, which commands the seas and is continuing the struggle."[15] His rallying cry was an incitement to act, and in spring 1941, Nathalie and Raymond joined Sartre's clandestine Socialism and Freedom group. This was almost certainly through Alfred Péron, who was married to Mania Lézine, whom Nathalie knew through family connections. Péron knew Sartre from their time at the École normale supérieure.

The group's efforts have since been much derided—not least by Nathalie—but its aims were, first, to create an alternative to the existing communist and Gaullist Resistance groupings and, second, to prepare a political future for a postwar France based on socialist principles. The prime movers of the group were Sartre and Maurice Merleau-Ponty, and between April and June it acquired around fifty members, most of them teachers, intellectuals, and students. They were organised into separate cells, which met in secret in a variety of locations to discuss the principles of a better world, a prospect which in 1941 must have appeared remote.

Nathalie was assigned to Sartre's cell, and this was the first time that she met the man who had written to her so encouragingly about *Tropisms*. The group, which included the philosopher and theorist of psychoanalysis Jean-Bertrand Pontalis and the philosopher Jean Cavaillès (later shot by the Gestapo), met in the Hôtel la Louisiane in the rue de Seine. Raymond was with Simone de Beauvoir in the cell led by Merleau-Ponty, which met elsewhere. Nathalie found the proceedings all too reminiscent of school, and the task she was set—a report on the conditions of workers in Nazi Germany—felt so much like a homework assignment that she never got around to writing it.

Members of the group were expected to co-opt new recruits, but when Nathalie approached a lawyer friend, Suzanne Lévy, she reported that Lévy's lawyer husband had advised that it was extremely unwise to meet in a hotel and that Sartre was putting the lives of his associates at risk by doing so. Nathalie immediately offered to host the next meeting in her home in the avenue Pierre 1ᵉ de Serbie, where the concierge could be trusted, and a date was fixed. However, no one turned up on the appointed day, and when she later came across Pontalis in the street he said he had never received notice of the meeting.[16] That was the last she heard of Socialism and

Freedom, which collapsed over the summer of 1941, Sartre and Beauvoir having failed to interest either Gide or Malraux, each of whom they visited in the course of an extended cycling holiday.

By the end of the summer, Nathalie had more urgent concerns. On 21 August Raymond had been arrested along with forty-one other, mostly Jewish lawyers—some of them very eminent—and taken to the recently opened internment camp at Drancy on the northeastern outskirts of Paris. Thanks to his divorce from Nathalie, Raymond had escaped classification as Jewish, and it seems very likely that he was detained on the basis of mistaken identity, and that the German authorities had confused him with a communist colleague of a similar name. The names of lawyers offering their services to communist militants in case of arrest had been seized by the police in February 1941, and they included one by the name of Sarotte.[17] He is also listed just above Joseph, Raymond, and Nathalie Sarraute in the official register of lawyers for 1938, where his first name is not given. Raymond's first name does not appear on the list of lawyers arrested on 21 August, whereas most of the other arrestees are recorded by both first name and surname. And unlike "Sarraute," most of those surnames are Jewish.[18] Without a first name for either individual (Sarraute and Sarotte), it would have been easy for the two men with such similar-sounding surnames to be confused. This confusion and the resulting arrest had, however, made Raymond Jewish by association.

The lawyers were not the only targets. Some 3,700 foreign Jews had already been rounded up in May, and between 20 August and 22 August a further 4,232 French Jews were seized in Paris, including the 42 *avocats* sent to Drancy. The internment camp was run under French prefectorial authority by the French gendarmerie, who made no effort to alleviate the dire living conditions. The buildings—an unfinished housing estate—were impossible to heat, and the winter of 1941–42 was one of the coldest on record. Inmates slept on wooden bunks, and some on the concrete floors. The food was barely enough to sustain life, with a daily ration of just two bowls of soup and 150 grammes of bread. Medicines, food parcels, and all contact from families were forbidden. Between 20 October and 5 November, some thirty inmates died of malnutrition and lack of medical attention.[19]

The authorities intended to make an example of the arrested Jewish lawyers. A newspaper article on the front page of *Paris-soir* on 12 September contained a gloating reportage devoted to the "celebrities from yesterday's Jew-infested Bar" held in Drancy, describing them as part of a "vast army of agitators and speculators in the pay of foreigners" and falsely portraying them as abject but well treated.[20] In the same month, the Palais Berlitz hosted an anti-Semitic exhibition titled "The Jew and France" designed to suggest that the Jews had surreptitiously taken control of all aspects of French life and that "the Jews had transformed the noble profession of lawyer into a shameless business, touting for clients in our prisons. The defender of widows and orphans had been replaced by the ally of crooks and murderers."[21]

Without any means of contacting Raymond, Nathalie had no information about life in the camp other than what she could glean from newspapers and rumour. She was unable to intervene directly on account of her own status as a Jew, and she sent Claude, who was fourteen at the time, accompanied by Lilo, to the headquarters of the Sicherheitspolizei in the Rue des Saussaies to plead for her father's release. Despite her repeated curtseys and tossing of her blond curls, Claude's only reward for this intervention was to be congratulated by the SS officers for being *ein tapfes Mädchen* (a brave girl). Nathalie then sent her to enlist the help of former president Millerand by reminding him of his friendship with Joseph Sarraute, but Millerand had long since lost all political authority and was in any case suffering from advanced Parkinson's disease.[22]

Other means were required to extricate Raymond from Drancy before things got worse. His release would now depend on documentary proof that he wasn't Jewish, but the only proof accepted by the authorities was evidence of religious affiliation, and Raymond had not been baptised. Atheism didn't count, and the fact that Raymond's mother had been Jewish now posed a serious problem. Eventually, a false certificate of baptism for Livcha was procured, almost certainly through Raymond's lawyer colleague Jacques Rabinovitch, who worked for the Comité Amelot and with whom Raymond subsequently wrote a book about the legal status of Jews in the period following the Liberation. The Comité was established in June 1940, initially to help Jewish immigrants and Jews who had lost their livelihood as a result of anti-Semitic legislation, and later on to find safe destinations for Jewish children. As part of its activities, the group specialised in producing false papers, either in situ in the rue Amelot or through local *mairies* in the Paris region. Dominique remembers a fake baptism certificate, which had been artificially aged with a mix of carrots and tobacco and was then left out in the sunshine to complete the process, while she and her sister Anne were told to keep an eye on it as they played.[23] The document must have had its desired effect because Raymond was subsequently released, and officially designated "Not Jewish." His revised status is noted on the file held by the Préfecture de Paris with an instruction that his record be destroyed.

However, on 28 April 1942 he was rounded up for a second time in an operation targeting left-wing figures. Launched by the German occupiers, its aim was to forestall potential trouble during the traditional May 1st celebrations for the Fête du travail.[24] This second, quite unwarranted arrest was the last straw for Joseph Sarraute, who died by his own hand on 7 May at the age of only sixty-eight. In a note addressed to his family, he writes, "The splendour of life is over . . . I have decided to take the decisive step."[25] It was an act of despair on the part of someone who had once been a spokesman for ideals that no longer had a place in occupied France.

Although the motive for Raymond's second arrest was political rather than racial, family memories conflated the two incarcerations. In Claude's recollection of events, Joseph's suicide was a response to being asked to declare whether or not his late wife had been Jewish. Considering it dishonourable to lie, but knowing that to tell the truth would have fatal consequences for Raymond and his family, Joseph had supposedly opted to take his own life. False as it may have been, the memory was clinched by the family's experience at Joseph's funeral in the conventionally bourgeois church of St Sulpice in Paris. As Raymond was still imprisoned and unaware of his father's death, Nathalie attended alone with her three daughters, only to be turned away by Joseph's family for reasons she interpreted—no doubt correctly—as anti-Semitic: Joseph's mistake was to have married a Jew and to have raised a son who repeated the error.

Whether in interviews or in the chronology she supplied for the *Complete Works*, Nathalie never alluded to Raymond's internment in Drancy. Nor did she mention her father-in-law's death, and these omissions are hard to interpret. She must have felt personal grief at the loss of Joseph since she had worked so closely with him during Raymond's enforced absences. But she also always maintained that she preferred not to make too much of her own experiences in the Occupation because others had fared so much worse. However, more was still in store for her.

CHAPTER FIFTEEN

In Hiding, 1942–44

OVER THE SPRING AND SUMMER of 1942, further anti-Semitic measures were introduced, impinging on all parts of everyday life for Jews in the Occupied Zone. A curfew prohibited them from leaving their homes between eight in the evening and six in the morning; they were banned from all public places, such as theatres, cinemas, parks, and sports stadiums; the time they could enter shops was restricted to one hour in the afternoon, when shelves would often have been emptied; they were confined to the rear carriage of the metro, and were forbidden to own bicycles, radios, and a telephone. An ordinance of 29 May 1942 required all Jews in the Occupied Zone, including children over the age of six, to wear a yellow star bearing the word *Juif*, attached to the left side of the chest, visible, and firmly stitched onto clothing. Wearing the star became compulsory after 7 June, and it was one of the few ordinances that Nathalie made any move to observe. Raymond Sarraute and Paul Tager describe the requirement as an "instrument of humiliation and isolation."[1]

Once again, the alphabet determined the date on which Jews were to comply with the latest edict, and for the letters S to Z it was Saturday, 6 June. The fact this was the Sabbath was not a problem for Nathalie, but there were inevitably those for whom it must have created difficulties. She presented herself at the Commissariat de police, where she took three yellow stars, declaring to the official that she had no intention of wearing hers and that she was taking them for her three daughters simply as a souvenir. (With Raymond's new status as non-Jewish, they had now also escaped classification as Jewish.) Nathalie was indignant that each star cost her two coupons against her textile allowance. One of her friends was later arrested for accidentally covering up the yellow star on her coat and was subsequently deported to a concentration camp where she perished.[2]

Jews in France were now confronting physical danger. The first deportations to camps in the east, which had begun in March 1942, were accompanied by further raids, one of the most notorious of which took place on 16 and 17 July, when 13,152 Jews, including 4,501 children, were rounded up, and several thousands of them herded into the Vélodrome d'hiver, where they spent five days without shelter or basic provisions of food and water. For Nathalie, survival had become a matter of urgency. Once Raymond had returned from Drancy cleared of any suspicion of Jewishness, it was possible to consider practical measures that would keep Nathalie out of harm's way. The solution was to rent a cottage for the summer in the village of Janvry, some thirty kilometres to the southwest of Paris in the Vallée de la Chevreuse, where the family had spent previous holidays. The nearest station at Bures-sur-Yvette was within cycling distance for Raymond, who had resumed his legal practice, and he joined the family at weekends. The house, belonging to the gardener at the château in Janvry, was on the village square, next door to the bakery and a café, both of which served the local population of some three hundred. Nathalie's father had occasionally been a paying guest in a fine house in the village by the name of La Chanson. Bought on behalf of the Russian singer Feodor Chaliapin by a rich Russian merchant, Leonid Golovanov, the house was run as a pension with a mainly Russian clientele by Golovanov and his wife after Chaliapin's death in 1938.

The gardener's cottage was a modest affair. It had only basic facilities, no bathroom, and the one lavatory, dubbed by Nathalie "Heaven's punishment," was at the bottom of the garden.[3] The house was full with the three children, Polina, and Nadine Liber, Lena's niece, to whom she had lent her married name, Gauthier-Villars, as cover for the girl's Jewish identity. Dominique remembers the house as "ugly," and she would escape to one of the farms in the village to help with the animals, while Nathalie took herself

FIGURE 15. The gardener's house, Janvry, June 2016. The house
next door is the former bakery. (Author's photo)

to the café, two doors along from the cottage, in order to write what
she later described as a sequel to *Tropisms*.[4] Away from Paris,
where mass roundups continued throughout the month of August,
a degree of normality could be maintained. When the school year
began, Nadine rejoined her family in Paris, and Claude went to live
with Raymond during the week so she could attend the lycée. Nathalie and the younger children remained in Janvry, where she
oversaw lessons by correspondence course for Anne and Dominique. By then, Lilo had managed to escape to the United States.[5]
Raymond was active in various Resistance groups, including one
supported by the lawyers at the Paris Bar, and the communist-
inspired Francs-Tireurs et Partisans led by Col. Rol-Tanguy, who
later nominated him for a decoration in acknowledgement of his
contribution.[6]

Sometime in early September Nathalie and Raymond were contacted by Mania Péron asking whether they could give shelter to Beckett and his partner Suzanne Deschevaux-Dumesnil. They were on the run after the Resistance group, the Réseau Gloria, to which both Péron and Beckett belonged, had been betrayed by one of its members. Péron himself had been arrested. Mania and Alfred, who both taught English in Paris lycées, were close friends of Beckett's, and for many years he consulted Mania about the French in his literary work after he started writing in the language. Claude Sarraute claims that Mania and Raymond were lovers at this time, while Nathalie chose not to know, and it may have been thanks to Mania that Claude found herself taking private English lessons with Beckett, who at that point was penniless and needed the money. She would visit him in his studio apartment where, at the age of fourteen, she had the benefit of a university-level education in the high points of the English literary canon, a far cry from the English she had learned from the English nanny with the penchant for drink and the betting shop.[7]

Nathalie had never previously met Beckett, but she had read *Murphy*, a copy of which was spotted by the Gestapo when they arrested Raymond and which, being in English, they had found suspicious.[8] The first encounter between the two came when Beckett and Suzanne spent ten days in the gardener's cottage in Janvry. However, Nathalie and Beckett, whose names would later be associated through the Nouveau Roman and the famous 1959 photograph, seem to have taken a hearty dislike to each other.[9] Raymond and Beckett got on well, but Nathalie found her guests ungrateful and discourteous. The two girls had relinquished their bedroom—the best room in the house—to Beckett and Suzanne, who didn't get up until midday, when Beckett would appear in the kitchen while Nathalie was eating lunch with Polina and the children, armed with his chamber pot on his way to "Heaven's punishment." When they left, with help arranged by Nathalie's friends Nahum and Sonia Liber, Beckett and Suzanne took some of the Sarraute family ration coupons with them. But what rankled most with Nathalie was Beckett's lack of interest in her literary activities. The antipathy was evidently mutual. In a letter of 1959 Beckett inserts an exclamation mark in brackets after Nathalie's name, and in 1962 he refers to her disparagingly as "la Sarraute."[10]

Before long, Nathalie had more urgent concerns. Mme Golovanov from La Chanson stopped her in the street one day and asked in Russian whether it wasn't dangerous for her to "roam around" without a yellow star. Nathalie replied, "No, because you're the only person who knows."[11] But villages thrive on gossip, and denunciations were rife, especially in a climate where anti-Semitic propaganda encouraged a desire amongst the population to track down "Jewish scum" in the name of "public hygiene."[12] The local baker, Nathalie's immediate neighbour in Janvry, was known for his denunciations, having previously informed on a couple of poachers and an escaped prisoner hiding in his parents' barn. He had noticed Anne and Dominique playing on the village square during term time and thought it odd that they weren't at school, but according to Nathalie it was Mme Golovanov who precipitated events in November by informing him that Nathalie's father was Jewish. The baker then mentioned this to Mme Lucas, the *patronne* of the local café, announcing that he would be off to the *préfecture* after the weekend to "clarify matters."[13] Mme Lucas, with whom Nathalie had become friendly, reported the conversation to her, never imagining that there might be any truth to his claim.

She couldn't risk staying in Janvry a moment longer. Raymond had arrived for the weekend and they made immediate plans for escape. Telephoning from a neighbouring village, they asked a friend to send a telegram to Mme Lucas's café with a message that Nathalie's mother had been taken ill, thus giving them a pretext to leave in a hurry without raising suspicion. And it was just as well that they did, because the *milice* turned up to arrest Nathalie the following Monday.

By then she had sought refuge in Paris with her friend Sonia Dobkovitch, and subsequently moved on to stay with Nahum Liber (Lena's brother) and his wife Sonia, hiding in their apartment on the avenue Charles-Floquet, and only using the service staircase. Anne and Dominique had returned to live with Raymond in the Avenue Pierre 1e de Serbie. Nathalie then took a room under a false name in the rue Molitor, in the sixteenth arrondissement.[14] Years later, in 1968, she received a letter from a man by the name of Joseph

Grebelsky, who, after reading an article about her latest novel in the press, recalled the help she had given him during the Occupation: "You came to my shop at 75, rue Michel-Ange to pay the rent for your room. It was on that occasion that you gave me the address of a lady who got me a German pass, which allowed me to cross into the Unoccupied Zone. I've never forgotten what you did for me, and it may have saved my life."[15] Although Nathalie evidently had the means to escape to the Unoccupied Zone where it would have been easier to avoid detection, this was an option that she chose not to pursue. It was more important to her not to be separated from Raymond and her three daughters.

But now that she was sought by the Gestapo, a longer-term solution was required. Under cover of dark one night, Raymond and Nathalie called on Fernande Elosu, Nathalie's friend from student days, who ran a pharmacy in nearby Passy and had been a frequent visitor to the Sarraute household, where she and Raymond would have animated political discussions. She had recently taken in a Jewish friend and equipped her with false papers. Nathalie and Raymond may have been aware of this when they asked if she knew anyone else who might provide Nathalie with a safe house. Renée, Fernande's Jewish friend, immediately suggested Madeleine Dieudonné, a former dancer at the Paris opera and the widow of the journalist and playwright Robert Dieudonné. She lived in the village of Parmain, forty-five kilometres north of Paris in the Seine-et-Oise, where she owned a large house and ran a small pension for children of the kind that the three Sarraute girls had often stayed in while Raymond and Nathalie went abroad. When Renée phoned to enquire whether she would be willing to take in a Jewish woman who needed to hide, Madeleine immediately accepted.[16]

Nathalie stayed in Parmain under a false identity from late 1942 to spring 1944, living at no. 93 rue du Maréchal Foch, a quiet street occupied by large villas whose mostly well-to-do owners kept to themselves behind fences, walls, and closed gates. The village lies on the bank of the River Oise across from the larger and older town of L'Isle Adam, and a train station connects Parmain to Paris in a little over an hour. L'Isle-Adam and Parmain had been the site of fierce fighting during the German invasion, and under the Occupation there was considerable Resistance activity. Through the secretary at

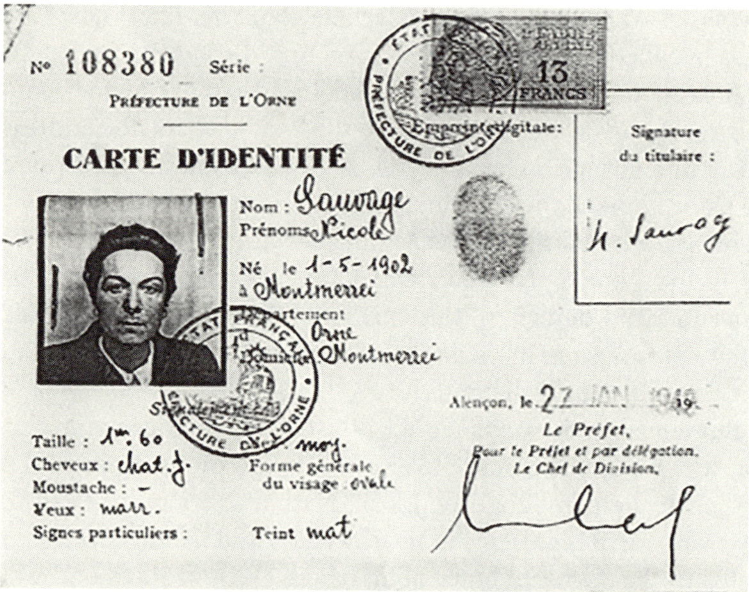

FIGURE 16. Identity card issued in the name of Nicole Sauvage.
(Fonds Nathalie Sarraute, Bibliothèque nationale de France)

the Mairie who was in the Resistance, Nathalie was equipped with a fake identity card under the name Nicole Sauvage, along with a birth certificate stating that she had been born on 1 May 1902 in Sées in the Orne department, making a small adjustment to her birthdate and allowing her to keep her initials. A suitably severe photograph stapled to the identity card corresponds to Nathalie's supposedly unmarried status and alleged profession as a primary school teacher. Raymond later obtained a variant of this identity card giving her place of birth in Algeria (where her father was deemed to have been a Latin teacher in a lycée) since, after November 1942, the French territory had been under Allied control, and there was no way of verifying this information. Nathalie's official status was tutor to the children in the pension where Anne and Dominique soon joined her, posing as her nieces. As their father, Raymond had a pretext to visit at weekends.

Madeleine, known as "Tatoune," was well liked by everyone. She was also an excellent cook and made the most of what had become very limited resources, occasionally supplemented by provisions obtained from farms in the surrounding countryside. Potatoes had more or less vanished from the start of the Occupation, and staples such as milk, butter, eggs, meat, sugar, and bread could be obtained only with ration coupons, while coffee and cheese had been replaced with unappetising substitutes. Tatoune was a generous host and the house would fill up at weekends when, in addition to Raymond, visitors included Fernande and Renée, along with the dancer Lycette Darsonval and Jacques Jaujard, deputy head of the Louvre who, on the eve of the German invasion, had organised the safe storage of the entire contents of the Louvre in locations throughout France.[17]

Nathalie would maintain and elaborate on her false identity for the benefit of these visitors, and everyone in the household called her Nicole. Anne and Dominique were to address her as "Tante Nicole," and when Dominique once let slip an inadvertent *maman*, she remained terrified that she had placed her mother's life in jeopardy. In private, Nathalie would entertain Fernande and Renée with comic accounts of her attempts to unscramble the imbroglios that the fictions about her life as Nicole Sauvage would occasionally generate. Fernande was captivated by Nathalie, describing her as having "a fascinating personality" and admiring the "elegance" with which she rose to the challenge of a life where she was in constant danger. She also remembered Nathalie coming downstairs, ecstatic after hearing news on the BBC of the German defeat in the Battle of Stalingrad on 2 February 1943.[18]

Despite its hardships and the constant risk of discovery, Nathalie later claimed that her time in Parmain had for the most part been happily spent. Raymond was there every weekend. She found teaching the children no special hardship, and Dominique recalls her mother being a far better teacher than any she ever had in school. During the Battle of Stalingrad, Nathalie taught Anne and Dominique the only Russian they ever learned: Россия победит Германию (Russia will defeat Germany).[19] The spring and summer of 1943 were gloriously sunny, and Nathalie would take the children for walks into the woods nearby, or along the River Oise, up the Sente au Beurre (Butter Path) and the Chemin de la Justice (Justice Lane), whose names were redolent of a better world, where food was plenty and equity reigned. She made regular clandestine trips to Paris to see Claude, who was a pupil at the Lycée Victor-Duruy. They would meet in the café opposite the school, Le Villars, later made famous by a photograph of that name taken by Robert Doisneau. Nathalie and Raymond visited exhibitions together, and in July 1943 they were in the audience for one of only three performances of Jean Vilar's production of Strindberg's *Dance of Death* in the Salle Vaneau, with Vilar himself in the role of the captain. The play was Nathalie's bedside reading over half a century later.

She was also writing, and she later recalled that she had more time to devote to her work when she was in Parmain than at any other point in her life.[20] Heating fuel was in short supply, and although the winter of 1942–43 was one of the mildest on record (unlike the two previous winters, both of which had been exceptionally harsh), most houses were cold. As her duties in the pension prevented her from going to the local café, she would write in her room in the Rue Maréchal Foch, where Dominique remembers her wearing two overcoats to keep warm while she wrote, one back to front and the other over her shoulders. At some point, she had decided to turn the continuation of *Tropisms* into a novel, having now reconciled herself to the genre which she felt could be adapted for her own preoccupations. This was very probably after Sartre's negative response to the six texts originally destined for *Volontés*, which she had shown him at the time of Socialism and Freedom. He had, however, repeated his earlier encouragement in his letter about *Tropisms* to try her hand at a larger project. A chance encounter with him on the Boulevard Montparnasse during one of her clandestine trips to Paris was further incitement to continue with the novel, which he said he would be interested to see once it was finished.[21] She kept the six *Planétarium* texts in their original form, no doubt still hoping to find another publisher for them, but those she had written subsequently were developed and integrated into the book became *Portrait of an Unknown Man*.

Sometime between June and September 1943, when the First Canadian Parachute Battalion was making preliminary forays into France, Nathalie was called upon by the local Resistance who had come to the rescue of a group of Canadian parachutists. They had been spotted in the woods nearby and were unable to speak a word of French. Nathalie was needed as an interpreter, so she joined the parachutists and a few members of the Resistance in the back room of the village café, while German officers drank at the bar out front. The Canadians were given civilian clothes to conceal their uniforms, and the following morning they were bundled into potato sacks and spirited away in the back of a vegetable delivery van. They later sent a coded message through the radio to say that they had reached safety.

However, a few days after this the Gestapo knocked at the door of no. 93 rue Maréchal Foch in the belief that Mme Dieudonné had sheltered the parachutists, whose recent presence in the village had been discovered. Nathalie was out with the children at the time, and it was Tatoune who had to confront the Germans. Their suspicions were aroused by the sight of Raymond's shaving things in the bathroom, which Tatoune had enough presence of mind to explain as having belonged to her recently deceased husband. (Robert Dieudonné died in 1940.) The map in Nathalie's room, with the progress of the Russian front clearly outlined on the basis of information illicitly gleaned from the BBC, and the shelf of books in English and Russian were also suspicious, but the Gestapo were satisfied with the explanation that Mlle Sauvage was a teacher. Tatoune herself was badly shaken by the episode and had been terrified that Nathalie would return while the Gestapo were in the house and hand herself in. Nathalie was also unsettled by her narrow escape from direct confrontation with the Gestapo.[22]

In late 1943, the secretary at the Mairie, who had supplied false papers to Nathalie, was shot by the Special Brigades, the French police force tasked with tracking down "internal enemies," and by spring 1944 Parmain was no longer safe. When the mayor telephoned to advise Nathalie to leave, she and Raymond agreed that the family should return to Paris. Once again they had to do so without raising suspicion, and instead of taking the train from Parmain they set off on foot for the next station in Valmondois, three kilometres and half an hour's walk away. Raymond then realised that they had left their ration book behind, and since it was impossible to survive without it, he went back to retrieve it while Nathalie and the children continued along the road with their suitcases, in dread that each black car that passed might be the Gestapo. However, they all reached Paris unscathed—and equipped with the indispensable ration book. Anne and Dominique returned to live with Raymond in the Avenue Pierre 1er de Serbie, while Nathalie took refuge with Mania Péron and her twin sons at no. 69 rue de la Tombe-Issoire, just down the street from the room where she used to write. Alfred had been deported to Mauthausen in September 1943. He later died having been fed too quickly on his release, an episode that haunted Nathalie, who often referred to it in later years.

The last months of the Occupation were as dangerous as ever, and despite the presence of the Allies on French soil from June 1944, repression was particularly violent. Jews were still being rounded up, and transports continued to leave for concentration camps almost up until the Liberation in August 1944. Nathalie would meet her children in public parks, dressed in widow's weeds, her face concealed by a black veil. On other occasions they would visit her in Mania's apartment. After the Allied landings began, it was decided that it would be safe for Nathalie to hide in the family home since the concierge was in the Resistance and could be counted on not to betray her.

Eventually, on 25 August, Paris was liberated as General Leclerc entered the city. Nathalie was jubilant, and, insisting that Claude, Anne, and Dominique witness the occasion, she took them up the Avenue Marceau to the Place de l'Étoile where they joined the crowds. Snipers were still firing from the top of the Arc de Triomphe, and they had to throw themselves to the ground when shooting started, Nathalie with both arms flung over her daughters to protect them while a few people around them were hit. But the collective euphoria was undiminished, and Dominique still recalls her joy at hearing the bells of Notre-Dame ring out over Paris.

The German Militärbefehlshaber in Frankreich had surrendered on the same day at the Hôtel Majestic, where Nathalie soon afterwards accompanied Raymond who was there on legal business. She was momentarily left in charge of a German prisoner, and with a rifle in her hand, she felt such overwhelming hatred for the entire German people that it was all she could do not to turn the weapon on her charge. What she resented wasn't only the German Occupation, with everything it had inflicted on her and others, but the fact that the occupiers had awakened such unwelcome murderous feelings inside her.[23]

In later life Nathalie said very little about these years, no doubt because, thanks to a combination of calculated caution, contradictory bravado, and the sheer arbitrariness of circumstance—she and her family had survived when so many others had not. Irène Némirovsky, who had also taken refuge in a village in the Occupied Zone, was arrested in the summer of 1942 and died soon after in Auschwitz, just one of some eighty thousand French Jews who were victims of genocide between 1940 and 1944. Nathalie, by contrast, was one of around two hundred twenty thousand—75 percent of France's Jewish population—who, despite the constant threat of arrest and the considerable disruption of their lives, had survived, whether by moving to the Unoccupied Zone, going into hiding, obtaining false papers, or relying on the help of Jews and non-Jews alike.[24] The Occupation had nonetheless imposed a Jewish identity on her that made her a social outcast and the target of a politics of persecution. Deeply marked by the experience, she took her daughters to visit the remains of the Jewish ghetto in Warsaw, where they could see for themselves evidence of the fate that could so easily have been theirs.[25] And in 1947 she wrote with vehemence about Hitler's Germany in an essay on Kafka, whose Jewishness she uncharacteristically specifies.

She credits him with having foreseen the fate of the Jews, and as having identified "certain fundamental traits of the German character," which led "the Germans" to devise "yellow satinette stars distributed upon receipt of two coupons cut from the textile ration-card" as well as the gas chambers where thousands died under the gaze of "well-cinched, booted and decorated gentlemen, sent on an inspection mission, who watched them through a glass-pane."[26] Later editions of the essay tone down this blanket condemnation and revise the wording to refer to "Hitler's Germany" and to "Nazis" rather than to Germans in general. Nathalie concludes her discussion of Kafka by saying that he had had the "superhuman courage" to go beyond both hatred and contempt to a place where all that remains is "a vast, empty stupefaction, a definitive and total incomprehension."

She eventually succeeded in tempering her lingering Germanophobia for people she could be sure had had no connection with Nazism. And, as if to imply that anyone could become susceptible to this way of thinking, she even momentarily ascribes to Alain Guimier, the central character of *The Planetarium*, the mind-set of an informer (like the baker in Janvry), driven by a desire to make people respect the law and exasperated by the defiance of Jews hiding under false names, gossiping on village squares, and drinking in the local café, just as she herself had done.[27] The image occurs again in her 1965 play, *The Lie*, where the action turns on the suspicions aroused by a character who claims to have been part of the Resistance and to have rescued a group of Canadian parachutists. As ever, nothing in the writing flags these moments as having any autobiographical significance, and Nathalie's lived experience is once again incidental to the exploration of a deeper psychological reality.

Raymond was also dealing with the experience of the Jews under the Occupation, addressing the issue from a legal standpoint in the two books he published in 1945. After listing all the anti-Semitic legislation under the Occupation in the first book, the second, *Examen succinct de la situation actuelle juridique des juifs* (A brief examination of the current legal situation for Jews), written with Jacques Rabinovitch, outlines the precarious status of Jews after the Liberation, as they sought to recover homes, businesses, and livelihoods from which they had been forcibly ousted by the legislation documented in the first book.[28] Both publications begin with strongly worded prefaces, where the authors do not refrain either from condemnation of "Nazi barbarians" or from the part played by Vichy and the French authorities in this barbarism.

Raymond's involvements continued to bear the traces of his wartime and postwar concerns with the publication in 1953 of *De la Libération à la répression. Étude sur la situation des immigrés en France* (From the Liberation to repression. An examination of the situation of immigrants in France).[29] He subsequently became secretary of the French Committee for the Defence of Immigrants, an organisation founded in 1949, which remained active until 1957.[30] His loyalty to the Freemasons, whose socially radical ideals he supported and whose weekly meetings he attended every Monday evening throughout his life, was of a piece with the values underpinning his professional writing.

The consequences of the Occupation also continued to make themselves felt for the Tcherniak family as Ilya returned from Switzerland and sought to reclaim his colourant factory in Vanves. The arrangements he had made to leave his business in safe hands despite its Aryanisation had finally unravelled when in April 1944 Demarteau took steps to acquire all shares outright and appropriated the business for himself. Like his near namesake in Nathalie's second novel *Martereau* (published in 1953), Demarteau, who had previously been regarded as the saviour of the Établissements Tcherniak, now appeared in a very different light as what the family privately called a *salaud*—a bastard or swine.[31]

Ilya was suffering from tuberculosis and at the age of seventy-five was in no fit state to seek restitution of his factory and to take the stagnating business in hand. However, Jacques, who had studied chemistry in Lausanne, obtaining a doctorate like his father before him, was ideally placed to step in and reverse Demarteau's takeover. He evidently succeeded, as a letter of 28 March 1946 signed by Jacques informs the Organisation for the Restitution of Property Belonging to the Victims of the Spoliation Laws and Measures that shares in the Établissements Tcherniak had been restored "by amicable agreement" to Ilya, Jacques himself, Nathalie, and Lili, who was still in Lausanne.[32] Nonetheless, despite this restitution, Demarteau's double dealing had left a scar, exacerbated for Nathalie when Ilya transferred the business to Jacques. This move was entirely logical, but it seems to have left Nathalie feeling that Ilya had chosen to designate Jacques as sole heir, a preference which may also have been implied in the absence of any financial provision for her. The affection she had previously felt for her younger half brother now evaporated, as another consequence—albeit indirect— of the Nazi Occupation of France.

Ambivalent Allegiances, 1944–58

CHAPTER SIXTEEN

Saint-Germain-des-Prés, 1944–47

NATHALIE'S LITERARY FORTUNES turned when she encountered Sartre again after the Liberation. The meeting took place in the Café de Flore, one of the venues in Saint-Germain that served as headquarters for Sartre and Simone de Beauvoir during and after the Occupation. Describing the episode in later life, Nathalie was unspecific about dates, but it was probably early autumn 1944, since it was warm enough for her to be sitting at a table on the terrace outside. She was there with two Russian friends, the Futurist painters of the avant-garde Natalia Goncharova and Mikhail Larionov, a point she frequently included when recalling the occasion, as if to stress her independence from Sartre's burgeoning literary hegemony. In various and not entirely consistent accounts of the meeting, she also suggests that it was Sartre who approached her, but given his status at this time, this seems unlikely, and it was almost certainly Nathalie who engineered the encounter.

Sartre nonetheless had good reason to be interested in her. He was intrigued by Russian women, having been besotted for a time with Olga Kosakiewicz, commemorated as Ivich in *The Roads to Freedom* and as Xavière in Simone de Beauvoir's eponymous novel *She Came to Stay*. Olga's sister Wanda also became Sartre's mistress, as did Natacha Sorokine, the daughter of white Russian émigré parents, who was Beauvoir's former pupil and lover. In a letter to

Beauvoir, Sartre claims that between the two of them they had explored the Russian soul "down to its deepest recesses."[1]

Nathalie, however, was not in the same mould as the couple's younger, mostly rather volatile Russian lovers, and Sartre was on the lookout for new literary talent. Conscious that an old literary order was on its way out, he was convinced that, as he said in his essay "The Nationalisation of Literature," the postwar literary order would not be the work of a particular school or movement, let alone of a single individual—or even of two (himself and Beauvoir)—but would emerge out of the multiple contributions of a new generation of writers finding their way in an unpredictable present. The essay appeared in the second number of *Les Temps modernes*, whose publication began in October 1945, and which quickly established itself as the leading cultural review of its time. Sartre's regard for Nathalie's work was genuine, as he made clear in an interview in 1960, when he said, "I've always found what Nathalie Sarraute does remarkable—and without any reservation," even if by then he had taken issue with the absence of any explicit social content to her work.[2] The extent of this literary divergence had become increasingly apparent over the course of the preceding decade.

In the winter of 1944–45 Nathalie found in Sartre a rare interlocutor with whom to discuss her writing. *Portrait of an Unknown Man*, which she had been working on since 1940, was not yet finished and still in fragmentary form. Sartre was keen to see it and she gave it to him to read piecemeal while she revised and rewrote it. He was an alert and attentive reader, as well as a good listener and, unusually for his time—or perhaps as a sign of changing times—he took women seriously as writers. In an interview for the *Paris Review*, Nathalie was adamant that there had been no physical attraction involved her relations with Sartre. "I liked him as a friend," she said, but although the physical aspect of a man was always very important to her, she added, "I found him physically one of the most repulsive men I had ever seen—it was terrible!"[3] What mattered was his attention, and in another interview she recalls that he had "the gift of making you feel more intelligent than you are thanks to . . . a sort of deference, which he accorded to absolutely everyone."[4]

At the time, she and Sartre had a number of common literary concerns, as is confirmed by Simone de Beauvoir in her memoirs, where she describes Nathalie as "an unknown woman"—possibly an echo of the title of the novel she was writing at the time—whose *Tropisms* had impressed them both: "Her vision of the world accorded spontaneously with Sartre's own ideas: she was hostile to all essentialism, she did not believe in clearly defined characters or emotions, or, indeed in any ready-made attitude."[5] For Nathalie, despite the growing public interest in Existentialism, Sartre was first and foremost the author of *Nausea*. When she read it in 1938, its first-person narrator Roquentin would have seemed to her to belong to the same family as Thomas Mann's Tonio Kröger or Rilke's Malte Laurids Brigge—an isolated introvert, alienated from a social world based in convention and prescription, and vulnerable to various forms of "psychopathological" disturbance. Her own anonymous (male) narrator in *Portrait of an Unknown Man* was a further addition to this family, whose members, according to her 1950 essay "The Age of Suspicion," also included Proust's Marcel, Céline's Bardamu in *Journey to the End of the Night*, along with the nameless narrators of Gide's *Paludes* and Jean Genet's *Miracle of the Rose*.

Sartre's awareness of the artificial character of narrative and his view of character as a social construction were welcome signs of an interest on his part in the formal features of fiction, which he saw as integral to what he had called the "metaphysics" of the novelist. He had elaborated this view in his critical essays of the late 1930s and early 1940s, notably in the one titled "François Mauriac and Freedom," published in the *NRF* in February 1939. Given Nathalie's interest in Mauriac's novels and her loyalty to the *NRF*, she is very likely to have read it then, and would undoubtedly do so in 1947 when it was republished in Sartre's first collection of essays, *Situations*. She may also have attended the lecture he delivered in autumn 1944, "Social Technique in the Novel," where he discussed the technical features of modern fiction. The young Michel Butor, future Nouveau Romancier, was in the audience, and later wrote, "I am absolutely certain that a good part of the *problématique* in my novels evolved out of the reflections prompted by that lecture."[6] For her part, Nathalie had already begun to reflect on many of these questions, but she was probably not acquainted with the American novelists discussed in the lecture.

Aside from the novelist and critic, Nathalie would also have seen in Sartre the author of *Reflections on the Jewish Question*, written in 1944 and published in 1946. He was one of the few French commentators to acknowledge the fate of the Jews under the Occupation, and his book is a powerful critique of French anti-Semitism. He condemns the imposition of a Jewish identity by means of the yellow star, which had obliged its wearers to "feel themselves perpetually Jewish in the eyes of others," and reduced every aspect of their existence to being an index of this single category.[7] His discussion of Jewish identity as the projection of an anti-Semitic viewpoint—"it is the anti-Semite who *makes* the Jew"—was particularly persuasive for Nathalie, who had herself been made Jewish by the Occupation, and whose *Tropisms* had already explored the susceptibility of the individual to the image of himself in the eyes of an interlocutor.[8] She later said that of all Sartre's books, the *Reflections* was the one with which she had been most in agreement.[9] He also has harsh things to say about those who denounced Jews, a view which she must have appreciated, having been on the receiving end of such denunciations. And although she professed to have no interest in Sartre's philosophical writings, it is more than likely that she read the pages in *Being and Nothingness* (published in 1943) dealing with *angoisse* (translated as *anguish*), the condition with which she was so familiar, even if his philosophical commentary did not entirely match her own experience.

After reading Nathalie's manuscript, Sartre offered to publish an extract from the as yet unfinished novel, and it appeared under the title "Portrait of an Unknown Man (fragments)," in the fourth number of *Les Temps modernes* in January 1946. The novel recounts its narrator's preoccupation with an old man and his adult daughter in a modern-day version of Balzac's *Eugénie Grandet*, where the narrator tests his sensitivity to the tropisms that pass between father and daughter, and between each of them and himself, while feeling his way towards a language that will convey this semiconscious, subterranean reality. The section chosen by Sartre omits passages dealing with the fictional painting of an unknown man as well as the narrator's own ruminations, and focuses primarily on the father, as his bluff exterior gradually breaks down under the pressure of an inner *angoisse*. The episode culminates in the old man's discovery that his daughter has been stealing soap from him, one of the rare features of the novel connecting it to its time when rationing had placed such commodities in short supply. By retaining the novel's title for the extract, the "unknown man" appears to refer to the father, rather than to the painting or to the narrator—an anonymous and socially insignificant individual. But, despite Sartre's cuts, the result is perfectly coherent, and apart from the excised passages, the extract corresponds word for word to the version that was finally published in book form in early 1949.

Although there was no contribution by a woman in the first number of *Les Temps modernes*, women were far better represented in the pages of the journal than they had been in the prewar literary press. Simone de Beauvoir was on the journal's editorial board (admittedly, the only woman for several years), and many numbers contained pieces by her. Work by Violette Leduc had appeared in both the second and third numbers, and the novelist Janine Bouissounouse contributed an article to the "Documents" section of the number containing Nathalie's piece.[10] Natacha Sorokine featured regularly under her married name, Nathalie Moffat, and an extract from a forthcoming book by Colette Audry was published in the seventh number of the journal, after which she too became a regular contributor. Most of the women associated with *Les Temps modernes* were friends of Simone de Beauvoir, and Sartre now steered Nathalie in this direction.

Sartre's support for women writers who were not his mistresses extended only so far, and he seems to have been content to allow Beauvoir to take charge of the female sector of their shared cultural empire. Nathalie was wary of Beauvoir's reputation as a philosopher, and *She Came to Stay* did not convince her of Beauvoir's talents as a novelist. (Beauvoir's subsequent novels did not alter this view.) In addition, perhaps recalling the changed relation with her father after his marriage to Vera, or her mother's exclusion of the child from the "team" constituted by husband and wife, she may also have been apprehensive that her relationship with Sartre would no longer be the same once Beauvoir was in the picture. Later experience confirmed this suspicion, and according to Nathalie, "When Sartre was there [Beauvoir] had an extraordinarily feminine way of behaving, which meant that she didn't say a word and let him talk. From time to time, he also seemed a little afraid of her, and would ask whether she agreed with what he was saying."[11] Beauvoir herself was unhappy about Sartre's enthusiasm for Nathalie's writing, and feared that it would undermine their shared literary aesthetic.[12]

These mutual reservations notwithstanding, Nathalie saw Beauvoir regularly over the winter months, knew her well enough to call her "Le Castor" (The Beaver), and through her made the acquaintance of Violette Leduc and Colette Audry. The four women first met in spring 1945, an occasion later described by Audry: "Simone de Beauvoir had invited the three of us for lunch. We were writers, and also women who had written books she thought interesting. She just wanted to introduce us to each other. I had probably already met Nathalie. At any rate, this was when I first met Violette Leduc."[13] The talk was of Faulkner's *The Sound and the Fury*, Kafka, and Virginia Woolf. Audry had known Beauvoir since the early 1930s when they taught at the same lycée in Rouen. She had also been a member of Socialism and Freedom, which was no doubt where she had encountered Nathalie, and she was soon to publish a collection of short stories, *On joue perdant* (A losing streak) which appeared in 1946. It was followed in 1947 by *Aux yeux du souvenir* (In the eyes of memory), an account of her early life viewed through abstract concepts such as boredom or happiness. Two extracts from the book appeared in the April 1946 number of *Les Temps modernes*. Leduc was also writing about childhood in her novel *In the Prison of Her Skin*. The topic, treated very differently by the two women, must have interested Nathalie, given her conviction that the key to writing lay in a deep-rooted attachment to childhood.

Her new female acquaintances were all a few years younger than herself. And compared to Nathalie with her lawyer husband, her three children, and her address in the well-to do sixteenth arrondissement, they were living in relatively unconventional personal circumstances. They were also sexually more adventurous. Colette Audry had a son, was recently divorced, and, like both Beauvoir and Leduc, was open to same-sex relations. Leduc, who was also recently divorced, had an obsessive—and unreciprocated—passion for Beauvoir, and intermittently, but with equal lack of reciprocation, for Nathalie. The four women were also bound together by broadly feminist convictions, which the belated granting of the vote in 1944 had by no means satisfied. Leduc wrote eloquently about the remoteness of the publishing world for women, and it had been a revelation to her when she first saw a copy of Beauvoir's *She Came to Stay* to see that women could write: "A woman writing such a big book. . . . It took me aback."[14] Beauvoir's *Second Sex*—an even bigger book—was published in 1949. (Nathalie owned a copy of the 1951 reprint, but not the first edition.)

A member of the socialist party in the 1930s, Audry went on to support a number of feminist initiatives in the 1950s and 1960s. After protesting against the invisibility of women writers in an article of 1963, she founded the series *Femmes* with the Éditions Gonthier, where she published translations of Betty Friedan's *Feminine Mystique* and Mary McCarthy's *Memories of a Catholic Girlhood*. She also published work by contemporary French women writers, including Charlotte Delbo's account of her experience of the camps, *None of Us Will Return*.[15]

Closer acquaintance with Beauvoir did not incline Nathalie to a warmer view, especially as Beauvoir kept aloof from the three other women. This left them to work out relations between themselves in the outer orbit of the universe whose centre was occupied by Sartre, Beauvoir, and *Les Temps modernes*. Sometimes Leduc would cook dinner for the other two in her apartment, and sometimes Audry and Nathalie would meet alone. Audry was wary of Leduc, as she later said to Leduc's biographer: "I thought I had (or could have) intellectually amicable (or at least cordial) relations with Violette Leduc. With Nathalie that was possible, but not with Violette. In her own way Nathalie was no doubt as difficult as Violette, but our mental structures were closer to each other."[16] The friendship between Leduc and Nathalie was the strongest bond to emerge out of the threesome, while Beauvoir remained the object of Leduc's jealous devotion.

Nathalie found in Leduc a fellow writer with whom she could talk about literature, exchange work in progress, and enjoy mutual encouragement on the fringes of a literary world still largely dominated by men. After all the years in which, until her recent meeting with Sartre, her only literary interlocutor had been Raymond, this collaboration was a new experience. In a rather formal note dated 7 June 1945, she thanks Leduc for sight of current work and is keen to see more:

> Dear Madame,
>
> Thank you for your kind note and for the manuscript—which I like enormously, much more than I dared to hope, despite all the positive things Simone de Beauvoir said to me. When can we talk about it face to face?
>
> I can't wait to read the story about the umbrella.
>
> with best wishes
> Nathalie Sarraute[17]

The manuscript she refers to was presumably the opening of Leduc's second novel, *L'Affamée* (The starving woman), since, as Leduc mentions in a letter to Beauvoir dating from October 1945, she had shown the first thirteen pages of the novel to Nathalie, and adds, "I tell her everything."[18]

In a later (undated) letter Nathalie writes to Leduc with even greater enthusiasm:

> Dear Friend,
>
> Thank you for the letter and the pages you sent. Of all those I've so far read by you, they are the ones I like best.
>
> I hope that one day others will enjoy the moments of pleasure—it would be more accurate to say of exhilaration, but I'm afraid of using a word you will find grandiloquent—that I have enjoyed, moments of the kind that are given to us by work of great quality.[19]

Her positive estimation of *L'Affamée* was genuine; she read the entire manuscript and provided essential encouragement.[20] As she recalled half a century later, long after Leduc had died of breast cancer in 1972, "The book I found admirable was *L'Affamée. In the Prison of Her Skin* wasn't bad, but it was a bit too influenced by Jouhandeau. I liked *La Bâtarde* [Leduc's autobiography] less. It was hugely successful, but it reverted to a more conventional outlook. I liked *L'Affamée* a great deal. She had considerable talent."[21]

In a letter to Nathalie after the publication of the extract from *Portrait of an Unknown Man* in *Les Temps modernes*, Leduc reciprocated with her own enthusiasm: "What a day! There was the T.M. with your text. . . . *It holds up.* . . . Everything is difficult, difficult but believe me: your efforts aren't wasted but your text is so depressing! Which shows that your aim was sure."[22] Nathalie may have been worried that the extract had been distorted by the cuts that Sartre made to the original, and it must have been reassuring to hear that the published result held together.

Nathalie and Leduc met regularly, at least once a week—and sometimes more—in cafés such as L'Ascot, a smart bar just off the Champs-Élysées, where they would spend the evening drinking whiskies (paid for by Violette) and talking about books, while Nathalie chain-smoked Gauloises. They would discuss Camus, Gide, and Kafka, Nathalie carefully weighing up the qualities of each, as she had at their first meeting over lunch with Beauvoir and Colette Audry, when she had agonised about the fact that she didn't care much for Faulkner, who was all the rage in the world of *Les Temps modernes*. "She explained again that she didn't like Faulkner all that much, she was sorry, it was a pity, that's how it was," while "she stared at the red tip of her cigarette, and continued, for her own satisfaction, to weigh the pros and the cons." In Leduc's account, Nathalie appears as "a fanatic, an Early Christian of Letters" and "a believer searching for truth in prayer." In sum, "It stared one in the face: literature was her reason for living. . . . It was what she loved most in the world."[23]

She would arrive at their rendezvous "half dead, consumed with torment," since "writing tortured her, writing made her ill."[24] Leduc would urge her not to upset herself over her work, and would drink recklessly in the hopes of impressing Nathalie, whose distress meanwhile enthralled her. In an unpublished passage of *L'Affamée*, which Leduc sent to Nathalie, she refers to her as "Hermine," the name she later gave in *La Bâtarde* to Denise Hertès, the supervisor and music teacher with whom she had had an affair at school. There was clearly an erotic undertow to Leduc's fascination, as she describes herself being "unsettled by Hermine's thoroughbred wrist" and physically excited by her friend's physically elusive presence.[25] The manuscript pages are roughly torn out of the exercise book in which Leduc wrote her novel, and they read like a declaration of love to their addressee—Nathalie—who may have insisted on their suppression, but kept them nonetheless, along with all the other equally scruffy communications she had received from Leduc.

The two pages contain a vivid portrait of Nathalie as she was in the mid-1940s, filtered through Leduc's captivated perspective:

> [Hermine] neutralises and buries her body under brownish coats the colour of ploughed earth. She wants to be physically insignificant. Her appetite is perpetually sated and her thirst quenched by things of the mind. Her body floats, and her mind crackles. It's fire and water. This cerebral being speaks to my viscera. The more disincarnate a person, the more they excite me. My body is prey to the body that's got rid of itself. Hermine has no lips. But her brown eyes are worth many mouths. When I'm with her, we're thrown out of cafés.

Nathalie's remoteness was an essential feature of her attraction, although it alternated with qualities that Leduc portrays as maternal: "She's too available and too unavailable, too open and too reserved. Too powerful and too powerless. She'd swallow me whole because she gives nothing. But her encouragement and her patience with me are extraordinary. She's a very affectionate anonymous creature."

Leduc was also alive to Nathalie's psychological vulnerability, whose effects she astutely identifies:

> She is intimately familiar with abjection. Her neuroses have the strength of tanks and their power of devotion. She is the one laid waste by them. . . . I'm far inferior to her. She lives only for literature. If she kicked her children out, she'd be a Madame de Staël. She's captivated by two contemporary writers. Her husband and children don't *affect* her. She remains intact despite being an admirable mother and an irreproachable wife. She wallows in her neuroses. A burning intelligence. A high-speed inner life.[26]

The comment about Nathalie's intelligence was echoed by others over the course of her life. In an undated letter to Nathalie (probably written in 1952) Leduc claims to have tried to impress Beauvoir by repeating, as if they were her own, remarks that Nathalie had made: "I don't have your level of intelligence. You didn't notice to start off with. You'd talk a lot and as my brain is weak, I'd take things, I'd steal them and I'd try to shine with S. de B. by using what you'd said to me, without mentioning you. You have been warned."[27]

Nathalie increasingly found herself caught up in a psychodrama of Leduc's making as she sought the affection and support of both Beauvoir and Nathalie. Looking back on these years in an interview she gave in 1987, Colette Audry offered her own comment on the relationship:

> There was an electricity between them, a sort of mutual fascination. Nathalie was simultaneously attracted and appalled. Often, when I had dinner in her house, she'd tell me with a mix of humour and horror about their meetings. She used to say, "You're strong, Colette, you can keep Violette at a distance." In my view, it wasn't strength. Nathalie was far braver than me because she'd face Violette every week. It's true that she got something out of it. The relationship fascinated her.[28]

Leduc certainly made demands on Nathalie, who came to the rescue when she was arrested for trafficking chocolate on the black market. Nathalie found her a lawyer who was able to get her off the charge by using the fact that Leduc was a writer and had letters from Camus—such was the respect for literature at the time.[29] On another occasion, Leduc turned up at 12 Avenue Pierre 1ᵉ de Serbie threatening to commit suicide because Beauvoir didn't love her. Nathalie took her in and gave her a bed for the night, but she stayed on for several days, disrupting the household by insisting that no one should go past her room because she was meditating. Later on, Nathalie was drawn into becoming the confidante for another of Leduc's unrequited passions, this time for the Greek painter Thanos Tsingos, whom she had met through Nathalie. Leduc would telephone at eleven o'clock in the evening or send up notes via the concierge insisting that Nathalie come down to speak to her.[30] Eventually these demands became too great and the friendship cooled. Recalling the period many years later, Nathalie explained, "[Violette] used to make scenes. She'd let rip in an incredible way. I put up with her. And then I had enough."[31]

She nevertheless sent Leduc a copy of *Martereau* in 1953 with the inscription, "For Violette Leduc and although she doesn't like it, with my affection," a reference to the fact that Leduc had claimed not to have appreciated the extract from the novel that appeared in *Les Temps modernes* in May of that year. But by then Nathalie was no longer as isolated in the literary world as she had been when the two women met in 1945. Their literary paths had diverged, and they no longer needed the support they had previously given each other.

CHAPTER SEVENTEEN

The Elephant's Child, 1947–49

BY THE BEGINNING of May 1946 Nathalie was putting the finishing touches to *Portrait of an Unknown Man*. "I'm working as much as possible," she wrote to Leduc, but adds that she is doing so "with dubious results."[1] Dubious or no, she delivered the manuscript to Beauvoir at the Café de Flore. Beauvoir had acted as intermediary for both Audry and Leduc, recommending their first books to Camus, who published them in his series *Espoir* at Gallimard. To judge by Beauvoir's own account, Nathalie does not seem to have benefited from the same degree of support when, in the course of a very busy day on Friday 10 May, Beauvoir took the manuscript not to Camus, but to Jean Paulhan at Gallimard, on her way to the editorial office of *Les Temps modernes* in the same building. She was pleased to find Paulhan alone, admired his handwriting as he inscribed Nathalie's name and the title of her book on the cover, and then turned her attention to a painting he had recently acquired. Nothing was said about Nathalie's novel, and after meeting up with several more people over the course of the afternoon, Beauvoir ended the day by drinking three gin fizzes in the Pont Royal Café to celebrate the appearance of the eighth number of *Les Temps modernes*.[2]

This was the third time that Nathalie had submitted her work to Paulhan's editorial scrutiny. Since there's no record of any correspondence on this occasion, one can only assume that despite the good word that Sartre subsequently put in with him, the outcome was a fairly rapid negative.[3] Sartre then intervened more decisively, and offered to write a preface for the book, since in his view it was difficult and she would have problems convincing a publisher to take it. The preface was the first and one of the finest of several that he wrote around this time. The endorsement was apparently effective, and by December 1946 Nathalie had a contract with the publisher Nagel, where Sartre's friend, the Hungarian-born journalist François Erval, worked as an editor. Nagel had published Sartre's best-selling *Existentialism and Humanism*, and further titles by both Sartre and Beauvoir were in the offing. On 17 December Nathalie signed a contract for *Portrait of an Unknown Man*, with a proposed print run of a thousand copies, royalties of 10 percent, a commitment to publish the book within twelve months, an advance of seventy-five hundred francs payable on signature of the contract, and a further seventy-five hundred on publication.[4]

However, dealings between Sartre and Nagel deteriorated. Sartre's preface became a liability, and Nathalie's novel was a casualty of this souring of relations. After a series of deferred promises from Nagel, Nathalie wrote on 11 March 1948—almost two years after finishing her novel—to say that in view of these failed commitments, she considered the contract to be void and she requested the return of her manuscript, Sartre's preface, and her blurb. She also demanded payment of the seventy-five hundred francs that she would have received on publication. No doubt, Raymond's legal expertise lay behind these demands and their careful wording, and the written material was restored to her. There's no record that her demand for payment was met.

By then François Erval was working as an editor for Robert Marin, a bookseller who had gone into business as a publisher after the Liberation, when there was a proliferation of new publishing ventures. Erval was one of a number of young editors taken on by Marin, who, for the duration of his brief existence as a publisher, acquired a reputation for signing up some of the most interesting and innovative writers of the period. In that sense he was a replacement for Robert Denoël, who had been murdered under mysterious circumstances in December 1945 following his acquittal on the charge of "collusion with the enemy" under the Occupation. (This accusation was levelled with varying degrees of explicitness at several publishers, Gallimard included.) Marin's list included Antelme's *The Human Race*, an account of his experience in Nazi concentration camps, and a translation of the antiwar novel *Stalingrad* by the German novelist Theodor Plievier, both of which Nathalie mentions in her 1950 essay "The Age of Suspicion."

Erval had teamed up with Maurice Nadeau, a young literary critic, and brought Nathalie's manuscript with him. Nadeau later acknowledged that he and Erval had no more idea than did Marin himself about running a publishing business, but they seized the opportunity to take on books and authors who interested them without worrying too much about practicalities. As a result, they created an adventurously cosmopolitan list that included titles by Virginia Woolf, Elio Vittorini, Raymond Queneau, and André Breton. Although Nathalie's subsequent frustrations didn't incline her to see it in this light, she found herself in interesting literary company.[5] On 23 March 1948 she received a letter signed by Erval in his capacity as literary editor and writing under his original name François Emmanuel, confirming acceptance of her manuscript with an expectation that the book would be published in September of that year. A contract dated 13 April 1948 duly followed, once again offering 10 percent royalties, and including an option on any forthcoming books. In fact, she had already started work on *Martereau*, which was announced as being "in preparation" when *Portrait of an Unknown Man* eventually appeared.

As proofs had still not arrived in mid-September, Nathalie sent a sternly worded letter to Erval where she says she fears a repeat of the prevarications she had encountered with Nagel and demands confirmation, by return, of Marin's intention to publish. She was evidently not aware of her young editor's inexperience, but she may have sensed that he was chronically disorganised.[6] Erval sought to reassure her, writing, "You know very well that I like your book very much and that I was very glad when you followed me to my new publisher. I would not have taken it, if I had not wanted to publish it."[7] He goes on to explain that production has been delayed because the book was to be set in a rare typeface that was being used for more lucrative projects to which Nathalie's book had to defer. More weeks passed, and still there was no sign of progress. She was finally promised a publication date of 1 January 1949. But, discouragingly, no sooner had she returned the proofs to Erval than she received a letter (dated 1 December 1948) from her previous publishers, Éditions Denoël, announcing their intention to delete *Tropisms* from their list and to pulp the remaining three hundred unsold copies. She negotiated a stay of execution after explaining that Robert Marin was soon to bring out a novel by her with a preface by Sartre, which referred to *Tropisms* and quoted passages from the book.[8]

Yet more weeks went by with no communication from Marin. On 31 January Nathalie wrote again to Erval to say that if the book had not come out by the end of February she would withdraw her manuscript, invoking the clause in her contract that promised publication within twelve months. In a slightly galling reply written on the following day, Erval once again sympathises with Nathalie's frustration but explains that the success of Plievier's *Stalingrad* had required a reprint, which used up the still very limited supply of paper. (There had been an acute paper shortage since the start of the Occupation.) *Portrait of an Unknown Man* was eventually published in March 1949, almost three years after it was finished, although the delay was masked by a copyright registration for the fourth quarter of 1948. To close the apparent gap still further, Nathalie added a final date of 1947 to the end of the text, corresponding to the composition of Sartre's preface rather than to that of her novel.

The book met with a certain amount of critical response in the weeks following its publication. It was reviewed on the radio in the lunchtime news of 4 May, and another review appeared in the *Figaro littéraire* of 7 May. The *Gazette des lettres* carried a short interview with Nathalie, and she was interviewed on the radio, as part of RTF's new policy of extended coverage of literary matters. Violette Leduc heard the broadcast and wrote to Beauvoir, "I heard N. Sarraute on the radio. It was so serious!"[9] The interview was also heard by a young medical student, André Hartemann, who was following Nathalie's fortunes with sympathetic interest, and wrote on 29 May to record his pleasure at the amount of attention her novel was receiving:

Your Portrait has made quite a splash. . . . In the space of a fortnight, I've heard the very laudatory comments about your book by Pierre Duma[y]et, on Wednesday May 4th on the 12.30 news—

read a rather less "understanding" article by Jean Blanzat in the *Figaro littéraire*

(the hero is a "neurotic," quite a *label*)

also read your interview in the Gazette des lettres (You don't have kind words for Heidegger [Nathalie had said that Heidegger 'bored her'], but I partly share your view, as he is sometimes boring).

And best of all I heard your interview on the radio two weeks ago last Tuesday, very well presented, but I didn't fully recognise your voice.[10]

Hartemann was an enthusiastic supporter of Sartre and *Les Temps modernes*, and had read Nathalie's contributions to the journal which evidently spoke to him. As a result, he initiated a correspondence to which she—uncharacteristically—seems to have responded, although unfortunately her letters have not survived. (Hartemann died by his own hand in 1959 at the age of thirty-six.)

The book was also reviewed by François Erval—its publisher—in *Combat*, which had started life as a clandestine publication during the Occupation. Leduc read the notice, and as she writes in another letter to Beauvoir, she was glad to see the positive reception of a novel whose painful composition she had witnessed at close quarters: "There was a good article about Nathalie Sarraute's book in the literary section of *Combat*. I'm pleased for her."[11] Erval offers a broadly perceptive and sympathetic account of the book, but, echoing Sartre's comment in his preface to the novel, describes it as "difficult" and "suited to a limited readership."[12] The review in the *Figaro littéraire* had made the same point, and in her interview in the *Gazette des lettres* Nathalie contributed to this estimation by declaring, "People don't understand it all. . . . It goes too much against current tastes."[13]

She nevertheless had the pleasure of a personal endorsement when she received a long and enthusiastic letter dated 4 May from André du Bouchet. He was beginning to establish himself as a poet and had just taken over as managing editor of *Transition*. There was also an encouraging letter from another poet, André Spire, with whom Nathalie may have been acquainted through Joseph Sarraute, whose contemporary he was. He had already expressed his admiration for the way she deployed an "impassioned scalpel" in her essay on Paul Valéry in *Les Temps Modernes* (on which more below) and he now wrote (in May 1949) with comments that must have pleased her: "One reads you word by word, line by line, living the *angoisse* of your characters, your own *angoisse*." He adds that he had been particularly struck by the complex imagery of the novel.[14]

In later years Nathalie tended to downplay the critical reception of her first novel, claiming that its appearance had passed virtually unnoticed. This was not quite the case, but her memory may have been coloured by subsequent events, because by November 1949, just a few months after the book's publication, her authorial standing was beginning to take a downturn. After selling only a further hundred copies of *Tropisms*, the Éditions Denoël decided definitively to delete the title from their list. Nathalie agreed to buy back the remaining two hundred unsold copies for fifteen hundred francs, the equivalent of a little over one hundred euros in today's money.[15]

Even more discouragingly, less than eighteen months later, on 9 May 1951, the managing director for Robert Marin wrote that in light of the continuing poor sales of *Portrait of an Unknown Man*, he intended to dispose of the remaining stock. The novel had sold two hundred and thirty copies in the first year, but only forty-eight in the second. Sales in these numbers were unsustainable since, like many of the publishers who had gone into business after the Liberation, Marin was now in financial difficulties. On 16 May Nathalie wrote to accept his terms and stated her intention to purchase two hundred of the remaining copies for 10 percent of the full price. At the age of fifty, just over two years after the publication of *Portrait of an Unknown Man*, and twenty years after the start of her writing career, Nathalie was the author of a grand total of two deleted titles and the signatory to two annulled contracts.

She was also increasingly ambivalent about her association with Sartre and Beauvoir. From the outset there had been a certain tension owing to the fact that Nathalie was Sartre's "find," but had been forcibly taken under Beauvoir's wing. Sartre's preface had also been a bone of unspoken contention between Nathalie and Beauvoir, who was quite simply jealous of their intellectual complicity. On the one hand, *Les Temps modernes* was, in Nathalie's own words, "the only place to get published," and, on the other, she risked finding herself alternately co-opted and excluded by a literary grouping—the self-styled "family"—with which she felt less and less affinity.[16] She was confronted once again with the old dilemma about where and to what extent she belonged.

In September 1945 a collective literary tone had been set by the simultaneous publication of the first two volumes of Sartre's *Roads to Freedom* about the run-up to war and the Occupation, and Beauvoir's second novel, *The Blood of Others*, portraying the same period. Nathalie received signed copies of all three books, with an inscription from Beauvoir which reads, "To Nathalie Sarraute, with my sure and loyal friendship. S. de Beauvoir."[17] Others were also writing about recent history. Elsa Triolet, who was now publishing in French, received the Prix Goncourt in 1945 for *A Fine of 200 Francs*, a collection of short stories about the Occupation. In the same year, another Russian-born writer, Romain Gary, won the Prix des Critiques for his first novel, *A European Education*, about the Polish Resistance. The literary ambiance surrounding all these publications was very different from the one that had nurtured the composition of Nathalie's novel, which continued in the vein of *Tropisms* and did not narrate the wartime experiences alongside which it had been written.

The transition to the longer format of the novel had been accompanied by her reading of (mainly) English fiction, borrowed from Sylvia Beach's library at Shakespeare and Company. Between 1939 and 1941, she took out Emily Brontë's *Wuthering Heights*, Charlotte Brontë's *The Professor*, and *Mill on the Floss* and *Romola* by George Eliot, as well as *David Copperfield* and *Nicholas Nickleby* by Dickens, Scott's *Waverley*, and Goldsmith's *Vicar of Wakefield*. She also read *Moby Dick* and Faulkner's *As I lay Dying*. (It may well have been this novel that inspired the misgivings she expressed about Faulkner over lunch with Beauvoir, Leduc, and Audry in the spring of 1945.) She later bought her own copy of *Wuthering Heights* and a French translation of Virginia Moore's biography of Emily Brontë, *The Life and Eager Death of Emily Brontë*. This English tradition was of no interest to Sartre or Beauvoir, whose Anglophone references were all to contemporary American fiction.

The preface Sartre wrote for *Portrait of an Unknown Man* certainly provided welcome validation. It was included in every subsequent edition of the novel, but Nathalie feared that it had come at the cost of misrepresentation, and she expressed increasing reservations about it. She even suggested that Sartre had actually done her a disservice by writing a preface rather than a review essay, which would have allowed more distance between her book and his commentary. These misgivings grew as she sought more and more determinedly to differentiate her work from the sponsorship from which it had nonetheless benefited. She rejected the philosophical pretension that Sartre's comments might have implied that she shared. And when asked about him in an interview in 1953, she replied in a distinctly double-edged fashion: "He discovered all sorts of intentions in my book that I'd never suspected myself," adding that if she had practised Existentialism, it was the way Molière's M. Jourdain practised prose, "without realising."[18] And while she credited Sartre with coining the term "sub-conversation," which she later adopted for herself, she repudiated others he had used, notably the label "anti-novel," which he had applied to *Portrait of an Unknown Man*.

By the late 1940s, Sartre's previous interest in literary technique had been subordinated to other concerns associated with "commitment." For Nathalie this was a serious lapse, indicating a lack of artistic integrity. When she recalled Sartre saying to her, "If you carry on writing like this, you'll be making the sacrifice of your life," she implied that in her view his literary choices had been driven by a desire for self-advancement, for which she held Beauvoir primarily responsible.[19]

This ambivalence towards her mentors was expressed in the three critical articles Nathalie contributed to *Les Temps modernes* between January 1947 and February 1950, where she presents herself as a dissident in a climate of critical orthodoxy. The first of these, "Paul Valéry and the Elephant's Child," takes a rather unexpected target in the figure of the grand old man of French poetry, Paul Valéry, whose death in July 1945 had been marked by a state funeral. She couldn't have known of the passages in his *Notebooks* where he used the word "tropism," and she had little interest in the classically formal and somewhat cerebral poetry written by Valéry. But he provides her with a pretext for rehearsing a certain stance in relation to the literary establishment.

Leduc was worried that Nathalie's attack would backfire, but admired the result: "I was afraid people would see her as an ant taking on the Pantheon, but I was moved by her sincerity, her rebelliousness, her energy, and her courage in debunking an untouchable."[20] In a diary entry for 11 May 1946, Beauvoir mentions having heard Nathalie talk about her plans for the article, and being amused by her temerity.[21] Nathalie's critique was directed not only at the conventional classicism she found in Valéry's poetry, but at "the ever-growing crowd of devotees" whom she portrays as submissively accepting Valéry's reputation as a great poet.[22] It is this unthinking consensus that she challenged by casting herself in the role of the Elephant's Child from Rudyard Kipling's *Just So Stories*, daring to ask questions about the merits of literary reputation and adopting a posture she describes as both insolence and sacrilege. It was an attitude she increasingly assumed in relation to *Les Temps modernes* itself.

This much became apparent in her next article, "From Dostoievski to Kafka," published in October 1947, where she defends the psychological novel against the "novel of situation" associated with the work of Kafka, Camus's *homo absurdus*, and the American novelists promoted by Sartre. She doesn't mention Sartre's own fiction, but coming just two months after the six instalments of Sartre's *What Is Literature?* published between February and July in *Les Temps modernes*, Nathalie was advancing a divergent conception of literature and a different literary history. At a time when she was still in search of a publisher for her first novel—and still dependent on Sartre's patronage—her intellectual confidence is remarkable as she outlines a conception of fiction that makes her own tropisms central to the entire tradition of the novel from Dostoevsky to the present day.

The third and last of the articles that she published in *Les Temps modernes*, "The Age of Suspicion," appeared in February 1950. (Its title was derived from Stendhal's remark that "The genius of poetry is dead, and the genius of suspicion has entered the world.") A dismantling of fictional character and a defence of first-person narration, the article is less overtly at odds with Sartrean literary theory than the previous one. But Nathalie later claimed that by then "Sartre had turned to committed literature and was no longer the least bit interested in what I was writing."[23] She also claimed that her piece was accepted only because Sartre had been away in Dakar at the time she submitted it, leaving Merleau-Ponty in charge of editorial decisions.

An extract from *Martereau* was published in the May 1953 number of *Les Temps modernes*, but a fourth critical article, "Conversation and Sub-conversation" (whose title recalled the term coined by Sartre in his preface to *Portrait of an Unknown Man*), was turned down after Nathalie submitted it to the journal in December 1954. She attributed the rejection to Beauvoir, who saw in it a critique of her own recent novel *The Mandarins*. When Nathalie asked Colette Audry to see if she could discover more, Audry reported that Beauvoir had responded with a peremptory, "We're not preventing her from writing. She shouldn't prevent us from writing either."[24] This marked the end of Nathalie's decade-long association with the journal.

There had always been a degree of personal animus between Nathalie and Beauvoir, and this gradually hardened into outright hostility. Nathalie was particularly sensitive to the unequal nature of their relations and was not afraid to say so. The day after Beauvoir had delivered her manuscript to Paulhan, Nathalie confronted her and Sartre in a scene recalled by Beauvoir in *Force of Circumstance*:

> Her hair beautifully waved and wearing a smart bright-blue suit, she explained quite soberly that we act as if we were Kafka's Castle; in our records, everyone has a number he knows nothing about; we allow so many hours per year to one person, so many hours to another, and it's impossible to obtain a further hour even by throwing oneself under a bus. We manage to convince her, after endless argumentation, that we like her. She confesses, moreover, that in her eyes we are pure abstractions, and that she doesn't give a damn about us as contingent, human individuals.[25]

Nathalie repeated her accusations in later interviews, but contested Beauvoir's recall on the matter of her physical appearance: she had always had straight hair, and she never wore bright blue.[26] Her account of other events supports this sense of having been assigned a place in a pecking order.

Beauvoir would talk in Nathalie's presence about her friendships with people she never introduced her to (Giacometti or Koestler), and Nathalie reports an occurrence when she was with Beauvoir at the Deux Magots café, and Jean Genet came over to their table. Beauvoir had previously introduced Genet to Violette Leduc, and the two had become friends, but in this instance—at least in Nathalie's telling—Beauvoir ignored her, until Genet finally addressed her directly by saying, "My name is Jean Genet. And yours?" On yet another occasion, Nathalie recalled that Sartre had invited her to a lecture he was giving at the Sorbonne and suggested that she join the party for dinner afterwards. But as they reached the restaurant, Beauvoir turned to her and pointedly said "Good-bye." For Nathalie that marked a limit, and it was the last time the two women had any active social exchange.[27] After this, there was no pretence of amicable relations between Nathalie and the Sartre-Beauvoir couple. But their paths continued to cross, and until the end of the 1950s—and beyond—Nathalie remained preoccupied by the image she had formed of Beauvoir, who haunts the pages of her third novel, *The Planetarium*.

New Horizons, 1949–53

IN ADDITION to the long-delayed publication of *Portrait of an Unknown Man*, the year 1949 brought major changes in Nathalie's private life, the most momentous of which was the death of her father on 23 August. He was almost eighty. After he and Vera had returned from Switzerland in 1945 they stayed for a time with Nathalie and Raymond in the Avenue Pierre 1ᵉ de Serbie, where Nathalie was able to care for him while he was treated for TB. And Raymond, with his expertise on the question of the restitution of Jewish property, was able to provide advice for recovering the Établissements Tcherniak from the duplicitous Demarteau.

It was also at this point that Nathalie's parents met for the first time since their divorce over forty years previously. After leaving Janvry in 1942, Polina had spent the remainder of the Occupation in a pension run by White Russians in the village of Osny in the Val d'Oise. She had survived unharmed through sheer bravado, categorically denying her Jewishness and declaring with equal aplomb that she had no children, thus removing a source of further potential threat from Nathalie's already risky situation. Summoned by the Gestapo, Polina had presented herself with a White Russian aristocratic friend and put on such a convincing performance that the German officer concluded the interview by apologising profusely and kissing the two ladies on the hand.[1] When she returned to Paris after the Liberation, Polina would regularly come to the Avenue Pierre 1ᵉ de Serbie for lunch, and take food home with her for the evening. No one was present when she and Ilya came face to face after years of sustained noncooperation, but it was Nathalie's characteristically romantic view that Ilya had never ceased to love his first wife, who took everything—whether exemption from anti-Semitic legislation, a permanent place at her daughter's lunch table, or the devotion of her ex-husband—as her due.[2]

Despite the difficulty created between Ilya and Nathalie by Jacques's position as de facto heir to the Tcherniak inheritance, her father came increasingly to rely on Nathalie as his illness progressed, regarding her as the only person who could be counted on to tell him the truth about his condition.[3] She relied equally on him, and the publication of *Portrait of an Unknown Man* was the occasion to acknowledge her long-standing debt to his encouragement. As her inscription on his copy of the book recalls, he had been her first reader: "To my dear Papa, with my immense affection and the hope that he will read this with the same indulgence with which he used to read the French schoolwork that I so loved to show him."[4]

There's no record of his response either to Nathalie's words or to her novel, where so much turns on the relationship between a father and his adult daughter, and where, in a portrait of the dying Prince Bolkonski from Tolstoy's *War and Peace*, unwonted words of affection are wrung from the old man by his quietly persistent daughter. Ilya himself was dying when he read Nathalie's novel, and although, as she often pointed out, there was very little resemblance between the fictional and real-life versions of father and daughter, the book was as strong an appeal as ever for his attention. This stands in sharp contrast to Polina's indifference to her daughter's writing. After Polina died, Nathalie discovered that the only part of *Portrait of an Unknown Man* her mother had bothered to read was Sartre's preface. The other pages had remained uncut.[5]

The most material legacy that Nathalie received from Ilya was the pulmonary tuberculosis from which he suffered, and in the summer of 1947 she became seriously ill with the disease for which the recent antibiotic cures were not uniformly effective. It was the condition with which Raymond had been misdiagnosed in his youth and from which his mother had died. Claude too became infected, but whereas she made a full recovery, Nathalie's recovery—in a TB preventorium—was slow, and she continued to suffer relapses for the next decade. The symptoms of TB include fevers, tiredness, sweats, difficulty breathing, uncontrollable fits of coughing, and bloody sputum. In Nathalie's case there was also a collapsed lung. The disease also has a long literary history, and many writers have been affected. The Brontë sisters had it, and Emily died of what was then called "consumption." So too did Chekhov, whose death is the subject of "Ich sterbe," one of the finest texts in *The Use of Speech*, published in 1980. Katherine Mansfield was another victim, and it was from her that Nathalie took the expression "this terrible desire to establish contact" (in English), which Mansfield uses in her diary to describe the response of her friend Ida Baker to Mansfield's own tubercular coughing. Nathalie quotes the phrase in her essay "From Dostoievski to Kafka," published in *Les Temps modernes* in 1947—at the point when she herself was in the grip of tuberculosis—to express the psychology of Dostoevsky's characters.[6]

Her own experience of coughing and gasping for air may well have left her with a heightened awareness of breathing as a bodily phenomenon, and it's tempting to speculate that this was the origin of her sense that her writing follows the rhythm of respiration. In later interviews she states that "the text has to breathe the way it does when I hear it," or explains that "punctuation helps me create a sense of breathing."[7] Her trademark ellipses— . . .—become integral to her style in her third novel, *The Planetarium*, much of which was written during a subsequent and protracted bout of the illness, as if the writing itself had needed to pause repeatedly for breath. At any rate, TB was another reminder of mortality, and it placed Nathalie very literally "between life and death," as the title of her fifth novel has it, when, over two decades later, she uses the image of a misted mirror as a test of whether writing is alive and breathing, or inert and lifeless.

After Ilya's death Nathalie ceased to have any contact with either Vera or Jacques, who was now married and had a child of his own. In later years she occasionally corresponded (in Russian) with Lili, who lived a lonely life in Lausanne, where her scientist husband spent most of the time in his laboratory. Nathalie's own family was growing up: Claude had left home after meeting and marrying an American, Stanley Karnow, who was establishing himself as a journalist. (This was the career Claude herself eventually chose following a brief spell as an actress.) In the autumn of 1949, Nathalie and Raymond invited the couple to move into the apartment in the Avenue Pierre 1ᵉ de Serbie until they found more suitable accommodation.

Karnow was fascinated by Nathalie, who encouraged him to call her Natacha and to address her using the familiar *tu*. He was wary of living alongside what he later called "her Slav temperament," and in his recollection, she could be by turns "uptight and relaxed, petulant and amiable, dour and jolly." But he appreciated the "intellectual electricity" of her company. Although dinners were "monastic," consisting of a dry omelette or chop, pallid vegetables, soggy salad, tired cheese, fruit, yogurt, and *vin ordinaire*, food was secondary to the ambiance, and the conversation, largely directed by Nathalie and generally on literary topics, was always stimulating.[8]

Home life acquired a new dimension when, in November 1949, Nathalie and Raymond bought a weekend house in the small village of Chérence in the Vexin region of Normandy, some seventy kilometres to the northwest of Paris. The money for the purchase came from the one-seventeenth share of a legacy that Raymond received from the sale of a property belonging to his father's family, a detail that Nathalie often repeated as if to contrast Raymond's inheritance with the absence of any from her own family. Chérence lies in the Val d'Oise, which was already familiar to Nathalie from the time she had spent in Parmain at the eastern end of the same *département*. And being just an hour's drive from Paris, it was easily accessible for weekends in the splendid Ford Nathalie and Raymond now owned.

They had stumbled on the place by chance on their way to the ancient *bourg* of La Roche-Guyon where they had originally planned to buy. On spotting a curious, stumpy stone cross at the entrance to the village of Chérence, they stopped to look around and were instantly charmed. After enquiring about the availability of houses for sale they were taken to a small stone farmstead attached to a barn, on the righthand side of the road leading out of the village, just like one of the houses visited in *Martereau*. (The house hunting that forms the backdrop to the novel, which Nathalie was writing at the time, was no doubt inspired by this experience.)

Although the money came from Raymond, the property was purchased in Nathalie's name, which, following her divorce under the Occupation, was still officially Madame Tcherniak. This arrangement was possibly for tax purposes, but in any case Nathalie was the

FIGURE 17. Chérence, April 2011. (Author's photo)

one who put her mark on the place. She threw herself into renova-
tions, incorporating the barn into the house, installing a simple
kitchen and basic bathroom, and creating a large fireplace in the
main room. All the internal doorways were fitted with oval doors,
just like the one on which Tante Berthe's anxieties are focussed in
The Planetarium, and Nathalie could talk for hours about the different designs of light switch while she deliberated.[9] When the
farmer who owned the land next door wanted to build a barn, she
intervened to insist that it be aesthetically pleasing, and the result
looks rather like a Russian wooden church, complemented by the
birch trees she planted in the garden as a reminder of Russia. She
was equally adamant and equally effective when, in later years, she
insisted that the concrete wall surrounding the village cemetery be
replaced with stone.

Chérence was a place for reading and going for walks across the
surrounding fields, one of which leads to the limestone cliffs from
which there is a view of the Seine as it loops around on its journey
west. Nathalie and Raymond, sometimes accompanied by children,
grandchildren, and the family cat Rio-Jim, went to Chérence at week-

ends, and almost always spent the month of July there before heading for the sun in August. They placed themselves on the electoral
register, and always drove there to vote, elections in France being
held on a Sunday. The village was close enough to Paris for visitors
to come for the day, and many of the letters from friends and acquaintances mention their visits, often with an acknowledgement
of how much the place meant to Nathalie.

Chérence became a hub towards which she would draw friends
who were increasingly remote from *Les Temps modernes* and Saint-
Germain-des-Prés. She soon persuaded Maria and Eugene Jolas to
buy a house in the same village, thereby cementing the growing
friendship between the two women. Betsy Jolas recalls Nathalie
tramping across the village in the afternoons to take tea with her
mother and listen while Maria read out her translations, before they
embarked jointly on detailed discussion and revision of the English.[10] Eugene Jolas died in 1952 and is buried in the cemetery.
Nadia du Bouchet bought a house in the neighbouring village of
Dampsmesnil, and Nathalie saw her often. Later on, in the 1960s,
when the novelist Mary McCarthy had become a friend, she too
came very close to joining the little Franco-American community
that Nathalie succeeded in creating around her, and which was
joined in even later years by Arno Mayer, a history professor from
Princeton University.

Nathalie thrived in Chérence, and it was hers in a way that the
first-floor rented apartment in the Avenue Pierre 1e de Serbie never
was. Whereas in Paris she had the impression that she was only ever
"passing through," in Chérence she felt she had "taken root," as if she
had "returned to a house from her childhood," and acquired the
home that had had never previously had.[11] It offered not so much
an escape from life as a place where she could be who she was, and
this included the writer she was. Her daily routine continued here
as it did in Paris, and she would spend her mornings writing in a
café in the neighbouring village of Vétheuil. From the square in Vétheuil there is a view of the church made famous by the multiple
paintings of it by Monet, who had lived there in the late 1870s before
settling in Giverny a few miles down the road. Strangely, Nathalie
never mentions this connection, as if she needed Chérence and its
surrounds to be virgin territory.

FIGURE 18. Nathalie with Maria Jolas in Chérence, 1960s. (Sarraute Family Collection)

It was in the café in Vétheuil that she wrote much of *Martereau* and *The Planetarium*. The name Guimier, given to the central character of *The Planetarium*, comes from a neighbour in Chérence whose tombstone can be seen in the cemetery. Nathalie Vierny, Anne Sarraute's daughter, remembers coming to fetch her grandmother from the café at lunchtime, when they would have an aperitif while Nathalie quizzed Nathalie Jr. and her brother Antoine about how they might have responded to various hypothetical situations she was exploring in her novel.[12] This writing routine finally came to an end when the café owner installed a jukebox and could not be persuaded to ban its use during Nathalie's visits. Instead, a cowshed attached to the house in Chérence was converted into a study for her. Although it could be reached from inside the house, the external door was retained and always used by Nathalie, who was thus able to preserve the precious sense that writing took place elsewhere, away from the demands of domestic life. In a letter written many years later, the writer Monique Wittig recognised that Chérence had provided Nathalie with a necessary alternative to Paris where she had never managed to find an intellectual environment that suited her. Does it exist? wonders Wittig, before answering her own question by saying that she has witnessed it in Chérence, where Nathalie and Raymond managed to create an atmosphere of relaxation and happiness without which, in Wittig's estimation, there could be no intellectual life.[13]

As Nathalie increasingly distanced herself from *Les Temps modernes*, other literary horizons were opening up, and when "The Age of Suspicion" appeared in *Les Temps modernes* in February 1950, she was already looking much further afield. Maria Jolas immediately produced an English translation of the essay and placed it with a new Dublin-based literary magazine, *Envoy, A Review of Literature and Art*, where it appeared in February 1951.[14] Created in 1949, the journal published contemporary Irish writers and "the best in international writing," before it suffered the fate of so many little reviews and folded after less than two years.[15] Maria had also begun translating *Portrait of an Unknown Man*, and tried to interest both UK and American publishers. She sent the novel and a translation sample to Harry Levin, who taught French literature at Harvard and had written on Joyce. He replied saying that he had been "much struck by the book" and promised to propose it and Maria's translation—"with a word of enthusiastic recommendation"—to the publisher New Directions, which specialised in modernist writing.[16] But the time was not yet ripe for an American readership.

Nathalie was also known in London, from where Miron Grindea, the Rumanian-born founder and editor of *ADAM International Review*, wrote to André Spire, "How fortunate that you know Nathalie Sarraute whose talent—as she knows—I admire!"[17] Spire reports this comment to Nathalie, who may have met Grindea through his Rumanian compatriot François Erval. But equally she may have come across him at one of the *décades* organised by Gilbert Gadoffre. Gadoffre was one of the founders of the Centre culturel de Royaumont, where he sought to relaunch French cultural life after the war. The *décades*—ten-day gatherings of writers and intellectuals in the grand surroundings of the Abbaye de Royaumont in the Val d'Oise—took their inspiration from the legendary prewar Pontigny *décades* attended by the literary elite of the interwar generation. He was also inspired by his experience of studying at Oxford in the 1930s, when he had been impressed by the community life of Oxford colleges, where fellows and students lived, worked, and ate in the same surroundings.

In addition to memories of Oxford, Gadoffre and Nathalie shared a love of Saint-Simon's *Memoirs* of early eighteenth-century court life with their cruel lucidity and the author's "ability to delve into the psychology of his interlocutor."[18] The similarities between the court of Louis XIV and the social world of Sartre and Beauvoir would not have gone unremarked by Nathalie. She and Gadoffre were also connected through Eugène Vinaver, whom Gadoffre knew before the war when he briefly taught in the French department at Manchester University where Vinaver held the chair. Gadoffre's *colloques* (as he dubbed them, introducing this sense of the word into the French language) brought participants from across Europe in support of a venture that aimed, in his own words, to "reduce the splits between different cultural nationalisms, generations, and disciplines."[19] This inclusive ambition was guaranteed to appeal to Nathalie.

Gadoffre had read and admired *Portrait of an Unknown Man*, and Nathalie was invited to several of his *décades*. In June 1950 she attended the gathering devoted to "Literature and Painting." Other colloquia from this period addressed "Le Mensonge" (Lies) (the title of her second play in 1965) and "Dialogue" at a time (1951) when her thoughts may already have been turning to her essay "Conversation and Sub-conversation." The participants assembled by Gadoffre brought her into contact with a different, much less partisan literary world than the one presided over by Simone de Beauvoir. It included Eugène Ionesco, who was just starting out as a playwright, the literary critic Gaëtan Picon, the novelist and Gallimard editor Marcel Arland, the scholar and literary critic Jean Starobinski, and the poet Francis Ponge, most of whom Nathalie met for the first time at Royaumont, around the green baize tables during the morning discussions and over the ensuing leisurely lunches. There were also evening concerts organised by the poet and playwright René de Obaldia and Boris de Schlœzer, a Russian émigré musicologist and translator of Dostoevsky, where Francis Ponge revealed his talents as a pianist.

Around the same time, Nathalie began attending lectures at the Collège philosophique, founded after the war by the philosopher Jean Wahl in something of the same spirit as Gadoffre's Royaumont colloquia. Conceived as an extracurricular alternative to the Sorbonne, the Collège aspired to a cosmopolitan interdisciplinarity where a spirit of intellectual nonconformism was the order of the day. Nathalie always kept her distance from philosophy as a discipline, but the cultural ambitions of the Collège appealed to her, and it was in these surrounds that she first encountered Michel Butor, who was Wahl's secretary at the Collège and helped to organise the programme of evening lectures.[20]

Other horizons were opening up through new friendships with a younger generation of political exiles from Greece. In 1945, when the Greek civil war was at its height, the French government granted scholarships to some 130 young Greek writers, artists, and intellectuals and brought them to France, where a number of them went on to make significant contributions to French intellectual and cultural life. Born in the 1920s, they were a generation younger than Nathalie, but they had much in common with the Russian exiles of early twentieth-century Paris. Nathalie and Raymond were in any case confirmed Hellenophiles, having taken summer holidays in Greece during the 1930s. They continued to do so in later life, and always retained a fondness for the country and its people.

Nathalie developed close friendships with two of these Greek refugees, Mimica Cranaki and Matsie Hadjilazaros. Cranaki had written a novel published in Greece and had a degree in philosophy, while Hadjilazaros was a poet who wrote in both Greek and French. In August 1950, *Les Temps modernes* carried a piece by Cranaki titled "An Exile Diary," where she described the sense of loss and disorientation suffered by exiles in terms that would have resonated with Nathalie, when she writes, "I will have nothing of my own, not a single thing, not even a plot of earth to love. I will belong nowhere."[21]

Thanos Tsingos, the painter for whom Violette Leduc acquired an obsessive passion, was another Greek friend, and he and his wife, the actress Christine Tsingos, were among the regular visitors to Chérence. On one occasion Matsie Hadjilazaros's partner Javier Vilato—also a painter—brought his uncle Pablo Picasso for the day, and Picasso went down in Sarraute family history when, in response to Nathalie's habitual extolling of the charms of the house, he declared, "Still, it's no château." He was forgiven for this heresy, and allowed to take away one of Nathalie's carefully chosen wicker wastepaper baskets because they reminded him of those he had known in his Spanish childhood.[22]

The friendships with Hadjilazaros and Cranaki both had a literary component. Nathalie would discuss matters of style with Hadjilazaros, while Cranaki's literary involvement took the form of critical discussion of her work. In a postcard from Mykonos dated September 1950, she reports, "I've published an article about you in a journal for young people. I'll show it to you after the summer. I did what I could, but I had to take account of a pretty imbecilic public, despite their youth. You can tell me what you think."[23] As with Maria Jolas's Irish connections, Cranaki's Greek outlets offered a chance for Nathalie to find a readership abroad, although in the event nothing further came of either venture. More effectively, Cranaki later wrote the first French book-length study of Nathalie's work with her partner the French philosopher, Yvon Belaval.

The intensity of Nathalie's social activities emerges very clearly from her engagement diaries for these years, and they give the lie to the claims she habitually made about her social isolation. She never "entertained" in any formal sense, as the wives of other lawyers did, and she had no interest in doing so on her own account, but she depended, both as an individual and as writer, on friendship and social contact. It was one of the ways in which she could avoid the doldrums that would otherwise descend in the early afternoon. The first of her little leather-bound engagement diaries dates from 1945, and is relatively empty. There are none for the years between 1946 and 1951, one for 1952, and none for 1953 and 1954. They resume in 1955, vanish for the following two years, reappear for the final quarter of 1958, and continue almost unbroken thereafter, providing a record—albeit incomplete—of Nathalie's numerous acquaintances and activities.

These are mainly social, but medical and dental appointments are noted, as are various medications as she keeps track of treatments, both for herself and for Raymond. From 1955 she notes payments for Germaine Wolk, who was employed as housekeeper for the family, where she became a fixture until her retirement. Visitors from overseas would ask to be remembered to "Madame Germaine," who enjoyed arguing about politics with Raymond over the breakfast table, Raymond defending left-wing positions against Germaine's greater conservatism.[24] From time to time, Nathalie uses the diaries to record personal and domestic expenditure: on 22 January 1955 she notes 1,150 francs spent on medicines and 590 on food, and there are several mentions of sums spent in the Deux Magots and other cafés. These entries are not systematic, but they reflect a certain anxiety about money, based on her view—inculcated in her three daughters—that women should pay their way in life, and not rely on the income of their husbands.

The extent of Nathalie's different involvements made the engagement diaries a necessity, and in his journal for 1958, Claude Mauriac describes her distress when, on one occasion, she had accidentally double booked herself.[25] (Claude, the writer son of François Mauriac, was associated with the Nouveau Roman and became a frequent visitor both in Chérence and the Avenue Pierre 1ᵉ de Serbie.) Names, times, and venues are noted in Nathalie's firm hand. The venues are almost always the hotspots of Parisian literary life, and after a morning's writing, she would often take the number 63 bus from the Place d'Iéna down to Saint-Germain-des-Prés, headed for the Deux Magots, the Flore, or Le Rouquet on the Boulevard Saint-Germain, and sometimes La Coupole on the Boulevard Montparnasse.

In addition to the friendships arising out of Nathalie's new literary engagements—who included the Swiss novelist Clarisse Francillon, sometime translator of Malcolm Lowry—she continued to frequent Colette Audry and Mania Péron. Lena, who had been widowed after the war, was now living in Nice, and made only occasional visits to Paris; but she and Nathalie remained close, keeping in touch by phone. There were other Russian friends, and Nathalie's engagement diaries from these years show that she regularly saw the painter Natalia Goncharova, who was present when Nathalie met Sartre in the Café de Flore in 1944; the psychoanalyst Léon Chertok, whose analysis with Lacan Nathalie would quiz him about; and the writer Nina Gourfinkel, who founded the Centre d'orientation sociale des étrangers (Social advice centre for foreigners).

The diaries also note several private views, testifying to the active interest in painting that Nathalie shared with Raymond, who no doubt accompanied her to these events. Entries for 1952 and 1955 include the names of Victor Brauner, Bram van Velde, Hélène de Beauvoir (Simone's painter sister), Françoise Gilot (painter and Picasso's former mistress), and Dora Maar (painter, photographer, and another of Picasso's ex-mistresses). She also knew the painter Greta Knutson, the Swedish-born former wife of Tristan Tzara, and mother of Christophe Tzara, Claude Sarraute's second husband. Another connection that came through her family was with Agnès Varda. Anne Sarraute was now working in cinema as an assistant director and editor, and it was through Anne that Nathalie met Varda, who invited her to a showing of *La Pointe Courte* in a letter where she offers Nathalie her "timid friendship."[26] This friendship became more substantial over the years. In 1985 Varda dedicated her film *Vagabond* to Nathalie, and in two of her later films she explicitly mentions her with great warmth. In a letter dating from 1992, she writes, "Dearest Nathalie, I write dearest because it's true. You are definitely the person (the artist) I think about most often but hardly ever see. The fault is mine."[27]

The roll call of names of women writers and painters that emerges from Nathalie's engagement diaries gives a sense of critical mass that must have provided her with a certain buoyancy as her own writing continued. The visibility of women in the cultural landscape of France in the mid-1950s was undoubtedly much greater than it had been two decades previously, although this was probably more evident to the women themselves than to the men, who still dominated most literary institutions, whether publishing houses or journals.

Nathalie also had literary friendships with men, none of which was ever amorous or physical, but which, on the contrary, were sustained by coupledom. Chief amongst these were her relations with Butor and his wife Marie-Jo, Gilbert Gadoffre and his wife Alice, Claude Mauriac and his wife Marie-Claude, and Francis Ponge and his wife Odette. There were visits to Chérence or reciprocal invitations to dinner, and in the case of Claude Mauriac, tea at no. 12 Avenue Pierre 1e de Serbie.

The friendship with Ponge was based on Nathalie's admiration for a writing that had something in common with *Tropisms*. *The*

Nature of Things, a collection of short prose texts midway between poetry and prose, was published in 1942 when Nathalie was still writing short texts of her own. Nathalie and Ponge were both associated with *Les Temps modernes* in its early days, appearing in it without being of it. Ponge's literary independence and the long years he had spent without recognition made him a kindred spirit for Nathalie, and she sent him a copy of *Portrait of an Unknown Man* inscribed "in homage."[28] Ponge reciprocated by giving Nathalie a signed copy of the limited edition of Eugène de Kermadec's lithographs based on Ponge's text, "Water in a Glass." (Nathalie knew Lucette de Kermadec from the Lycée Fénelon.) Nathalie and Ponge continued to send each other copies of their new books, always inscribed to both husband and wife. Ponge's response to *The Golden Fruits* in 1963 conveys the nature of the bond that united them:

> I shan't bore you with critical reflections about this new offspring of yours. Between people (there aren't many of them, after all) who are able to bring some thing into the world (you will recognise me in *thing. . .* , a very inadequate word) it's not done, and never has been.
>
> Let me just tell you that we thought it had a perfect, admirable constitution; more harmonious than any of the others; and that it resembles you to a T.
>
> In a word, we love it and we wholeheartedly congratulate you.[29]

Nathalie replies in similar terms to the volume Ponge sent her in the same year, conveying a tacit literary understanding, mutual respect, and grateful affection:

> You've known my feelings about your work which go back to my first and now distant contact with it. They have merely developed as your accomplishments are progressively revealed in the light of day. It's a true—and rare—joy.
>
> And you also know how fond I am of you both. Knowing that you are always there, just the way you are, does me good and often consoles me.[30]

Such "consolation" was a necessity for Nathalie. This was something that Claude Mauriac clearly understood when, even though she had by then acquired considerable literary recognition, he noted in his diary for 1958, "Exquisite, touching. She doubts herself, no proof of her success will set her mind at rest, she needs constant reassurance—this is what she expects from me, eliciting compliments, not out of vanity, but rather because her inner peace depends on it."[31] In the early 1950s, after the disappointments and frustrations of her recent dealings with the Éditions Denoël, Nagel, and Robert Marin—not to mention the previous rejections she had received— she regarded all publishers with mistrust. They were, however, a necessity.

CHAPTER NINETEEN

A Gallimard Author,
1953–56

BY THE END of November 1952 Nathalie had a completed manuscript of *Martereau*, and she submitted it to Marcel Arland at Gallimard. This was her third attempt to find a home with the publishing house from which she continued to seek consecration. Her chances of acceptance had, however, much improved after meeting Arland at Royaumont, when he encouraged her to send him her novel once it was finished. She had also been placed on the invitation list for the Gallimard's monthly cocktail receptions, and her engagement diaries for 1952 record her attendance in March and November.[1] She nevertheless took precautions against a further rejection and explored alternative possibilities when she met Georges Lambrichs in *Les Deux Magots* on 2 December.[2]

Lambrichs was the literary editor at the Éditions de Minuit, created during the Resistance, and which, under his guidance and with the active encouragement of its new owner, Jérôme Lindon, was publishing innovative writing by young authors. These included Beckett, whose *Molloy* and *Malone Dies* appeared in 1951, followed in 1953 by *The Unnamable*. Alain Robbe-Grillet and Michel Butor were also making their literary debut with Minuit. However, Nathalie's backup plan proved unnecessary as Arland instantly accepted *Martereau*, and she received a contract on 16 January 1953. Gallimard was also now actively looking to publish innovative writing, a policy signalled by the resurrection of the *NRF* as the *Nouvelle nouvelle revue française* in January 1953.[3] (The journal was suspended after the Liberation, having been under the editorship of the Nazi collaborator Drieu la Rochelle.)

Nathalie's novel was associated with this new departure, although its central figure, Martereau, harks back to Nathalie's experience of the Occupation, both through his name, which so closely echoes that of Demarteau, and through his suspected double dealing under the guise of doing an old friend a favour when he acts as a straw man for the purchase of a house. But these autobiographical resonances—which include Nathalie's recent acquisition of the house in Chérence—are not made explicit in the novel, whose chief concerns lie elsewhere. The narrator's obsessive interest in Martereau isn't based in any desire to uncover hidden motives or to explore the psychology of a possible swindler. Instead, the question is whether Martereau is the solid character he appears to be, or whether he, like the narrator, is subject to the shifting internal dramas of the tropism. What might have been a forensic quest for a single, unitary truth becomes instead a proliferation of speculation and alternative realities—including four different versions of a single scene—providing graphic equivalents for an elusive psychological reality.

The book came out on 22 June in Gallimard's classic *Collection blanche* series, with its cream cover and instantly recognisable black and red typeface: black for the author's name, red for the title. The speed of this turnaround was very different from the three-year wait Nathalie had endured with *Portrait of an Unknown Man*, and the novel was reviewed in the Parisian literary press by the leading critics of the day, some more sympathetically than others who had no patience for what they dismissed as the narrator's pathological sensitivity. Colette Audry wrote a perceptive article for the journal *Critique*, it was discussed on the radio, and an interview with Nathalie was published in *Les Nouvelles littéraires* under a rather forbidding photograph of the author.[4]

The book received coverage in the foreign press, where it was picked up by the *New York Herald Tribune*. It was also reviewed in Switzerland for the *Journal de Genève* and for the German-language *Neue Zürcher Zeitung*, which described it as "one of this summer's most important new French publications." Nathalie wrote to the reviewer, Gerda Zeltner, partly to express her appreciation of Zeltner's comments, but also in the hope of acquiring a Swiss publisher. Zeltner, who subsequently became a friend, replies by saying, "Like you, I thought that your work should be made available abroad," but she goes on to explain that since Swiss German-language publishers were not interested in translations of French literature, she had sent a copy of *Martereau* to a German publisher in Stuttgart.[5] Perhaps fortunately for Nathalie, who was not yet ready to make her personal peace with the German nation, nothing came of this initiative.

She had every reason to be pleased with the recognition she had received at home for *Martereau*, and Michel Butor remembered her from this time as a much-respected figure in the literary world of Saint-Germain-des-Prés, where she was seen as a leading representative of the literary avant-garde.[6] Success was, however, a prospect to be greeted with a certain caution. In Simone de Beauvoir she had witnessed what she saw as the pursuit of success for its own sake, obtained through a constant demand for adulation from her captive acolytes. For Nathalie, failure in the public eye had the advantage of providing an insurance against becoming like Beauvoir and the consolation of continuing literary integrity. It was perhaps for this reason that she tended to exaggerate the problems she had had in finding a publisher and to overstate the negative reactions of the critics. But any failure had to be on her own terms, and she remained acutely sensitive to the possibility of misrecognition, or even outright condemnation by others. This sensitivity was especially marked in her dealings with Gallimard, where her new acceptance does not seem to have effaced her memory of previous rejections.

After the publication of *Martereau*, she was invited by Jean Paulhan to contribute an article to the *NNRF*. This was no doubt on the recommendation of Marcel Arland, the journal's joint editor, to whom Nathalie must have mentioned her essay "Conversation and Sub-conversation," recently refused by *Les Temps modernes*. *Les Temps modernes*'s loss was Gallimard's gain. Paulhan wrote to Nathalie in December 1954 saying, "I very much like *Conversation and sub-conversation* and I am keen to read the sequel, the *Trompe-l'œil* article you told us about. Could I ask you for it before *Conversation* ... appears in the nrf?"[7] "Trompe l'œil" became "What Birds See," and was included in the volume of

Nathalie's essays *The Age of Suspicion*, along with "Conversation and Sub-conversation" and two of the pieces originally published in *Les Temps modernes*, "From Dostoievski to Kafka" and "The Age of Suspicion." The volume was Arland's suggestion, and when it appeared in March 1956, it clinched Nathalie's position as a Gallimard author. This status was further reinforced when *Portrait of an Unknown Man* (whose rights Nathalie was now free to dispose of) was republished by the same house in 1957, giving her three Gallimard titles in less than four years.

However, relations with her publishers were never easy. Arland was a somewhat reserved individual, and Nathalie never felt at ease with him. This sentiment was shared by the Swiss-born novelist Clarisse Francillon, who had been published by Gallimard in the 1930s, but whose novels were rejected after the war. In a letter to Nathalie, she describes Arland as "the person with the least human warmth I've ever encountered, charmless, and incapable of connecting with other people."[8] Despite the role he had played in establishing her with Gallimard, Nathalie suspected that this lack of human warmth was directed in particular at her. She voices these suspicions in a letter to the Belgian critic René Micha in 1963, when she writes, "I beg you to keep it to yourself, and never tell Marcel Arland the name of the friend who said that Marcel Arland didn't like me."[9] The identity of this friend is not revealed.

The complications and the suspicions were even greater in the case of Jean Paulhan, and here too Nathalie was not alone in her nervousness of the man whom Michel Butor described as "the high priest of French literature" and whom, as a young writer starting out in the early 1950s, he had found "very intimidating."[10] Paulhan was tall and physically imposing, and the power he exercised in the Gallimard publishing house was widely acknowledged. Dominique Aury—Paulhan's editorial assistant, mistress, and, as of 1950, the first and only woman on the editorial committee—describes him as having had "something simultaneously affable and sarcastic in his expression."[11] Nathalie's mistrust was so great that she was unable to take at face value the enthusiastic letter he wrote to her about her article, and was always convinced that his messages bore a underlying coded meaning. On a later occasion when Nathalie and Paulhan

FIGURE 19. Dominique Aury, Jean Paulhan, and Marcel Arland in
Paulhan's office at Gallimard, 1953. © D.R. Coll. J. Paulhan / Paris.

passed each other in the labyrinthine corridors of the Éditions Gallimard in the rue Sébastien-Bottin, Paulhan stopped to say that he
had the impression that she didn't like him, to which Nathalie re-
torted, "And you? Do you like me?"[12]

She also suspected Dominique Aury of having played a part
in the previous rejection of *Portrait of an Unknown Man* by offering to help get it accepted, but then blocking it behind the scenes.
She entertained friends with an amusing account of an awkward

encounter with Aury under the hairdryer at a *salon de coiffure* in rue Jacob, when she took Aury's abrupt departure as proof of her animosity. How much basis there was for these speculations is impossible to say and, as Robbe-Grillet commented in response to Nathalie's anecdote, she was apt to construct elaborate fabrications on the flimsiest pretext.[13] But she clearly remained uneasy, and in a letter to Butor in 1964 she thanks him for his reassurance over some matter about which Dominique Aury was allegedly spreading alarming rumours.[14] Their content is not revealed.

As Claude Mauriac had observed, reassurance was the thing of which there was never enough and which Nathalie never felt she could count on. There were high points, as when Gaston Gallimard reportedly said to her in 1958, "Rest assured that I will never let you go. Never. So, tell me your conditions and I'll agree to them in advance."[15] But the effects of these reassurances didn't last, and a letter of 26 May 1961 shows Gallimard trying to assuage Nathalie's concerns after another unspecified problem: "As you must have sensed, I was very affected by our last conversation. You know how devoted I am to your work, and how important it is for me, and I don't want there ever to be any misunderstandings or problems between us."[16]

Claude Gallimard, Gaston's son, was less adroit in his dealings with authors and found himself threatened with Nathalie's defection when his failure to return a phone call convinced her that the Éditions Gallimard had no faith her work. The draft of a letter to him dated 15 June 1966 conveys her sense of precariousness, due in part to the mismatch between the brisk pace imposed by the practicalities of publishing and the slow agonies entailed by her writing:

> I thought you had enough appreciation of my work and enough friendship towards me to respond within a decent period of time.
>
> I now see that this is not the case,
>
> Under these circumstances I do not feel comfortable either with you or with your collaborators and I do not wish to set foot in your offices again.
>
> I need to feel that my publisher has confidence in my ~~somewhat atypical~~ books, supports them and promotes them at least as much as those that ~~require less effort~~ appeal to a general readership. . . .

I realise that you have reduced me to the ~~sad~~ role of the ousted author ~~for whom one is not there available~~ and to whom one does not even bother to reply.

It's a role that I have no wish to ~~re~~learn.

I did not and do not wish to initiate a showdown with you, but I have to tell you that under these circumstances ~~and whatever the cost to me~~ I have taken a firm decision to offer my radio plays and my next novel to another publisher.

I think you won't care ~~in the slightest~~, but for my part, it's a relief to ~~say~~ let you know about it now.

Claude Gallimard's handwritten reply conveys in turn his sense of having been unjustly accused of indifference when in reality he had been away from his office because of ill health. He continues, somewhat defensively, "I believe that I have given you proof on many occasions of my esteem and the confidence I have in your work. You cannot forget all that just because an unfortunate contretemps prevented us from speaking on the telephone." He concludes that he would very much like to see Nathalie, and signs off as "Your good friend."[17]

She did not defect and, apart from a momentary loss of nerve (related below in chapter 20), she remained with Gallimard for all her subsequent writing. Her books never sold in sufficient numbers to justify a regular retainer, and even as late as the 1990s, her engagement diaries contain notes of sums received from the publisher, suggesting that money continued to be an object of concern. Meanwhile, each submission raised anew the fear of rejection, and Nathalie Vierny recalls her grandmother's acute anxiety when, in 1997, Antoine Gallimard—Gaston's grandson who took over from his father in 1988—called at no. 12 Avenue Pierre 1ᵉ de Serbie to collect the manuscript of what proved to be her last published book, *Ouvrez*. It was Nathalie's eighteenth publication with Gallimard, and to date, some 2,350,000 copies of her work have appeared under its imprint.[18] Her books have all been published in their own paperback collection, *folio*, and in 1996 her complete works appeared in the prestigious Pléiade series. In sum, she was nothing if not a Gallimard author.

CHAPTER TWENTY

The Nouveau Roman, 1956–59

WITH THE PUBLICATION of *The Age of Suspicion* in March 1956, it seemed that Nathalie's time had finally come, and she began, almost overnight, to win widespread recognition. The year had already started well. Four of the six short texts which should have appeared in *Volontés* in 1939 and which Paulhan had turned down for *Mesures*, were published under the title "Le cercle" (The circle) in the December 1955 number of the *Monde Nouveau*, where Georges Lambrichs was now literary editor.[1] (After learning of Pelorson's collaboration during the Occupation, she may in retrospect have been very glad not to have featured in *Volontés*.) Paulhan himself published "Conversation and Sub-conversation" in the January and February numbers of the *NNRF*.

When the volume appeared in the bookshops a month later, Nathalie was described in the accompanying publicity as "one of the most original and gifted writers of our time," and the book was billed in the blurb as "a true *ars poetica* for the contemporary novelist . . . which anyone with an interest in contemporary writing . . . is duty bound to have read." The essays, written two, six, and nine years previously, were originally conceived by Nathalie as a means of explaining her own novels in response to what she saw as an absence of critical recognition in a world dominated by *Les Temps modernes*. Collected in a single volume, the same essays were now seen as giving voice to very topical concerns and as setting an agenda for a new generation of novelists.

This sense of a changed literary climate was picked up by Gilbert Gadoffre, who, in July 1956, organised a *décade* under the rubric "A Break with the Post-war Moment." As well as Nathalie, he invited Alain Robbe-Grillet, whose novel *The Voyeur* had recently caused a stir. The *colloque* was held at the Château d'Eu, near le Tréport on the Normandy coast, and Nathalie travelled there with Robbe-Grillet, who was keen to make her acquaintance. He had just published an article in the July number of the *NNRF*, titled, in the spirit of the times, "A Path for the Novel of the Future," with an epigraph taken from *The Age of Suspicion*. He had also acquired the position of chief literary adviser at the Éditions de Minuit, where, after being turned down by Gallimard, he had published two novels of his own. He later dated the origins of the Nouveau Roman to this meeting with Nathalie: "The face to face discussion with this openly revolutionary author, her keen intelligence, and her humour, immediately convinced me that we should form an alliance. . . . In the train that took us to Eu, Nathalie said to me with a smile . . . : 'In short, we'd be a bunch of hoodlums!' "[2] The label "Nouveau Roman" did not yet exist, and Robbe-Grillet is looking back from a distance of almost four decades to a moment that marked a significant turning point in the history of the novel, whose future became the object of major cultural debate.

The Château d'Eu was a somewhat incongruous setting for these concerns. Built on the grand scale in the sixteenth century, it had belonged to the Orléans branch of the royal family, whose presence remained in the form of numerous portraits and framed photographs. Writing to his future wife, Catherine, Robbe-Grillet describes the setting as "wonderfully majestic," and the amenities as "monarchist life in all its splendour."[3] The Comte de Paris himself chose the wines, and the conference participants ate off china bearing the arms of the last emperor of Brazil, who had briefly owned the château before passing it on to a group of Brazilian businessmen. The weather was glorious, and in the breaks between discussions, guests wandered in the formal gardens which anticipate the setting of Alain Resnais's film *Last Year in Marienbad*, for which Robbe-Grillet wrote the script. Nathalie writes with less cynicism and more exclamation marks to her family than Robbe-Grillet, describing the royal history of the château and the deferential behaviour of one of the old retainers and reporting that guests had to be accompanied from their bedrooms since the château was so vast that they risked losing their way. She also comments that she finds Robbe-Grillet "very modest." This modesty had not, however, prevented him from telling her that his novel *Le Voyeur* illustrated her theories and was consequently a failure.[4] The Nouveau Roman was pulling in two different directions from the very start.

There was also a sizeable Russian-speaking contingent, which included the musicologist and translator Boris de Schloezer, his niece Marina Scriabin, composer daughter of the composer Alexander Scriabin, and Dominique Arban, the Russian-born literary journalist at *Le Figaro*. They created their own drama one night when they gathered in the imposing Salon Noir to test the local rumour that the ghost of La Grande Mademoiselle, niece of Louis XIV and onetime owner of the château, returned to haunt the place at midnight. As the hour struck, Dominique Arban took fright and fled screaming, followed by the others. Gadoffre, who reports the episode, doesn't say whether Nathalie was among them.

The gathering was certainly a very cosmopolitan affair. Gadoffre, who was once again teaching at Manchester University, had gathered a broad assortment of writers, artists, and musicians from France, Germany, Belgium, and England, with the aim of discovering, "what point we had reached in history, whether we were still in the post-war phase, or whether we were moving towards a more constructive period than the previous one, and if so what it was."[5] This was an ambitious agenda, and according to the report in *The Observer* by the British novelist and journalist Philip Toynbee, the participants spent their days in heated argument. The future of the novel was at the centre of these debates, and Toynbee comments that "by the end of the congress each side in this particular dispute had healthily upset the assurance of the other, and all the delegates had come together on the most important point of all: the traditional novel is dead, and there is a fatal triviality about all attempts to revive it."[6]

Despite their newly hatched alliance, the differences between Nathalie and Robbe-Grillet became explicit when he published a long review of *The Age of Suspicion* in the journal *Critique* later in the summer. He endorses Nathalie's assertion of the need for con-

FIGURE 20. With Robbe-Grillet, 1963. (Sarraute Family Collection)

temporary forms of fiction, and he is equally positive about her condemnation of the character types inherited from the nineteenth-
century realist novel, but he concludes by implying that the value
she places on psychology binds her to what he calls the "old myth of
depth."[7] While portraying her as his ally in the creation of new forms
of fiction, he defines the contemporary novel in terms that correspond to his own practice of descriptive objectivity, and implies that
her writing lagged behind his on the path to a literary future.

However, since he never sought to hide what Nathalie saw as his
shameless self-promotion, their relations remained broadly positive.
He teased her mercilessly and, with no regard for *galanterie*, would
comment on the number of her wrinkles in relation to the number
of books she had written. She referred to him once in a letter to
Claude Simon as "that monster Alain," but as Claude Mauriac noted,
their dealings were mostly characterised by "the joking tone mixed
more or less with seriousness (less with Robbe-Grillet, more with
Nathalie) that is *de rigueur* in their relations."[8] They both had a
strong sense of humour, and Nathalie once described driving home
with Robbe-Grillet after a dinner, which he talked about with such
"irresistible hilarity" that they "drove haphazardly around the streets
of Paris to prolong their high spirits."[9]

She found herself once again associated with a literary coterie, but it was very different from the one she had experienced with Sartre, Beauvoir, and *Les Temps modernes*. Whereas previously she had been confined to the margins, she now had a role as a founder member of what was nonetheless never a school, but a loose grouping with a broadly avant-garde identity. She was happy to allow Robbe-Grillet to exercise his talents as publicist and impresario, for which his position at the Éditions de Minuit provided a base. Minuit published Michel Butor's first three novels, and when *Second Thoughts* won the Prix Renaudot in 1957, this clinched the legitimacy of innovative writing, as Robbe-Grillet drew others— Robert Pinget, Claude Simon, Claude Ollier, and Marguerite Duras—into the Minuit orbit. Between them, these authors and their novels confirmed the sense of a new literary phenomenon, prompting critics to come up with a variety of labels and definitions—*l'école du regard*, *l'école de Minuit*, *l'école du refus*, or Claude Mauriac's specially coined *alittérature*—before the term "Nouveau Roman" took hold.

Nathalie herself was a willing beneficiary of Robbe-Grillet's editorial energies when, ignoring any rights to it that Gallimard might have had by virtue of her current contract with them, Minuit republished *Tropisms* in March 1957. Following Robbe-Grillet's meeting with Nathalie at the Château d'Eu, Jérôme Lindon had sought her out with a note expressing an enthusiastic wish to meet her on one of the Tuesdays when she was said to be found at Les Deux Magots.[10] This kind of interest from publishers was new and flattering, and in a letter of 1964 to Lindon, Nathalie records "my gratitude for your enormous kindness towards me when you published 'Tropisms' and helped me so often and so effectively."[11] On its appearance, no mention was made of the book's former publication with Denoël, the previously unnumbered texts now bore Roman numerals, and the volume included the extra six items that were to have appeared in 1939 in *Volontés* under the title "The Planetarium." One of the original Denoël texts was omitted since, with references to interwar Russian and German finances, it betrayed its date of composition in the 1930s. Nathalie also judged it to be formally less satisfactory than the rest.

Robbe-Grillet's own novel, *Jealousy*, was published in May of the same year, and although it was very different from *Tropisms*, the two books were reviewed together. Nathalie's book had been written two decades previously and was not in fact a novel, but in their matching Minuit jackets, they inspired the introduction of the term "Nouveau Roman." After a hostile review of both publications in *Le Monde* by the critic Émile Henriot ("from the Académie française") under the heading "Le nouveau roman" (The new novel), the expression caught on, and featured as the running title in the much more sympathetic article by Maurice Nadeau in *Critique* of August and September of the same year. It was used again—still positively, but in quotation marks—on the cover of a double number of the review *Esprit* in August and September 1958, devoted to new fictional writing and showcasing ten novelists, Nathalie being listed third.[12]

She had acquired a parallel identity as a Minuit author, the rest of whom were mostly a generation younger than herself. In February, Lindon invited her to join the group of writers that met regularly at his home on the Boulevard Arago, where they were tasked with establishing a "Vocabulary" of key words—*subjectivity/objectivity, plot, form/content, character, reality, object (things), action, event, description*, and so forth—with a view to creating a "Dictionary of the nouveau roman." Lindon includes a list of eighteen topics with his letter, and explains that participants were expected to submit contributions for each of them. The topic for the session scheduled for 26 February 1957 was *object (things)*.[13] Nathalie's engagement diary for 1957 has not survived, and there's no way of knowing whether she attended this or any other of these meetings whose theoretical abstraction and potential for conformism were probably not entirely to her taste. In any case, the project eventually collapsed, and a funeral oration for the venture was delivered by Roland Barthes.[14]

The association with Minuit was certainly congenial enough to prompt Nathalie to seek to extricate herself from Gallimard, so that she could bring out her third novel, *The Planetarium*, with a publishing house where, in her view, the book would be provided with a more supportive literary environment. An undated set of notes for a projected letter to Gaston Gallimard gives a flavour of her thinking and includes the manifestly unjustified claim that *The Age of Suspicion* had met with a poor critical reception:

> My book [*The Planetarium*] will soon be finished.
>
> It's been a long and difficult labour. Difficult to make oneself understood. No material result. Social security—refused. I'm not considered to be a writer. It's only now that I am beginning to be understood.
>
> Because I published The Age of Suspicion where I set out my ideas about the novel.
>
> Ideas taken up by R.G. and Lindon who created a movement for the modern novel. R.G. to promote his own work and Lindon to promote his own authors.
>
> Lindon asked me for Tropisms which are in line with the new movement. This has been very useful because R.G., by promoting his own work, and Lindon, by promoting his own authors, explained my work, and people are beginning to know me. My books are beginning to sell abroad.
>
> My new book—I'm anxious because it's difficult. It needs to be explained and promoted.
>
> I don't feel I have strong enough support here for my book to be appreciated and defended.
>
> N.R.F. Tropisms refused.
>
> Very bad critical reviews of age of suspicion.
>
> No reference to this movement.
>
> My work needs a lot of explanation. Tropisms helped to make my work known.
>
> I wondered whether it wouldn't be a good idea for you to lend me to Lindon for the next book.[15]

It's possible that she never actually sent the letter, since her archive contains no trace of any reply, but whether it was the result of choice or contractual constraint, she remained with Gallimard, and it was they, not Minuit, who published *The Planetarium* in May 1959.

Nathalie's connection with Minuit continued by other means, and most tellingly in the so-called "Nouveau Roman photograph," taken in October 1959 outside the Éditions de Minuit in the rue Bernard-Palissy. It was the work of an Italian photographer, Mario

FIGURE 21. The Nouveau Roman photo. © Mario Dondero / Ed. Minuit / Leemage.

Dondero, and had been commissioned by the Milan-based cultural review *Illustrazione italiana*, where it appeared in February 1960. Lindon, who features in the photograph framed in the Minuit doorway, orchestrated the event. Claude Mauriac was the only writer present not to have published with Minuit, but his recent book, *L'alittérature contemporaine* (Contemporary a-literature) included discussions of several Minuit authors, including Beckett, Robbe-Grillet, and Nathalie. Butor is missing from the photograph because he arrived late, by which time Beckett had already left.[16] (He appears in separate photos taken on the same occasion with Robbe-Grillet, Claude Simon, and Nathalie.) She is the only woman, and stands uncomfortably next to Beckett, talking neither to him nor to Claude Ollier on her left. Her ankles are crossed because, as she later said, alongside Beckett's gaunt features she was acutely conscious of her own plump cheeks—a side-effect of medication she was taking at the time—and she was trying to suck them in. In some versions of the photograph, she has exercised a female prerogative to have the image retouched to show her feet apart.[17] When it was reproduced in the French literary press—beginning with *Le Figaro littéraire* in June 1962—the photograph encapsulated the identity of the Nouveau Roman, now forever associated with the Éditions de Minuit.

Nathalie's new prominence spawned other involvements, and she was appointed to the committees of two new literary prizes, the Prix de Mai and the Prix Médicis, both created in response to the new literary climate. The critic and novelist Bernard Pingaud convened the first meeting of the jury for the Prix de Mai in April 1957, where four contenders were discussed. Aside from Pingaud, the jury consisted of leading representatives of contemporary writing, with Roland Barthes, Georges Bataille, Maurice Blanchot, Maurice Nadeau, Louis-René des Forêts, Robbe-Grillet, and Nathalie. Dominique Aury and the literary critic Marthe Robert were co-opted the following year, when the prize was won by Marguerite Duras for *Moderato cantabile*. But by then, the Prix Médicis had been established and it soon eclipsed its short-lived rival, taking Nathalie and Robbe-Grillet with it, much to Pingaud's chagrin.[18]

The Médicis was the creation of Jean-Pierre Giraudoux, son of the novelist Jean Giraudoux, and the Russian-born Gala Barbizan, a former actress, who had left the Soviet Union in the mid-1930s to marry an Italian industrialist, and who used her husband's money to sponsor literary projects. She was eccentric and known for outrageous behaviour. The Médicis committee saw a fairly rapid turnover, but it always had a significant representation of women, who soon included the society literary hostess Denise Bourdet, the biographer and critic Francine Mallet, and, from 1960, Marguerite Duras. Although their role as arbiters of literary quality was proportionately greater than the number of women writers rewarded by it, their presence was a sign of women's changing status in the Parisian literary world. Nathalie's diaries for 1959 and 1960 record several meetings with Gala (with whom she sometimes communicated in Russian), and she attended a Médicis cocktail party given by Denise Bourdet in the run-up to the final deliberations over lunch at the imposing Hôtel de Crillon in November 1959.[19]

The first beneficiary of the prize was the Minuit author Claude Ollier. Robbe-Grillet took credit for this success, and the predominance of the Nouveau Roman continued the following year with Claude Mauriac's *The Dinner Party*. As time went on, tensions emerged because some felt that Robbe-Grillet was seeking to direct the committee's choices to endorse his own editorial policy. The selection of Colette Audry's *Behind the Bathtub* (Gallimard) over Robert Pinget's *The Inquisitory* (Minuit) in 1962 brought matters to a head, when Robbe-Grillet wrote to the members of the committee to protest that the prize, created with the aim of encouraging a "renewal of the novel," had nonetheless failed to reward both Pinget's novel and Claude Simon's *The Flanders Road* two years earlier. In his reply Giraudoux accuses Robbe-Grillet of dictatorial behaviour and, somewhat misogynistically, of using his influence over the three allegedly malleable women on the jury to impose his own preferences.[20]

The brief covering notes that Robbe-Grillet appended to the correspondence copied to Nathalie certainly suggest that he counted on her support; but it was willingly given. This much is clear in a letter from Nathalie, written two years previously, where she reports on the jury's deliberations, from which he had been absent:

Obviously, I'm wholly in favour of "The Flanders Road," and I'm very sorry that you're not here. I've just come away from the last lunch before the prize—and things are going badly. Claude Simon has: my vote, Gala's, Denise Bourdet's, and yours. All the others are for Henri Thomas's "John Perkins." And when I say that it's weak (John Perkins) they reply that the prize is being given to an underrated author, that Simon has had a lot of success, and will get the Goncourt another time! etc. . . . But the big argument is: we can't give the prize to the "nouveau roman" every year. Gala irritates them, as you know. I think—as does Gala and also Barbizan, who is an intelligent man—that if we give the prize to Thomas (as a consolation for the Goncourt where he got 3 votes!), the Prix Médicis will rapidly go downhill. Gala is going to try to lean on Claude Roy again, and Denise Bourdet on [Félicien] Marceau, but I don't think they'll succeed. There's nothing to be done—obviously— with Pierre Gascar (this year), [Pierre] Albérès and Giraudoux. So that's the news. It's not good. The Prix de Mai—and, now, the Prix Médicis—

have proved to me that there's no room for people like us in prizes. Anyway, we shall see.[21]

The formulation "people like us" wasn't strictly coterminous with the Nouveau Roman, and in any case, although Nathalie was sometimes referred to as "leader" or "abbess" of the Nouveau Roman to Robbe-Grillet's "high priest," she always insisted that there was never a school. As she wrote in 1962 to the Portuguese critic, Artur Portela,

> There is, strictly speaking, no nouveau roman movement, if by that you understand a school or even a group with a programme and a common plan of action. It represents novelists who are working in very different domains and exploring in directions that are sometimes quite opposed. What unites them is a common attitude towards novelistic convention, a common conviction that in order to remain alive, the art of the novel, like all art, requires a constant renewal of its forms, and consequently of its substance. . . .
>
> The nouveau roman does not propose any pre-established form or impose any rules. Except for one: the need to regard the novel not as a source of entertainment or information, but as an art.[22]

The label nevertheless had its uses, and while Nathalie was mostly content for Robbe-Grillet to take charge of its public image, she nonetheless claimed precedence for some of the ideas associated with it. In 1958 she wrote in outrage to the editors of the *Evergreen Review* in the United States and *Akzente* in Germany, both of whom were due to publish translations of a series of articles by Robbe-Grillet, which had originally appeared in *France-Observateur*, to demand that they insert an acknowledgement that his article was a restatement of ideas that had first been expressed by her. In the case of the *Evergreen Review*, she was particularly galled that they had accepted Maria Jolas's translation of "The Age of Suspicion" for publication before then deciding to publish an essay by Robbe-Grillet in its place.

It was an understandable but somewhat undignified action on Nathalie's part, which changed nothing. Instead, it gave Robbe-Grillet the chance to write to her in morally superior tones, saying that he had written to Barney Rosset, editor of *Evergreen Review*, exactly as she wished, but that despite his compliance, "I don't have the impression that you will be satisfied this time, because your dissatisfaction will be provoked by any new instance (French or foreign) involving the articles from France-Observateur."[23] When she could, Nathalie subsequently contented herself with dropping comments about her own antecedence into interviews where, for some time to come, the question of the Nouveau Roman was almost invariably on the agenda.

These changes in Nathalie's literary standing took place against a background of equally momentous developments in her private life, very little of which was visible on the public stage. The first of these events was the death of her mother in May 1956, at the age of eighty-nine. In an uncanny parallel with Ilya's death, which had occurred a few months after the publication of *Portrait of an Unknown Man*, Polina's death followed the appearance of *The Age of Suspicion*, but as with *Portrait of an Unknown Man* it's unlikely that she showed any interest in it. Nathalie was undoubtedly a better daughter than Polina was a mother, supporting her financially, paying her rent, and providing her with regular meals.[24] It's impossible to gauge what impact this death had on Nathalie, who was now succeeding as a writer to a degree and in terms very different to any that Polina had known.

She was also developing serious health problems, and in 1956 she endured a kidney stone operation. Raymond and Nathalie remarried in December, a move which may have been a response to these events (Polina's death, Nathalie's illness), although Nathalie herself always claimed that it was simply for tax purposes. Despite her publications, she was still officially categorised as being "unemployed," or as the French expression goes, "sans profession." The following year she suffered a serious relapse of TB and was given only weeks to live. Raymond was distraught, and perhaps on the recommendation of her doctor friends (Nadia du Bouchet, Lena Liber, or Sonia Dobkovitch), Nathalie was referred to a specialist in drug-resistant strains of TB, Dr Boris Kreis. He had developed a technique for identifying the individual profile of any given case of resistance, so as to be able to prescribe a targeted combination therapy of antibiotics, while keeping patients regularly monitored for the TB bacteria known as Koch's bacilla.[25]

With a curious absence of apparent alarm at the prospect of her own death, and perhaps as a sign of her confidence in Kreis, Nathalie wrote a comic poem about these microbial entities, which she called "the B.K.s."[26] (Unfortunately, the poem has not survived.) Kreis insisted on complete rest, but when she announced that it would be impossible for her to stop writing, he allowed her to spend her mornings on the divan in her study at home. But as Claude Mauriac observed, Kreis assumed that she was writing a novel "the way other women do knitting," and permitted her "this innocent obsession, without suspecting that she tires herself out more by writing hunched over on her bed than at her desk—which is now piled high with manuscripts."[27] This was in June 1958. In August, Nathalie wrote from Chérence to Claude and her husband, who were on holiday in Ibiza, to say that "the B.K.s have finally 'hoisted sail' as Domi says," but that she was still being treated, and still suffering symptoms. She nevertheless hoped to join them, and asks them to find accommodation for herself and Raymond in a version of their usual Mediterranean summer holiday. Her ideal was

> a room in Formentera where I can rest and work, and from where, without too much effort, I can drag myself to a shaded spot or as far as the sea. . . . Too much heat—and no shade where I could spend most of the day without getting tired—will make Raymond anxious and he'll tell me all the time that I've made a big mistake; when in fact I'm afraid more than anything else of
>
> -a return of the B.K.s.
>
> -spoiling Raymond's holiday and yours.
>
> So don't telegraph us to come unless you really think I can do so without giving up my title of right royal pain in the neck and taking on that of Emperor of Pains in the Rear.[28]

The plan evidently came off, but Nathalie's engagement diary for the last quarter of 1958 has several entries with the word "ill," and some days are marked with a cross, presumably indicating a symptom, such as coughing up blood, extreme fatigue, or high temperature. The handwriting is frequently unrecognisable, perhaps because Nathalie was too weak to hold a pen properly, or because she was trying to write lying down. However, these entries alternate with outside activities, including several theatre visits, while treatment continued—as witness the effect on Nathalie's cheeks in the Nouveau Roman photograph. Life gradually reverted to normal, with a full engagement diary for 1959, and in May, the publication of *The Planetarium.*

Golden Fruits, 1959–70

CHAPTER TWENTY-ONE

"One of the Great Novelists of Our Time," 1959–62

THE APPEARANCE of *The Planetarium* in May 1959 was heralded by advance publicity in the form of two published extracts from the novel and three interviews with Nathalie. The first extract was published in 1957 in the October and November numbers of Maurice Nadeau's journal *Les Lettres nouvelles*, followed a year later in October 1958 by a second under the title "La rencontre" (The meeting) in the *NNRF*. Denise Bourdet, whom Nathalie knew from the Prix Médicis committee, published an interview in the *Revue de Paris* in June 1958, when Nathalie was still suffering from TB (described as pleurisy in the article). There is no mention of the Nouveau Roman. Instead, the focus is on Nathalie in her own right, with her own biography, her Russian origins—"between Moscow and Siberia"—her apartment, her husband, her literary tastes which, for a writer of the mid-twentieth-century avant-garde, include the unexpected examples of Saint-Simon and Rousseau, and, most importantly, her reputation. This last Bourdet summarises enthusiastically by saying, "Nathalie Sarraute's name is now familiar to the general public who know that she is one of the major writers of today."[1]

A second interview, with Nathalie's friend and fellow novelist Clarisse Francillon, was published in the *Gazette de Lausanne* in

November 1958. It too is an occasion to retrace the history of Nathalie's writing from *Tropisms* onwards, and for her to explain her literary aims, while she once again stresses her isolation. Echoing Bourdet, Francillon concludes with the statement that "Nathalie Sarraute is one of the great novelists of our time." A third interview, with Geneviève Serreau, another friend who was also the managing editor at *Les Lettres nouvelles*, is the occasion, on the eve of the novel's publication, for Nathalie to explain that her fiction doesn't derive from some prescriptive theoretical formula, but from a creative impulse that has its roots in the unconscious mind. And, she adds, each writer needs to invent his own literary tools for giving form to that impulse.[2]

In Nathalie's case, these tools are developed and adapted from one novel to the next. In *The Planetarium*, the perspective of the single male narrator in the first two novels is dissolved and distributed among the shifting viewpoints of the various characters, who are seen both from within and from without—as others see them and as they experience their own engagement with others. The book's title, originally intended for the projected sequel to *Tropisms*, and still used in the early stages of the composition of *Portrait of an Unknown Man*, reflects this dual perspective.[3] As Nathalie later explained, "A planetarium is not the real sky, but an artificial one." And correspondingly, "the characters and the things they are pursuing, such as living in a nice apartment, or being famous, or anything else, constitute the surface beneath which the true impulses take place, the real, microscopic dramas that have nothing to do with the manifest content."[4]

Family relations once again provide a context for the underlying psychological dramas as they play out between husband and wife, mother and daughter, father and son, aunt and nephew, brother and sister, mother- and son-in-law. The issue is not the family roles as such, but the volatility associated with the intimacy of these relationships, where emotional registers can shift from one moment to the next, closeness becomes distance, and hostility replaces mutual understanding. Or vice versa. And despite external differences, the motif that runs through the text, right up to its closing words, is that, when it comes to psychology, "somewhere, farther down, everyone is alike, everyone resembles everyone else."[5]

Questions about writing and writers are a major preoccupation, and the experience of Alain Guimier, a young art historian with literary inclinations, is offset against the figure of Germaine Lemaire, a famous novelist, who is constructed out of raw material drawn from the example of Simone de Beauvoir. This was the closest Nathalie ever came to the inclusion of an identifiable biographical source in her work. The motivation was not so much an undeniable personal animus, as a desire to get to grips with the question of what the proper stuff of literature should be, and what it takes to be a writer of such literature. (These issues would return in later novels.) Whereas Nathalie found a certain comfort in failure—as long as it was on her own terms—Beauvoir exhibited all the features associated with the pursuit of the world's idea of "glory," placing herself on a pedestal, and illustrating the phenomenon whereby people will happily accept the self-image that such self-regarding individuals construct and project.

The Planetarium contains a number of clues identifying Beauvoir: Germaine Lemaire's association with a review called "L'ère nouvelle" (The new era)—a transparent variant of *Les Temps modernes*—her collection of male disciples, and the mantilla she sports at one point. (Beauvoir later told her American lover, the writer Nelson Algren, that she recognised herself in Nathalie's novel, and noted the mantilla.)[6] But the key issue turns on aesthetics, and Germaine Lemaire is described as a Madame Tussaud, the creator of waxwork figures, which have a superficial resemblance to living beings, but which in reality are as artificial as the fake stars in the painted sky of a planetarium. (The Planetarium and Mme Tussaud's are neighbours on London's Marylebone Road.) This artificiality is related to a second element in Nathalie's critique, namely Germaine Lemaire's preoccupation with her own celebrity, portrayed as a constant demand for adulation. This demand presupposes a hierarchical conception of human relations and is the very reverse of the psychology of the tropism, which posits the existence of an entirely egalitarian underlying similarity between individuals, however different they otherwise appear to be.

The essay "Conversation and Sub-conversation" (rejected by Beauvoir for *Les Temps modernes* in 1954) started the argument by reaffirming the place of psychology in fiction against those who dismiss it as a thing of the past. It also defends the search for new forms against the repetition of inherited literary formulae. Although Beauvoir assumed that the article was an attack on *The Mandarins*, Nathalie hadn't read the novel at the time of writing, but she certainly had Beauvoir in her sights.[7] In any case, *The Mandarins*, published in October 1954, had itself declared hostilities by ascribing literary concerns that are recognisably those of Nathalie—the defence of generically indeterminate writing, the search for new forms, the condemnation of a "tediously classical" realism—to the character Paula, a neurotically anxious and talentless individual.[8] Beauvoir's portrait was a timely incentive for Nathalie to respond in fictional kind as she worked on *The Planetarium*.

The dispute between the two writers continued even after the publication of Nathalie's novel. Beauvoir retaliated in 1963 with the next volume of her memoirs, *Force of Circumstance*, when she writes that in *The Planetarium* she "once again found Nathalie Sarraute's paranoid little bourgeois," and defends *The Mandarins* against the critique of "Conversation and Sub-conversation." Just as for Nathalie, the novelist who ignores "the dark places of psychology" is condemned to produce nothing more than "a *trompe l'œil*," so for Beauvoir the bracketing out of social realities in favour of what she calls a "outmoded psychologism" precludes any "valid aesthetic system."[9] The opposition between the psychology that Nathalie had first outlined in the pages of *Les Temps modernes* and the *engagement* with which the journal had subsequently become associated had irrevocably hardened.

As Nathalie approached her sixtieth year, the "glory" she had explored through the figure of Germaine Lemaire was now in prospect for her. After *The Planetarium* came out in May, she was called upon for further interviews, including one for *Vogue* magazine. She was photographed by Richard Avedon for the American literary review *Harper's Bazaar*, which published an extract from *The Planetarium* in translation. She was also photographed by the Studio Harcourt, whose glamourizing house style was the target of one of Roland Barthes's 1957 *Mythologies*. She featured in two separate talk shows on the radio to discuss topics of general interest, such as whether morning is the best time of day. She was interviewed in the Jewish journal *L'Arche* and was one of several writers in a special number of the Marxist *La nouvelle critique*, which published replies to the question "In 1960, what, in your view, is your purpose?" In the same year, the first number of the new avant-garde journal *Tel Quel* included her reply alongside thirty-one others to the question, "Do you think you have literary talent? how do you recognise it?" She used to think she had it, she says, when she wrote her French compositions in school, because of the ease and the pleasure with which she did so. But, she continues, both have long since vanished.[10]

This level of exposure was obviously a welcome alternative to the relative indifference with which her first publications had been met, but it assumed skills that Nathalie had yet to master, as well as some that she might never wish to. At a gathering of students and poets who had come to hear her, Claude Mauriac, and Robbe-Grillet speak in a café one evening in June 1958, she was reduced to stammering two or three inaudible sentences in response to the questions addressed to her, and did so with an air of such evident distress that the audience left her in peace for the remainder of the proceedings.[11] She was still ill with TB at the time, but a year later things hadn't much improved, when in his portrait of Nathalie, the journalist Pierre Démeron comments that she "is not yet at ease with journalists. She nervously clasps and unclasps her hands, her smile and her gaze collapse suddenly to reveal distress." As she then explains, this nervousness is due above all to a fear of misrepresentation, and in justification of her wariness, she shows him a photograph (almost certainly the one by Avedon) that had appeared in an American journal where—whether according to Démeron or to her—she looks like "an Eskimo returning from a successful fishing trip." She adds that the text accompanying the photograph was no better.[12]

The sense of vulnerability to misrepresentation is also evident in Nathalie's claims that the success of *The Planetarium* was based on a misperception on the part of readers, who saw the novel through the lens of the kind of realist characterisation that her writing sought to undermine. This was certainly the case in the enthusiastic review by the seventy-three-year-old François Mauriac, whose novels exploring family relations had been such a revelation to Nathalie in the 1920s. Writing jointly about her and—strangely—his own son Claude, Mauriac singles out the way that each of them succeeds in portraying the consciousness of their characters, and he confesses himself "dazzled" by the distinctive means in which they each do so. However, against the logic of Nathalie's writing, he goes on to maintain that these states of consciousness are necessarily dependent on the memorable quality of the fictional individuals with whom they are associated.[13] It must nevertheless have been gratifying for Nathalie to have the benevolent attention of a writer she had long admired, and after meeting her at a dinner one evening, Mauriac noted in his diary, "Nathalie Sarraute and I felt very close to each other, over and above any words we exchanged."[14] No doubt the feeling was mutual, and in subsequent years they sent each other signed copies of their new books.

In 1960 Gaëtan Picon, the literary critic whom Nathalie had first met at Gadoffre's *décades* in Royaumont, and who had written about her work in his review *Mercure de France*, suggested putting her name forward for the Légion d'honneur. He had been appointed Directeur général des Arts et des Lettres by the minister of culture, André Malraux, who also supported her nomination. But, as her response very clearly indicates, this honour offered recognition on terms that she could not accept:

Dear Gaëtan Picon,

My sincere thanks for your letter which touched me greatly. You know how much your rare and generous understanding has meant to me, how much encouragement it has given me, and continues to do so. I would be only too glad to be able to please you.

Unfortunately, I cannot do so—it's not so much about "wearing a robe that ill suits me," as having to behave in a way that would go against the—perhaps anti-social and absurd—way I have behaved throughout my life.

It's too late for me to change.

I hope you can sense how sorry I am about this, and that you believe in my grateful and loyal friendship.

Nathalie Sarraute[15]

Her default position was one at odds with the establishment, rather than as part of it.

Her occasional public involvement in political causes reflected this stance. The first of these involvements arose in connection with the Algerian war when she signed the *Manifesto of the 121* in September 1960. This *Declaration on the Right to Insubordination in the War in Algeria*—to give it its full title—was an open letter signed by 121 intellectuals and writers, calling on the French government to recognise the Algerian war as a legitimate struggle for independence, and demanding the right of conscientious objectors to refuse to torture or to take up arms against the Algerian people. The declaration's assertion that "the cause of the Algerian people . . . is the cause of all free men" chimed with Nathalie's own libertarian instincts. In the same month she appeared for the defence at the trial of the so-called Jeanson Network, which had supported the National Liberation Front in Algeria. In her statement, she declared,

> In times like those we are living through now, patriotism appears in the guise of rebellion. I believe that these Frenchmen [the defendants] are genuine patriots. The day is not far off when their actions will be judged according their true worth. Their self-abnegation, their courage and their respect for the great principles that have been inculcated in us ensure that they will be esteemed and respected by all, as they deserve to be.[16]

She gave a fuller account of her views in a subsequent interview with the journalist Madeleine Chapsal, where she explains her own—deeply patriotic—reasons for signing:

> I feel infinite love and gratitude towards France. For me, the face of France is the one I have always known: the face of liberty. It's the one that, despite everything, France still has all over world. It's still the country of the French Revolution, the Rights of man, the Liberation of peoples, the Dreyfus affair, the Resistance. In 1952, in Morocco, members of Istiqlal [Morocco's first independence party] recited words by Mme Roland in front of me. I'm sure that for the people fighting us, the words of the *Marseillaise* have retained their full force, their full meaning. Make no mistake, this is the real prestige that France enjoys throughout the world. She will lose everything, if it disappears. I think it's right, at a critical time like this, not to remain silent. It's important to know that for many French people, these principles have retained all

their force and that many French people are ready to demonstrate their respect for those who expose themselves to risk and sacrifice in order to defend those principles. . . .

I think agreement between the French and the Algerians is possible, and that brotherly acts such as these are the only remaining means of bringing this about. Otherwise all is lost. . . .

I think that the spirit of this Declaration corresponds to the feelings of a great number of French people. It's taken time for people to realise this. During the Resistance too, there were very few people involved to start off with, but then it materialised, and it snowballed. I'm convinced that the great mass of the population wants peace and friendship with the Algerian people.[17]

As for many of the other signatories, Nathalie's perspective on the Algerian war was filtered through her experience of living under Nazi Occupation, with the French army now in the role of the German occupants. Her mention of the Dreyfus case also carries echoes of her experience of anti-Semitism, and the Algerians' demand for independence would almost certainly have suggested parallels with the Russian revolutionary politics of her childhood. It would not have been hard to imagine Uncle Yasha fighting with the FLN.

Her public participation in the affair was, however, a risky strategy for someone who always insisted that her writing was not political, and that politics and literature were separate spheres. This was one of the issues on which she and Beauvoir—who also signed the *Manifesto of the 121*—were most opposed. As Nathalie said in the interview she gave to *L'Arche* in 1959, "There is no connection between my political sympathies and what I do in literature." But, in a telling rider to this comment, she went on to say, "but I don't think, either that there is any contradiction."[18] Her political views were ultimately grounded in the conviction that informs the psychology portrayed in her novels, namely that, as she stated so clearly in *The Planetarium*, "farther down, everyone is alike." For Nathalie, the Rights of Man sanction this fundamental resemblance, all French people share the same principles at heart, and—though the claim sounds a little naïve—Arabs subscribe to the republican sentiments of the Marseillaise.

The holiday in Morocco in 1952 had already given Nathalie a glimpse of Arab life in the North African French territories, and she wrote to Maria Jolas to say that she was contemplating an article for *Les Temps modernes* on the subject:

> There'd be an interesting article to write for the T.M. about Morocco, but I don't know if I would be up to it. People I've met here have told me all sorts of things and promised to provide me with documentation. The poverty in the souks and the backward state of the population are unimaginable. You constantly have the impression that you've taken a leap back in time and that you're living in the Middle Ages.[19]

The letter provides no further hint as to what the article might have said, and Nathalie may have decided not to set herself up as a commentator on political matters—particularly in the pages of the *Les Temps modernes*—for fear that it would skew the perception of her literary writing. But from time to time she did go public with her views.

Another such occasion arose after a visit to Cuba in July 1961. The invitation to visit the country had probably come on the recommendation of the Cuban poet Nivaria Tejera, who had been appointed Castro's secretary of state for culture after living in exile in Paris where she and Nathalie had become acquainted. Utterly captivated by what she saw of Castro's socialist revolution, Nathalie gave a long interview to Louis Aragon's communist newspaper *Les Lettres françaises* extolling what sounds like utopia. Sartre and Beauvoir had visited Cuba the previous year during what they called the "honeymoon" of the socialist revolution, which they described in the press on their return. Nathalie's uncharacteristically nonliterary interview in the uncharacteristically chosen communist newspaper may have been an attempt on her part to challenge—or at least to match—Beauvoir on her own territory.

During her stay, she gave lectures, visited model farms, hospitals, and museums, and attended a writer's congress, but it was Castro himself who embodied her most fervently held ideals. She saw in him a leader who exemplified radically egalitarian principles: "There isn't a hint or the least trace in his behaviour of pride, no sense of self-importance, no need to impress, no awareness of producing an effect." He places himself on an equal footing with his people: "He's one of them. A man like them, the same as them." In sum, Nathalie's Castro was everything that Germaine Lemaire (aka Simone de Beauvoir) was not.

Nathalie also attributes literary virtues to his famed eloquence, which she sees as exhibiting the very qualities she sought in her own work: "a nascent attempt to express himself and communicate, as thought and feeling take shape in front of everyone, emerging directly from their source, without alterations, corrections, or revisions, and then land deep inside everyone in the place where feelings and thoughts originate."[20] Since she didn't speak Spanish, this assessment must have been based on her observation of his delivery and its reception by his audience. She was particularly charmed by his use of the word *nosotros*, which she heard as meaning *nous autres* (we all), and which, to her ears, encapsulated the inclusiveness of the racial equality she observed. She also singles out Cuba's cultural aspirations for special praise, and claims that Cuban writers are free to support the revolution in any form they choose. She had apparently encountered no refutation of her own view that the revolutionary authenticity of a work of art has nothing to do with the overt political convictions of its creators.

But disenchantment subsequently set in, and in 1964 she wrote directly to Castro—as one equal to another—to intervene on behalf another writer friend, Flora Díaz Parado, against whom a number of false accusations had been made, and whose "total and constant dedication to the Cuban Revolution" could be not be placed in doubt. She closes with a statement of "the profound admiration and the enthusiasm with which I have followed everything that you have achieved and which provides a measure of how far nobility of the soul and the power of the human spirit can extend."[21] But this admiration was already becoming a thing of the past, and from then on Nathalie's relations with Cuba were confined to friendships with Cuban writers, most of whom—including the playwright Eduardo Manet—eventually returned to exile in Paris following their own disenchantments.

CHAPTER TWENTY-TWO

Nathalie Abroad, 1959–64

THE PUBLICATION of *The Planetarium* was the cue for widespread foreign interest in Nathalie's work, with contracts for translation and invitations to give talks and lectures. In a climate of growing international curiosity about the Nouveau Roman, she had a distinctive profile thanks both to her command of the English language and to Maria Jolas's links with publishers in the United States and the United Kingdom. Maria's earlier attempts to persuade English-language publishers to take on a translation of *Portrait of an Unknown Man* had met with no success, but in 1957 things began to change. Nathalie acquired a literary agent in the United States, Renée Spodheim, who reported that enquiries about a translation of *Portrait of an Unknown Man* had come from the London publisher, Peter Owen, and from George Braziller in the United States.[1] Owen was then preempted by John Calder, who took an option in the same year on all work by both Robbe-Grillet and Nathalie. Calder was a tireless promoter of new French writing, and he and Braziller remained Nathalie's English-language publishers from the moment that *Portrait of an Unknown Man* was published in the United States in 1958 and *Martereau* in the United Kingdom in 1959.

Nathalie's facility in English nevertheless had its downside, making her more sensitive than her monolingual compatriots to the way she and her work were represented abroad. She was particularly exercised about Braziller's proposed blurb for *Martereau*. Following "a desperate phone call" from Nathalie, Maria acted as go-between in discussions with the publisher, explaining that Nathalie objected to what she saw as the socioeconomic emphasis of the draft, and was dismayed that her own description of the book's intentions "appears not to have been understood by the person who wrote the blurb." Braziller's editor replied laconically to say that he was sorry the jacket displeased Mrs Sarraute, and it's not clear how much—if any—of the original version was altered in response to her alarm.[2]

Despite these anxieties, the translations met with enthusiastic coverage in the American literary press. *The Planetarium* received several reviews, it was advertised as a "chef d'œuvre of the subconscious," and the *New Yorker* introduced its author to the American reading public with a colourful portrait: "born in Russia, . . . long resident in Paris, married to a French lawyer, and mother of three grown daughters, . . . still foreign-looking in her way, with her black hair combed back in the Russian style, above extraordinary eyes as black as black cherries—an impressively quiet, observant, international-looking intellectual."[3] In the same year, *Portrait of an Unknown Man* was translated into Italian and *Tropisms* into both Danish and German. A Polish translation of *Martereau* was under way and another in Serbo-Croat.[4] Thereafter, all Nathalie's work appeared in both English and German. Her misgivings about publication in Germany had been allayed thanks to her German translator Elmar Tophoven, with whom she had detailed discussions of his drafts, just as she did with Maria Jolas. These collaborations, made possible by Nathalie's familiarity with both languages, were essential for her confidence in the translated versions of her work.

She was also invited to give lectures, most often to student audiences in universities outside France. Lecturing was a new experience, but it revived her relish of the *conférence du stage* thirty years previously, and she saw these occasions as a chance to explain herself to audiences who came without preconceptions. She was also convinced that she received a better hearing abroad than she did at home. One of the few pieces of biographical information she remained happy to give out was a list of the dates and places she had been invited to lecture, and she kept copies of all the foreign translations of her work displayed on a table in the entrance to her apartment in the Avenue Pierre 1ᵉ de Serbie.

There was considerable enthusiasm for avant-garde writing in Italy, and one of the first of these lecture invitations took Nathalie to Milan in September 1959. She shared a platform with several contemporary writers and critics, including Giuseppe Ungaretti and Elio Vittorini at an event organised by the publisher Feltrinelli, who had recently brought out the first ever edition of Pasternak's *Doctor Zhivago* (in Italian translation). Although she had been invited to talk about the Nouveau Roman, Nathalie was quite explicit in denying the existence of any group programme, and she used the lecture instead to give an account of the development of her own writing and her own aims.[5]

A few months later she was in Switzerland, where she spoke in Geneva, the city she had briefly visited aged two, en route with her mother from Ivanovo-Voznesensk to Paris, and where her parents had been students. She also spoke in Lausanne where her father had lived during the Occupation, and where Lili was now a permanent resident. Her topic for these lectures was "The Novel and Psychology," a defence of her own terrain against its detractors. A letter to the Russian-born Jean Blot, who was French consul at the time and later became a close friend, conveys her appreciation of the welcome she felt she had received:

> I would like to say how touched and comforted I was—because for a shy person like myself it was quite an ordeal—by the support you gave me and by the very great kindness that you and Madame Blot showed towards me.
>
> Now that those moments I experienced in Switzerland are, alas, just memories settling in my mind, the evening I spent with you in that strange cellar with the young troupe who performed with such fervour and such conviction, has lingered as an intense impression: it's like the secret and persistent pulse of the life of a city, a country—which without you I would never have glimpsed.[6]

It was also during this tour that Nathalie became reacquainted with Jean Starobinksi, the literary critic and author of an influential study of Rousseau, whom she had first met at Gadoffre's *décades*. It was the start of a lifelong friendship.

The success of the Danish translation of *Tropisms* led to an invitation to speak in all three Scandinavian countries in the autumn of 1960. The tour was initially cancelled when the French government withdrew funding because of Nathalie's involvement in the *Manifesto of the 121*. Writing to her host in Copenhagen she explains the situation: "As you perhaps know, I signed the manifesto of the 121 against the Algerian war and my presence in Denm[ark], Norway and Sweden, even to talk about the novel, appears undesirable to our government. We are living through troubled times."[7] Alternative sources of finance were found, and the trip went ahead. But it was an irony of history that Nathalie should find herself in Sweden at a time when, like Yakov Tcherniak half a century earlier, she had been designated persona non grata at home. She was overjoyed when her hosts in Göteborg (the city from which Yakov had made his last fateful journey) sent her a copy of the front page of a booklet about Yakov Tcherniak published in Sweden in 1907, *Den mystiska Tscherniak-affären: Brott eller olyckshändelse?!* (The mysterious Tcherniak affair: crime or accident?!). Her gratitude is evident in the letter she wrote to Ingrid Mesterton: "What joy you have brought me! I am deeply touched that you looked for the document, that you found it, and made a copy to send me. It's very precious to me, and relates to things that I hold very dear."[8] Like her visit to Geneva, her lecture in Sweden brought back memories of her family's past.

The programme of talks and lectures continued unabated, and in February 1961 Nathalie spent two weeks in the United Kingdom on a tour masterminded by John Calder in the company of Robbe-Grillet and Marguerite Duras. Nathalie's name was already familiar to readers of the *Times Literary Supplement* where, in February 1959, she was discussed in an article devoted to "The Anti-Novel in France," which elicited a reply from her, published the following week (in French) correcting the statement that she was opposed to psychology. A review of the translation of *Tropisms* appeared in January 1960, where the novelist Rayner Heppenstall presented Nathalie as having been influenced by English women novelists—Virginia Woolf and Ivy Compton-Burnett—and as influencing others in turn. He concludes by saying that "what passes as novel-writing here is so abject that the merest flicker from abroad is likely to be seen as a ray of hope. Madame Sarraute is more than a flicker."[9] The article became the basis for a chapter in Heppenstall's book on the comparative literary traditions of England and France, and Nathalie wrote to him to say, "It is a great pleasure to me to think that my books are read in England. I have great affection for the country, which for many reasons is *very* close to me."[10]

In June 1960, the *TLS* carried a short, previously unpublished article by Nathalie titled "Rebels in a World of Platitudes," which was included a year later in *The Writer's Dilemma*, a volume edited by the poet Stephen Spender.[11] In July, she spoke on BBC radio in a programme devoted to "The Work of Younger French Writers," and the producer wrote afterwards to say that he was delighted with the result and would welcome a further contribution.[12] Despite her sixty years, she was young in literary spirit, and her ease in English combined with her familiarity with English literature made her an ideal representative of new French writing for a British audience.

Calder's tour capitalised on this growing interest in contemporary French culture, which now included the *nouvelle vague*, with films such as Alain Resnais's *Hiroshima, Mon amour* for which Marguerite Duras wrote the screenplay. Calder ensured maximum publicity for the two-week visit, which attracted considerable attention. One event had an audience of over eight hundred and lasted for more than three hours, as the three writers took it in turn to respond to questions from the audience—Robbe-Grillet, a couple of sentences at a time, which Calder translated into English, Sonia Orwell doing the same for Duras, and Nathalie speaking in what Calder describes as "careful and faultless English."[13] Their itinerary took them to several universities, including Oxford, where Nathalie had been a student exactly four decades previously, and where one of the dons tried unsuccessfully to seduce Robbe-Grillet at a party given in their honour. They recorded a programme for television, and another for the radio with the novelist William Golding, where Nathalie's English gave her the edge over Robbe-Grillet, who was otherwise inclined to dominate the proceedings. She recorded a separate radio programme about her own work which was then published *The Listener* magazine.[14]

Robbe-Grillet dropped out of the tour halfway through the second week, much to the relief of the two women. As Calder recalls, "He had constantly made little jokes at their expense which they did not appreciate and they had formed a solid feminist resistance to his self-confident masculinity."[15] Nathalie knew Duras from the Médicis jury, and their numerical advantage over Robbe-Grillet on this occasion was largely unprecedented. Their own relations, which continued over many years, took the form of an exaggeratedly jokey but nonetheless keen rivalry, which the writer Jean-Pierre Faye later described as "a comical hatred."[16]

The tour received generous coverage in the press, and for Nathalie it reestablished links with a country of which she had fond memories. As she wrote to an English admirer of her work, "My tour through England renewed all my love and sympathy for this country. The country is beautiful. Wonderful villages, cottages, beams, roofs, meadows, children and young people. And lovely old people too."[17] The slightly bizarre mention of "lovely old people" may well be a tacit reference to Ivy Compton-Burnett, whom Nathalie visited at her home in London in the company of Sonia Orwell, who was a friend of the seventy-six-year-old novelist. Nathalie had briefly discussed the novels of Compton-Burnett and Henry Green in her essay "Conversation and Sub-conversation" as examples of modern uses of dialogue in fiction. Sonia Orwell, who had been married to George Orwell for three months before his death, was a highly effective literary editor at *Horizon* magazine, and as a great Francophile, had many French writer-friends. (She and Nathalie had a common link in Eugène Vinaver.) There's no record of the date of this visit, but it almost certainly took place during Calder's two-week tour, when Sonia Orwell acted as Duras's interpreter.

Nathalie often mentioned her meeting with the author of *Parents and Children*, which in her telling has all the features of the England she recalled from Harrow-on-the-Hill and Oxford. Or even, as she suggests, the Victorian novels she read as a student at the Sorbonne.

When she was herself in her nineties, she wrote an account of the visit for Compton-Burnett's biographer:

It is difficult for me to say anything about Ivy Compton-Burnett that would not appear like a reminiscence from a Victorian novel.

I was taken to see her by Sonia Orwell. She did not seem to have the slightest idea as to what I might be doing in life. Neither did she seem to know that I had written anything about her books. I believe that if she had known it, she would not have cared.

We found her in a Victorian drawing-room, dressed like a Victorian lady, with a velvet ribbon around her neck [in fact she wore the ribbon in her hair], sitting in an old English armchair near a coal-fire. After a while, we went to the dining-room, where a real English tea was served by a parlour-maid with cap and apron, on a table covered with old silver, buns, scones, and so on. The conversation ran on the rising costs of food, wages and rent.

Miss C.B. told us that when her name first appeared in the papers, her maid came back from the grocer's saying that he had been shocked to see the name of a lady like Miss C.B. printed in a newspaper. "But, said she, with a sigh, what could I do, I had to earn my living."

I asked whether she had known V[irginia] W[oolf]. She said: I met her two or three times but I disliked her: she was a terrible snob, you know!! And I remember her also saying that it made her smile to see what ridiculous precautions young people took when they spoke to her about homosexuals . . . as if that could have shocked her.

Before we left, she put her hand on my arm and said: "Do you girls want to go along the passage[."] We declined the offer, shook hands with her and left.

But maybe all this was just one of my delightful dreams about England?!

Just ask Sonia Orwell, when you meet her, if all this is true. At any rate it shows once more that Proust was right when he wrote: ["]a man of genius generally inhabits a very ordinary man" or something like that.[18]

Nathalie was always most charmed when her experiences of England coincided with the idealised image that had first drawn her to the country, its language, and its people. The mention of homosexuality nevertheless strikes a slightly incongruous note, hinting at her admiration for the older woman's decidedly un-Victorian social attitudes. (Nathalie was aware that Compton-Burnett had lived for thirty years with another woman.) But what the scene encapsulates above all is the image of a writer—Compton-Burnett—who, though in reality "one of the great novelists of her time," found politely English ways of ignoring all the trappings of this position and, unlike Germaine Lemaire, embraced ordinariness in her everyday life.

There was no mistaking Nathalie's own growing importance, which was amply fêted in the course of a two-month lecture tour of the United States in February and March 1964. It took her to over a dozen major universities between both coasts of the country, beginning in New York and ending in Washington six weeks later. Contemporary French writing was the object of considerable enthusiasm in American universities where, unlike France at the time, there was no ban on teaching living writers. Students were taking courses on contemporary French fiction, doctoral theses were being written on the Nouveau Roman, and in 1959 the academic journal *Yale French Studies* devoted a special number to the "Midnight Novelists" in a nod to the Éditions de Minuit. Butor taught at Bryn Mawr for a semester in 1960, and Robbe-Grillet arrived for a lecture tour in late 1963.

An invitation to Nathalie had been on the cards since 1960, when the writer André Berne-Joffroy wrote from Harvard to say, "Your fame here is considerable. On the day I arrived, the members of the Humanities Section, which I belong to, all received a typed copy of your article in the *Times Literary Supplement*."[19] Once again, Nathalie had an advantage over most of her compatriots, thanks to her ability to speak English, and thanks also to a certain familiarity by proxy with the United States through her friendship with Maria Jolas. Her old friend Assia had settled permanently in New York, where she worked for the French Cultural Services and was closely involved in the arrangements for the lecture tour. Maria accompanied Nathalie for the first part of the trip.

Nathalie and Maria were in the habit of communicating in a mix of English and French, and one of Nathalie's letters to Maria written in 1960—in anticipation of a visit to the United States—is a very convincing pastiche (in English) of J. D. Salinger's *Catcher in the Rye*:

Darling Maria,

I think that guy Salinger *is* a swell. His book is simply terrific. It just kills me.

We are driving all day long on those goddam roads, to that goddam country, Yougoslavia.

"For Chrissake, what the hellya gonna do there?" you might ask.

"I dunno. Sure, only crazy fools like us would go so far to find that stinking place." Before I left Paris, I got a letter from that phoney, Richard Heppenstall, telling me that goddam stuff, "The Labyrinth" by Alain R.G. made some people in London puke and all the morons there laugh like hyenas, because the translation was so damn lousy. Now don't you think this will give that bastard Howard the helluva pain in the ass?

That same guy Heppenstall says he met Crook at a goddam party and they discussed the stuff I wrote in the T.L.S. Crook said Heppenstall had "paved the way to it for me." Those were his goddam words. I do hope this Crook will send you the dough. Even a crook can't be *that* tough?

You see, I am practising in English for my lectures on that bastard old Tolstoi and that sonuvabitch Dostoievski. I am sure all those dopes, old Peyre and old Levin will laugh their asses off when they hear me delivering all my crap. I am not kidding.

With oodles of kisses from both of us, as a boy [perhaps one of the English students from the Mont Blanc climb in 1923] with whom I sometimes doubledated when I was a babe, used to say.

Natacha.[20]

All this gave her an excellent rapport with students and her various hosts, as is confirmed by Germaine Brée, one of several French natives teaching in the United States, who wrote after Nathalie's subsequent return to the University of Wisconsin–Madison: "You seem to me to have the gift of deeply affecting the people who are able to come into contact with you—and it's rare. I think you have been liked here as no one else from France. And it's far more helpful to us than the negative and arrogant attitude that Sartre has towards the United States."[21]

Nathalie's attitude to the United States was indeed anything but negative, and the ecstatically telegraphic letters she wrote to Raymond during her stay (a rare instance of personal correspondence) testify to her enchantment with the country. She loved its energy and its modernity, and she had a particular fondness for New York:

> Fantastic sky-scrapers, like vast jewels, their layout, the Hudson, the East River, the ocean, the Greek skies, better than Greece, the light, the life and the joie de vivre on Broadway and Park Avenue, the variety, the old Georgian streets with their little houses, everything, just everything is fantastic. The view from the top of the Empire State Building is the real surprise here, in all my life. I've understood the beauty of the architectural art of the future and I've seen the most beautiful sight in the world.

It was winter when she arrived at the beginning of February 1964, and after a heavy snowfall, Boston brought back memories of Russia. She remarks that Russian émigrés love the United States, and she herself instantly warmed to Americans, amongst whom she found many of the qualities that she had met in Russia on a recent trip (about which more in chapter 25). As she wrote to Raymond, "I receive so much affection, so many charming compliments about my eyes, my face, my voice, my attitude (like in Russia!). The same affection, spontaneous generosity and candour." In sum, "People are delightful, pleasant, cheerful, without any vulgarity. Everything we imagine about them is so untrue!"[22]

The English translation of her fourth novel, *The Golden Fruits*, had just come out in the United States, and was receiving notices in the press, where it was listed in *Time*'s "Best Reads." This no doubt contributed to the popularity of Nathalie's lectures, which attracted large numbers, filling venues not normally required for talks by French writers and generating great enthusiasm. She had a portfolio of talks, including one on "The Novel and Reality" and one on Flaubert, which she had worked up for her tours. She gave them alternately in English and in French, juggling them so as to avoid giving the same one twice in the same place. The fees were beyond her previous imaginings: "It's as if it rains dollars every time I open my mouth. I'll be paid 1,000 dollars here. Oh, miracles of human destiny!" (This was in Madison where she spent two weeks, and the sum she received was the equivalent of around eight thousand dollars in 2018.) In the hopes of convincing Raymond to join her for the Easter holidays, she insisted that she was earning enough for the cost not to be a problem. In fact, she said, "I'm bursting with dough."[23]

She was treated like royalty and taken to the best restaurants, such as the Carlyle in New York, where President Lyndon Johnson was due to dine later the same day. "I'm invited everywhere, people adore me," she writes to Raymond, adding in mimicry of Salvador Dali's inflated pretentions, "everyone now knows that 'je souit un génie.'" And, she observes sardonically, "It's a change from Paris." In the United States she could—with amused self-mockery—enjoy the regal role she deplored in Simone de Beauvoir, as on the occasion when she was taken to visit a physics laboratory in Madison: "Her gracious majesty smiled, and opined, 'Oh ! I see . . . How interesting . . . ,' uttered thanks, held out her gloved hand . . . didn't understand a word, but pretended to examine curves, currents, radioactive apparatus . . . laboratories where her most brilliant subjects manipulated levers and came to greet her." In response to Raymond's scepticism, she continues in the same vein, "You tell me I've become 'a touch megalomaniac'!! but in fact the population of the entire continent is charmed by my regal modesty and simplicity."[24]

Beauvoir was, however, far from forgotten, and rather strangely Nathalie engineered a meeting in Chicago with Beauvoir's former lover Nelson Algren. There's more than a hint of rivalry in her portrait of Algren, whom she finds nothing like Beauvoir's depiction of him as Lewis Brogan in *The Mandarins*, and she implies that she has more in common with Algren than Beauvoir did, describing him to Raymond as "not attractive, looks like an old Jew: ([Ilya] Ehrenburg), but delightful, nice, spontaneous, adores me!!!" He accompanied her on a distinctly un-royal tour of Chicago, which, contrary to any idea of her as a Parisian *bourgeoise*, Nathalie took in her stride: "Night-clubs, Black and Indian slums which were dreadful and fantastic (nightmare, Bosch). Searched by police who were pursuing a murderer and had surrounded the area. Ate in a restaurant run by Al Capone's cook! Saw apartments belonging to millionaires, all glass, on the fortieth floor with a perfect view of illuminated skyscrapers!!"

Beauvoir was dismayed to hear of Nathalie's visit, and wrote to Algren to say so: "How strange Nathalie Sarraute wanted to see you! She hates me, a fascinated hate; she painted me as a ridiculous, untalented writer in *The Planetarium*. Did she let this hate appear? I am curious to know how things went between you."[25] If Algren responded to Beauvoir's curiosity and provided his own account of the occasion, she never made it public.

Despite the verve with which she imitated Salinger's literary idiom—whose oral qualities would certainly have appealed to her— Nathalie does not seem to have taken much interest in contemporary American culture. What captured her attention was the race question. The civil rights movement was at its height, supported by Lyndon Johnson (whom Nathalie narrowly missed seeing at the Carlyle restaurant in New York), and opposed, amongst others, by George Wallace, the governor of Alabama, whom she did in fact see—also in a restaurant—and whose lecture on the topic of segregation she attended at the University of Wisconsin–Madison. Elsewhere she notes that segregation is an "urgent problem for everyone. Blacks on the up and up. Whites terrified."[26]

In New Orleans she observed the way desegregation on public transport was only very tentatively taking effect: "In trams, young Blacks come and sit bravely among silent Whites. The reverse very rare, Whites prefer to remain standing when black places free. Blacks pleasant and charming." And she reports a comical but telling conversation with "a white lady of New Orleans":

ME: "They are often very good-looking."

[THE LADY]: *Oh! Are they?*

ME: *Yes, don't you agree?*

THE LADY: *I confess, I never look at their faces.*

ME . . . *Oh!* . . .

THE LADY: *I believe they have sometimes lovely bodies. . . . But, you see, they are so lazy in their movements and so slow in everything they do! Though I have nothing against them, of course. They are often quite nice.*[27]

Nathalie had a sharp ear for the coded forms through which racism was expressed.

In New York she persuaded a young journalist to take her to a Gospel church service in Harlem, where they were the only whites present. And a few years later, she went back to Harlem—this time accompanied by Raymond—to see an all-black production of *Cindy*, an adaptation of Cinderella by the black actor and theatre director, Maxwell Glanville, at the American Community Theatre on 125th Street. As a counterpart to "black is beautiful," the ugly sisters were white, and the actors chanted "whites are ugly," to which the audience responded with more chants of "U.G.L.Y.: UGLY." Here too, Nathalie and Raymond were the only whites in the audience, accepted, according to her, because they had followed the advice of friends and made it clear that they were French.[28] Nathalie's own experience of anti-Semitism gave her an instinctive sympathy with American blacks, which she assumed, perhaps a little optimistically, they would recognise.

The main literary acquaintance Nathalie made outside the university context was Hannah Arendt, who published a long, perceptive, and sympathetic review of *The Golden Fruits* in the *New York Review of Books* at the beginning of March, and invited Nathalie to dinner at her home in New York on 30 March.[29] Arendt, being as cosmopolitan as Nathalie, but differently so, was a link between modern-day America and the Europe familiar to assimilated Jews like Nathalie. As with Algren, Jewishness provided a tacit connection, and in a letter to Karl Jaspers, Arendt describes Nathalie as a "French novelist and Russian Jew—just like at home; we hit it off so well from the first moment."[30] Having lived in Paris as an exile from Hitler's Germany in the 1930s, Arendt spoke French as well as English, and they had a mutual friend in Nina Gourfinkel.

Nathalie may well have been nervous of Arendt's reputation as a philosopher, but she must have been aware of Arendt's book on the Eichmann trial in Jerusalem, which had recently been published in the United States. Arendt genuinely liked Nathalie's novels, and after reading *The Planetarium* in 1960, she had written to her friend, the American novelist Mary McCarthy, "By the way: Do you know the work of Sarraute? I am reading the Planetarium in French, very very amusing and witty, excellently done, great sense of sarcasm and humour. Don't believe anything about the anti-roman talk or that this has no plot. It has a beauty of a plot—a young ambitieux who tried by hook and crook to get his old aunt's apartment." Arendt's own interest in thought processes and the "whole question of inner life, its turmoil, multiplication, the splitting-into-two (consciousness), the curious fact that I am One only in company," as she put it in another letter to McCarthy, gave her a natural affinity with the psychology of Nathalie's tropisms.[31]

They also had shared literary tastes (Kafka and Rilke) and a shared scepticism with regard to Sartre. Over and above these literary and intellectual connections, they seem to have taken a spontaneous liking to each other. They had a similar sense of humour, and as Arendt later remarked to McCarthy, "One can laugh with her and one laughs about the same things—delightful."[32] The two women continued to meet for a number of years, either in Paris or in New York, and their friendship is documented in the correspondence between Arendt and McCarthy, who had moved to Paris, where, through the intermediary of Arendt, she too became acquainted with Nathalie.

Nathalie's US tour ended on 6 April after a short holiday with Raymond. He had finally made arrangements to join her in the United States, despite the fact that his initial application for a visa had been turned down on the grounds that the French Committee for the Defence of Immigrants, of which he was the secretary, was (wrongly) assumed by the Americans to have been a communist organisation. Membership—current or erstwhile—of the Communist Party and venereal disease were the two nonnegotiable criteria for the withholding of visas. This bureaucratic delay didn't dampen Nathalie's enthusiasm for the United States, and she made thirteen further visits over the course of the next thirty years, the last one at the age of ninety-five in 1995. They were a tonic on which she continued to rely.

CHAPTER TWENTY-THREE

A Reading Public,
1963–66

IN MAY 1964, after seven years as a judge of literary prizes, Nathalie herself became the recipient of one such prize. This was the Prix International de Littérature, awarded for *The Golden Fruits*, which had come out in April of the previous year. Officially known as the International Publishers' Prize, the award was overseen by a committee of prestigious representatives from France (in the form of Gallimard), the United States, the United Kingdom, Germany, Spain, and Italy. Its purpose was to promote avant-garde literature by authors "of any nationality whose existing body of work will, in the view of the jury, have a lasting influence on the development of modern literature."[1] The Italian publisher Guido Einaudi described the prize as an "anti-Nobel," and its reach was as broad as that of its long-established counterpart. The first recipients were Borges and Beckett, who shared the prize in 1961, Borges for *Ficciones* and Beckett for the English version of his *Trilogy*. They were followed in 1962 by the young German novelist Uwe Johnson, and in 1963 by the Italian writer Carlo Emilio Gadda. Nathalie was the first and only French writer to receive the short-lived international award. (It was discontinued in 1968.)

In 1964, the German hosts (Rowohlt) selected the grand surrounds of the Mirabell Palace in Salzburg as the venue for the deciding debates, which were held in public. The list of some sixty nominees, each of whom had published a novel within the previous three years, included Nathalie's fellow Nouveaux Romanciers Claude Simon and Robert Pinget, as well as Yukio Mishima and Alexander Solzhenitsyn, both of whom she was up against in the final round. Nathalie carried the day thanks to interventions from Michel Butor, her onetime editor François Erval, and Dominique Aury from Gallimard, supported by Mary McCarthy speaking for the United States, the Franco-German journalist François Bondy for Germany, and Alberto Moravia for Italy. Dominique Aury's defence was particularly eloquent. Although Nathalie's diary indicates that she had no other major engagements for the dates in question, she didn't attend the award ceremony to receive the ten-thousand-dollar prize (equivalent to around seventy-four thousand euros today), which brought with it the prospect of translation and publication in all the countries represented by the awarding committee. By 1964 Finland, Holland, Canada, Latin America, Portugal, Denmark, Norway, and Sweden had been added to the list.[2] These rewards were particularly gratifying to Nathalie who, at the age of sixty-three, was finally beginning to earn relatively substantial amounts of money. And the international recognition reinforced her sense that her work was better appreciated outside France than at home, where she was still perceived as having what one critic called "a big name [and] a small readership."[3]

Violette Leduc heard the news in a radio broadcast, as she reported in a letter to Simone de Beauvoir: "I heard on the radio this evening that Nathalie Sarraute got the grand Prix International de Littérature and I started Sartre's *Situations IV* [his fourth volume of essays] with the preface to *Portrait of an Unknown Man*. What a lot of success!"[4] Nobody remarked on the fact that Nathalie was the first—and as it turned out, the only—female recipient of the prize. Such gendered recognition might, however, have come at an unwelcome price, since the journalist Bernard Pivot commented not on the books but on the looks—and the legs—of the twenty-seven-year-old German novelist, Gisela Elsner, who won the Prix Formentor (awarded for previously unpublished work) on the same occasion.[5]

There's a nice irony in the fact that the novel that won Nathalie the prize was itself the product of her own involvements with the Prix de Mai and the Prix Médicis, where she would have heard and contributed to the sort of literary debates that provide material for the overt exchanges in the book. In it, a fictional novel, also called "The Golden Fruits," is discussed by a series of anonymous voices, as it grows in popularity and then declines into near oblivion. The idea of turning this kind of literary trajectory into the subject of a narrative had come to Nathalie while she was writing *The Planetarium*. As she told Germaine Brée, "I had just completed a passage about Germaine Lemaire, the writer, and I thought that it would be very interesting to do something about the literary text itself. I thought of *The Golden Fruits*. It would be interesting to take a book, which would become the true hero of the novel, and follow its destiny as it rises and falls and especially to examine the tropisms which its publication generates around it."[6] The phenomenon is also the subject of her essay "What Birds See," published in 1956 in *The Age of Suspicion*, where she associates this kind of popularity with conventionally realist novels, whose lack of inherent literary value will ultimately disappoint. Like the birds who were taken in by the realism of Zeuxis's grapes in the apocryphal story about the Greek artist, readers of such novels will eventually find that they have, metaphorically, been trying to sink their teeth into hard metal instead of succulent fruit. Whence the choice of "The Golden Fruits" as the novel's title.

What interested Nathalie was the fact that, as she says in the essay, the collective hysteria sometimes generated by a novel will cloud the judgement of even the most discerning critics, who "praise to the skies a work that is devoid of all literary value, as will be proven, some time later, by the indifference, and then the oblivion into which its weakness will inevitably lead it to slide."[7] She had her own axes to grind, sharpened by years of critical neglect, but Zeuxis's trompe-l'oeil grapes weren't her own sour grapes. To be sure, there is an element of satire in some of the language ascribed to the novel's fictional critics, whether in such chestnuts as the claim that banal writing is "done on purpose," or in the cliché that the mark of a good novel is its ability to express "the spirit of our times," or even in the wonderfully vacuous pastiche of the new quasi-structuralist critical discourse of the period, "We have here a movement that abolishes the invisible by blending it with the ambiguity of the signified," and so on.[8]

For those in the know, there may even have been glimpses of recognisable figures, such as the speaker of the statement just quoted in whose bony features and barely moving lips Robbe-Grillet once said he recognised the critic Maurice Blanchot.[9] However, in his illuminating discussion of the novel, there is no hint that Blanchot saw himself depicted in any of the utterances or portraits it contains. The letter Nathalie wrote to him in response to his review expresses genuine gratitude for his perceptiveness: "You have cast light as you know how on what has always seemed to me to be the essential issue." And she continues, "I think that writing is like repeatedly casting a line to reel in something that slips off and hides, and, when you have hauled it up, when it's there, laid out in the light of day, it dies. And then one starts all over again."[10] It was a process she felt Blanchot had understood.

In her view, literary authenticity could be achieved only through sustained exploration and a refusal of the temptation to settle into a single literary formula. In the case of *The Golden Fruits*, this led to the complete elimination of consistently defined characters, and the scenes that make up the novel are populated by unnamed figures who are the bearers of both the critical pronouncements and the tropistic responses to which they give rise. For those on the receiving end, these pronouncements are frequently perceived as dictatorial "arguments from authority." Human relations take the form of power relations, disagreements are construed as heresy or defection, justifying violent reprisal: "We always finish off the wounded, that's the rule here, there's no mercy."[11] Nathalie is not making a case for one kind of fiction (formally and psychologically exploratory) against another (conventionally realist), as she did in the essay, and in the end it is private reading—as distinct from public criticism— which proves to be the ultimate test of literary authenticity.

Reading had always played a vital part in Nathalie's own life. She read slowly and with great concentration, often returning to the same authors. She wasn't interested in "keeping up" and frequently complained about having to read and respond to books sent to her by friends and literary acquaintances. With the exception of one very short review of Michel Butor's *Histoire Extraordinaire* about one of Baudelaire's dreams, she never wrote critical articles about other writers, whom she mentions only incidentally in her essays in order to illuminate aspects of her own work. What mattered to her were readers, and as she later told Isabelle Huppert, "Once I've published something, what I want is for other consciousnesses to say to me: 'It's true.' One reader would be enough."[12]

She kept letters from readers who wrote to say how much her writing had meant to them, that they had discovered literature for the first time through her books, that in them they had found an echo of what they themselves feel, and that her books had become part of the fabric of their lives. When the son of Algerian immigrants wrote from *la banlieue* to say that her books were the only sustenance he had in a cultural desert, Nathalie immediately sent him further copies.[13] One of the most touching and characteristic testimonies comes from an academic critic, Sabine Raffy:

> I think I feel what you write, in the deepest part of what I am, or have become through your books, and I think I feel it accurately. I have an intimate sense of not being mistaken, of knowing exactly where you're leading me, towards what strange places within us, strange and entrancing places. I feel I have grown a great deal inwardly. The first time I read you, when I knew nothing about you, it came as a shock that I shall never forget: am I dreaming, am I inventing what I'm reading, or does someone, at last, somewhere on earth, really feel these things, understand them, see them, write about them? Have I finally encountered a real human being who can give meaning to existence? You opened up a universe in which, finally, I recognised everything, with an overwhelming gratitude.[14]

Nathalie treasured—and frequently repeated—the responses of readers who didn't belong to the cultivated bourgeois world that Beauvoir accused her of portraying. (The detail of the anecdotes varies with each telling.) In addition to the son of Algerian immigrants, there was the Russian worker who told her that *The Planetarium* reminded him of his mother who had a grocer's shop and had always wanted to buy an antique set of table and chairs, but had been prevented from doing so by her husband until he died, at which point she went out and got them. And there was the young man who came to interview her and said, "I'm Tante Berthe, I've just got married, and I get up at night to look at the doorhandles."[15]

The publication of Nathalie's work in paperback editions placed her books within the reach of readers with limited financial resources, including a new student market. *Martereau* came out in this format in 1964, *The Planetarium* in 1965, and *The Golden Fruits* in 1969. *Portrait of an Unknown Man* appeared in the recent 10/18 paperback imprint which specialised in contemporary writing, and *The Age of Suspicion* was one of the earliest titles to be published in Gallimard's *idées* collection launched in 1962 under the general editorship of François Erval. It included a new preface by Nathalie. Subsequent novels appeared in Gallimard's own paperback collection, *folio*, launched in 1972. It was just this kind of democratisation of culture that Nathalie had admired in Cuba's literacy programmes, and which also made her a strong supporter of television.

One of the complaints she would make about critics was that they reviewed her books without actually having read them. Critics and criticism were, however, a reality to which she paid close and anxious attention. The letters she wrote to critics whose reviews she appreciated show how much she relied on their responses for external validation, without which she remained prey to doubt and crippling anxiety. In a letter to Olivier de Magny she begins with an exclamation of relief at being understood: "At last! What reassurance, what security! With rare lucidity, you have understood where my efforts are directed."[16] She expresses a similar sense of relief to Gaëtan Picon after his review of *The Planetarium* in the *Mercure de France*: "After so much doubt and anxiety, which slowed my work down for weeks, I'm finding it difficult to get used to the new happiness you have brought me. Thanks to you I feel, for the first time, that I have finally managed to come close to everything towards which my efforts have for so long been directed. Illuminated and justified by you, my most obscure and tentative aims seem to me now to have become a reality!"[17] Matthieu Galey's review of *It's Beautiful* in 1975 at the Théâtre d'Orsay gave her the reassurance which, even at the age of seventy-five, she still needed "for the threat of death to be removed, and for the thing that at times seemed to have died to receive a life which can never again be taken from it."[18] This dependence on critical recognition didn't spring from vanity, but as Claude Mauriac had sensed, and as she indicates here, was experienced by her as a matter of life and death.

By the same token she could be savage with critics whose views she took issue with. An article by the Russian-born poet and critic Alain Bosquet prompted an indignant phone call from Nathalie, to which he retaliated with equal force by letter: "The other day on the telephone, you gave vent to recriminations which I regard as completely inappropriate." He continues,

> With a lack of subtlety that astonishes me, you divide critics into nice people and nasty people, as if our job consisted in talking about writers on the basis of a sensibility—I'd go so far as to say a susceptibility—that is utterly childish. I beg you to believe that each time it's a task that aims at objectivity, where the author's personality is neither here nor there, and where the sole aim is to report on the true value of the work, an object available to everybody.

Although he defends the principle of a critical objectivity independent of authorial personality, he goes on to say,

> I know you have a sensitivity that people say is pathological; this is unfortunate, especially as I am undoubtedly the last person you have any right to complain about. For the past six years, I have talked constantly about your work in all the countries where my lectures for the Alliance Française have taken me, universities, etc. . . . If I have some reservations about your last novel, "THE PLANETARIUM," it's not out of ignorance or with the imagined aim of wronging you in any way.

In an undated draft Nathalie responds vehemently to the charge of pathological sensitivity:

> What can I say? I do not like making what the English call "personal remarks" in which they correctly see an elementary lack of courtesy, and your letter contains plenty of these. . . .
>
> As for your reproach that I am pathologically sensitive—this is rich coming from the pen of a critic addressing a writer. I assume that the "people" who say I am pathologically sensitive can only refer to readers

who confuse characters in novels with their authors. Surely no critic, as I don't think any has ever received the least word of reproach from me, and you are the first to whom I have spoken my mind: your inconsiderateness has finally driven me to it. I'd be curious to know if there is an author, the happy possessor of a "normal" sensitivity who, after an article like yours would continue to number you among his friends.[19]

Things were evidently patched up between them—as they almost always were after this kind of falling out—and a few years later Nathalie thanked Bosquet warmly for a volume of his poems which bore an "inscription by which I was very touched."[20]

Others who were not directly involved had more perspicacity about her sensitivity to critical comment about her work. One such was the novelist Béatrix Beck, whom Nathalie met on one of her North American lecture tours. Beck's 1978 novel *Noli* portrays Nathalie in the character of Prisca Darfeuil. Far more sympathetically delineated than Beauvoir's Paula, Prisca is credited with "a discovery as important as [Stendhal's] cristallisation or [Proust's] intermittences of the heart"—i.e., the tropism—and insightfully described as having "such an anxious, demanding nature, because she doubted herself so powerfully, and admired my admiration for her."[21] This admiration for those who admired her work was genuine and generous, if often tinged with anxiety. At Nathalie's instigation, many of these critics became personal friends. The literary critic Georges Raillard recalled that his own friendship with her began when, the morning after the publication of his essay on *The Planetarium* in the journal *Littérature* in 1971, he received a phone call from Nathalie, whom he didn't know personally, to say that they should meet.[22]

In addition to acknowledgement that her books were "true," she appreciated comments that illuminated dimensions of her work, which she had not herself been fully aware of. While she considered that the creative impulse had its roots in the unconscious and could be destroyed by excessive clarity, she treasured—and would repeat—insights such as Yvon Belaval's comment that *Tropisms* captured "creation in its nascent state."[23] Perhaps on the strength of his review, Belaval and his partner Mimica Cranaki were commissioned by Gallimard to write the first monograph on Nathalie's work. It appeared in the publisher's new *Bibliothèque idéale* series aimed at "a general literary readership" and devoted to the great contemporary writers who "should be in every good [personal] library."

The book came out in 1965. As long-standing friends of hers, the authors had ample opportunity to consult Nathalie and to involve her in the selection of extracts from her work, which make up almost half the volume. She supplied all the photos, and must have contributed substantially to the bibliography, which contains a striking proportion of articles by critics in Germany, the United Kingdom, Denmark, Portugal, the United States, Switzerland, Belgium, Yugoslavia, and even one from the Soviet Union, as if to emphasise the extent of the recognition she had received outside France.

Although the series usually addressed "the life" as well as "the work," Nathalie resisted any discussion of the life, and categorically rejected Belaval's suggestion that she contribute "a small Confession . . . , in the style of Jean-Jacques [Rousseau] (less brazen, no doubt), running to 10 or 12 pages," which he had fondly imagined would be interesting for her to write and, which, being previously unpublished, would add to the appeal of the volume. She evidently also rejected his alternative proposal for a "montage" of information about her to be culled from interviews, articles, and her work.[24] With the exception of a brief biographical sketch—whose contents were presumably supplied by its subject and do not include her date of birth—the monograph is entirely devoted to the work. Only the photographs, which include several from Nathalie's childhood, one of the group at the summit of Mont Blanc, another of her three children, and one of her in 1940, several of Chérence, and one with the Russian poet Victor Nekrasov, tell their own unspoken biographical story. The frontispiece is the portrait photograph from *Vogue*.

At around the same time she was in regular contact with the Belgian literary and art critic, René Micha. After hearing from Marcel Arland that Micha was preparing an article about her for the *NRF*, she had requested that he get in touch before writing the piece.[25] There ensued an active exchange of letters in which Nathalie expressed appreciation of his critical acumen and answered questions from him before he submitted a draft of his article for her approval. She subsequently thanked him for taking account of her ideas, which had been enhanced by his own insights along with his "constant and generous friendship."[26] For her, this combination of perspicacity, generosity, and friendship was the ideal component of any critical response to her work.

However, convinced that her books were all too often read on the basis of assumptions that falsified them, she continued to provide Micha with commentary about her writing—mostly in the form of letters—on which he drew for two further articles and for his own book-length critical study, published in 1966.[27] He clearly understood the importance of these letters, which he later donated to the Bibliothèque nationale. Nathalie once again supplied the bibliography, and for the unavoidable biographical component she directed Micha to the Belaval and Cranaki volume, with all the diffidence that is conveyed in her remark that "As regards biography— I find nothing quite as deadly."[28] Her request to see the book in proof seems not to have been met, but she was pleased by the published result, and read it carefully enough to note the mistranscriptions of quotations from her work, a list of which she passed on to its author.

CHAPTER TWENTY-FOUR

Friendships

FRIENDSHIPS HAD ALWAYS MATTERED a great deal to Nathalie, and, apart from her family, friendship constituted the emotional focus of her life. As life and work became ever more inseparable, critics became friends, and friends were more and more likely also to be critics. Or, in some cases, fellow writers. The exceptions to this combination were Nathalie's oldest friends, particularly Lena, Nadia, and Assia. The death of Lena in March 1961, just as Nathalie was emerging from TB and her own brush with death, was an enormous loss.[1] Lena had been a link to a now distant past, when Nathalie was escaping from family life into independence through Oxford, mountaineering, and the apartment in the Boulevard Raspail, all of which they shared. There is little material trace of this friendship, which Nathalie later said had been of great personal and moral as distinct from intellectual importance.[2] As Lena lived in Nice, contact was maintained by telephone and the occasional visit. Nathalie had consulted her about the difficulties with Simone de Beauvoir, but Lena was too far removed from Nathalie's literary world to understand its intricacies. However, perhaps as a kind of talisman, Nathalie took her friend's spectacles with her to the United States in 1964 and wore them to deliver her lectures.[3]

After Nadia du Bouchet returned from the United States in 1947, she and Nathalie saw each other frequently in both Chérence and Paris, where Nadia, who was now widowed, worked as an anaesthetist. She was, however, connected to the literary world through her son, André du Bouchet. Relations between Nathalie and André soured at some point during the 1950s, as is indicated in an anxious letter from André, whose perplexity and distress are familiar from other instances of Nathalie's apparently inexplicable repudiations:

> I feel I am on a very slippery slope, at whose end I will have lost your friendship. This would affect me more than I am able—or apparently have been able—to tell you. Anyway, perhaps, if you were willing to see me in Paris rather than in Chérence—and if there is still time, I will tell you, even if your complaints are justified a thousand times over, how much it means to me. I will telephone you, and you can tell me if it's worth meeting.[4]

The rift may have been due in part to the breakup of Du Bouchet's marriage to Tina Jolas. However, good relations were eventually restored, and in later years Nathalie wrote with evident affection to "My dear, most dear André," to say, "You know how much you exist in my life and that doesn't change, which you also know."[5]

Friendship with Nathalie was often precarious, and several friends—particularly women friends—found that, like André du Bouchet, they had inadvertently crossed some invisible line and incurred Nathalie's wrath. The postcard to which it is a reply has not survived, but a letter from Mimica Cranaki is typical of the bafflement that others later expressed in the face of Nathalie's opprobrium:

> Quick, quick, quick. I've just received your card. Several hypotheses:
>
> 1) Either you *really* believe what you say and that grieves me greatly. Because I didn't think that this kind of fantasy could re-emerge, at least not between us. What can I tell you that you don't already know? Not a day passes where we don't think about you, talk about you (dually), watch out for the least article, the least reference to you (Natacha). Yvon [Belaval] can tell you how proud I am to do so. . . .
>
> 2) Or else you don't believe a word of what you say, and you're just teasing me. But in that case, you're rubbing salt into the wound: I've been meaning to write to you for weeks now, and I feel guiltier about it every day. I try to console myself with the idea that per-

haps, down there, in the sun, my God, the memory of your Paris friends might fade. Which leads me to my third hypothesis.

3) It's a mix of the two, i.e. you don't seriously think that . . . but you like people to keep telling you. I understand so well! . . .

Are you reassured now?[6]

On this occasion too, things were evidently patched up, but the pattern recurred.

Assia was Nathalie's oldest friend, and their relations were more volatile than those with Lena and Nadia. Although Assia had settled in New York, they remained in regular contact. Shortly after the war Nathalie wrote to Assia to remind her of the deep attachment she always felt for her, and promised to help her find an apartment if she came to Paris. In the course of a conversation in 1986, Nathalie told her friend that "our meeting is something very special in life." However, Assia notes that her relationship with Nathalie was the most troubled of her own close friendships, and after one of their transatlantic telephone calls, she remarks on "the irreparable ambivalence of our relations."[7]

This ambivalence surfaced on the occasion when Assia stepped out of the role of friend and took on that of critic, publishing two articles about Nathalie's work in academic journals in the United States. Signed in the name of Anne Minor, they are remarkably perceptive and elegant pieces of writing, but to judge from one of the few surviving letters from Assia, Nathalie wasn't happy about this intervention: "Will you be in Paris in the 2nd week of June? Do you want to see me? would you like to meet somewhere else? You could work and I would read. We'll finally be able to talk. . . . My great wish is to see you again. I have thought about you a lot. Agreed—and you will probably never forgive me for it—to write about your books."[8] This was in 1961, but their friendship recovered, and Assia was instrumental in facilitating Nathalie's trip to the United States in 1964, when Nathalie found her "adorable" and was very touched by her affection.[9]

The friendship with Maria Jolas, who was also her translator and informal literary agent, seems never to have suffered from such ambivalence. Meanwhile, Nathalie's new literary involvements brought new friendships, one of the least troubled being with the novelist and militant feminist, Françoise d'Eaubonne, who wrote a long review of *The Planetarium* for *Les Temps modernes* which—predictably, given relations between Nathalie and Simone de Beauvoir—never appeared. D'Eaubonne's close friendship with Beauvoir didn't hinder her amicable dealings with Nathalie, because she appreciated her work on its own terms and was clear-sighted enough to see that the antipathy between the two writers derived—at least in part—from incompatible literary principles. She later described her meeting with Nathalie as "the most decisive event of 1959," and she considered Nathalie to be "the greatest [female] prose-writer of the century."[10]

They met regularly in the 1960s, exchanged books, and defended each other in public as circumstances required. When d'Eaubonne was sued for defamation by another writer for the way he had been portrayed in her recent memoirs, she asked Nathalie to provide a deposition "protesting that my book is good, that I'm a respectable author, an honest person, etc." She adds that "signed with your prestigious name, it would give me precious support [in court]." D'Eaubonne returned the favour several years later when—almost certainly at Nathalie's request—she sent a letter to *Le Canard enchaîné* objecting to their review of the 1993 production of Nathalie's plays *Silence* and *It Is There*, which the irreverent journal had described in as "a liturgy of boredom."[11] Nathalie admired d'Eaubonne's energies, which were devoted as much to politics as to literature: she signed the *Manifesto of the 121*, cofounded the French Women's Liberation Movement (the MLF), participated in the *Manifesto of the 343* demanding the legalisation of abortion, created the Homosexual Front for Revolutionary Action (the FHAR), coined the term *phallocrat*, and was one the founders of ecofeminism. Her politics were more extreme than Nathalie's, but d'Eaubonne's generosity and lack of self-importance were qualities that she always appreciated.

Many of Nathalie's new friends were more than a generation younger, being the same age as her children, and in some instances even younger. Geneviève Bollème, author of an unpublished article on *The Golden Fruits*, born in 1927, was the same age as Claude.

She and Nathalie were introduced through Gaëtan Picon, for whom Bollème acted as assistant, both at the *Mercure de France* where he became editor, and at the École Pratique des Hautes Etudes, where she completed a thesis on Flaubert. Many of the literary-minded women of her generation combined academic work with literary journalism, and their own creative writing. This was the case with Lucette Finas, Béatrix Beck, Monique Wittig, and, later on, Françoise Asso, all of whom also wrote about Nathalie, and all of whom became personal friends. Letters from Bollème, which start in 1959, suggest a close and affectionate relationship with both Nathalie and Raymond, but she too found herself on the receiving end of one of Nathalie's rebuffs when Nathalie accused her of overfamiliarity, remarking rather brutally, "Nous n'avons pas gardé les chèvres ensemble" (*lit.* We never looked after goats together). Bollème later wrote a book, *Parler d'écrire* (Speaking of writing), where she recognises that the curiosity of the non-writer or the would-be writer might be felt by the actual writer as an attempt to appropriate his carefully guarded secret. Perhaps this was the case with Nathalie.[12]

It was not a concern that Nathalie needed to have with either Mary McCarthy or the English writer Christine Brooke-Rose, since both were already established as novelists when she made their acquaintance in the 1960s. Mary McCarthy had moved to Paris in 1961 where her husband worked for the Organisation for Economic Cooperation and Development. In June 1962 she wrote to Hannah Arendt to say that "the only French person I'd really *like* to meet is Nathalie Sarraute."[13] McCarthy and Nathalie then became acquainted—thanks to Arendt—and by December they had struck up a friendship, which nonetheless retained a degree of mutual wariness. Although McCarthy supported *The Golden Fruits* for the Prix International de Littérature in 1964, their literary talents had little in common, McCarthy's being, in the words of her biographer, essentially critical, and Nathalie's inventive. McCarthy herself spontaneously acknowledged that her writing was not in any way experimental.[14] The two new friends saw each other regularly, often for lunch, sometimes with other writers, including Monique Wittig, whom McCarthy met through Nathalie. McCarthy mentioned to

FIGURE 22. Mary McCarthy interviewed by Jean-François Revel, *New York Times*, 16 May 1971. © Bruno Barbey, Magnum Photos.

Hannah Arendt (with whom she says Nathalie was "smitten") that they had discovered similarities between Nathalie's mother and Mc-Carthy's Morganstern grandmother, right down to their face-lifting scars.[15] She also met—and took to—Jean-François Revel, Nathalie's writer-journalist son-in-law (Claude's third husband), who published an interview with McCarthy in the *New York Times* in 1971.

Nathalie's dislike of Simone de Beauvoir made a "strangely unpleasant impression" on McCarthy, who, in another letter to Arendt, says that when the subject arose there was "malice in [Nathalie's] sharp face [which] was like a kind of voracious greed." Arendt takes a more sympathetic view, and responds by saying, "I think I can understand Sarraute's 'malice'; to live somehow together with these characters in power and command must not be easy." A couple of months later (in 1965) McCarthy writes, "Nathalie and I have become much more easy with each other."[16] And in July 1969, helped perhaps by this rapprochement, McCarthy published a long and appreciative review of the English translation of Nathalie's fifth novel, *Between Life and Death*, in the *New York Review of Books*.

Nathalie was reportedly "very, very enthusiastic, oh yes, *deeply, really*."[17] In return, she had recommended one of McCarthy's novels to Gallimard, but apparently with no success, since *Birds of America* eventually came out with Laffont (very likely thanks to Revel) in 1972. It was at this point that McCarthy seriously considered buying a house in Chérence. Two letters to Nathalie in July and October 1969 speak enthusiastically of the prospect, but practical complications eventually put paid to the plan.[18] Had the sale come off, the relationship with Nathalie might not have foundered the way it eventually did.

Tensions arose over their differences with regard to Israel (on which more in chapter 29), but the friendship came to an end in April 1973 following a hostile review of the English translation of *Do You Hear Them?* in the *New York Review of Books* by the English critic and academic John Weightman. Nathalie had met Weightman at Gadoffre's Château d'Eu gathering in 1956, but she held both McCarthy and Arendt responsible for having failed to recommend a more sympathetically inclined reviewer to the *NYRB*—not that either of them as occasional contributors to the journal had any say in what was an editorial matter. A decade later Nathalie's sense of betrayal was undiminished, as is spelled out in somewhat inappropriate detail in a letter to Robert Silvers, editor of the *NYRB*, where She accuses her erstwhile friend of having expressed insufficient indignation about the review and, more generally, of possessing "a certain aggressiveness towards me." She adds that McCarthy had not responded to Nathalie's subsequent overtures and had refused to view her outrage about the review as simply being "part of the kind of 'Spring-cleaning' that maintains friendship."[19]

According to McCarthy, the problems were more general: "[Nathalie] wanted to break with me. I think that she perhaps just got sick of me, of our friendship and those weekly lunches. . . . Maybe this is true of many of her friendships; a moment comes when she wants to break, and with a paranoid psychology it's not hard to find a reason." With more ambivalence she adds, "I liked her as a person, I still do, except that she's mad, and of course it's really obvious in the books, too. . . . But she has a really pleasing voice and a marvellous face."[20] After McCarthy died in 1989, Nathalie reciprocated with her own perspective on their friendship, tempered no doubt by the fact that the record was now posthumous:

> There was a time when Mary and I didn't see much of each other. And then we saw each other again. I began to see her again because with time you forget things and I liked her very much. I loved her in a way. I was so sorry when I heard how ill she was. The last time I saw her, when I went to her house for dinner, she really looked tired. Mary seemed to know that life was unbearable, but she had parties anyway. She was more than brave. She was gallant.[21]

The literary differences between the two novelists were matched by differences in temperament. McCarthy was brisker and more pragmatic than Nathalie, whose vulnerability and fear of misrepresentation inclined her, as Béatrix Beck had observed, to demand unconditional endorsement from those she assumed were in a position to provide it.

Nathalie's friendship with the English novelist Christine Brooke-Rose was considerably less fraught. They first met in England during the 1961 tour organised by John Calder at a time when Brooke-Rose was still writing in the style of the British fiction that Rayner Heppenstall had deplored in the *Times Literary Supplement*. She then changed literary direction, and, inspired by the example of the French Nouveau Roman, became one of the few English novelists to adopt an experimental approach. Writing to Nathalie in 1964, she tells her, "You have influenced me greatly, along with Robbe-Grillet and Samuel Beckett."[22] She also asks whether Nathalie would be willing to read the manuscript of her latest novel (*Out*) and consider recommending it to Minuit. There's no record of Nathalie's reply—this was not the sort of role that she enjoyed—and it was several years before any translation of Brooke-Rose's work appeared in France, even after she had settled there permanently in 1968.

In 1966 Brooke-Rose wrote to Nathalie to reiterate that, despite her interest in Robbe-Grillet (about whom she had written and some of whose work she also translated), her admiration for Nathalie was unalloyed:

> Dear, dear Nathalie, . . . please believe how much I admire you and owe to you, I have said it and will say it again. It is possible as you know to

admire different writers for different things or in different ways. . . . It is also possible to admire a writer without adopting his solutions—like you vis-à-vis Ivy Compton-Burnett for instance. Your essays and your work (especially *The Planetarium*) were a revelation to me. And if I later also read other French writers and other essays on the New Novel, the first impetus, the first hunger to know, to think, to rethink everything I had been doing, was due to you.

Nathalie evidently agreed to write a report for Gallimard on Brooke-Rose's 1966 novel, *Such*, but as with Mary McCarthy's *Birds of America*, her word didn't carry enough weight to convince the publisher to take on either of these Anglophone authors.[23] Along with her commitment to literary experiment, Brooke-Rose's difficulties in finding a publisher in France and an audience in England were more than sufficient reason to elicit sympathy rather than suspicion from Nathalie. There is little written record of Brooke-Rose's critical appreciation of Nathalie's fiction, but Nathalie's engagement diaries indicate that their acquaintance continued at least up until 1977. For her part, Brooke-Rose's letters reveal a keen and confiding friendship, and her literary and personal temperaments combined to make her one of the critic-friends on whom Nathalie felt her work depended.

Brooke-Rose was appointed to the new Université de Vincennes, created after May 1968, where she was one of an innovative group of teachers and writers whom the writer and theorist Hélène Cixous assembled in the department of literature. These included Lucette Finas, who published an article on Nathalie's work in *Tel Quel* in 1965 and became another of Nathalie's critic-friends, or as she aptly styled herself in a letter to Nathalie in 1980, "your faithful Lucette— *lectrice amicissima.*" An earlier letter from Finas about *The Golden Fruits* pinpoints very astutely the qualities exemplified in Nathalie's work, along with those that it required of loyal reader-friends: "Your books are . . . prohibited for those who have not been seared by anxiety [*inquiétude*] (especially the rare and exalted form of anxiety that is yours: a sensitivity towards ideas, and their metamorphosis in the opinions of others). Only anxiety attaches such value to contact and assent."[24] Finas's comment provides a more insightful gloss on the phenomenon that Alain Bosquet had dismissed as Nathalie's "pathological sensitivity." Contact, endorsement, and a shared experience of anxiety were qualities that predisposed readers to Nathalie's fictional world where, to quote the title of Mary McCarthy's review of *Between Life and Death*, things were always felt to be "hanging by a thread."

The most enduring and undoubtedly the most important of Nathalie's friendships from this period of her life was with Monique Wittig, who was her junior by thirty-five years. Wittig's first novel, *The Opoponax*, won the Prix Médicis in 1964, when Nathalie was still on the prize committee. The book bears no obvious resemblance to Nathalie's writing, but in a long letter dating from 1992, Wittig recalled her decisive encounter with Nathalie's work at the age of twenty-six. After buying *Tropismes* in a bookshop in the Latin Quarter, she opened it immediately and was so affected by the power of the words she read that she almost fainted in the street. What she appreciated above all was Nathalie's treatment of language. For her it was a unique experience, which nourished her for years, filling her with a desire to understand it in ways that didn't interest linguists, or literary critics, or semiologists. In Nathalie she had found the ideal guide for her own writing.[25]

Wittig's literary debt is explicit here. But there was something else, a more extreme version of the response to Nathalie's writing that other readers described, and which, in an earlier letter Wittig defines quite simply as "love." (She was one of the few friends other than those Nathalie made in childhood with whom Nathalie used the *tu* form.) This was more than the sense of having something in common with another writer, and much more than admiration on the part of a novice for a writer she regarded as incomparable. When they had finally met following the Médicis award ceremony, the reality of Nathalie in person proved to be the same as the Nathalie of the writing. It was a deeply moving experience for Wittig and the start of a lifelong friendship. A note in Nathalie's hand on Wittig's letter specifies "Keep."[26]

Marguerite Duras and Claude Simon, who were also on the Médicis committee, both published articles about Wittig's novel, as did Mary McCarthy when the English translation came out. But true to her reticence in these matters, Nathalie never wrote about either

FIGURE 23. With Monique Wittig, Chérence. © Sande Zeig.

The Opoponax or any other of Wittig's books, and she confined her-self to mentioning in interviews how much she had liked the novel for the originality of its portrayal of childhood. In reality, she had a deep and unwavering admiration for *The Opoponax*, which in her view was in a class of its own in contemporary French fiction. As she wrote to Wittig, "I admire your exceptional talent very deeply. If you had written nothing else, your book would be an entire oeuvre in itself."[27]

The friendship with Wittig lasted for the rest of Nathalie's life, and proved to be the deepest and the most unambivalent of those that date from these years. In a rare declaration of private feeling, she writes, "You matter a great deal to me." Their relations were both literary and personal, and Nathalie's literary admiration was matched by an equal admiration for Wittig's existential ethic: "I admire the way you are, the strength and rectitude with you choose and conduct your life. I think all this very sincerely." Wittig was everything Beauvoir was not, and despite the three-and-a-half-decade age difference, it was a relationship of absolute equals. As

Nathalie comments, "I can see nothing but perfect equality and reciprocity in our friendship. Years—and it's very heartening—make no difference to this."[28]

It's striking how cosmopolitan many of these friendships were. Nathalie never lost her awareness of wider horizons lying beyond the confines of the Parisian literary world. Lena, Nadia, and Assia were Russian; Assia was now in the United States; Maria Jolas was American but domiciled in France; Mimica Cranaki and Matsie Hadjilazaros were exiles from Greece; while Mary McCarthy and Christine Brooke-Rose were in self-chosen exile from the United States and the United Kingdom respectively. In 1976 Wittig, who didn't have the *agrégation* (the prerequisite for an academic post in France), became another of these voluntary exiles when she moved to the United States, where she taught in various universities.

The majority of these friendships were with women. Despite their growing presence in the literary and cultural world, women continued to be perceived as peripheral, pushing a number of them to political action. Both d'Eaubonne and Wittig joined the MLF in the late 1960s and both were openly lesbian, which compounded their marginal status as women. Despite her bourgeois address in the sixteenth arrondissement and her lawyer husband, Nathalie felt a natural kinship with all forms of marginality.

Where men were concerned, friendships tended to be cooler. Nathalie placed less demand on her male friends for endorsement of her work, and friendship was not incompatible with a certain literary reserve on their part. This apparently applied to Ponge, about whom Nathalie later said, "There is someone I liked a great deal as a writer, and as a man too, and that's Francis Ponge. We had nothing in common. I'm even convinced that he didn't like what I write. But that didn't matter to me."[29] (This was despite his positive written responses to her books.) Jean Blot, whom Nathalie first met on her lecture trip to Switzerland in 1959, never concealed his reservations about her work, but this did not spoil the friendship that she and Raymond had with Blot and his Russian wife Nadia, as they met regularly for dinner and holidayed together on the Greek island of Skyros.[30]

Another of these friendships was with Gaëtan Picon. Nathalie appreciated Picon's reviews of her novels, and he felt a particular affinity with her writing. This mutual appreciation became the basis for a closer personal affinity, where Picon would confide in Nathalie about the difficulties of his official responsibilities as Directeur gé-néral des Arts et des Lettres in the Ministry of National Education and director of the École des hautes études en sciences sociales, which, as he confessed in a letter to Nathalie in January 1963, he found increasingly burdensome. His distress elicited an immediate response from Nathalie:

> I received your letter this morning. Will you believe me this time? I'm unable to express myself in a letter. However sincere my feelings, as soon as I try and express them in a letter, I find them somewhat stiff, contrived and artificial. I just want to tell you that I think I understand you thoroughly, that I feel everything you feel—completely—and not because I have some gift of second sight, but because I have experienced almost to the limit the same distress (the word is very feeble). In the end I gave up trying to choose and decided to live as best I could on two levels. . . .
>
> ~~I am very aware that what was required of me externally cannot be compared to what is required of you. But I have and still have the impression of being threatened with destruction whatever I do one way or another~~
>
> It was as if you were talking all about me. One feels so terribly confined and isolated here. You have managed, with such generous spontaneity, to knock a hole in the wall between us: and I must restrain the impulse to rush through and join you.
>
> I'm afraid of importuning you with this letter. There are times when one doesn't want contact of any kind. Perhaps this is what you feel at the moment. In which case, forgive me.
>
> All I ask is that when you feel a need to talk about yourself ~~i.e. us~~ you remember that I am close to you and that I like you very much.
>
> Nathalie[31]

Nathalie was capable of offering a sympathetic ear to friends who found themselves in emotional distress. Tina Jolas was one such, and in letters to Nathalie, she speaks of "the trust and the secret understanding between us" and describes her as "mysteriously benevolent and consoling."[32] Friendship, on which Nathalie thrived, brought out many sides of her character, which Tina's daughter Paule du Bouchet recalled as being essentially "multicoloured."[33]

CHAPTER TWENTY-FIVE

"The Heroine of Post-Stalin Russia," 1960–67

A NEW DIMENSION was added to Nathalie's life when, with the easing of the political climate in the Soviet Union, she renewed contact with the country that she had left half a century previously and of which she had had a brief and horrified glimpse in 1935. This reconnection began tentatively in August 1956, when she spent a week as a tourist visiting friends and family. The trip was almost certainly prompted by Polina's death in May, and it allowed Nathalie to renew links with surviving relatives whom she had not seen for twenty years: Lola Shatunovskaya, the daughter of Nathalie's Uncle Grisha from Kamianets-Podilskyi, Berta Petrovna Tcherniak, a Tcherniak cousin, and two of Berta's nephews who in later correspondence address Nathalie as "Tyotya [Aunt] Natacha."[1] Berta was the daughter of Pierre Tcherniak, whom Nathalie had met on her visit to the Soviet Union in 1936. Her return in the summer of 1956 was undoubtedly facilitated by the "thaw" that followed Stalin's death in 1953 and was made unofficially official by Khrushchev's denunciation of Stalin in the so-called Secret Speech at the Twentieth Congress of the Communist Party of the Soviet Union in February 1956.

The brief stay left her with two very different visions of her native country. The first was of a Soviet Russia bearing few signs of any relaxation despite the thaw. "Stalin was dead," she recalled in a later interview, "but it was horrible."[2] The letter she wrote to Sartre about Russia in November 1956 suggests that her view was coloured not only by the Soviet invasion of Hungary in October, but by the discoveries she had recently made through members of her family about the deportations of the 1930s, confirming everything she had intuited on her previous visit.[3] The other vision was of a traditional and timeless Russia, vividly captured in a scene she described to Claude Mauriac:

> With friends, on the terrace of a dacha, by a lake, like in *The Seagull* ... one friend wearing the traditional embroidered shirt with the closed collar.... An old lady who had always been there ... and, although there was no samovar (they don't exist any more in the USSR, it takes too long to make tea with them, you have to get up early, and gas is more convenient), there, with these friends, I had such an extraordinary sense of being in an eternal Russia, that I closed my eyes with emotion, in ecstasy.[4]

Who these friends were she does not say, but the sense of connection with a Russian past is palpable. In a radio interview in 1960, she mentions having returned to the place where she grew up (now Leningrad) and having encountered smells she remembered from the years she spent there as a child: "the mustiness of some of the rooms from my childhood, the way people smell, the furs." She was also reminded of the more direct form of human relations favoured by Russians:

> When I go back to Russia, ... I'm struck by the abrasive honesty of my compatriots. Their liking for truth makes them say things straight out. If someone doesn't like you, you know immediately. The first time I went back to Russia, I was still young, but when they saw me my cousins burst out: "God, you've aged!" In France, even after a long absence, people would have said: "You don't look a day older." It might not have been true, but it would have been kinder.[5]

Back in Paris, she saw Eisenstein's *Alexander Nevsky* and *Battleship Potemkin* in October 1958, attended a Soviet Music Hall show in November 1959, heard a BBC concert of Soviet choirs in March

1960, and, in 1961, visited a Soviet exhibition, saw more Soviet films, and went to a performance of Soviet ballet. These were all signs of a general revival of Franco-Soviet relations, and are noted in Nathalie's engagement diaries where in every case the "Soviet" specification is hers.[6] Yet despite her apparent appetite for Soviet culture, an article on Tolstoy, published in the communist newspaper *Les Lettres françaises* in September 1960, is a pretext for Nathalie to condemn Socialist Realism, which she sees as modelling itself on the falsely realist aesthetic of Tolstoy's fiction, and ignoring the greater, more challenging realism of Dostoevsky's writing.[7]

Thanks to the thaw (so called after Ilya Ehrenburg's novel *The Thaw*, published in 1954), Socialist Realism was also being undermined on Soviet territory. Ehrenburg himself challenged the orthodoxy in a speech at the Soviet Writers Congress in the same year, and his views were echoed in 1956 by the writer Konstantin Paustovsky in a speech whose text then circulated privately. In 1959 Andrei Sinyavsky, who worked at the Gorky Institute for World Literature in Moscow, smuggled a harsh critique of Socialist Realism to the West, where it was published under a pseudonym. Nathalie subsequently became friends with all three.

The renewal of her links with Russia soon led to an introduction to Soviet literary circles. From 1959 Nathalie was in contact with one Olga Kraevskaya at the Union of Soviet Writers, and it was probably through Kraevskaya that arrangements were made for her to visit the Soviet Union in 1960.[8] In the course of this stay, about which no details have been preserved beyond a mention in the Chronology for the *Complete Works*, she became acquainted with a number of Russian writers. Several of them then visited Paris and refer in correspondence to having met Nathalie there. They include Boris Agapov, who started life as a constructivist poet and later became a travel writer; Nikolai Pogodin, a playwright whose first play had been about the building of a tractor plant; and Lev Sheinin, author of detective novels noted for their compliance with party ideology, and a onetime supporter of Stalin and senior prosecuting investigator, who had been arrested on Stalin's orders before being freed to investigate Jews accused of Zionism. All three were sufficiently well regarded by the Soviet regime to have acquired permission to travel abroad, and they all maintained contact with Nathalie by letter. (Unlike her exchanges with correspondents in other countries, which she conducts almost exclusively in French, Nathalie's letters to Russians are always in Russian.) Agapov writes in January 1961 asking her to send him copies of her books, and invites her to visit when she next comes to the Soviet Union.[9]

This took place in December 1961, when she spent three weeks in Moscow and Leningrad as a guest of the Union of Soviet Writers. The stay transformed Nathalie's view of Soviet Russia. In an article she wrote in Russian and published in the *Literaturnaya Gazeta* in January 1962, she comments in glowing terms on changes that have taken place since her visit in 1956: the standard of living has risen significantly, the appearance of streets, shops, and theatres has vastly improved, and people are much better dressed. (She always noticed how people dressed.) But what strikes her most is the change in human relations. Social divisions have altogether vanished, there is "evident equality in relations between people," and absolutely no sign of any "exclusion."[10]

These were issues that mattered to Nathalie, and her remarks about the Soviet Union on this occasion are very similar to those she made about Cuba a few months earlier. As in Cuba, she was impressed by the cultural appetite of the Soviet population. She admired the apparent devotion to literature, supported by generous provision of books in factory libraries, and shared equally by "men and women, young and old, engineers and workers."[11] Her hosts would have ensured that contemporary Soviet life was shown off to its best advantage, and Nathalie herself was no doubt aware that an article in the official organ of the Union of Soviet Writers was expected to strike a positive note. But this new perspective on the Soviet Union contributed to making her, in the words of Jean Blot, if not actively pro-Soviet, then quite definitely not anti-Soviet.[12]

The three weeks spent in Moscow and Leningrad gave her opportunities to meet many more Soviet writers, critics, and journalists. She visited the Institute for World Literature where she would have come across Andrei Sinyavsky; the editorial office of *Literaturnaya Gazeta*; and the offices of the journal *Inostrannaya Literatura*, which later published short extracts from *The Planetarium*, albeit accompanied by a somewhat negative introductory gloss. An editor's note appended to Nathalie's article in the *Liter-anurnaya Gazeta* also comments on the alleged shortcomings of the Nouveau Roman, but overall, Nathalie found "a very lively and benevolent interest in all the new things that are happening in French literature."[13] She was invited to lecture on 28 December and mentions interest on the part of the Philological Faculty in Leningrad University.

But it was the personal links that counted most. Nathalie's engagement diary for these three weeks is filled with names and telephone numbers, noting, amongst others, a visit to Sheinin in his dacha, dinner with Pogodin, and a meeting with Agapov. She also saw somewhat less conformist writers, such as Ilya Ehrenburg, whom she may already have met in Paris. Viktor Nekrasov, whose photograph she included in the Cranaki and Belaval monograph, was another new and even more nonconformist acquaintance, as his novels were a clear departure from Socialist Realism and had become markedly anti-Stalinist. Perhaps after discovering how much their past had in common, Ehrenburg gave her an inscribed copy of the French translation of his memoirs, *Men, Years, Life*, published in 1962, where she could read his evocations of émigré Paris at the turn of the century and Berlin in the 1920s.

Nathalie's ability to speak Russian—which by all accounts, including that of the poet Yevtushenko, she did very well—set her apart from most other French writers. And it facilitated her entry into Soviet literary life, where, as the French writer Jean-Pierre Faye put it, she knew "everyone" and became "the heroine of post-Stalin Russia."[14] Between 1961 and 1967, she made frequent visits to the Soviet Union, almost always to Moscow or Leningrad, and once to Kiev, where her father had studied, and where she was warmly received by the Ukrainian poet Nikolai Bazhan and his wife Nina. In her way, Nathalie had become as much part of the Soviet literary world as her mother had been in Saint Petersburg half a century previously. She was there often enough for John Calder to recall several lunches at 12 Avenue Pierre 1ᵉ de Serbie, where they ate caviar that Nathalie had brought back from the Soviet Union.[15]

She does not seem to have been unduly intimidated by Soviet surveillance, a reality she was confronted with on the occasion when, having gone out without her spectacles, she returned to her hotel room to fetch them from her suitcase, which she had left locked. Mystified to discover that when she put the glasses on she couldn't see, she put them back, re-locked the suitcase, and left, only to find normal vision restored on her return in the evening. Her Soviet minder had accidentally exchanged her own spectacles with Nathalie's during a search of her possessions.[16]

Back in France, her links with Soviet writers also acquired a semiofficial component. After publishing a French translation of Pasternak's *Doctor Zhivago* in 1958, Gallimard responded to the growing French interest in Soviet culture by expanding their list of Russian authors. Brice Parain, a long-standing member of the editorial committee who also read Russian, was charged with identifying suitable titles. Nathalie knew Parain through his Russian first wife Natalia Tchelpanova—an illustrator—and from 1961 she and Parain met regularly after she was co-opted for this venture. In 1962 Gallimard appointed Louis Aragon to edit a new series devoted specifically to Soviet writers, which subsequently published titles by Vasily Aksyonov and Konstantin Paustovsky, both of whom figured among Nathalie's Soviet acquaintances. There was no love lost between Nathalie and Aragon (nor between her and his Russian-born wife Elsa Triolet), and it's not clear how seriously she took her role as editorial advisor, but in letters to Claude Gallimard she reported briefly on a number of books, and as late as 1969 Paustovsky's translator sent Nathalie a list of titles in response to her request for recommendations.[17]

The high point in Franco-Soviet literary relations came in August 1963 with an international conference of European writers held in Leningrad. Organised by COMES, the short-lived Community of European Writers, whose aim was to promote opportunities for authors on both sides of the Iron Curtain to explore issues of common interest, the subject of the 1963 meeting was "The Modern Novel." Invitations were issued to one hundred participants, and the names of Nathalie Sarraute, Robbe-Grillet, and Butor, put forward by the French, were accepted by the Union of Soviet Writers, who hosted the occasion. As Butor was unable to attend, the French delegation consisted of Nathalie, Robbe-Grillet, the poet André Frénaud, and Bernard Pingaud, secretary of the French section of COMES, whom Nathalie knew from her brief association with the Prix de Mai.

Sartre and Beauvoir received separate invitations from the Union of Soviet Writers, and Sartre gave the closing address.

The occasion was one of the last in the "decade of euphoria" marking Soviet interest in Western literature. Its death knell had already been sounded by Khrushchev in March, when he gave a speech condemning formalism and abstraction in literature and the arts, and singled out Ehrenburg, Nekrasov, and Yevtushenko for particular opprobrium.[18] (All three were friends of Nathalie's.) The conference nevertheless went ahead, and over the course of ten days participants were lavishly entertained by their Soviet hosts with tours of the Hermitage and the Peterhof Palace, a grand reception in each of Leningrad and Moscow, an excursion to Tolstoy's estate at Yasnaya Polyana, and a trip to the Soviet-built Moscow Canal.

The three days set aside for the conference proper saw the expression of very divergent views, and, with their confidence no doubt boosted by Khrushchev's recent speech, many of the Soviet participants gave vent to denunciations of Western European modernist writers as sterile, decadent, and immoral. In fact, very little modernist literature was available in Russian translation, and such instances as existed were mostly offered as negative examples, designed to discourage any Soviet emulation. The samples of work by Nathalie and her fellow Nouveaux Romanciers published in January 1963 in *Inostrannaya Literatura* were a case in point. The twentieth-century French-language authors most commonly read in the Soviet Union at the time were Romain Rolland, André Maurois, Saint-Exupéry, and Simenon. Though translated into Russian, Proust was barely known and most definitely frowned upon.

Nathalie was undaunted by Soviet criticism of her work, which she would have found intolerable on home territory. She was confident that she was addressing readers who shared her sensibility. As she had already said in a radio interview in 1960, "I'm convinced, because I've talked to Soviet people about it, that they have the same sensations, the same impulses and they understand these tropisms completely because they experience them."[19] Her talk at the Leningrad conference, titled "Two Realities," sought to clarify for the benefit of her Soviet audience the difference between a known, documented reality and the unknown, invisible reality that is the novelist's quarry. She defends the freedom of writers to pursue their own literary path but acknowledges that there are works of great literary merit based on visible reality that address social, political, and moral problems. This might sound like an uncharacteristic concession to literary values that she repudiated elsewhere—not least in connection with *Les Temps modernes*—but she may well have been thinking of Solzhenitsyn's *One Day in the Life of Ivan Denisovich*, which had been published the previous year. It was a book for which she had great admiration, and which in her view could not be judged by the criteria that prevailed in France.[20]

Ehrenburg, whom Nathalie had already introduced to her fellow Nouveaux Romanciers at her home in Paris, took a more conciliatory line than most of his compatriots. While admitting that he wasn't much attracted by the "theories" of the Nouveaux Romanciers, he respects their work, describes Nathalie as "a good writer," and acknowledges that the separation of literature from politics can make sense in the West in ways that it does not in the Soviet Union.[21] In any case, he observes, writers in both East and West rely too much on hearsay about each other's work, and he sees more points of contact between the two sides than much of the polemic had allowed. In the spirit of the declared aims of the conference and of the COMES itself, he calls for the translation of as many books capable of "touching their readers" as possible. And, appropriately, the text of Nathalie's talk was published in both Russian and French, appearing in *Inostrannaya Literatura*, *Le Monde*, and the special number of *Esprit* devoted to papers from the Leningrad conference.[22]

Nathalie and Ehrenburg were probably the only participants in the conference to have had firsthand experience of the culture of both East and West. Both had been born in Russia, both knew the émigré world of Russian political exiles in Paris, and although Nathalie lived in France and Ehrenburg (mainly) in the Soviet Union, each had one foot in the other country and spoke the languages of both. Ehrenburg's experience of multiple and contradictory identities—"Russian in France, French in Russia, Jewish as much in France as in Russia or Germany"—was also hers.[23] These alternative identities were both positive and negative: at times a pretext for exclusion, and at others an opening onto wider horizons.

Ehrenburg's call for more translation was answered for Nathalie in 1968 with the publication of a section of *The Golden Fruits* in

Novy Mir, the most liberal of the Soviet literary journals. But by then Nathalie's visits to the Soviet Union had ceased. Brezhnev had ousted Khrushchev in 1964 and set about reversing the cultural freedoms introduced under his predecessor. The effects on writers were almost instantaneous. Solzhenitsyn was no longer able to publish in the Soviet Union, the manuscript of *Gulag Archipelago* was seized by the KGB, and in 1969 he was expelled from the Writers' Union. He was deported to West Germany in 1974 after the *Gulag Archipelago* was smuggled to the West, where it was published (in Russian) in France. In parallel with this, the writers Yuli Daniel and Andrei Sinyavski were detained and charged in February 1966 with seeking to "subvert or weaken the Soviet regime." Both were found guilty and sentenced to hard labour in the kind of camp described in Solzhenitsyn's novels. Condemnation in the West and protests from several leading Soviet authors—including Ehrenburg, Aksyonov, Paustovsky, and Yevtushenko—who demanded the release of the two writers, were of no avail. A new, repressive cultural policy was now in place, and Nathalie's last visit to the Soviet Union took place in 1967, when she and Raymond spent a month holidaying on the Black Sea.

Thereafter, as she later explained in a letter to Roland Husson, the French cultural attaché in Helsinki, she felt unable to return. Husson had suggested to her that she might wish to make a brief trip to the Soviet Union during a forthcoming visit to Finland (this was in 1984), but Nathalie tells him why this was now out of the question:

It's not possible, after my repeated refusals, for me to go to the USSR at the moment. I'd immediately be obliged to meet officials from the Writers' Union and the press. I couldn't say what I think, and silence implies consent.

There isn't a single person who comes to France from the Soviet Union who doesn't insist that I go. I would have access to substantial sums of money there, thanks to the publication of "The Golden Fruits" and "Do You Hear Them?" My stay would be facilitated in all sorts of ways. And I always refuse.

How could I go without getting in touch with any of my friends? It would be impossible for me.

I hope you understand, and can sense how hard it is for me to turn down your proposal whose kindness and consideration towards me I much appreciate.[24]

Things got worse in 1970 with the return of overt anti-Semitism, when in a show trial seven Jews who had expressed a desire to emigrate to Israel were accused of treason and desertion to the enemy. The presence of a circular letter from the French Committee for the support of Jews in the Soviet Union dated 18 December 1970 and a clipping of a newspaper item from *Le Monde* of 17 December amongst Nathalie's papers testify to her concern.[25]

The exchange of letters with many of her former correspondents gradually petered out, partly because there were no more visits to the Soviet Union, and partly because the writers themselves were growing old: Ehrenburg died in 1967, Paustovsky in 1968, and Agapov in 1973. However, Nathalie maintained a Soviet presence by proxy through translations of her work. As early as 1962, her links with the Soviet Union had generated spasmodic translation of her work into Russian, when the first of her translators, Tamara Ivanova, wrote to say that she had started on *Tropisms*, but the translation never appeared. The idea of having Russian readers meant a great deal to Nathalie, and even before winning the Prix International de Littérature in 1964, she sent copies of *The Golden Fruits* to Olga Kraevskaya at the Union of Soviet Writers and the translator Rita Raït-Kovaleva, with whom she soon struck up a close friendship. In January 1965 Raït wrote to Nathalie to say that she would like to translate the novel for *Novy Mir*, but feared that the reputation of the Nouveau Roman as "difficult" would create problems. However, the long extract published in the journal in 1968 was followed in 1969 by the publication of the entire novel by the state-owned publisher Progress, which specialised in Western literature and social science.

Nathalie was blessed in her translator, with whom she had close personal affinity. Born in 1898 into a Jewish family, and with modernist tastes in literature, Rita Raït had lived a life in the Soviet Union parallel to the one Nathalie had lived in France. She mostly translated from English (including Salinger's *Catcher in the Rye*, which Nathalie had once so stylishly pastiched), but she rose to the challenge of Nathalie's French. "The translation is strikingly good," Nathalie wrote in response to the book manuscript, "and it is a great pleasure and an honour for me just to think that my work will appear—and has already appeared—before Russian eyes in such a favourable form." She worked with Raït much as she did with Maria Jolas and Elmar Tophoven, commenting "mercilessly" at Raït's invitation on a draft of the full-length version, but leaving it to the translator to decide which suggestions to implement.[26] Despite the political distance now separating her from the Soviet Union, Nathalie was particularly gratified by the book in its Russian guise. As she wrote later, "One of the best receptions of 'The Golden Fruits' was the Russian one, when it appeared in *Nov[y] Mir*, and then in book form with the comment: 'From now on when we praise a book or a play, etc. to the skies and then denigrate it, we will call it "The Golden Fruits." ' "[27]

On the back of this venture, Raït expressed an interest in translating Nathalie's next novel *Between Life and Death*, but was doubtful about her chances of persuading a publisher to take it on, since they all had a long backlog.[28] (The novel is still unavailable in Russian.) In the meantime, Nathalie had acquired a new translator, Lena Zonina, which created a curious twist in her relations with Sartre and Beauvoir. Zonina had been assigned to Sartre as his interpreter during his visits to the Soviet Union, which began in 1962. He had fallen passionately in love with her, wrote to her frequently, and proposed marriage, which she refused when she saw the strength of his relationship with Beauvoir. But she modelled her appearance on Beauvoir—right down to her trademark turban— Sartre dedicated his autobiography *Words* to her, and she translated the book into Russian. Nathalie's own involvement with Zonina placed her in close proximity to this complicated emotional triangle, which may explain why her relations with Zonina were somewhat cooler than those she had with Rita Raït.

Their acquaintance, which began in 1960, predated Sartre's encounter with his Russian interpreter. Jewish, highly intelligent, and extremely cultivated, Zonina was born in 1922 and named Lenina after the founder of the Soviet State. She was Ehrenburg's secretary

for a time and a specialist in French literature. She published articles on *The Planetarium* and *The Golden Fruits* in 1963, before embarking on translation of Nathalie's work with three texts from *Tropisms*, which appeared in a Russian anthology of French short
stories in 1973. She translated the essay "The Age of Suspicion," and
kept up this momentum with *Do You Hear Them?*, which came out
in 1983 (with a preface by Yevtushenko, who had become personally
acquainted with Nathalie). She then turned her attention to the
translation of *Childhood*, which was completed by her daughter,
Maria (Masha) Zonina, after Lena died in 1985. Published in 1986,
just three years after its French appearance, the Russian-language
account of Nathalie's childhood in Ivanovo-Voznesensk and Saint
Petersburg paved the way for her long-delayed return in 1990.

In the meantime, Nathalie continued to receive Russian visitors,
who were glad to have the invitations that were a prerequisite for
travel abroad. Many of these visitors were translators, notably Margarita Aliger, whom Nathalie had known since 1962. Aliger was fe-
rociously energetic and maintained an active network of friendships
between translators and writers, who passed on news of each other
in their letters to Nathalie. Aliger had come to fame in her youth
after winning the Stalin prize in 1943 with "Zoya," a poem about a
young woman hanged by the Nazis. She also had a daughter by
Alexander Fadeyev, founder of the Union of Soviet Writers. This
past presumably gave her a certain immunity, thanks to which she
visited Nathalie frequently in Paris and Chérence. In 1973 she was
still hopeful that she could persuade Nathalie to return to the Soviet
Union, tempting her with four different plans involving a steamer
trip, for which Nathalie had once expressed enthusiasm.[29] Apart
from anything else, as she pointed out in her letter to Roland Husson, a visit would have given her a chance to claim and spend the
five hundred roubles owed to her from Progress publishers for *The
Golden Fruits*.

But as time passed, more and more of Nathalie's Russian acquaintances were finding themselves exiled from Russia. In 1973
Andrei Sinyavsky, whom Nathalie later said she knew "very well"
and whose shrewdness she admired, settled in Paris after serving
his sentence for hard labour, and Viktor Nekrasov moved there in
the following year. Vasily Aksyonov emigrated to the United States,

from where he made regular trips to Paris.[30] Masha Aliger, Margarita's daughter, also lived in the United States during her unhappy marriage to the German poet Hans Magnus Enzensberger, before settling in London where she eked out a living as a translator. Nathalie's correspondence and engagement diaries testify to active relations with all of them. The Russian dimension of her life was once again a world of exiles and émigrés, excluded by force or by choice from a country that had been home, and for which they once had hopes of better things.

CHAPTER TWENTY-SIX

Radio Plays, 1962–72

NATHALIE'S ENERGIES in these years were apparently inexhaustible. With the delays and disappointments of the previous three decades behind her, she was throwing herself into fresh ventures as if she were twenty or thirty years younger. By happy coincidence, the 1960s were a decade in which novelty was more widely in the air, awakening appetites for change across the Western world to which she was quick to respond. The connections with readers and audiences abroad were a further stimulus, and in 1962, contact with Germany, which she had for so long thought herself incapable of, led to a new departure as she embarked on writing plays for radio. She had already begun to acquire a German readership thanks to Elmar Tophoven's translations. She admired Tophoven's integrity, which had made it possible to conceive of a Germany other than the one she had known during the Occupation. Her friendships with the German-speaking Swiss critics Gerda Zeltner and François Bondy also contributed to this softening of her attitude. So, when in February 1961 she received a lecture invitation from Max Bense, professor of philosophy at the Technische Hochschule in Stuttgart, she accepted. Bense was something of a maverick and had been a confirmed anti-Nazi, which disposed Nathalie in his favour, and she flew to Germany from Le Bourget on 30 May.

The most decisive encounter was with Werner Spies, a young German art historian and journalist, who lived in Paris and wrote for the German press. Acting on behalf of the Süddeutscher Rundfunk (SDR), he was commissioning radio plays from avant-garde French writers in the medium known in German as *neue Hörspiele* (new radio plays). He had already signed up Michel Butor and Robert Pinget when he approached Nathalie. This was at the suggestion of Philippe Sollers, editor of the journal *Tel Quel*, who had reportedly said, "Try with Nathalie," but warned, "in any case, it won't work."[1] A meeting at the Café de Flore proved Sollers right, when she immediately explained that the sub-conversation which formed the substance of her novels could in no way be recast as theatrical dialogue.

Spies was not the first to raise the question of writing for the theatre. When she was asked in an interview in 1959 whether she had ever been tempted to write for the stage, she replied very firmly that "it's difficult to be both a novelist and a playwright." And, she added, "To each his own language. I cannot imagine Strindberg writing novels or Proust writing plays!" In 1960 she turned down an invitation from RT France to contribute to a series of broadcasts under the title "*Carte blanche*." The producer, Lily Siou, explained her conception for the series: "The idea is for writers to choose a subject that suits them, either an original one or something from one of their novels, and to make a radio play out of it. . . . An hour and ten minutes of text, around 60 typed pages." But the writers she listed as having already contributed—Marcel Jouhandeau, Jean Giono, Jacques Audiberti, Félicien Marceau (whom Nathalie knew from the Médicis prize committee)—had little in common with her, and would not have inspired her to take up the challenge.[2]

The *neue Hörspiele* were a different proposition, and experiment was positively encouraged. Reluctant to take Nathalie's "no" for an answer, Spies tried once again to interest her by stressing the innovative character of the venture. She recalled him saying, "Make it as modern and as difficult as you like. We don't mind—on the contrary!" and, as she observed, "No one else said that."[3] These discussions almost certainly took place during the meetings with Spies noted in Nathalie's engagement diaries for the last quarter of 1962. But with no indication of a change of heart on her part, Spies assumed that his urgings had fallen on deaf ears. In the meantime, he had contracted several other Nouveaux Romanciers: Claude Ollier, Claude Simon, Marguerite Duras, and Claude Mauriac.

However, at some point in the following year Spies received a phone call from Nathalie inviting him to come and collect the manuscript of a radio play she had written in response to the suggestion she had initially rejected. This was *Silence*, which she read aloud to him in the presence of Raymond, with whom she must have discussed the pros and cons of this move into a new literary genre. She had finished *The Golden Fruits* in January 1963, and dispatched both sets of proofs by mid-March for publication in April. With the Leningrad conference scheduled for August, this was an ideal moment to contemplate an alternative, shorter project before embarking on the next novel.

The *Hörspiel* venture coincided with further German engagements: a talk delivered in German by Nathalie herself—"Werden wir richtig informiert?" (Are we correctly informed?)—was broadcast by Swiss radio in January 1963 and subsequently rebroadcast by Bavarian radio, before appearing in print in both Switzerland and Germany.[4] She was invited for a second visit to Stuttgart, and further invitations Germany were under discussion.[5] In December of the same year, François Bondy published an interview with her in the German monthly *Der Monat*. How much of all this was originally conducted in German and how much translated isn't clear, but Nathalie's knowledge of the language—from the Lycée Fénelon, from her time in Berlin, and from her reading of Rilke and Thomas Mann—enabled her to speak faultless German, despite having vowed after the Occupation never to usc thc language again.[6]

Over the course of 1963, Nathalie saw Spies on several further occasions, having warmed to the young German whose age she been careful to establish on their first meeting: born in 1937, he was too young to bear the taint of Nazism. He became a lifelong friend, and Nathalie later told him that it was thanks to him that she had finally been able to reconcile herself with a younger generation of Germans. He acted as an intermediary in her dealings with the SDR and went with her several times to Stuttgart to discuss arrangements for the broadcasts of *Silence* and the other radio plays that followed, all of them translated by Elmar Tophoven.

Despite Nathalie's insistence that theatre and fiction were quite separate domains, this move into theatrical writing was not entirely unheralded. The discovery of Pirandello and Chekhov in the theatre had been an important stage on her path to writing in the 1920s. Jean Vilar's production of Strindberg's *Dance of Death* had made a deep impression on her during the Occupation. And as she said in the interview for *Les Nouvelles littéraires* in 1959, "Beckett's Waiting for Godot was a real revelation to me; as regards Ionesco, if he counts so much for me, it's undoubtedly because his domain is adjacent to my own hunting grounds!"[7] She knew both dramatists personally, Beckett from his unfortunate stay in Janvry in the autumn of 1942, and Ionesco from Gilbert Gadoffre's Royaumont colloquia. Then, towards the end of the 1950s, she became more directly and more actively involved in theatre herself. Through her friend Geneviève Serreau (managing editor on Maurice Nadeau's journal *Lettres nouvelles*) she met Jean-Marie Serreau, Geneviève's theatre director husband. The engagement diaries for 1958 and 1959 contain several mentions of the Théâtre de Lutèce, where Serreau was staging *Le Cadavre encerclé* (The encircled cadaver) by Kateb Yacine, an Algerian living in Paris, and *Picnic on the Battlefield* by the avant-garde Spanish playwright Fernando Arrabal.

Arrabal's name also appears several times in the diaries for the last quarter of 1958 (the only engagement diary to survive from that year). These entries refer to Serreau's rehearsals at the Lutèce and meetings of Arrabal's own personal *cénacle*, which Nathalie attended at his home in Paris, often silently accompanied by Raymond. Arrabal was an exile from Franco's Spain, and in addition to the shared experience of exile, he and Nathalie had TB in common at a time when Nathalie was in an acute phase of the illness. (She later came to Arrabal's rescue when he ran into trouble with the authorities in the United States for his nude appearance in one of his plays, which she defended as an artistic necessity.)[8] It was also around this time that she got to know Paule Thévenin, devoted editor of the complete works of Antonin Artaud, whose theory and practice had revolutionised French theatre in the 1930s.

There are several diary entries during the same period for the Théâtre Récamier, which had been taken over by Jean Vilar. She was at the Récamier almost daily in December, often with Arrabal. Intriguing notations of "pistol," "costume," and "manuscripts" in the diaries suggest that she may have had some practical involvement in the production of either Armand Gatti's theatrically provocative

The Buffalo-Toad or Boris Vian's *The Empire Builders*, which opened on 22 December. In one way or another, during these months she had intensive exposure to contemporary avant-garde theatre. This was also the theme of the "Defence of Theatre" held at the Théâtre Récamier in December, and the subject of a book by Geneviève Serreau published a few years later and which she almost certainly discussed with Nathalie on the numerous occasions when they met in the autumn of 1958.[9]

With the exception of Gatti and Ionesco, all these dramatists give the lie to Nathalie's claim that it's impossible for novelists to write plays (and vice versa). Their plays were, however, written for the stage and not specifically for radio. As far as Nathalie was concerned, the appeal of the *neue Hörspiele* was that they called for experiment in a medium whose domain was the ear, not the eye. This aural focus could be grafted from her fiction, where every word was spoken in her head as she wrote, and where language is very often the medium in which the drama between characters takes place. As Nathalie remarked in her 1954 essay "Conversation and Sub-conversation," words are "the daily, insidious and very effective weapon responsible for countless small crimes" because "there is nothing to equal the rapidity with which they affect the other person at the moment when he is least on his guard."[10]

In the radio plays, the ravages caused by these verbal exchanges could be explored as characters register the effects of an uncomfortable silence (*Silence*), a possible lie (*The Lie*), a pronunciation (*Izzum*), or a conventional expression of aesthetic appreciation (*It's Beautiful*). The characters, almost all designated simply as HE, SHE, or W 1, M 2, and so on, are barely delineated, and exist as voices rather than as individuals. The plays are language acts *in extenso*, but these acts are explored in a new form of dialogue as the characters themselves articulate responses which in the novels would remain at the level of the semiconscious, unspoken sub-conversation. The inherent drama of the tropism had found a new medium, and Nathalie a new literary language.

Jochen Schale, producer at the SDR, accepted *Silence* with enthusiasm and wrote to say that her *Hörspiel* would be "the most important event of our season."[11] His prediction was confirmed by the response to the broadcast on 1 April 1964 (Nathalie was still in the United States), and he wrote again on 22 May to report on this success and to say that other radio stations were certain to take the production.[12] The broadcast on Bayerischer Rundfunk was followed by a reading of an extract from *The Golden Fruits* in German translation, and in August the Hessischer Rundfunk broadcast included a text on the emergence of the tropism read by Nathalie herself. The play's success in Germany contrasts with the absence of any sign of interest in France. Nathalie met Lily Siou in December 1963, but no French broadcast was forthcoming, and its publication in Gaëtan Picon's *Mercure de France* in April 1964 was the only sign of the play's existence in French.[13]

The German response was nevertheless enough to convince Nathalie to continue in this new creative vein, and *The Lie*, written in 1965, was broadcast by SDR on 2 March 1966. On this occasion it aired simultaneously on France Culture in the series *Carte blanche*, whose invitation she had turned down six years previously. The play was then published with a short introduction by Nathalie in the April 1966 number of the *Cahiers Renaud Barrault*, edited by Barrault's literary consultant Simone Benmussa for the Renaud-Barrault theatre company at the Théâtre de l'Odéon. The text of the play had in fact been promised to Marcel Arland for the *NRF*, and Nathalie seems to have treated him rather shabbily by failing to tell him, despite repeated enquiries on his part, that *The Lie* would be appearing elsewhere. After having announced the play for over a year as forthcoming in the *NRF*, it was left to Arland to discover for himself its appearance in the *Cahiers Renaud Barrault*. His upset is understandable when he writes, "Allow me to tell you that, however unfortunate it is for the journal, it affects me even more directly in the friendship I have always felt for you."[14] There was already a hint of evasiveness in the letter Nathalie had written to Arland the previous June, where she says, "I am touched by the interest you have always shown in my work and I will be very happy to give you this text, or another, when I am able to."[15] But having failed to give him *The Lie*, she made no effort to offer him any alternative.

The Renaud-Barrault publication was nonetheless a fortunate move. Simone Benmussa recommended the play to Jean-Louis Barrault for the opening of the small auditorium at the Théâtre de l'Odéon, the Petit Odéon. Barrault took up the suggestion, and

The Lie was performed in a double bill with *Silence*, which received its belated French premiere on 17 January 1967. Barrault directed both plays, and Madeleine Renaud took the part of W.1 in *Silence*, thus launching an unintended career for Nathalie as the author of stage plays.

The plays were well chosen for the Petit Odéon venue, as Barrault indicated in an interview at the time. He stressed the intimate dimensions of the auditorium, which seated only 120, and where the L-shaped stage made it possible to "study the inside of the human heart like a surgeon."[16] This arrangement called for a very particular kind of theatrical writing, which Barrault found in Nathalie's radio plays. She attended rehearsals, providing guidance to the actors on intonation and the implications of the dialogue, but no more. The rest was Barrault's business, and she was pleasantly surprised by the transition of her plays from aural to visual performance: "With his gift for mime, and that imagination which allows him to bring the whole stage to life, [Barrault] was able to show people moving on the stage, and making all sorts of quite rich and varied movements. I must say these movements fascinated me. I saw my text integrated with stage movements in this way, borne along and amplified by gestures, with all the astonishment of a hen who has just hatched a duck."[17]

She also enjoyed being part of a group because, as she explained in an interview, "the atmosphere created by Jean-Louis Barrault, Madeleine Renaud and the rest of their troupe is admirably full of understanding and kindness. I felt as if I was in a very dear and very unified family and I was sorry when the rehearsals came to an end."[18] It was certainly a very different kind of "family" from the one she had known at the time of her association with *Les Temps modernes*; and her willingness to trust directors and actors was quite different to her surveillance—however well intentioned—of the translations of her work, or the anxious suspicion with which she followed its reception by the critics. The plays received mixed notices, and some critics were unconvinced that theatre was Nathalie's medium. However, the review by Simone Benmussa, who had the advantage of an insider's perspective and with whom Nathalie would later collaborate, underscored the vital role given to the spoken word in these plays where "language alone introduces danger on the stage."[19]

Despite the experience of having her work performed at one of Paris's most respected theatres, Nathalie continued writing for radio rather than for the stage. Her next two plays both received their premieres on the airwaves, *Izzum* simultaneously in France and Germany in 1970, and *It's Beautiful* on France Culture alone in 1972. The writing of the plays alternated productively with Nathalie's other work, but they never supplanted her main activity as a writer of prose fiction, from which many of the plays took their initial inspiration. They were a form of relaxation, simpler and more fun to write. The theatrical dialogue, which Nathalie had once thought an impossibility, had proved to be far easier than the sub-conversation which she still found the greatest challenge. Changing its name to "pre-dialogue," as she did at this time, did nothing to lessen its demands.

CHAPTER TWENTY-SEVEN

The Writing Life, 1964–68

WRITING WAS ALWAYS DIFFICULT, but not writing was worse: "It's not even a form of suffering. . . . It makes me feel as if I'm not alive, I don't exist. As if I weren't breathing."[1] Day-to-day life was therefore arranged around this basic existential necessity. Domestic preoccupations and family responsibilities were kept to a minimum and served primarily as a stimulus for writing. She kept to a disciplined routine, working every morning, Sundays included, for two or three hours. Phone calls were made before nine o'clock each morning, and anyone wishing to contact her was advised accordingly. She would then leave the house and spend the morning writing in a café five minutes' walk away from home. Le Marceau on the Avenue Marceau had a very different function in Nathalie's life from the cafés in Saint-Germain-des-Prés: the time she spent there had no social purpose, visitors were not welcome, and the children were forbidden to disturb her except in the case of dire emergency. The café proprietors were Lebanese, and while life would go on around her, the conversations were mostly in Arabic and not a distraction. In fact, they contributed to the pleasant impression of being abroad, which was itself a catalyst for writing.

She always sat at the same table, and always placed the same order—a small cup of coffee and a jug of hot water—before lighting a cigarette. She wrote on loose sheets of plain paper, which she brought with her in a small brief case, along with an exercise book for notes, and two biros in case one ran out. She never fetichised writing materials, and used biros until the late 1960s, when she adopted the recently introduced and equally disposable felt-tip pen. Since she voiced every word, her writing would be accompanied by a low murmuring that went unnoticed in the surrounding hubbub. She wrote slowly, and the results were subject to repeated correction. Visitors and friends who caught sight of her work in draft were struck by the number of crossings out and revisions; the self-correction that was a feature of her written style was also the means of its genesis. Some passages were revised as many as fifty times, and each of her novels—none of them long—took up to five years to write.

They all had a geometrical shape in Nathalie's mind:

> *Portrait of an Unknown Man* appeared as enclosed space, with an internal agitation created by the clash of two consciousnesses. *Martereau*, by contrast was a single monolithic block destined to disintegrate on contact with consciousnesses outside it which are agitated by these movements. *The Planetarium* was a circular space where the movements were directed towards its periphery. *The Golden Fruits* was a rising and then a falling curve.[2]

The books would take written shape only after "pages and pages of fairly formless attempts," and the beginning had to be in place for the rest to follow. She would then write a complete draft, establishing a rhythm for the novel as a whole, as well as for each chapter and each sentence. (The rhythm was important.) This process would take about two years, after which she would revise exhaustively, before giving her manuscript to Raymond to be typed. She then worked on the typescript, which Raymond retyped piecemeal, while maintaining his other role, which was to listen to the work in progress as Nathalie read it to him. Correcting proofs was always an ordeal.

Given that she never had—and never wanted—a single replicable formula, each book represented a new departure. As she explained, "I always feel I'm wandering aimlessly, alone, without support. I don't know where I'm headed." Although her quarry remained the tropism, its manifestations took many forms, and were by definition elusive: "If I'm interested in something, it's precisely to the extent that I don't know what it is."[3] A further source of difficulty was the susceptibility of the writing itself to a fixity which is only discovered on rereading. This fixity is the "death" of the title of the novel, *Between Life and Death*, which portrays the phenomenon in a scene where the fictional writer returns to a passage he had previously been satisfied with, only then to realise that it is lifeless. (A similar scene is ascribed to Germaine Lemaire in *The Planetarium*.) The delicate process of revision is about bringing a moribund text back to life without definitively destroying it through overcorrection.

After a morning writing in Le Marceau, the solitariness of work would be offset by human contact. This mostly took the form of engagements for lunch, coffee, or dinner with friends and professional acquaintances in the cafés and brasseries of Saint-Germain-des-Prés. Nathalie would often arrange to meet her adult children here, as she liked to see them individually away from home. From time to time Raymond's sister Véra would come to the Avenue Pierre 1ᵉ de Serbie for dinner, and there were occasional visits from Raymond's cousin Gabriel Sarraute, who had gone into the church. He followed Nathalie's work and published a few books of his own: a novel, a children's story, and a study of the poet Joë Bousquet, who had written one of the few reviews of *Tropismes*.

She would also see visitors at home, mostly in the late afternoon. The salon was used only for formal occasions, and she preferred the intimacy of her study. The walls were hung with brown velvet curtains, and the window looked out onto the back of the Musée Galliera (a museum of fashion and fashion history) with its adjacent garden. Visitors occupied chairs while Nathalie sat on the divan, where she would also read in the afternoons when she was on her own. A tinted engraving of the Kremlin hung on the wall above the divan, a reproduction of Van Gogh's *Night Café* on another. Her personal library—which included Russian authors in Russian—occupied the rest of the wall space. Her preferred time for such visits was five o'clock, when she would make tea for her guests. Claude Mauriac describes her preparing "delicious tea, without a samovar, but nevertheless in in most orthodox manner possible."[4] This was in 1958. In later years tea was replaced by whisky mixed with Perrier water, while Nathalie's taste in cigarettes evolved from the Gauloises recalled by Violette Leduc to American brands. She smoked in mod-

eration and never inhaled. With friends she indulged in uncon-
strained gossip.

She received journalists in her study, and many of the photographs accompanying interviews and articles were taken in this
room, creating a public image for the writer "Nathalie Sarraute."
They contributed to her visibility, while the setting underscored
the isolation that she so often emphasised to interviewers. She did
not enjoy posing for the camera and stated quite categorically to
the American photographer Jill Krementz, "I hate being photographed."[5] She never cultivated a feminine appearance: her hair
remained short, straight, and practical. Her clothes were equally
functional: a plain, open-neck blouse, a jacket, very often a silk scarf
round the neck, and—at least in the 1960s—a skirt somewhat more
often than trousers. She never wore makeup or jewellery, and she
sported a man's watch.

Her ambivalence about photography was partly an ambivalence
about her own appearance. As she said to Simone Benmussa, "I
don't know what I look like. I just don't know." And thinking back
to her youth, she adds, "I was more conscious of my body. I could
see it. But my face was more difficult because it changed. I had a face
that could be hideous in one mirror and beautiful in another. It was
extremely variable. Dreadful on one photo, not bad on another. My
body was the only thing I liked. It had flaws which I didn't like, but
overall, I could look at my body."[6] But whether passable or hideous,
her self-image was something she never felt able to control: "Seeing
yourself in the eyes of other people and imposing a particular image
of oneself. There, I'm completely blind, and have always been so. I'm
quite unable to imagine what other people see."[7] She makes these
remarks in the course of interviews which are themselves one of the
chief means devised for constructing such images. But unlike a photograph, a conversation can be adjusted and its record corrected for
publication, which Nathalie always did.

The experience of seeing oneself in the eyes of others was an issue
she had explored in her writing from *Tropisms* onwards, but with
the increasing mediatisation of authors, literary celebrity gave it
special relevance. The reality wasn't always negative: Nathalie had
basked in the compliments that she received on her tour of the

United States and enthusiastically embraced the role of "gracious majesty." But she was also very sensitive to any hint that she had been placed in a subordinate position to others, particularly Robbe-Grillet. In June 1966 she wrote twice to her English publisher John Calder to protest about the way she was presented in his latest catalogue, where she was listed in fifth place. In his reply he attempts to assuage her concerns:

> I am sure that all the trouble comes from a misreading of the catalogue.
>
> In the introduction we say that some of our best authors have passed through "the stages of critical disdain, philistine attack and slow acceptance, until many of them are now internationally recognised as the outstanding creative minds of modern literature," we included not only the first four names [Beckett, Burroughs, Ionesco, Robbe-Grillet] which are at present the more commercial, but also the seven names that follow and which are headed by yourself. . . .
>
> Where you are concerned we have to depend entirely on the value of your prose as we would have to do if you were Proust or Kafka. You are simply more difficult to publicize and your sales are correspondingly lower, but it is not through lack of effort.

And he concludes, "I really feel you have been unfair to us. . . . In referring to certain writers as being less established, we are not talking about their importance but the fact that they are known to fewer people. / We are doing everything possible to magnify your reputation all the time in the face of a largely hostile literary establishment who are opposed to everything you stand for in the novel."[8] She continued to feel vulnerable to the way she was portrayed in the public eye. As she jokingly reported to Matthieu Galey in later years, she once sent Raymond out to the bookshop to compare the amount of space devoted to her and to Robbe-Grillet in the standard history of French literature by Lagarde et Michard, with the instruction, "If what they say about me is reasonable, you can buy it, if not don't tell me!"[9]

Meanwhile, in her fiction, she explored these questions in a different mode. Following *The Golden Fruits*, which dealt with the fate of a novel, *Between Life and Death* examines the fortunes of a writer. This, her fifth novel, comprises a selection of scenes from a writer's life, but there's no attempt to construct a coherent portrait of a single individual. The writer, in all his various and sometimes contradictory guises, is always male, but his experiences are those that many writers would recognise. Most turn on encounters with others—interviewers, visiting acquaintances, mother, father, former schoolteacher, curious readers, other writers—where he is confronted with the image of himself as A Writer uncomfortably reflected back to him.

There's no escaping these images, which are generated on the least pretext. There's a would-be writer who is accused of only ever talking about writing; a novice who tries to duck out of the limelight in the presence of a more established literary figure; and a new writer who meets with scepticism from his father on one occasion and anxious pride from his mother on another. There's a writer who is witnessed on a bus fulminating excessively about a new ticket system, and another who finds himself accused by readers of portraying them in his book. Some readers claim to have identified the source of the pointed fingers of one of his characters, and others worry that he will use the things that they say as material for his work. Another extravagantly praises his book for an episode that doesn't actually appear in it. And so on.

What emerges time and again is the writer's own inadvertent complicity in the images of himself that these exchanges inevitably produce. In the opening scene where—as Nathalie herself often did—he tells an interviewer how difficult writing is for him, he ends up merely mythologising the process of literary creation and then launches into a self-aggrandising account of his family background. A second writer finds himself caught out by his claim to have been sensitive to words from an early age, when he is accused of trying to portray himself as a "predestined child."

In many ways the novel is a continuation of the issues raised through the figure of Germaine Lemaire in *The Planetarium*, but they are developed here with greater subtlety, and Nathalie draws on experiences from her own life for several of these vignettes. One writer describes a writing routine that entails working every day, Sundays included; another recalls a school composition on the topic of "My First Sorrow," just like one she once wrote in primary school; and yet another is idolised by visitors for the way he made tea for them, as Nathalie did for her own visitors. But as ever, there's nothing confessional about the novel, which uses Nathalie's own experience strictly as material for further literary exploration. There are extreme and often very comic analogies for the moments when the writer becomes trapped in his self-image. The one who recalls his love of words as a child and is accused of posing as a "a predestined child" is portrayed through an extended image where he is rounded up by his accusers in what feels like an ambush, summarily stripped of his clothing and handed the obligatory uniform of pretentious genius. The disproportion between the fleeting remark and its extended figurative interpretation is both clarifying and humorous in its exaggeration.

But the core of the novel is entirely serious, when in two separate scenes the focus switches from the writer figure to writing itself. Being "A Writer"—with capital letters—does nothing to facilitate the writing process, which works by going beneath the visible surface of the writer's life. Perhaps recalling Yvon Belaval's characterisation of *Tropisms* as "creation in its nascent state," Nathalie seeks to capture this emergence in her depiction of the process of writing as it happens. This is not in order to celebrate the supposed mysteries of creation—one of the self-dramatizing topics targeted elsewhere in the novel—but to explore the knife edge that separates life and death in writing, and of which Nathalie was always acutely aware.

As she said in an interview with Geneviève Serreau shortly after the book's publication, "It's a book that was contained in embryo in all the others. As a result of having discovered it progressively in my other books, I think that the position of the writer 'between life and death' is for me the most revealing of all. It's the ultimate experience and it's linked to the partial experiences of all my other novels."[10] For this reason, *Between Life and Death* was the book she liked best of all her work. But it was also the one that received least attention on its appearance. Published at the end of April 1968, its reception was almost immediately eclipsed by the events of May, when the world—the literary world included—turned its attention elsewhere.

CHAPTER TWENTY-EIGHT

Revolution and May 68

ONCE AGAIN HISTORY had intervened, but on this occasion Nathalie was a willing participant. The word "revolution" was in the air, bringing with it a distant echo of the ambitions of the Socialist Revolutionary refugees of her childhood, but applied now to the literary domain. In 1966 she had told the *New York Times Book Review*, "It is a happy symptom, a reassuring symptom, that the idea of revolution—indeed of revolutions—in literature is spreading more and more. It is especially reassuring as far as the novel is concerned, since, not long ago, the idea of revolution seemed to have been forgotten." For her, "[literature's] span of life is marked by successive revolutions," achieved not through any representational content, but by means of a constant renewal of literary form.[1]

The political climate was also taking a revolutionary turn, and Nathalie initially became involved through the growing protests against the American war in Vietnam. On visits to the United States in 1964, 1966, and 1967, she observed growing student revolt against the war, which was shared by her American friends. In 1967 Mary McCarthy published a forceful indictment of America's role in Vietnam in the *New York Review of Books*, while Maria Jolas was an active member of the Paris American Committee to Stop War, which met in her apartment on the rue de Rennes. In December 1965 Nathalie joined the European Artists' Protest against War in Vietnam, and in 1966 she contributed to a volume edited by Cecil Woolf (a nephew of Virginia Woolf by marriage), which appeared in 1967 under the title *Authors Take Sides on Vietnam*. In her brief contribution Nathalie describes the situation in Vietnam as the consequence of a popular uprising against oppression and proposes a somewhat idealistic solution:

> I think that the conflict in Vietnam stems from a popular revolt against an oppressive régime. The American intervention which, having provoked that of North Vietnam, has led to "escalation," [and] is consequently quite unjustified.
>
> The only possible solution of the conflict therefore seems to me to be the suspension of bombing, followed by the withdrawal of American and North Vietnamese forces, accompanied by the neutralization of the whole of Vietnam.[2]

In January 1968 she sent a small donation to the Paris-based Conseil National du Mouvement de la Paix which backed the struggle of the Vietnamese people for independence, and in March she signed a letter in support of the Journée des Intellectuels pour le Vietnam.[3]

Other forms of discontent were rising to the surface in France with student protests and intermittent strikes. Things came to a head in spring 1968, when the students' appeals for solidarity met with positive response from intellectuals and writers. Nathalie was drawn into events by Jean-Pierre Faye, whom she knew as a member of the editorial committee of *Tel Quel*. After a meeting organised by students on 3 May in the Latin Quarter, Faye telephoned Nathalie to canvass her support and then visited her at home, where she observed, "You're getting me into things," and asked, "Do you have a Lenin?"[4] She didn't take much persuading, and was one of some thirty signatories to a communiqué dated 8 May expressing support for "the world-wide student movement—the movement that, at this glorious moment, has suddenly shaken the so-called prosperous society, so perfectly incarnated in France," and encouraging those same students to resist the established order with a "a rejection capable . . . of opening up a future."[5] Other signatories included Sartre and Beauvoir, Marguerite Duras, Maurice Nadeau, and Maurice Blanchot, whose names, like hers, had also appeared on the *Manifesto of the 121* in 1960.

From the beginning of May the Sorbonne was occupied alternately by students and the police who ejected them; barricades were erected in the Latin Quarter; and a general strike was called for 13 May. On 18 May the new solidarity between writers and students led to the creation of the Comité d'action étudiants-écrivains révolutionnaire (Students' and writers' revolutionary action committee), known by the acronym CAEE, which met in in the Sorbonne. Nathalie attended the meeting with Jean-Pierre Faye. He later recalled her saying that she regretted not having returned to Russia in 1917, but in his view, despite her enthusiasm for revolution, "she didn't know what it was."[6]

There was, however, more to her support than simple enthusiasm. The movement of May 68 was driven primarily by students, and Nathalie had developed strong sympathies with those she had encountered on her lecture tours in the United States and elsewhere. She was also galvanised by the CAEE's demands for change in the economic status of writers, and was one of the signatories to the resolution calling for a transformation of "the conditions that allow the exploitation of writers by publishers, and with the agreement of all Book workers, in order to arrive at a new economic and social definition of the relation between writers and society."[7] Two days later, on 20 May, the CAEE launched an appeal calling on intellectuals to boycott the ORTF, the French radio service. Once again, Nathalie signed.[8]

On the following morning, Tuesday 21 May, she was one of a group of some fifteen writers who occupied the Hôtel de Massa, an eighteenth-century building in the fourteenth arrondissement, seat of the Société des gens de lettres (Society of writers). This somewhat toothless organisation oversaw the unsatisfactory editorial and remunerative conditions about which writers were now protesting. Faye was one of the instigators of the action, along with Maurice Roche, cocreator with Faye of a new review, *Change*. Initially reluctant to involve himself, Michel Butor joined the group when he learned that Nathalie had agreed to participate, because, as he later said, "I couldn't leave her to this adventure on her own."[9] Others included the Oulipo poet Jacques Roubaud and Pierre Guyotat, whose provocative novel about the Algerian war, *Tomb for 500,000 Soldiers*, had caused a scandal the previous year. At twenty-eight, Guyotat was the youngest of the group, and at almost sixty-eight, Nathalie was the oldest. She was also the only woman.

Despite its revolutionary intent, the occupation of the building was a soberly conducted affair. Much to the bemusement of the office staff, the group simply walked in, established themselves in the

FIGURE 24. Occupation of the Hôtel de Massa, 21 May 1968.
Nathalie third from the left. © René Pari, *Le Figaro*.

elegant surrounds of the Salon Victor-Hugo, and embarked on intensive deliberations, which resulted in the creation of the Union
des écrivains (Writers' union), abbreviated to UE. An alternative to
the CAEE, the union was named in honour of the Czech Writers'
Union and the Prague Spring. A banner was hung from the upstairs
windows, and a statement issued later in the day declared, "Open to
all who regard literature as inseparable from the current revolutionary action, this Union will be a permanent centre of contestation of
the established literary order." The group also announced the UE's
intention to "give writers a new status in a new society."[10]

Nathalie was one of the declaration's fifteen original signatories,
to whom several more were added over the course of the day. These
included Sartre, Beauvoir, Maurice Nadeau, Marguerite Duras, and
Geneviève Serreau, who had published an interview with Nathalie
in the *Quinzaine littéraire* on 1 May. The interview was devoted
entirely to literary issues and made no reference to the political circumstances that were brewing. One section, however, was headed
"Everything must be destroyed," which taken out of context read like
a call to arms and was echoed by Duras the following year in the title
of her novel *Destroy, She Said*.

Over the next few days, a steering committee firmed up an agenda for the UE, resulting in a break with the CAEE. Nathalie, who had become unwell, took no part in these discussions, and never returned to the Hôtel de Massa. But she continued to lend her name to further declarations from both the UE and the CAEE, notably one drawn up by Maurice Blanchot on 26 May in which the group, consisting of some sixty writers, expressed "solidarity with the anger of the young," adding "we're all rioters, . . . we're all criminal hoi polloi."[11] Another statement on 18 June affirmed that the student uprising "has struck at the heart of the system of exploitation and oppression that governs this country," and demanded that these same students not be subject to criminal proceedings. Once again, Nathalie was one of some one hundred signatories.[12]

She never spoke about her participation in May 68 and discouraged others from doing so. (I was obliged by the editor at Gallimard to delete all mention of it from my account of the critical reception of *Between Life and Death* in the *Complete Works*.) Her reticence was no doubt designed to deflect any political interpretation of her writing, whose revolutionary ambitions lay entirely in the literary domain. She continued throughout her life to assert, "I have political involvements as a citizen, not as a writer," but the politics of May 68 were different to most, since they were as much concerned with writers as they were with citizens.[13]

By July she was already regretting having taken part in the occupation of the Hôtel de Massa, and she told her friend the novelist Dominique Rolin that she was "extremely annoyed about having got involved in the Hôtel de Massa business."[14] Her growing disenchantment with the Soviet Union—especially after the Soviet invasion of Czechoslovakia in August 1968—may retrospectively have tempered her revolutionary zeal. Comments she made a decade later convey considerable political caution: "I loathe mobs. I loathe processions. Public demonstrations. Political meetings. Military and non-military parades. Anything with banners. Anything displaying a sign, any kind of sign. Anyone who feeds off crowds, whoever he is: Stalin, Hitler, Mussolini, Mao, etc. People like that are a sign that the paranoia of a tyrant has spread throughout a world." She had never taken to the streets during May 68, the group that occupied the Hôtel de Massa could hardly be called a mob, and the *Evénements* never had the Lenin she asked Jean-Pierre Faye about, but she was now very conscious of the way that revolutions could backfire: "I think crowds shout the opposite of what they mean. When they shout: 'Freedom!' they mean: 'Authority!' When they shout: 'Liberation!' they mean: 'Terror!' When they shout: 'Revolution!' they mean: 'Dictatorship!' Revolutions always lead to tyranny." And she concludes, "Revolution means dictatorship. Revolution means terror. I hate terror."[15] She was frequently prone to such second thoughts after an initial political enthusiasm.

Yet May 68 had struck a chord, as Nathalie acknowledged in 1972, when she said, "What happened then was a catalyst for my feelings, without my intending it. I experienced them more powerfully, but as spontaneously as ever. I never try to make a show of them."[16] She was speaking after the publication of her next novel, *Do You Hear Them?*, which, without being a direct record, captures the spirit of May 68. It's one of her finest novels, and one of the most important literary responses to the events that inspired it. She wrote it fast, carried along perhaps by the euphoria of the moment, and with its depiction of the clash of artistic cultures, the novel completes the triptych dealing with literary and aesthetic issues—the critical reception of a novel having been the subject of *The Golden Fruits* and the figure of the writer that of *Between Life and Death*.

Do You Hear Them? is set in a house in a village, a long way from the street demonstrations in the Latin Quarter, the barricades and the student occupations, the declarations and the manifestoes, or even the various demands made in the name of writers by the CAEE and UE. The action, such as it is, takes place in a domestic setting between a father and an unspecified number of children of equally unspecified age and sex, and is triggered by a neighbour's interest in a primitive stone sculpture owned by the father. The narrative content is minimal as the neighbour, visiting after dinner, takes the sculpture from the mantelpiece and places it on a coffee table, while the children retreat upstairs from where their irrepressible laughter can be heard. The novel repeatedly returns to this moment which sets the scene for the ensuing confrontation, as the neighbour's admiration for what he considers to be a museum piece comes up against the children's irreverent modernity. The children disdain all "authorial amour-propre" in favour of collective production, and live in a disposable culture of comics and pop music, making a ruffle for the sculpture out of the lining of a biscuit tin or using it as a support for an ashtray.

This wasn't the first time that Nathalie had used the plastic arts as a vehicle for her own preoccupations. The painting in *Portrait of an Unknown Man* is a turning point for its narrator-protagonist, and in her critical writings, she frequently quotes painters, and claims that the visual arts are more progressive than their literary counterparts. But the sculpture in *Do You Hear Them?* isn't modern; its provenance is obscure, its shape ambiguous. The children's irreverence is offset by the solemnity of the neighbour's devotion to Art with a capital A and his response to the sculpture's aesthetic qualities. But nothing in the novel is stable: neither the sculpture, whose shape remains indeterminate, nor the laughter of the children, which is by turns "innocent" and "sly," nor even the conflict that seems to separate adults from children. Positions constantly shift as the father wavers between the attitudes of his connoisseur friend and his own offspring, and the ingredients of the novel's central configuration are reworked and reinterpreted in a series of variations and extended analogies. It is in these analogies that the novel's real energies lie, exemplifying through their extensiveness and the sheer exuberance of the writing one of the core slogans of May 68: "All Power to the Imagination."

Published in January 1972, the novel was well received. Several critics remarked that it was Nathalie's most successful work to date, and some made the link with May 68. But the period of the novel's composition had been marked by a very different kind of political engagement on Nathalie's part, when she came to the defence of the state of Israel, and found herself in a very different relation to the spirit of the times.

CHAPTER TWENTY-NINE

Israel, 1969

IN JANUARY 1969 Nathalie cancelled a government-sponsored lecture tour to Israel. As she explained to her prospective hosts, "My total disapproval of the French government's current policy towards Israel prevents me from going to Israel under the aegis of our diplomatic services."[1] She was responding to the French condemnation of Israel following an attack on Lebanon by the Israel Defense Forces in December 1968, which prompted De Gaulle to announce a blanket embargo on arms sales to Israel. This break in Franco-Israeli relations had been preceded by some unfortunate comments made by De Gaulle in November 1967, when he described the Jews as "an elite people, sure of itself and domineering," and the state of Israel as liable to "transform into a burning, conquering ambition the deeply moving wishes held for nineteen long centuries."[2] Public recognition of the part played by the French in the persecution of Jews during *les années noires* was still a decade away, and De Gaulle's remarks appeared to license a revival of French anti-Semitism. For Nathalie this was exacerbated by the fact that the left in France was now actively supporting the newly decolonised Arab states and the Palestinians displaced by the creation of the state of Israel.

She had never previously shown much interest in the country whose name was also that of her father: no Tcherniaks, no Shatunovskys, and none of her friends had immigrated there. The idea of a Jewish homeland had never held any attraction for her, and assimilation had always seemed preferable to the assertion of a positive ethnic identity. She made this position clear in the interview she gave in 1959 to the Jewish journal *L'Arche*: "During the Occupation I felt Jewish, which is to say unjustly persecuted, but not at all involved in a culture and a religion which I know nothing about. . . . I still believe that Judaism, as a sign of separateness and a solitary destiny will wane." She regarded the existence of Israel as a means of erasing Jewish identity rather than affirming it: "I'm 'for,' 100% for, literally 'over the moon' about this great achievement. . . . Israel seems to me to indicate, almost as of now, an end to the eternal 'Jewish problem.' In the sense that Israelis escape the eternal alternative between victim and renegade, martyr or traitor, Israelis are no longer Jews. This is, without doubt, the way to be 'no longer Jewish.'"[3] A visit to Israel would have allowed her to witness for herself the dream of not having to be Jewish, but in 1959 she had no plans to do so, and her support for Israel was no impediment to her endorsement of the Algerian cause in the *Manifesto of the 121* in 1960.

A cryptic note in her engagement diary for 27 October 1964 records some uncertainty about the issue: "What more did I expect of this State? is Israel's existence an accident or a historical necessity / value of journalism / homeland of the atomic Age? universal attitude / belief in an abstraction—abstract attitude."[4] These jottings (of which there are very few in the diaries) date from a period when Israel was remilitarising and had failed to comply with an agreement to repatriate and compensate Palestinian refugees. But in 1968, Nathalie's curiosity about Israel was piqued for quite other reasons after Dominique Sarraute returned from a spell working in a kibbutz, full of enthusiasm for the beauty of the landscape and deeply impressed by the regeneration brought about by the Israelis.

It was a young country, and Nathalie always responded positively to youth. Coming at the same time as the return of anti-Semitism in the Soviet Union, the French condemnation of Israel in 1969 made her determined to visit, but she did not wish to do so in any capacity that might imply complicity with the French government. So, with the help of the Israeli cultural attaché in Paris and the France-Israel Friendship Association in Tel Aviv, she made independent arrangements to spend two months there over the summer of 1969.

The result was a semiofficial stay during which Nathalie and Raymond visited the Dead Sea and the Golan Heights, as well as Jerusalem, Tel Aviv, and Haifa, where she gave the lectures she had previously cancelled. They also spent some time in the kibbutzim of Revivim in the Negev desert and Merhavia in the Jezreel Valley, where Nathalie was given work weighing and sorting eggs while Raymond packed flowers. She described this experience in a glowing account of kibbutz life published in the *Quinzaine littéraire* on her return to France in October.

The picture she paints has many of the features she had admired in Cuba and the Soviet Union in 1961. She was struck by the absolute equality in the living conditions of the kibbutzniks, and by the absence of any distinction between men and women, Jew and non-Jew. She glosses over a Palestinian attack on the kibbutz airstrip, and insists that local Palestinians were welcomed on an equal footing. The kibbutz appears as the embodiment of Nathalie's ideal of a world where Jewishness becomes invisible in a thoroughly cosmopolitan society, which included a young Dutch couple, an old lady born in Czechoslovakia, a beautiful young English woman in Wellington boots, a student from Nanterre university, and two Catholic priests. As in the case of Cuba and the Soviet Union, she remarks on the quality of the cultural life of the kibbutzim where, in addition to libraries, film projections, and dance and theatre performances, artists were given studios and writers were able to devote several days a week to their creative work.

Her views were doubtless influenced by the friends she made during her stay, since all were veterans of the kibbutz movement. These included the poet Tuviah Ruebner and Avraham Yassour who were both veterans of Merhavia kibbutz. Yassour later published *The Kibbutz: Vision and Daily Life*. Alexander and Yonat Sened, early settlers in Revivim, wrote about kibbutz life in the novels they jointly authored. Gad Shahar was one of the founders of Regavim kibbutz which Nathalie also visited, and after her return to France, he wrote to say, "Here in Regavim, no one has forgotten your visit." She sent books for the kibbutz library in Merhavia, while letters from Yonat

Sened continued to relay news about children and grandchildren. Almost all the Israelis she met belonged to a generation whose culture was essentially European: she spoke French with the Seneds, German with Ruebner, English with Yassour, and Russian with Jacob Tsur, former Israeli ambassador to Paris and author of a memoir titled *The Saga of Zionism*.

The interviewer for the *Quinzaine littéraire*—Erwin Spatz—was a journalist and translator who knew Israel well, and he asks Nathalie whether her account of the kibbutz isn't overly enthusiastic, to which she replies emphatically, "I was really impressed . . . and it was a unique experience for me." She comments on the pragmatism of life in the kibbutz, where ideology is subordinated to practical needs: "The strength of the kibbutzim comes from the fact that they're the product of necessity, not the application of abstract theories. The advanced social ideas of the early founders merely invigorated and reinforced what was geared towards the greatest effectiveness." And she concludes with a sideswipe at French socialists: "I would advise people who are genuinely interested in socialism to share in kibbutz life for a while. They might be encouraged to reflect on this concrete experiment."[5] The kibbutzim were an embodiment of socialist ideals, achieved without recourse to the slogans whose promises of freedom and revolution so often ended up, in Nathalie's view, with tyranny and dictatorship.

Her Israeli hosts treated her Jewishness as a given. An article in a Tel Aviv newspaper reported her visit to the city under the headline "Nathalie Sarraute's Jewish Soul"; another describes her as a "French Jewish writer"; and yet another speaks of her returning to her "Jewish origins." She herself was more ambivalent and confessed to Denise Goitein (who taught French literature at Tel Aviv University) that in Israel she felt ashamed of being Jewish, "inferior and ineffectual compared to the [Israeli] Jews."[6] She was also very conscious of her lack of familiarity with Jewish culture and religion.

Despite her ambivalence about her own Jewishness, she expressed unalloyed support for Israel, and on her return to Paris she wrote an unsolicited article in impassioned defence of the country. Her state of mind is described by Mary McCarthy in a letter to Hannah Arendt:

> Nathalie came by for tea yesterday and stayed for more than six hours, in a tremendous emotional state. She was back from Israel and full of passionate partisanship for the Israelis, which she has expressed in a very polemical letter to the *Nouvel Observateur*. . . . I've never seen her so excited, so unlike herself . . . ; she's obsessed by the *survival* of Israel, as though it were a beloved person in danger.

McCarthy doubted the wisdom of publishing the article, "afraid it would not convince anybody, being much too justificatory in tone," especially as Nathalie's views proved to be more nuanced in discussion:

> Mainly reservations about the Israeli way of life and the kibbutzes, which she was half in love with and half repelled by. Or maybe I should say a quarter repelled by. . . . She was impressed by the *voluntary* communism of the kibbutzes, though acknowledging, somewhat later in the conversation, that this amounts to rule by your neighbours . . . who decide whether you merit a trip outside the country or should be allowed to devote yourself to painting or writing. . . . I said I thought it might be preferable to be ruled by the state, which at least would leave you the psychic freedom of disagreement.[7]

Though Nathalie took McCarthy's criticism very well, "indeed admirably," she maintained her determination to publish the piece, and dispatched it to the *Nouvel Observateur*.

When it failed to appear, she became suspicious and demanded its return, although, according to the editor, the article's nonappearance was due simply to an internal failure of communication.[8] She sent it instead to *Le Monde*, where it was published on 11 November under the title "Deux poids et deux mesures" (Double standards), alongside a contribution of equal length by an anti-Zionist Israeli, Eli Lobel, defending the rights of the Palestinian people. Nathalie's article sought to dismantle a series of prejudices about Israel: its alleged colonialism, its supposed dependence on American money, and its apparent failure to support Palestinian refugees. She argues that Israel is held to standards that don't apply to Arab countries, and she attributes the plight of the refugees to Fatah and those same Arab countries. Most of all, she condemns the refusal by Arab states to recognise Israel's right to exist. This, in her view, threatens Israel with "extermination," and she concludes by placing blame for the present and responsibility for the future squarely with the Arabs:

> Everything becomes possible, on the other hand—and how often did people say this to me!—as soon as Israel is assured of living in safety. Everything—and I believe this, because I never saw the least sign of hatred towards the Arabs, but always, on the contrary, a sincere desire for mutual understanding, and for working together in peace. But, how do people not see this, what use is all the advice lavished on Israel, all the exhortations and admonishments? Peace lies in the hands of the Arab States, and theirs alone.[9]

The interview in the *Quinzaine littéraire* and the article in *Le Monde* were also published in the Israeli press, and both met with approval.[10] But in France the article in *Le Monde*—predictably—produced widely divergent reactions. Clearly wishing to avoid controversy on the issue, the editor forwarded readers' letters to Nathalie with the suggestion that she reply to them privately. In a supportive note which must have greatly touched her, one of her father's former colleagues wrote, "I thought about your father Илья Евсеевич and how proud he would have been of your courage in speaking the truth under current circumstances and also of the way you expressed it."[11] A note from the writer Hélène Cixous reads, "I wanted to tell you that I liked your letter in Le Monde about Israel, for the cry it raises, and for your voice. Thank you."[12]

Another expression of support came from Roger Errera, a jurist at the Council of State, who wrote endorsing Nathalie's comments about the French left. She received criticism mainly for her views about the Palestinians, to which she responded privately at some length. Jérôme Lindon, who was himself half Jewish and had been a moving spirit behind opposition to the French war in Algeria, wrote to express his disagreement on the issue. Nathalie's adamant reply triggered a further, more conciliatory letter from him where he expressed equal concern that neither the Jews nor the Arabs should face extermination. He signs off in his usual formulation as "Your friend."[13]

There's no record of the conversations about Israel that Nathalie almost certainly had with Hannah Arendt, but Arendt makes some perceptive observations in a letter to Mary McCarthy, when she writes, "Nathalie's reaction to Israel [is] quite understandable. I still remember my first reaction to the kibbutzim very well. I thought: a new aristocracy. I knew then, of course, as she probably does too, that one could not live there. 'Rule by your neighbours,' that is of course what it finally amounts to. Still, if one honestly believes in equality, Israel is very impressive." On the other hand, she is critical of Nathalie's attitude: "Nathalie's partisanship is naïve and childish, she talks like any unreflected [*sic*] Jew. But it is quite characteristic that she has reflected upon herself almost excessively and still it never occurred to her to examine herself qua Jewess."[14] This is no doubt a fair comment, but for Nathalie, the Jewish question—whether applied to herself or to the state of Israel—had always been focused through the lens of anti-Semitism. Her visit to Israel was not the occasion to embrace a positive Jewish identity, and she could never forget that under the Occupation the designation "Jew" had been a prelude to the threat of extermination. In her eyes Israel was the victim of an equivalent anti-Semitic attitude, which she sought to rectify through her article. Unlike her participation in May 68—or even her support for the *Manifesto of the 121*—this was a lone mission, where she found herself going against the grain of a majority consensus.

She continued to feel strongly about the issue, as is evident from a letter to her from Monique Wittig, written two years later following a discussion about the Palestinian question. When Wittig had commented that she could never fall out with anyone for political reasons, Nathalie had responded with astonishment to say that she herself could quite easily fall out with someone for political reasons. Hearing it from Nathalie, Wittig had then found the assertion entirely logical.[15] However, despite her feelings on the matter, Nathalie made no further pronouncements about Israel, and returned only once, briefly—in 1977—for a tour of readings from her work for student audiences. She kept all the correspondence related to her 1969 visit and to her article in *Le Monde*, but these documents were not included in the papers she donated to the Bibliothèque nationale.

The disparity between the undoubted strength of her views and her subsequent reserve is curious. But in the end, perhaps, she had maintained the assumptions of her parents' generation and considered that there was simply no way of talking about Jewishness without raising the ever-resurgent spectre of anti-Semitism.

On Her Own Terms,
1970–99

{≈≈≈W≈≈≈}

CHAPTER THIRTY

The End and Afterlife of the Nouveau Roman, 1971–82

IN JULY 1971, the Nouveau Roman was once again given collective visibility in the form of a *décade* at the Château de Cerisy-la-Salle, in the rural surrounds of Lower Normandy. The château regularly hosted conferences run by the daughter and granddaughters of Paul Desjardins, founder of the prewar Pontigny *décades*. For the event devoted to *Le Nouveau Roman: hier, aujourd'hui*, the organisers assembled five of the seven novelists who appeared on the famous photo of the Nouveau Roman: Robbe-Grillet, Claude Simon, Claude Ollier, Robert Pinget, and Nathalie. A sixth participant, Michel Butor (who had in any case arrived late for the 1959 photo), was unable to attend in person, but he sent a contribution to be read by a stand-in, and was present in spirit. The seventh was Jean Ricardou, one of the conference organisers, and the representative of a new generation of Nouveaux Romanciers. The event was a very different affair from the *colloque* at the Château d'Eu, fifteen years earlier. The austere seventeenth-century protestant château outside the village of Cerisy-la-Salle is considerably less grandiose than the Château d'Eu, and its surrounds are rustic rather than formal. More significantly, the Nouveau Roman had long since acquired a name, a reputation, and a number of established representatives.

It had also acquired a certain theoretical orthodoxy, with which, increasingly, Nathalie did not concur. Whereas Butor had stopped writing novels altogether, Robbe-Grillet had formalised his approach in 1963 with the publication of his critical essays as a single volume under a title—*For a New Novel*—which had the unmistakeable ring of a manifesto. In the early 1960s, the Nouveau Roman was supported by the avant-garde journal *Tel Quel*, founded by the young novelist and critic Philippe Sollers. Nathalie was initially drawn to the journal's ambitions and activities, which were launched in 1960 with a powerfully anti-Sartrean "Declaration." This statement of intent rejected all theories based on ideological content in favour of allowing literature to "be concerned just with itself, its own fate and its particular rules."[1] These words would have been music to Nathalie's ears, and she had every reason to take an interest in an enterprise whose editor—Sollers—was close to Francis Ponge, and whose first number included Virginia Woolf's essay "The Moment" as well as two of Ponge's own prose poems. Nathalie herself was present in the form of her contribution in answer to the question, "Do you think you have literary talent?," and *The Planetarium* was among the twelve recent publications to which members of the editorial committee gave marks out of twenty. Despite the editors' comment that the results illustrated the arbitrariness of all critical judgement, it's nonetheless telling that only Robbe-Grillet's *In the Labyrinth* and Maurice Blanchot's volume of essays *The Book to Come* scored consistently higher marks than Nathalie's novel.

The journal was also a very youthful enterprise: Sollers and his cofounder Jean-Edern Hallier were only twenty-three when the first number appeared. Hallier had taken an early interest in the Nouveau Roman, and the support given to it by *Tel Quel* was reinforced when Sollers's novel *The Park* won the Prix Médicis in 1961. Nathalie was clearly charmed by Hallier, the good-looking renegade son of a French general, and something of a maverick, whose name appears frequently in her engagement diaries between 1960 and 1963, when he parted company with Sollers. In a later interview he recalled, "I had friends in the nouveau roman gang, I saw less and less of Simon, I saw Robbe-Grillet often, and Sarraute, whom I liked a lot, very often. I used to visit her in her large apartment on the Avenue Pierre Ier de Serbie, and I traditionally saw her every Monday evening from six until eight on the first floor of the Flore."² It was no doubt in conversation with Hallier that the questions were devised for a written interview with Nathalie, published in *Tel Quel* in spring 1962 in the series "Literature, today."

She was also on friendly terms with Sollers. He was the lover of the novelist Dominique Rolin, whom Nathalie had known for many years, and she would occasionally meet Sollers for lunch in a restaurant in the rue des Saints-Pères. He had liked *The Age of Suspicion*, especially for the notion of sub-conversation, and gave *The Planetarium* a high mark (16/20) in the *Tel Quel* listing. And while he had some reservations about her work, he appreciated her awareness of the "unconscious malice of human beings" and what he saw as her fundamental cruelty—amply illustrated in her writing.³

Until 1964, several numbers of *Tel Quel* carried announcements for a forthcoming contribution from Nathalie, and there were also promises of an article about her work by Jean Lagrolet, whose name had been associated with the Nouveau Roman in the early days. (He was the first recipient of the Prix de Mai.) Neither piece ever appeared. It seems likely that Nathalie's contribution would have been the text of the lecture she regularly gave on Flaubert, but as her views on the author differed from those of the structuralist-minded critics increasingly associated with *Tel Quel*, she offered it to *Preuves*, whose editor François Bondy was in greater sympathy with her own approach. The article duly appeared under the title "Flaubert the precursor" in 1965.⁴ Whereas the structuralists' Flaubert was a producer of sentences and gratuitous descriptions, her Flaubert was the first writer to make inauthenticity the subject of fiction.

As far as the Nouveau Roman was concerned, Sollers was primarily interested in Robbe-Grillet, as was Jean Ricardou, who joined *Tel Quel* in 1962 and became the self-appointed spokesman for a *new* Nouveau Roman. This version stressed the formal, purely textual component of literature, summed up in Ricardou's much-quoted formula, according to which a novel is "less the writing of an adventure, than the adventure of writing."⁵ When Sollers changed his position on the Nouveau Roman and broke with Robbe-Grillet in 1964, Ricardou remained close to Robbe-Grillet, who was more than happy to subscribe to a Nouveau Roman #2. Its theorisation was set out in Ricardou's *Pour une théorie du nouveau roman* (Towards a theory of the Nouveau Roman) published just a few months before the Cerisy conference in July 1971.

Against this background Nathalie found herself in circumstances that recalled her association with *Les Temps modernes*, where an initial convergence of outlook had come asunder. It's therefore not surprising that she had at first been reluctant to take part in the *décade*. As she explains in her talk, "I knew that I would once again find myself, as I have so often in my life, in rather singular situation. In an isolated position, which I am not complaining about—it has probably been necessary for me—but it is not pleasant enough for me to actively seek it out."[6] Ricardou, whose face was always disconcertingly hidden behind dark glasses, set the agenda for the proceedings, and delivered the opening address in which he sketched out the history of the Nouveau Roman from "yesterday" to "today" in reference to the title of the conference. Nathalie was respectfully relegated to "yesterday," credited with having initiated the dismantling of character which other Nouveaux Romanciers had subsequently continued by other means.

However, one of the participants wrote to Nathalie later saying that in her view the conference had succeeded in relegating the entire Nouveau Roman to "yesterday," and she observes that "the whole thing was actually the funeral oration for the 'nouveau roman,' because it was clear that the name no longer meant anything and that people were talking about individuals, not a movement." In fact, she adds, the discussions had been little more than "a great game, an exchange of *politesses* with knives held at the ready behind people's backs."[7]

Nathalie was a beneficiary of these *politesses*, but the deference had its own marginalising effects which she turned to advantage in her talk by distancing herself from the language of contemporary structuralist linguistics with its "signifiers," its "signifieds," and its "scriptors." Whereas the new orthodoxy proclaimed the self-generating nature of literary language, untethered from any representational purpose, she asserted the necessity of going in pursuit of as yet unnamed realities. And she insisted with equal conviction on the need to resist the tyrannies that are so easily exercised by language itself:

FIGURE 25. With Jean Ricardou, Nouveau Roman Colloquium,
Cerisy-la-Salle, July 1971. © Archives Pontigny-Cerisy.

Where language extends its power, there arise rote-learned ideas, des-
ignations, definitions, psychological categories, sociological categories,
moral categories. It drains, hardens, and separates something that is
just fluidity and movement. . . . As soon as this formless, trembling, wa-
vering thing tries to emerge into the light, language, with all its power
and its weaponry, always ready to intervene and reestablish order—its
order—pounces on it and crushes it.[8]

She could have been talking about Brezhnev's Russia, or the way
that revolutionary slogans backfire, or even the very literary ortho-
doxies by which she was once again confronted. Literature and politics were not so far apart when looked at from the perspective of
power relations. But in the literary domain, the orthodoxy she condemned provided her with more potential for the personal anarchy
on which, as she confessed to one interviewer, she thrived: "I prefer
order to disorder, because a social order permits personal anarchy."[9]
She was still the Elephant's Child, drawing attention to truths that

no one wanted to hear, and being "slapped down" for her pains. (The word is repeated in the Cerisy talk.)

While the young Turks talked of "generators" (the individual words that engendered entire texts in the manner of those of Raymond Roussel, Pierre Janet's onetime patient), or took part in the sexual activities organised by Catherine Robbe-Grillet in the attics of the château, Nathalie kept a low profile.[10] She didn't join in any of the discussions, except the one that followed her own talk, where she took issue with comments in a paper about her work given by the critic Micheline Tison-Braun. And she left after only three days.

In a rather more extreme measure, she later demanded a reprint of the entire volume in which her talk appeared because the text of the discussion hadn't been submitted to her for approval. Although her many corrections were purely stylistic, the volume was pulped and a new one printed in its stead. Nathalie's fear of misrepresentation often expressed itself in corrections of this kind, and on this occasion her sense of being out of step with Jean Ricardou had made her even more apprehensive. A letter from Anne Heurgon-Desjardins, daughter of Paul Desjardins and founder of the Centre Culturel in Cerisy, offered some consolation for this incompatibility:

> How did I feel about the incident over the publication of the "Discussions about the Nouveau Roman?" A little differently from you. I'd said to my daughter Edith [Heurgon], when she and Jean Ricardou were preparing the publication: "I know you don't usually show the texts to each of the participants, but I beg you to do it for Nathalie Sarraute, she's so sensitive!" . . .
>
> When the book came out I only read one text, yours, followed by the discussion. Unlike you, I liked it. It brought back your voice in the library with that certain something that's Russian, that's you. Your presence, your sincerity. Without anticipating any conflict, I wanted to write and tell you this. With the others in the Nouveau Roman, it's contrived, calculated, and I'm not touched by it. With you it's like the memories I'm trying to record of our great friends at Pontigny, it's alive, it's sensitive, it restores life and transcends death.[11]

Nathalie found a considerably more sympathetic environment when she escaped from Cerisy to take part in one of Gilbert Gadoffre's

Rencontres in Loches, where he now held his annual gatherings. She delivered a short paper ("Is Proust Topical?") and took active part in the ensuing discussion.[12] Both the topic—Proust—and the company were far more congenial to her than those she had found in Cerisy.

Her differences with the *nouveau* Nouveau Roman, structuralist theories of language, and the French left on the matter of Israel all revived her long-standing resistance to what in *The Golden Fruits* are called "arguments from authority," imposed by the rule of force and attracting the unthinking support of the crowd. It was a theme she returned to in her novel *"Fools Say,"* published in 1976. The utterance of the title is ascribed to an anonymous "Maître" who dismisses dissenters with the label "fool," and the novel explores the politics of such verbal categorisations. It makes little difference whether these categorisations are superficially innocent (a grandmother is repeatedly described as "sweet") or experienced as hostile (a child is described as "jealous") or frankly negative (another character is dismissed as "gifted, but not intelligent"), since they all exert some form of power.

The elucidating imagery is often violent, showing how easily such use of language supports a reign of terror. Despite the number of concrete instances that Nathalie had encountered in real life, and the hints she dropped to friends and acquaintances that the expression in the title had been used by someone she knew personally, her aim is not to portray particular individuals or any given convictions. And she avoids setting herself up as an alternative "Maître" by leaving it to the anonymous voices in the novel to comment on the verbal action, just as the characters so garrulously do in the plays—*It's Beautiful* and *It Is There*—that she was also writing during the 1970s.

The novel consolidated Nathalie's break with what had become of the Nouveau Roman, which nevertheless enjoyed a long afterlife despite the obsequies that the Cerisy conference proved to have been. This was largely thanks to its shift of gravity towards the academic world, which was already in evidence at the Cerisy *décade* where, except for the novelists themselves, almost all the participants held university posts. Two of the three organisers—Françoise van Rossum-Guyon and Raymond Jean—taught at the universities of Amsterdam and Aix-en-Provence, respectively. Other speakers came from the United States, Italy, Germany, Canada, the United Kingdom, and as far afield as Japan. From the late 1950s the Nouveau Roman had been the subject of courses, theses, and academic publications in the United States, and several other countries had subsequently followed suit. Nathalie took an active interest in much of this academic work, answering questions, supplying suggestions for further reading, correcting misconceptions, arranging to meet thesis students at her home in Paris, and very occasionally commenting on manuscript drafts of books for academics she knew and liked.

She was often helpful to younger scholars, writing a letter of support for a tenure application, and giving permission to Shulamith Weissman, whom she had met in Israel, to publish a letter from her as a preface to Weissman's book.[13] In 1993, she attended the doctoral viva of a young French scholar, Françoise Asso, whom she had come to know personally. Indeed, she became friends with a number of academic Sarraute specialists, and contributed a grateful encomium to the *Festschrift* for Valerie Minogue (author of one of the first English-language monographs devoted to her work), citing the bonds of friendship that united them along with "her constant and generous support over many years, and her very great, invariably penetrating and subtle attention to my work."[14] So many of these contacts and friendships were made abroad that in 1972, Bernard Pivot remarked that Nathalie's reputation as "a writer of exceptional quality" was perhaps greater outside France than it was at home.[15] Double-edged as it may sound, there was some truth in Pivot's comment, and she certainly never appeared on his famous long-running literary TV show *Apostrophes*.

She seized every opportunity to lecture, and these invitations took her abroad at least twice a year, and sometimes a good deal more often. The long train journeys of her childhood had left her with a taste for travel, added to which the lecture fees were a welcome boost to her income. The trips to Italy, Switzerland, Scandinavia, Cuba, Germany, the United States, and the Soviet Union in the late 1950s and early 1960s were just the beginning. In 1966 she visited Mexico, where she met the poet Octavio Paz, and in 1968 she went to Chile, Uruguay, and Argentina, where she met Jorge Luis

Borges and Victoria Ocampo, who edited the influential literary magazine *Sur*. Although interest in the Nouveau Roman was often the trigger for invitations, Nathalie made it clear from early on that she would not share a platform with other writers, whether Nouveaux Romanciers or not.[16] She needed these encounters to be on her own terms

In 1970, a two-month tour took her first to India and then to Japan, one of the few countries whose language she didn't speak—with disconcerting results, as she later recalled in an interview:

> My most comical memory is of Japan. They always ask you to write your lecture in advance so it can be translated. So, when I arrived in the lecture hall all the students had my text. I was seated next to the professor, on the podium and he began to read my lecture. Obviously I didn't understand any of it. But at one point, quite a long time after he had started, I heard the name Mallarmé which was near the beginning of my talk. I was panic-stricken. In fact, the professor was commenting on my text while reading it. When he finished two hours later, it was my turn to speak. But this was in 1978, and very few students in Japan spoke either French or English at that time. I wasn't allowed the usual back-and-forth of questions.[17]

The lecture in question—"Language in the Art of the Novel"—was one she had not previously given, but in response to the growing preoccupation with linguistics and structuralist theory, she was beginning to stake out the position she set out more fully in her talk at the Cerisy conference. In any case, unfamiliarity was not in itself a barrier, and as she told Sonia Rykiel, she threw herself into new environments in every way she could: "When I arrive in a country, I have to imbibe the food . . . as a way of assimilating and integrating. In Japan, I liked the raw fish, and in England the porridge."[18] Sushi is a far cry from porridge, but the function of each was the same, and in Tokyo she and Raymond took part in a tea ceremony, Nathalie appearing considerably more at ease on a floor cushion than her rather less supple husband.

A visit to Czechoslovakia was cancelled in 1970 at the behest of the Ministry of Culture, which was clamping down on the international activities of the Czech Writers' Union. Nathalie had spoken there the previous year, and she visited Poland in 1971.[19] She returned several times to Germany, and a two-week tour of Italy in 1970 included a lunch hosted by the French ambassador in the grand surrounds of the Palazzo Farnese. She made many further trips to the United Kingdom, where during a visit to Manchester in 1981 she was able—thanks to Gilbert Gadoffre, who now held the chair of French in the university—to include a trip to Haworth Parsonage, the home of Emily Brontë. Raymond often accompanied her on these tours as he scaled down his own professional activities. He would oversee the travel arrangements (some of the itineraries are written in his hand), and for each of her lectures he drew up a set of "speech notes" of the kind lawyers use. She kept these notes alongside the written text to enhance the oral character of her talks, which made them such a success with their audiences. And despite having heard them many times, Raymond would attend each and every one.

Nathalie had a portfolio of material in both French and English versions where she elucidated issues relating to her own work: "The novel and reality," "Flaubert," and "Form and content in the novel," to which she added the lecture on language in the novel first given Japan, and a short talk, "The Happiness of Man," also given for the first time in Japan.[20] A discussion of her theatre, "The Inside of the Glove," was first delivered at the University of Wisconsin–Madison in the United States in 1974. The lectures reflected her concerns as these evolved from the debates about the nature of the reality depicted in fiction that followed her disagreements with both *Les Temps modernes* and Robbe-Grillet to her preoccupation with language in the latter part of the 1960s and the less contentious topic of her theatre in the 1970s. With the exception of "The Happiness of Man," she regarded them all as providing sufficiently illuminating commentary of her work to merit inclusion in her *Complete Works*.

The lectures were an experience that Nathalie relished, since, somewhat counterintuitively, they were a chance to communicate without anxiety:

> I love giving lectures to students. I don't find it intimidating. I always
> have the sense that we are having a conversation, and that what we're
> talking about interests them as much as it interests me. They're glad to
> be there and to talk with me, or rather to talk about the topic, because

> I disappear completely. I don't see myself on the podium and I abso-
> lutely can't see how they see me. I don't think about it. . . . When I give
> a lecture to students, I'm always very free because I don't exist. Words
> come out of me and go towards them, and they'll be accepted because
> they're bearers of something that I feel is sincere and true.[21]

This slightly odd combination of contact and invisibility prompted her to introduce a different format for her talks, as she replaced formal lectures with readings from her work, followed by *causeries* (informal conversations), a model she proposes in correspondence prior to a lecture tour in the United States in 1974.[22] Also somewhat oddly, the readings she offered were always from her radio plays, which involve different voices for the different roles, and are not easily conveyed by one person. But as she explained, "I have the impression when I read them aloud that I'm rediscovering what I hear when I write. Because when I write, I hear all the words, I hear the rhythm of the sentences; it's a sort of internal murmur. And I have the impression that no one except me can capture that. When actors read them, it often sounds wrong to me."[23] Between them, the lectures and the readings allowed Nathalie to take her audience as close as possible to the experience of "creation in the nascent state," to cite Yvon Belaval's formula. It helped that she had a very charismatic reading voice, and the American academic Roger Shattuck once remarked on the "deep, intimate, vital sounds that come from the throat of this modest yet resolute woman."[24] In due course, on the back of the success of the readings to live audiences, she made audio recordings of several of her books.

It was a voice and a communicative stance that found their way into her writing with *The Use of Speech* published in 1980, where a first-person authorial speaker addresses a singular or plural inter-locutor, anticipates queries, and includes the reader in a shared endeavour as he examines a series of linguistic exchanges. The volume reverts to the short format originally adopted in *Tropisms*, but the ten unrelated encounters are portrayed with an equanimity very different from the anxieties through which the tropisms were registered in her first book. Each turns on an apparently innocent, incidental remark—"See you very soon," "And why not?," "Aesthetic," "My dear," and so forth—which is revealed to have unexpectedly powerful effects on its recipient. Much like the plays, which are also constructed around linguistic events, the ten short texts demonstrate just how much is at stake in the use of speech, the phrase so aptly chosen for the book's title.

The first of these texts is, however, a little different from the others. It places Chekhov's dying words—*Ich sterbe*—under the microscope to re-create the mind-set of the Russian writer, as he imparts his own medical diagnosis to the German doctor attending him. Chekhov himself, speaking in the first person, provides the commentary. The scene had unspoken personal resonances for Nathalie, which were not necessarily shared by her presumed audience who, unlike her, were not alive when Chekhov died in 1904, had not lived in exile, had not suffered from the TB that killed the Russian playwright, and were very probably not afflicted with Nathalie's preoccupation with death. Her own recording of the text is one of her finest.[25]

In addition to the lecture tours, Nathalie received invitations for longer stays at individual universities. Most of these were in the United States: the University of Texas in Austin where she stayed for over a month in 1967, a stay of a similar length at the University of Laval in Quebec in 1970, Princeton University in 1972 (where she gave the prestigious Gauss Lectures, which Hannah Arendt came to hear), the University of California, Irvine in 1975 and UC Santa Cruz in 1976, and in 1977—the same year as her brief return to Israel—a three-week residency as Distinguished Visiting Professor at the American University in Cairo. There was never any question that she would do any formal teaching. As Roger Shattuck at the University of Texas explained, "Above all, we will hope to have your reactions as a practicing writer . . . without following any predetermined scholarly or critical method. Your authority would be that of a novelist and human being, not of a professor."[26]

In the event, Nathalie joined his seminar on Flaubert, visited almost every undergraduate course on French literature, and directed students in a performance of her play *Silence*. She also gave an electrifying reading of a violent episode from Michelet's *History of France* and some extracts from Saint-Simon's *Memoirs*. She threw herself into faculty life, making friends with Christopher Middleton, poet, professor of German, and translator of modern German literature, gossiping unashamedly, and constantly asking personal questions about students, faculty members, and other Austin residents whom she met.[27] At the University of Laval in Quebec she joined Béatrix Beck, the Belgian-born French novelist, who was teaching a course on the Nouveau Roman. It was this visit that Beck recalled in her novel *Noli*, where Nathalie is given the name Prisca Darfeuil and described as a "distinguished guest."[28] Raymond was a discreet but supportive presence, as one witness recalled in a letter to Nathalie: "It was great having you here in Chicago and most pleasant to meet your charming husband. I can still see him smiling as he listens to the rush of Americans talking to him and always about some aspect of something while he never really let them know what he was thinking."[29]

At Irvine Nathalie had an unexpected encounter with Olivier Tcherniak, the son of her half brother Jacques. He had a postdoctoral position in the Department of Economics at nearby UCLA, where he was also doing some teaching in the French Department. It was here that he met the aunt whose books he and his parents had read, but with whom they had had no contact since the death of Ilya in 1949. Aunt and nephew established a warm rapport, and since Raymond had not accompanied Nathalie on this occasion, they spent a great deal of time together. Nathalie talked about Russia, the Tcherniak family, and Uncle Yasha, while Olivier was struck by her anxious preoccupation with death. He was also surprised to observe that, despite her considerable renown (this was 1975), she was greatly intimidated by Michel Foucault, who was visiting Irvine at the same time.[30] The relationship continued after Olivier's return to France, but it was not enough to deter Nathalie from misrepresenting Jacques's achievements in the *Chronology* for her *Complete Works*. Rather than failing in his studies, as she reports, he had obtained a doctorate in chemistry, built up Ilya's business after succeeding his father to the point where—in another of history's ironies—it was taken over by a German firm during the 1960s, with Jacques retaining directorship. When he died in 1976 Nathalie did not attend his funeral.

The culmination of North American interest in the Nouveau Roman came in late September 1982 with a three-day conference in New York organised by Tom Bishop, director of NYU's Center for

French Civilization and Culture. Under the title "Three Decades of the French New Novel," Bishop brought together Robbe-Grillet, Claude Simon, Robert Pinget, and Nathalie. Borrowing the formula used at the Cerisy conference in 1971 (where Bishop himself had spoken), each of the novelists gave a talk, followed by a paper from one of the academic participants. The emphasis in 1982 was far more on the individual novelists than on any monolithic Nouveau Roman. There was considerable wariness about "theory," and the novelists had most to say about their own particular concerns. Nathalie's talk was entirely autobiographical, as she recounted the emergence of her work against a background of incomprehension and resistance, and Monique Wittig provided a penetrating account of language as action in Nathalie's work.[31]

Bishop described the conference as a "retrospective," while also asserting that the Nouveau Roman was "THE major emanation of the French novel in the second half of the twentieth century, an erstwhile avant-garde that [had] become for many the major mode of novelistic production not only in France, but in other European and American cultures as well."[32] A roundtable of four contemporary American novelists was there to support his claim. But as the Nouveau Roman became mainstream, the autobiographical slant of the Nouveaux Romanciers' own remarks prefigured a turn soon to be taken by both Robbe-Grillet and Nathalie when they embarked on overtly autobiographical ventures. In *Le Miroir qui revient* (The returning mirror), published only two years after the New York conference, Robbe-Grillet quite explicitly presents this development as a challenge to the orthodoxy that had attached itself to the Nouveau Roman, whose original raison d'être had been anything but orthodox.

CHAPTER THIRTY-ONE

Plays on Stage, 1972–88

AS SHE ENTERED HER SEVENTIES, Nathalie's writing for the theatre continued to provide her with concerns that took the language of the tropism in new directions. Her third play, *Izzum, or What Is Called Nothing* was published with *Silence* and *The Lie* by Gallimard in 1970. As alert as ever to the effects of language, she explores the effects of the pronunciation of the suffix *-isme* as *-isma* (*-izzum* in English) in words such as "*capitalisme*," "*syndicalisme*," or "*structuralisme*." The play was picked up by the theatre director Claude Régy, who staged it at the Espace Pierre-Cardin, inaugurating an association that lasted to the end of the decade, and clinching Nathalie's growing reputation as a dramatist. They had shared theatrical interests in Chekhov, Pirandello, and Strindberg, whose *Dance of Death* Régy directed in 1969. His conception of theatre was particularly well suited to Nathalie's writing and facilitated the transition from an auditory to a scenic medium. He regarded theatre primarily as "a mental space, an open space rather than stage-set," and his productions exemplified a pared-down form of theatricality, with scarcely any movement on the part of the actors, who mostly stood face-on to the audience.[1] This ethos was much appreciated by Nathalie, who later said, "I always agreed with Claude Régy's productions. They really succeeded in bringing out language in the pure state."[2]

By giving visual form to the anonymous, disembodied voices of the radio plays, there was always a risk that an audience would focus on the gestures and physical appearance of the actors, and view them as having conventionally realist, socially defined attributes. For this reason, Nathalie sought as much neutrality as possible in her characters, who were predominantly and unremarkably male, in middle years, and with no discernible social identity. (She once reprimanded a director who wanted the actors each to have a glass in their hand.)[3] Her reluctance to use female characters stemmed from her conviction that it was impossible for a woman to be heard on air or to appear on stage without being endowed with all the trappings of a female identity that was irrelevant to Nathalie's concerns. Female roles in her plays are primarily a means of introducing variety in the different voices of her largely anonymous characters.

The actors for the 1973 production of *Izzum* included Michael Lonsdale and the young Gérard Depardieu, both of whom participated actively in the rehearsals which Nathalie described as "a meticulous and very sensitive peeling-off and laying bare of each vibration of the language."[4] The production was generally well received, and the critic Mathieu Galey, who had an intuitive grasp of the principles of Nathalie's theatre (and became a friend), praised "her extraordinary ear for the idiocy of everyday language, and the muted but real comedy with which she reconstructs it." He also singled out "the power of Gérard Depardieu in this exercise, the slightly menacing unease which he manages to introduce, the astonishing talents that he allows us to glimpse on the threshold of a great career, [along with] the merits of Michael Lonsdale, who is incomparable in his stammering emotion, whose abrupt shifts one follows on his virtually impassive face."[5]

Nathalie's involvement with Régy helped to sharpen her own understanding of her theatre, which she outlined in the short essay "The Inside of the Glove," originally delivered as a lecture at a conference on modern theatre held in April 1974 at the University of Wisconsin–Madison. She describes how her writing for the theatre—which she first thought impossible—had required her to find a way of turning unspoken sub-conversation into articulated conversation, so that "the inside became the outside," like the "glove" of her title. She observes that the resulting contrast between the "unusual" content of the dialogue and the familiar conversational medium through which it was articulated was often the source of considerable comic effect, and she confesses that she frequently found

FIGURE 26. *Isma*, directed by Claude Régy. With Pascale de Boysson, Gérard Depardieu, and Dominique Blanchar, 1973. © Archives Nicolas Treatt.

herself laughing out loud as she wrote.[6] (The drawback of Régy's staging, as she later acknowledged, was that it tended to downplay the humour in her work.)[7] She also acknowledges her debt to both Régy and Barrault, and to the actors who had performed her plays. In contrast to her usual remarks about her isolation in the literary world, she portrays theatre as an essentially collaborative enterprise, which achieved creative results not otherwise available to the writer.

Boosted perhaps by these collaborations, as well as by the growing recognition of her status as a dramatist, Nathalie wrote another play—*It's Beautiful*—which was published in 1975 in the *Cahiers Renaud Barrault*. Although the piece was conceived for radio, Régy immediately took it on, and produced it for the stage in the small auditorium at the Théâtre d'Orsay, where the Renaud-Barrault Company was now based. It opened in October 1975, with Emmanuelle Riva in the role of SHE. The drama is built around themes explored in Nathalie's previous novel, *Do You Hear Them?*, as a son

resists the blandishments of his parents (SHE and HE) to acknowledge that some unspecified item is "beautiful." In addition to the text
of the play, the October number of the *Cahiers Renaud Barrault*
included the text of Nathalie's lecture "The Inside of the Glove" and
an article by Régy about *It's Beautiful* where he discusses the sense
of impending disintegration contained in Nathalie's dialogues.[8] Performances ran until January 1976, and it was Galey's review in *Les
Nouvelles littéraires* which rescued Nathalie from "the threat of
death" to which she always felt her work was vulnerable.[9]

The alternation of her writing between prose fiction and theatre
continued, as *"Fools Say,"* which came out in December 1976, generated its own theatrical progeny in 1978 with *It Is There*. This time,
the text was published by Gallimard in a volume titled simply
Théâtre, containing all five of Nathalie's plays in reverse chronological order, giving *It Is There* pride of place. Once again Régy responded to the publication of a new play by Nathalie, which, as she
later told Gilbert Gadoffre, she had conceived for the first time with
the potential for a stage performance in mind.[10] Régy's theatrical
style had no doubt helped her to imagine her play in scenic form,
and he scheduled a production for November 1978 at the Centre
Pompidou, which had opened the previous year to worldwide publicity. However, in the course of rehearsals, he decided to cancel the
production and rethink his approach.

Paradoxically, and despite Nathalie's anticipation of a stage production, this rethink took the form of a radio version, which Régy
characterised as a "sound performance."[11] The play had already been
broadcast in German on Radio Cologne in January 1978, but Régy's
was the first French radio version. It aired on 4 May 1980 on France
Culture in an extended programme, which included readings by
Nathalie, an interview with Régy, and another between him and
Nathalie. In the intervening eighteen months, the detour via radio
had allowed him to devise a stage version of the play, which built on
the sense of interiority initially developed for radio performance.
This version ran from January to March 1980 in a return to the
small auditorium at the Théâtre d'Orsay. The largely positive press
included another perceptive response from Matthieu Galey, who
applauded Régy's attempt to allow the audience experience the
drama from within.[12]

Although Nathalie was now well outside the orbit of Robbe-Grillet and the *nouveau* Nouveau Roman, her involvement in the theatre had brought her into closer proximity to Marguerite Duras, whose work had been directed by Jean-Louis Barrault, Claude Régy, and Simone Benmussa, performed by some of the actors who also performed Nathalie's work (Madeleine Renaud, Michael Lonsdale, Gérard Depardieu, and Emmanuelle Riva), and staged at the same theatres (the Théâtre de l'Odéon, the Théâtre d'Orsay, and the Théâtre du Rond-Point). In autumn 1975, plays by the two authors were being performed concurrently at the Renaud-Barraults' Théâtre d'Orsay—Nathalie's *It's Beautiful*, and a revival of Duras's *Whole Days in the Trees*. A *soirée d'hommage* for the two writers was arranged for 17 November, during which, in the mix of complicity and rivalry that characterised their relations, rivalry came to dominate. Nathalie later regaled Matthieu Galey with an account of the event, although she mistakenly recalls a single occasion as two separate ones:

> I was asked to read a page from [Duras's] *L'amour*. I wasn't too keen. But I'd read the text, and I found it beautiful, so I did it. After which, I went and sat down in a corner. No thank-you, no nothing. It didn't bother me.
>
> I found it odd, that's all.
>
> A few months later, it was my turn and Madeleine insisted that Duras do the same for me and read a page of mine. She arrived, in a foul temper: "I've got a film on the go, I had other things to do, this is inconvenient." And once she was on the stage, she stepped forward and announced that she wouldn't read anything, she didn't know what to choose, that she didn't like all those little grey words, but if anyone wanted to ask questions about her own work, she'd reply![13]

In Nathalie's view, Duras couldn't bear to see anyone else in the limelight, and the event led to a breakdown in their already precarious relations. Things were patched up nine years later, when Nathalie expressed her admiration for Duras's *Savannah Bay* at the Théâtre du Rond-Point. "As soon as I admire her . . ." she remarked acerbically to Galey. In conversation she would often hark back to Duras's reference to her "little grey words," which she contrasted with Duras's one-word estimation of her own work as "sublime."[14]

Their relations had always been marked by rivalry, and in later years Nathalie would insist that "we had nothing in common." Unlike Nathalie, Duras had never been reluctant to flaunt her femininity and also to advertise the biographical basis of her writing, which Nathalie privately regarded as "trashy."[15] But in stressing their differences she was primarily resisting the widespread assumption that women writers should be judged by comparison with each other. In more nuanced remarks made towards the end of her life when Nathalie had mellowed with regard to Duras, she commented, "I like Marguerite Duras very much, but what exasperates me terribly are the continual comparisons made between women, which women themselves also make. It's impossible to imagine work more unlike hers and mine. . . . Why compare two writers like her and me who have nothing in common, except that we are women. It's so tiresome. Women create rivalry between each other which I find tiresome."[16] However, whether they liked it or not, their paths had frequently crossed: in the Éditions de Minuit and the Nouveau Roman with which Duras had somewhat ambivalent relations; on the lecture tour to the United Kingdom in 1961; and on the committee for the Prix Médicis which Duras had joined in 1960. Duras had supported Wittig's *L'Opoponax* for the prize and written an influential article about the book. In then seeking Wittig's friendship, Duras once again found herself competing with Nathalie, and as Wittig later confided to Nathalie, Duras had never forgiven her for becoming Nathalie's friend rather than hers.[17]

Relations between Nathalie and Duras nevertheless had their positive moments. In a note to Nathalie written in December 1968, Duras writes "with all my affection." For her part, Nathalie was willing to acknowledge the talent of her unwanted rival, about whom she nonetheless had a clear-sighted view. Speaking on one occasion about "dear Marguerite," she comments, "If I had an ounce of her self-confidence, the certainty she had about her own talent I would have been a happy woman. She loved compliments. And she mostly deserved them."[18]

It Is There was the last of Nathalie's plays to be produced by Régy, who always felt that he had never found a way of doing justice to her work, despite holding it in the highest esteem.[19] She continued, nonetheless, to write for the theatre, and *The Use of Speech*, published in February 1980, was immediately followed by *For No Good Reason*, which has since become her best-known and best-loved work for the stage. Like many of the texts in *The Use of Speech*, the play turns on a single utterance examined in the context of an encounter between two old friends as they discuss a remark—"That's . . . good"—once made by one of them to the other. Taken as a put-down, its implications are forensically and exhaustively unpicked in the dialogue that follows its recall. (Greenroom gossip has it that the play's origins lay with Robbe-Grillet who had allegedly once responded to Nathalie with the same comment.)[20] The play was broadcast on Radio-France in December 1981, and published soon after in a single volume by Gallimard. Strangely, it didn't receive a stage performance for another five years, when Simone Benmussa directed an English-language version at the Beckett Theatre on West Forty-Second Street in New York.

Nathalie's acquaintance with Benmussa dated back to Jean-Louis Barrault's production of *Silence* and *The Lie* in 1966. A friendship had developed between them, based on a shared literary sensibility explored in a documentary film, *Regards sur l'écriture: Nathalie Sarraute* (A look at writing: Nathalie Sarraute), made by Benmussa in 1977, and developed a decade later in the book-length conversations published as *Nathalie Sarraute: Qui êtes-vous?* in 1987. She had also become a theatre director in her own right, and her 1982 production of Virginia Woolf's light-hearted, satirical *Freshwater* was performed entirely by writers, including Ionesco, Robbe-Grillet, the poet Michel Deguy, the philosopher and novelist Jean-Paul Aron, the surrealist poet Joyce Mansour, the essayist Viviane Forrester—with Nathalie in the (masculine) role of a visionary butler. For once, she was on stage in her own right. Ionesco, as the Victorian poet Tennyson, sported a long white beard, but since he could never remember his lines, he would make such absurd faces that Nathalie had difficulty maintaining the solemn demeanour required of her role. She relished the experience of acting so much that at the curtain call she intercepted the bouquet destined for Simone Benmussa, graciously accepting it for herself. After a first performance in Paris in December 1982, NYU provided the venue for a New York staging of the play in October 1983, exactly one year on from the NYU conference on the Nouveau Roman whose organiser,

Tom Bishop, also had a part in the production. It was performed again in Spoleto in July 1984, and a few months later in November it had a final outing in Paris.

Benmussa returned to New York in May 1985 with her premiere of *For No Good Reason*, translated by the Australian radio producer Kaye Mortley. It was performed in a double bill with a stage adaptation of Nathalie's autobiographical *Childhood*, published in 1983 (on which more in chapter 32). The adaptation of *Childhood* had already been performed in the original French in February 1984 in the small auditorium at the Théâtre du Rond-Point, where the Renaud-Barrault company was now based. Benmussa had been given a free hand by Barrault, and she used it to explore new theatrical ideas with avant-garde work. Like Régy, she was interested in creating a theatre of inwardness, or what she called "dramatic poetry," which she found in Nathalie's writing. They established a mutual understanding, and as Nathalie explained in an interview in 1986, "I have complete confidence in Simone Benmussa, we're very alike. We have the same sense of humour. People who read me don't always notice this humour, but it's there, it exists. It comes out well in production."[21] As time went on, this humour was increasingly evident in her relations with others.

It was Benmussa's interest in the inner life that led her to adapt nontheatrical texts for the stage. Nathalie later regretted agreeing to the adaptation of *Childhood*, but she contributed to the production by recording the portions of the text where the narrator's alter ego intervenes to challenge the narrator's memories of childhood. This recording provided a voice-off in dialogue with the onstage narrator, whose costume was designed by Sonia Rykiel. Glenn Close, who was soon to acquire fame for her role in the film *Fatal Attraction*, starred in the New York production, where the double bill with *For No Good Reason* received only a muted reception.

The French reception of Benmussa's production of *For No Good Reason* at the Théâtre du Rond-Point was a very different affair. The play ran for six weeks from 17 February 1986, and was well served by Benmussa's responsiveness to the humour in the script, held in perfect equilibrium with the much darker elements that also surface between the two friends. The text was equally well served by the actors Samy Frey and Jean-François Balmer, who alternated the parts of M.1 and M.2. The mostly very positive reviews defined the play as the culmination of Nathalie's career as a dramatist, and the critic in *Le Monde* wrote, "Alongside her, other writers are deaf. . . . She makes drama out of every word, however transitory. . . . The play . . . is hugely comic. And at the same time, it's a terrible tragedy." He concludes, "This is great theatre, performed by great actors [and] a major event."[22] The production returned to the Théâtre du Rond-Point for a further two-month run in November.

In the summer of 1986 the play was performed at the Avignon Festival in a separate production by Michel Dumoulin, who, in a celebration of Nathalie's work, also directed the actress Maria Casarès in *It Is There*, along with readings from *Tropisms* and *The Use of Speech*, staged in the intimacy of the Collégiale Notre-Dame in Villeneuve-lez-Avignon. All this ensured a high profile for Nathalie at France's leading theatre festival. Dumoulin had already filmed *It's Beautiful* for television in 1980, and went on to make a film version of his Avignon production of *It Is There*, which was televised the following year. In a further transition from stage to screen (originally promised to Simone Benmussa), Jacques Doillon created a masterly film version of *For No Good Reason* in 1988 with Jean-Louis Trintignant and André Dussollier. In Doillon's recall, the eighty-eight-year-old Nathalie was "wild with joy" when she saw it.[23] And justifiably so: frequently rescreened since its first showing, it secured Nathalie's place in the French theatrical repertoire, where the play continues to be regularly performed.

CHAPTER THIRTY-TWO

A Life and a Death, 1983–89

FOR NO GOOD REASON was Nathalie's last play. By the time it received its first French stage performance February 1986, her reputation had already been sealed by the publication of *Childhood* in April 1983, and it was no longer possible to say, as Bernard Pivot did a decade previously, that her qualities as a writer were better appreciated abroad than they were at home.[1] French recognition had in any case been unequivocally conferred on Nathalie the previous year, when, as only the second woman recipient in its thirty-one-year history, she was awarded the Grand Prix national des Lettres by the Ministry of culture. (Marguerite Yourcenar was the first.)

Childhood has remained the book for which she is now best known. There's nothing on the title page to define it as autobiography, and it's only in the opening exchange between the narrator and her alter ego that the formulation "childhood memories" is reluctantly accepted. Each of seventy unnumbered fragments captures a moment from Nathalie's childhood, as she relives experiences that since *Tropisms* had nourished her writing. The project is explicitly of a piece with her previous work: made of the same substance and still in pursuit of something that's "still faintly quivering . . . outside words . . . as usual . . . little bits of something still alive."[2] Although this turn to autobiography was a new departure, it had a long prehistory. Over the years, Nathalie had recounted several of the episodes to friends. Michel Butor remembered her telling a story about her mother at one of the gatherings at his home in the 1950s and being angry when one of the guests laughed. She also told Werner Spies about the time she stabbed a pair of scissors into a silk-upholstered sofa in defiance of her Swiss nanny. Her interviews had also become increasingly autobiographical in content, and in a filmed conversation with Francine Mallet in 1976 she described two of the childhood attempts at writing narrated in *Childhood*, one of which she had already mentioned to a journalist in 1959.[3]

Despite the familiarity of the narrative material, the venture was not a case of childhood recollected in the tranquillity of old age. This much is spelled out as the narrator denies that she is taking the easy option or that her powers are in decline. In fact, Nathalie was particularly exercised about the use of the autobiographical "I." The manuscript reveals her worry that the recourse to an "I" might appear a capitulation "after so often deriding the seductive displays of all those 'I's' and 'me's' . . . after believing so little in all that frank and generous confiding." There was also the risk that the seasoned adult "I" would eclipse the younger one, whose tentative experiences were precisely those she was seeking to capture: "Thinking about it, I realise that what I was obscurely afraid of, was that the 'I' of today would immediately work its way in, that it would take up residence and refuse to leave, that this socialised, burnished, replete and weighty 'I' would pass itself off for the untouched, downy, feathery, and insubstantial 'I' that it was so long ago."[4] The "I" of the anecdotes retailed to friends and journalists could not be used for the book, and it is replaced by two others: that of the child Natacha living each moment in its confusion and immediacy, and that of the adult narrator who is further split, as she is repeatedly challenged by her alter ego, who launches the text with the question, "So are you really going to do it? 'Recall your childhood memories.'"

This use of dialogue as a means of narration is an extension of the growing presence of dialogue in Nathalie's work. The model of her lectures in the form of "conversations" had been adapted for *The Use of Speech*, where the narrator directly addresses readers as "you." Dialogue in the plays had also been pared down to become a to-and-fro between M.1 and M.2 in *For No Good Reason*. And like the exchanges in *The Use of Speech*, almost every one of the seventy fragments in *Childhood* is based on a word or an utterance, whose charge is registered semiconsciously by the child, and its implications probed as they are brought back to life after almost eight decades.

The book was written relatively quickly by Nathalie's usual standards, and she finished it in a little over two years. The writing nonetheless entailed a good deal of revision and redrafting. In his analysis of the manuscript of the second section of the book, the critic and theorist of autobiography Philippe Lejeune identifies at least ten versions as Nathalie repeatedly revised her text. Sheila Bell, an English academic, spent a week examining the manuscript in the apartment at no. 12 Avenue Pierre 1ᵉ de Serbie, noting that the original order of the sections had been changed, and that an early list of contents contained scenes that were subsequently abandoned.⁵

The speed of the book's composition may have been due to a new sense of urgency. The working title—*Before They Vanish*—indicates a desire to record memories before they are lost to the oblivion of death or incapacity, and, since *The Use of Speech*, Nathalie's working method had altered to accommodate this eventuality. Instead of completing a first draft of the whole before embarking on the process of revision, she now wrote her books section by section, perfecting each before moving on to the next. This ensured there would always be something publishable to salvage from a work in progress, should it be cut short. These revised writing practices were a strategy designed to outwit death.

While the narrator of *Childhood* hotly denies that her strength is failing, the effects of age had nonetheless begun to make themselves felt, and Nathalie had been consulting an ophthalmologist about cataracts since 1978. The loss of her sight would have been catastrophic, since for her, a life without the ability to read and write was unthinkable. She was operated for cataracts in February 1983, an intervention that was presumably deferred until *Childhood* was completed and safely in production. The operation was a success, but the procedure was less refined than it has subsequently become, and Nathalie was obliged thereafter to wear glasses with thick bottle-bottom lenses, which magnified her eyes out of proportion to the rest of her face. Conscious of her appearance, she wore them as little as possible and took them off in company.

On its publication, *Childhood* met with an enthusiastic reception, and was widely and warmly reviewed. Several critics found the portrait of Natacha "endearing"—and a number of publications carried examples of the always enchanting photographs of the author as a child. (This was presumably at the suggestion of Gallimard's publicity department, but Nathalie must have acquiesced.) Jacqueline Piatier in *Le Monde* wrote, "Nathalie Sarraute should rest assured: *Childhood* is not a product of old age, but one of her major creations." She nevertheless concludes that "more than ever, she has given us reason to love her." Nathalie was no longer portrayed as a difficult writer who appealed to a restricted readership, and *Le Nouvel Observateur* placed *Childhood* at the head of its recommended reading for August 1983.[6]

The review in *Le Monde des livres* was part of a larger feature devoted to Nathalie—including an interview with the novelist and photographer François-Marie Banier. Similar features combining articles, reviews, and interviews appeared in other publications, notably the June number of the *Magazine littéraire*, whose cover carried a large pencil portrait of Nathalie. The March 1984 number of the journal *Digraphe* was entirely given over to her work, as was the autumn number of *L'Arc* in the same year. This attention was a mixed blessing, and Nathalie used many of the interviews that followed the book's publication to counter its seductive effects, dissociating it from the category of autobiography and declaring, "I don't like autobiographies . . . as a literary genre [because] it's impossible to talk sincerely about oneself." And she is adamant that "the one thing I didn't want was to write an autobiographical narrative. I just wanted to capture unrelated, isolated moments."[7]

In a long interview with Marc Saporta for *L'Arc*, she repeatedly tries to steer him away from her biography, and she always felt that the popularity of *Childhood* had come at the cost of a misreading of her intentions. She was also afraid that by writing directly about the childhood in which all her writing had its origins, she had jeopardised the possibility of ever writing again.[8] These fears proved unfounded, and while Simone Benmussa was producing a version for the stage, and the book was rapidly being translated into several other languages, Nathalie had already embarked on a new venture—*You Don't Love Yourself*—which is both a sequel to and a repudiation of *Childhood*.

Childhood nevertheless retained a special place in her heart. In addition to the usual signed copies given to friends, she also showed the manuscript to a number of other people. This offer of access to unpublished drafts was unprecedented. She never normally shared work in progress, and like all the manuscripts she donated to the Bibliothèque nationale, *Childhood* remains inaccessible to readers until 2036. Georges Raillard remembered receiving the manuscript—unsolicited—from Nathalie; Françoise Asso had it for a while; Sheila Bell was granted permission to consult it; Philippe Lejeune was loaned all the drafts of the second section; and Nathalie gave several pages to Werner Spies. Her reasons for this openness—in which she took most of the initiative—are unclear. With the exception of Philippe Lejeune, the recipients were all personal friends, and she could trust them to appreciate that, as she said to Lejeune, "It's work."9

Childhood was the last book that Raymond saw to completion. His health was less robust than Nathalie's had proved to be after she recovered from TB. In correspondence she complains quite frequently of flu and exhaustion, and she seems to have suffered from chronic gingivitis, but she had no major health problems. Raymond suffered a thrombosis in October 1977 from which he rallied.10 But he developed a heart condition requiring treatment and tests, many of which are noted in Nathalie's engagement diaries from 1980 onwards. Their shared life nonetheless continued. They drove to Chérence for weekends, both taking the wheel at the same time in a somewhat risky-sounding practice. This wasn't the first Nathalie was known for: although she had been driving since the 1930s, Michel Butor remembered accepting a lift from her in Paris in the 1950s and being terrified as she sailed through every intersection in the belief that women drivers were automatically granted priority.11 Nathalie and Raymond continued to spend the month of July in Chérence and August in the Mediterranean sun, very often with Jean Blot and his wife Nadia, who had a house on the Greek island of Skyros.

Raymond's condition gradually worsened, first with a sarcoma on the leg, which limited his physical capacities (putting an end to the Skyros holidays, amongst others), and then with dementia, which showed in the form of memory loss. Mathieu Galey describes its effects in his account of a visit to Chérence in October 1984: "I find them both sitting by the fire. Raymond slightly out of it. His wife sends him to fetch ice for the whisky. He gets up, flustered, and says amiably: 'I'm sorry, but with these memory problems, I can't remember where the kitchen is.'"[12]

His death was a terrible prospect. Age and growing awareness of its inevitability hadn't lessened Nathalie's lifelong horror. As she said to Isabelle de Vigan in 1982, "The fact of being a mortal being, who will cease to see this and cease to see that, and worse still, who knows that people around him will die, is an unbearable thing." For her, "the only way not to feel that angst is to work." In her case this meant writing, since for her "writing is work like any other."[13] Indeed, there was no reason ever to stop writing, and in a letter to Monique Wittig she expresses her astonishment at seeing Sartre and Simone de Beauvoir announce in a television interview that they could no longer write and that their work was now behind them. "I'm dumbfounded," she comments, appalled at this resignation: "I don't feel anything that I didn't feel before, the same anxieties, the same difficulties, the same moments of relief."[14]

However, the strain was beginning to show. In January 1984 she was taking medication for anxiety, and as she wrote to Wittig in May, she had suffered from a series of ill-defined ailments all winter which kept her in a state of permanent nervousness. She mentions that Raymond's memory was deteriorating, but as she lists these woes, she confesses herself disgusted by her "moral weakness."[15] But all the while she kept working, and attended rehearsals for Benmussa's adaptation of *Childhood* at the Théâtre du Rond Point before its opening on 8 February. The diaries are filled with engagements, and she made a brief trip to Milan to give a lecture in June. *Freshwater* took her to Spoleto for a week at the beginning of July. In September, she flew to Helsinki and then to Oslo for ten days (it was on this occasion that she turned down the opportunity to visit the Soviet Union), and at the end of October she left for Stockholm and Copenhagen to give more lectures. But when Raymond became seriously ill at the start of November she cancelled a two-day trip to Arles and a lecture tour in the United Kingdom. The engagement diaries trace Raymond's worsening condition as his weight drops, while Nathalie's, noted alongside his, remains steady at around fifty-two kilograms. She records measurements for his swollen knee, and keeps track of medical appointments, two separate operations, and his transfers between various hospitals and clinics which she oversaw.

All this—the lecture engagements, the medical details—was a way for Nathalie to distract herself from the reality of Raymond's decline, which she found hard to confront, while the children took turns to keep their father company in hospital. But the end was inevitable, and she marks it in her diary simply with a note of the time—"2am."—on 2 March 1985. It was a Saturday. Raymond was buried five days later in the cemetery in Chérence in a plot where Nathalie would eventually join him. The numerous letters of condolence she received all stress Raymond's qualities—"his grace, his kindness, his smile," "his competence, his lucidity," "his deep and subtle intelligence, his tolerance, his exceptional charm"—and several mention the special character of the relationship between him and Nathalie.[16]

She had lost her companion of over sixty years, alongside whom she had become both the person and the writer she needed to be. Since the death of her father, Raymond had been the living being who mattered to her the most, and his unwavering support for her writing had always been vital. It was the ground on which their relationship was built, and despite the decline in his mental capacities, she had continued to rely on his presence, and she completed seventy pages of *You Don't Love Yourself* before he died. With his death she found herself, for the first time since the interruption to *Tropisms*, quite unable to write.[17] Her engagement diary for the following month records almost continuous visits from her children and some close friends and a gradual return to outside activities, beginning with the private view of an exhibition by Árpád Szenes at the Galerie Jacob on 26 March. But without Raymond's knowledgeable commentary, such occasions could not be the same. Practical matters also required her attention as she sorted out finances with the family accountant, and dealt with a cruelly timed burglary in Chérence.

She had always appreciated the familial ambiance of the theatre, and in April she attended rehearsals for Monique Wittig's play *Le Voyage sans fin* (The journey without end) at the Théâtre du Rond Point in a production by Wittig and her partner Sande Zeig. The English productions of *Childhood* and *For No Good Reason* were also in preparation, and Nathalie had frequent meetings with Benmussa and her partner Erika Kralik, who had the lead part in the French production of *Childhood* the previous year. Benmussa's productions then took them both to New York at the end of May, and Nathalie combined the trip with a lecture at Amherst College. When Assia Gavronsky came to France in June, Nathalie had an opportunity to share with her oldest friend memories of the years when she and Raymond were young. In September, she went to Brussels for a reading of *For No Good Reason*, and in October she spent a week in Athens for talks and readings, where she met up with another old friend, Matsie Hadjilazaros.

She was now living alone, which she had never previously done, and she ensured that she saw people every day, sometimes several. There were regular visits from children and grandchildren, especially Anne Sarraute's children, Nathalie and Antoine Vierny, and Claude's youngest son, Nicolas Revel, who at the age of twenty-one was beginning to look more and more like Raymond. Wittig and Sande Zeig spent July in Chérence, as they would for the next ten years.

Over the course of 1986, Nathalie's renown provided its own momentum. In January, Gallimard brought out two of her essays ("Paul Valéry and the Elephant's Child" and "Flaubert the Precursor") in a single volume. Simone Benmussa was rehearsing *For No Good Reason* with Samy Frey and Jean-François Balmer at the Théâtre du Rond Point, where Nathalie attended rehearsals in the run-up to the play's opening on 17 February. February also took her to Düsseldorf and Munich in the company of her German translator Elmar Tophoven, and in April she flew to Spain in response to invitations to lecture in Madrid and Barcelona. In July she went to Avignon with Sande Zeig for Michel Dumoulin's festival productions of *For No Good Reason* and *It Is There, Tropisms*, and *The Use of Speech*. In September she flew to New York at the invitation of Tom Bishop, and gave talks at NYU, Columbia, and Wellesley

College. In December, the Russian translation of *Childhood* by Lena and Masha Zonina was published in *Inostrannaya Literatura*. And in the same month she recorded the wide-ranging conversations with Benmussa, which were published in book form the following year.[18]

But 1987 started badly with the death of Maria Jolas at the age of ninety-three. Chérence—where Maria was buried in the cemetery alongside her husband Eugene—was not the same without her. Nathalie had lost one of her oldest and closest friends, and the translator who for nearly forty years had accompanied and promoted her work. In November, she was once again taking medication for acute anxiety. She had however resumed her writing, and continued to work—albeit slowly—on *You Don't Love Yourself*, which was eventually published in September 1989. With Raymond no longer there, her routines had been adapted. She still went every morning to Le Marceau to write, but the typing was now done by her daughter Anne Sarraute in the time she had spare from her job as managing editor of *La Quinzaine littéraire*, which she ran with tremendous efficacy under the appreciative oversight of Maurice Nadeau. Anne's daughter Nathalie Vierny also shared the typing duties, and Dominique Sarraute provided the listening ear for work in progress, being of Nathalie's three daughters the one who, in her own estimation, resembled her the most.

The new book was conceived as a counterweight to the autobiographical appeal of *Childhood*. One of the blank pages in Nathalie's engagement diary for the last quarter of 1983 contains a quotation from Beaumarchais, "What is the self [or I] that occupies me? A [shapeless] assemblage of unknown parts," taken from Figaro's soliloquy in the last act of *The Marriage of Figaro*. Her literary interests were turning increasingly to the eighteenth century, as she added Diderot to her old loves, Saint-Simon, and the Rousseau of the *Confessions*. There's no knowing whether she had seen a performance of the play, read it, or simply heard the line in some other context. But it formulates very precisely the principle on which she conceived *You Don't Love Yourself*, where she resumes her long-standing debunking of the "seductive displays of all those 'I's' and 'me's'" to which she was afraid *Childhood* might appear to have succumbed.

The "I" of *You Don't Love Yourself* is dismantled from the outset, refusing the consolidation that is presupposed by the reflexive forms of self-love, self-awareness, self-description—or the self-narration of autobiography—and supporting Nathalie's own comment that she couldn't imagine ever saying, "I'm like this or that. . . ." This is because, as Beaumarchais's Figaro had already intuited, "There's always a multitude inside us, because we are so numerous." In a disavowal of all autobiographical ambition, she adds, "As soon as I say 'I,' I never have the impression that I'm talking about me, or rarely. I never say what I'm like because it would be untrue."[19] In the novel, "I" takes the form of a multitudinous "we" to whom Nathalie's writing gives voice by means of the extended dialogue which comprises the entire text.

The dialogue form of the theatre is adopted for the prose writing, where the voices are as anonymous as those of the early radio plays, having neither face nor body and, in this case, not even gender. In the book's twenty-five unnumbered sections, the "we" discuss how to respond to the various situations in which they find themselves, volubly dispatching a selection of delegates or spokesmen to negotiate on their behalf in the absence of any coherent "me." Some of these situations involve encounters with powerful personalities who seem to have no problem loving themselves or saying "me, I," while other circumstances are created by labels such as "Paranoid. Persecuted," which have been imposed on the "me" who is actually an "us."[20] Comedy is never very far away, as when the "we" debate how to respond to an invitation to spend a month's holiday with a "strong personality" and wonder which representative would be best suited to provide appropriate company, only then to see him carried away by the role of favoured houseguest, as he stands on the host's terrace reciting mediocre poetry with exaggerated emphasis and unnecessary gesticulation.

While resisting any overt self-narration, many of the scenes tacitly draw on Nathalie's own life. She herself was often accused of being paranoid and acting persecuted. The holiday episode implicitly recalls her invitation to Wittig to spend a month in Chérence whose landscape is evoked in "lucerne fields and meadows on one side, and ripening corn on the other," which the host briefly pauses to contemplate.[21] At other points, as one character lays claim to twenty years of happiness and another to "a mutual love," there are echoes of the phrases Nathalie must have heard from well-meaning sympathisers after Raymond died. But she and he had spent sixty years of something that it was impossible to characterise with the simplification and complacency of "happiness" or "a great love" with its obligatory rituals of "'I love you,' 'Do you love me?'"[22] Such autobiographical material is put to decidedly un-autobiographical use, and anyone expecting a continuation of *Childhood* would have been disappointed. Indeed, although there were positive reviews from critics who were already familiar with Nathalie's work and could appreciate both her irony and her ear for language, several expressed impatience with the novel's anonymous dialogue. The artistic probity for which Betsy Jolas (Maria's composer daughter) admired her had once again placed Nathalie in the class of a "difficult" writer.[23]

CHAPTER THIRTY-THREE

The Last Decade,
1990–99

ONE OF THE HAPPIEST CONSEQUENCES of the publication of *Childhood* was Nathalie's trip to Ivanovo in October 1990. She had in fact made a brief, anonymous visit in 1965 when it was still a closed city, but hadn't been able to locate the house where she was born or find any trace of her father's factory. In 1989, thanks to the changing political climate brought about by *glasnost*, and to the interest kindled inside Russia by the recent translation of *Childhood*, a local journalist had gone to search the holdings of the Ivanovo Regional State Archives for documentary records of Nathalie's Russian origins. He sent her a copy of the resulting article published on 5 March 1989 in the local newspaper, *Rabochiy Krai* (Workers' region).[1] Under Gorbachev, a visit to the Soviet Union had become politically, morally, and practically feasible, and so Nathalie flew to Moscow on 15 October 1990 for a ten-day visit, accompanied by the Russian-born Ania Chevalier, who worked for Gallimard.

They dined at the French embassy, and for Nathalie it was quite like old times. She had an invitation from the Writers' Union, met several authors and journalists from *Inostrannaya Literatura*, and visited her indefatigable translator friend Margarita Aliger. She also managed to see a few remaining members of her family, and during her stay, received news of the death—that very week—of her cousin Lola Shatunovskaya. But the high point was the return to Ivanovo.

Nathalie and Ania Chevalier took the overnight train from Moscow, arriving on the morning of 19 October for what proved to be a very full day before returning to Moscow that same night. After visiting the house on the Ulitsa Pushkina, Nathalie was taken to the museum and the House of Literature, gave interviews to the press, radio, and TV, met professors and students in the French department at Ivanovo State University, and was photographed and welcomed as Ivanovo's most famous writer.

The trip by no means marked the end of Nathalie's travels. She visited New York in 1993, spent four days in Berlin in the same year, returned to New York in 1995, and went twice to the United Kingdom, first in 1991 and again in 1996. She was usually accompanied by her daughter Dominique, who now had a career as an artistic photographer of industrial objects, and since 1988 had been working from no. 12 Avenue Pierre 1^e de Serbie, where she had her studio, and where, on returning from her travels, Nathalie would resume her old habits.

There was always a supply of whisky and Perrier water for Nathalie's five o'clock visitors, of whom there was one almost every day. Viviane Forrester, the essayist and literary critic, had become a close friend, and describes "[Nathalie's] look each time she opens the door to me, which surprises me with its extreme youthfulness . . . but without the least trace of ingenuousness or naivety." The ensuing exchanges would be marked by Nathalie's analytical penetration, "which shows in every gesture, the way she laughs, her irresistible way of telling stories, attentive to the most imperceptible movement, stories which, told by her are so hilarious that you laugh till you cry; with a very special laughter thanks to her gift for observation and mimicry, and her incredible perceptiveness."[2] These anecdotes were the stuff of novels for which Nathalie evidently had the talent, but of a type she did not consider worth writing. She could also let rip on occasion, and the young novelist Marie Darrieussecq, who became a regular visitor after a disastrous (unpublished) interview with Nathalie for the magazine *Les Inrocks*, was taken aback to discover that Nathalie also "liked speaking ill of people."[3]

Her oldest friends were gradually disappearing. Nadia du Bouchet died in June 1992. Transatlantic phone calls with Assia in New York continued intermittently, but as Assia observed, there was an ineradicable ambivalence in their relationship.[4] (She outlived Nathalie by just two months.) Elmar Tophoven, her German translator, died in 1989. Even the children of her oldest friends were disappearing. In her diary for November 1997 Nathalie notes the death of Lena's son Gilles Gautier-Villars at the age of only fifty-nine, and two years later she records that Tina Jolas was seriously ill. In fact, Tina died just a few weeks before Nathalie. Old age has its own forms of loneliness.

There were nevertheless several long-standing friends: Jean Blot and his wife Nadia, and Alice Gadoffre, especially after the death of Gilbert in 1995. Georges Raillard visited regularly, and in June 1998 Nathalie notes in her diary that he kissed her. These signs of affection mattered. Most of the visitors were considerably younger than her. The names that appear regularly in her diaries for these years include Kaye Mortley (the Australian-born radio producer who had translated *For No Good Reason*), Mathilde La Bardonnie (a journalist and theatre critic at *Le Monde*), Monique Gosselin (who taught at Nanterre University and wrote a book-length study of *Childhood*), Géralde Nakam (a specialist of early-modern French literature at Paris III and a regular at the kibbutz in Merhavia), Christine Jordis (writer and journalist who was also the editor for English fiction at Gallimard), Rolande Causse (who later published a record of their five o'clock conversations), Gilberte Lambrichs (writer and translator, and the widow of Georges Lambrichs who had published the later texts of *Tropisms* in *Le Monde Nouveau*), Françoise Collin (a feminist philosopher who wrote about Hannah Arendt), and Chantal Thomas (a historian, novelist, and author of several books on the eighteenth century), among many others. Nathalie continued to work with her translators: Erika Tophoven, who had taken over from her husband after his death, and the excellent Barbara Wright, whose British English rang changes on Maria Jolas's transatlantic renderings.

After the film version of *For No Good Reason*, Nathalie became friendly with Jacques Doillon and his English-born partner, the actress Jane Birkin. François-Marie Banier (the novelist and photographer whose friendship with another old lady, the L'Oréal heiress Liliane Bettencourt, later brought him into disrepute) was a particularly frequent visitor, and he saw Nathalie several times a month for twenty years. He was well-connected, good-looking, and amusing. In April 1999 Nathalie wrote a reminder in her diary to "phone François-Marie to laugh with him." He invited her out to restaurants, and they would have lengthy discussions about books. He also took some particularly fine photographs of her. There were lunch engagements with the novelist Jorge Semprun, visits from the Argentine-born French author Hector Bianciotti for whom Nathalie was an exemplary writer, and telephone conversations with the novelist Dominique Rolin and Max Dorra, a writer and doctor who admired her work. There was also a last conciliatory telephone call from Marguerite Duras (who died in March 1996), where she told Nathalie that she had the impression that all the organs in her body were giving out.[5]

Aside from these social contacts, Nathalie made regular visits to the theatre and the cinema, the latter sometimes in the company of her granddaughter Nathalie Vierny, who works in film and recalls Nathalie's attentiveness to the detail of the movies she had just seen. She kept up, seeing mostly international films including *My Own Private Idaho, Howards End*, and Woody Allen's *Shadows and Fog* in 1992 (Woody Allen was always a favourite of hers); *Breaking the Waves* and *Un Air de famille (Family Resemblances)* in 1996; *The English Patient* and *The Sweet Hereafter* in 1997. She also saw Fellini's *8½*, for which she had a long-standing admiration.[6]

In April 1999 she noted in her diary, "*Still hanging on to the old routines. . . .* What else can you do with your life?" But the old routines were sustaining, and always had been. The visits to Chérence continued. Françoise Asso and her partner would often drive Nathalie there for the weekend. And until 1997, Wittig would be there for the month of July, joined for some of the time by Sande Zeig. Days in Chérence followed a long-established pattern. Mornings were devoted to work, and Nathalie would retreat to her cowshed to write. Afternoons were for walks or reading, Nathalie lying on her bed propped on one elbow in her favourite posture, which, as she explained to Isabelle de Vigan, allowed her to forget her body.[7] Discussions about books could go on for hours, and Nathalie spent one summer reading Trollope. (With the passing years, her literary tastes became predominantly pre–twentieth century, and she had always been an avid reader of Balzac.) Arno Mayer called by almost daily during the summer, and recalls Nathalie's accounts of the authors she had just been reading—Proust or Dostoevsky—about whom she also had bad dreams, where neither author paid her any attention or showed the least interest in her admiration.[8] Meals were often taken in nearby restaurants, where Nathalie and Wittig celebrated their birthdays, which both fell in July.

The month of August was spent in the sun as had always been the case, and Nathalie's daughters would join her, one week at a time. For several years they went to Venice, where a friend lent her an apartment on a canal just behind the French consulate. She was a keen swimmer, and would take the vaporetto every day from the Accademia to the Lido, recording details of each of these outings in her diary: "Heavenly swim 25 min.," "Nice swim algae 15 min.," "Rain—thunderstorm—good swim 30 min.," "Waves 10 min."[9] She also kept a note of restaurants where she ate, churches visited, and paintings seen. There was a Tiepolo in the Accademia—either *The Discovery of the True Cross* or *The Scourge of the Serpents*—which she visited each year because, as she told the writer Marianne Alphant, "It puts me in a state of joy, euphoria, which radiates from the entire painting."[10] Her interest in eighteenth-century literature had been matched by a new enthusiasm for the painting of the period, and Rolande Causse recounts Nathalie's delight at visiting the Louvre one Tuesday, when the museum was closed to the public and she could enjoy to her heart's content the Watteaus, the Fragonards, the Bouchers, and the Chardins, the last of which she had a particular affection for.[11]

Her acquaintance with the visual arts had come through Raymond, but she had no interest in art history per se. Nor, on her own admission, was she "a visual person."[12] She never described a painting in any detail, and her responses were affective rather than analytical. What she appreciated above all was the capacity of painting to escape or transcend the passage of time: "I remember a Picasso exhibition in 1937. It made a big impression on me and I thought: How lucky he is to be able to show a face full-front and in profile at the same time, and without it spoiling the perception you have of that face. In literature, when you want to express the same thing, you have to do it successively, never simultaneously."[13] (There are three portraits that correspond to Nathalie's description—*Portrait of Dora Maar, Seated Woman (Marie-Thérèse)*, and *Woman in Hat and Fur Collar*—all painted in 1937.) In her own work Nathalie sought literary means of achieving this simultaneous presentation of different perspectives. Later, when the passage of time made itself felt through old age and the deaths of those around her, the atemporal virtues of painting took on a more existential quality. As she told the writer and journalist Danièle Sallenave in 1992, "A painting is calming, it has something that fixes the moment, and gives it the appearance of eternity, it exudes a very powerful sensation which fills you with stillness, like something infinite held motionless in the picture; whereas in music there's a flux which gives me angst."[14]

Painting was also a welcome reprieve from the traps set by words, and a guarantee of authentic aesthetic experience, a view Nathalie expressed with the somewhat tendentious claim that "people who read novels are very often not much interested in art; what they're looking for is a notion of life, love, or things that have nothing to do with art. Whereas people who look at paintings want to satisfy aesthetic needs."[15] Only slightly less tendentiously, she always portrayed painting as embodying artistic standards against which literature could be measured and most often found wanting. She continued to maintain that painting was more innovative than literature.

She had a number of painter friends over the course of her life— Natalia Goncharova, Eugène and Lucette de Kermadec, Javier Vilato, Thanos Tsingos, Greta Knutson—but none was particularly close. Nor does she appear to have taken much interest in their activities or to have owned any of their paintings. However, in her nineties, she made the acquaintance of Pierre Soulages. He had contributed the cover to the special number of the journal *Digraphe* in 1984, and explains in the same number that while he didn't know Nathalie personally, he had great admiration for her writing, "because it seemed to me to be literature in what it has that's specific, richest, and most powerful. Literature, and a literature that is hers alone."[16] Nathalie, for her part, mentions Soulages as one of the painters she appreciates; and they had in common the fact that, while each valued the medium of the other, they saw the two as quite distinct. At some point he sent her a little gouache which she hung above the table in the entrance hall where she kept the translations of her books, but later transferred to her bedroom. In 1995 she sent Soulages a copy of *Here*, and their brief correspondence at this time testifies to their mutual admiration and a shared sensibility.[17]

One of the advantages of Nathalie's advancing years was the freedom to dress as she pleased, and to find ways of inhabiting the gender-neutral role to which she had always aspired. In her conversations with Benmussa in 1986 she adopts the term *le neutre* (neuter), corresponding in her mind to the word *tcheloviek* in Russian or *der Mensch* in German, or, more awkwardly in French, *l'être humain*. This affirmation of gender neutrality was a resistance to the *écriture féminine*, which had emerged in the 1970s with its positive assertion of female difference. Nathalie may well have been encouraged in this stance by Monique Wittig's politically inflected lesbianism, which Wittig portrayed as a refusal of heterosexuality and its inevitable oppression of women. As she announced in 1978, "Lesbians are not women."[18] From the mid-1970s, in line with this refusal of femininity, Nathalie had called Wittig by the ungendered name Théo, which Wittig had taken to using in preference to Monique.

Nathalie's own gender neutrality was an expression of her longstanding egalitarianism. She now always wore trousers, unisex cardigans, a silk cravat, flat shoes, and men's shirts—but in an echo of her fashion-conscious twenties, she bought them from Dior or Pierre Cardin. Sensitive to the cold, she had a cashmere shawl and a camelhair coat, both of the best quality. Her hair was still cropped and she continued to abjure makeup. But with age she also lost the severity that is often seen in the photographs of her middle years, and she acquired a beauty that was only enhanced by her wrinkles. In her 2008 film *Les Plages d'Agnès*, Agnès Varda describes Nathalie as having had "the deeply scored face of an Indian, the nobility of a Sioux or an Apache." Many people commented on Nathalie's eyes, whose expressiveness was undiminished by the cataract operation, and was described by Viviane Forrester as a mix of "derision and affection."[19] The seductiveness of the charm she exerted was felt by almost everyone who came into contact with her.

FIGURE 27. Nathalie in the 1980s. © Daniel Psenny.

In these years she was also accumulating honours of various kinds. In July 1989, on the eve of the publication of *You Don't Love Yourself*, she was the subject of a *décade* at Cerisy, which assembled participants from all over the world. She attended for the first two days, and when she left, it was without the disaffection inspired by the Nouveau Roman *décade* eighteen years previously. The proceedings were published under the title *Autour de Nathalie Sarraute*, and other conferences and other volumes devoted to her work followed.[20] Books and theses continued to appear. A student wrote in 1992 mentioning that one of the texts in *The Use of Speech* had

been set for her oral exam in the *baccalauréat*, and another correspondent recalled that when she was at school she had been given
a passage from *The Golden Fruits* as a source of examples of the
imperfect subjunctive.[21] Monique Wittig had written a thesis at the
EHESS under the supervision of Gérard Genette, where she advanced views about the material character of language, which challenged the dominance of structuralist theory and gave Nathalie's
work pride of place. Completed in 1986, the thesis was revised and
scheduled for publication in November 1999 as Wittig's own *ars
poetica*. But it was also intended as an homage to the writer with
whom she felt the greatest personal and literary rapport.[22]

In 1991 Nathalie received an honorary doctorate from Oxford
University. She had already been awarded an honorary doctorate
from Trinity College, Dublin (Beckett's alma mater) in 1976, and
another from the University of Kent in 1980, and was familiar with
the requests for information about her height and head circumfer-
ence so she could be fitted with the appropriate ceremonial robes
and caps. True to her embargo on sharing a platform with others,
she insisted on a date when she would be on her own, thereby missing the opportunity to meet the other honorands and to take part
in the robed procession through the streets of Oxford that she knew
from her time as a student. On 18 May, she was a diminutive figure
in the university's ceremonial building, while a speech about her
accomplishments was read in Latin, in a distant echo of the honorary doctorate awarded to Queen Mary in 1921 and her own enrolment in the same building seventy years previously.

On her return to Paris she received a letter from Jacques Lassalle,
artistic director of the Comédie française, which led to a renewal of
her theatrical activities. The Comédie française had recently taken
over the Théâtre du Vieux-Colombier, known in the early years of
the twentieth century for its promotion of contemporary writing for
the theatre. (Nathalie may have seen some of Pitoëff's productions
there in the early 1930s.) The building was being restored after years
of neglect, and Lassalle was hoping to stage one of Nathalie's plays
to mark its reopening. As he explains in the letter,

> In December 1992 the Théâtre du Vieux-Colombier, will open refur-
> bished after a long escheat and will become the second auditorium for

the Comédie Française. You will be aware that this theatre represents the happy, fertile and innovative conjunction . . . of literature and the art of the stage. For this reason, as well as for others that are less historical and more personal, I should like the first season of the Comédie française troupe at the Vieux Colombier to open with the performance of one of your plays. . . . Perhaps there is an unpublished one?[23]

The original plan was a double bill with a play by Michel Vinaver, the playwright nephew of Nathalie's old friend Eugène Vinaver, but nothing came of the Vinaver proposition. Since she had no unpublished work, preparations went ahead with her own suggestions of *Silence* and *It Is There*.

There was, however, a problem, and once again Nathalie's involvement in the theatre led to a betrayal. In March 1991 she had renewed the exclusive performance rights first granted in January 1989 to Michel Dumoulin following his productions of *For No Good Reason* and *It Is There* at the Avignon festival in 1986. The draft states, "I the undersigned, Nathalie Sarraute, authorise Michel Dumoulin to stage 'Silence' and 'It is There' or 'It's beautiful' in the theatre of our joint choice. / This authorisation is exclusive for a period of three years and renewable by tacit agreement."[24] The Vieux-Colombier production clearly broke this agreement, and in July Dumoulin wrote to Nathalie in bewildered dismay: "After everything that has happened to me, in the exhausted state I find myself in, what you said to me the other day on the telephone astonished me so much that I thought I had misheard. . . . I do not think that all my efforts since 1988 . . . can be negated. . . . And I need to earn my living like everyone else. . . . For me, the understanding we have had for so long (since 1965, I believe) until the last agreement between us should not become any different."[25]

No doubt advised by Lassalle, Nathalie failed to respond, even when in May 1992 she received a letter from Dumoulin's lawyer threatening action. Lassalle brushed aside Dumoulin's claims, telling him, "This document [the agreement with Nathalie] has nothing to do with me, and I have made it clear to Mme Nathalie Sarraute: for this project, as for all the others, I preserve the entire initiative."[26] There's no record of whether Dumoulin ever received the compensation he demanded. It was a sorry episode.

Lassalle was the fifth director Nathalie had worked with, and like the others, he had a keen appreciation of both her work and her person. For her, the project was a chance to rediscover the creative and collaborative ambiance that she always relished in the theatre. She joined Lassalle and the actors around the table for the first rehearsals, answering questions and regaling them with anecdotes and personal memories. She insisted that the actors not speak too fast and that the women tone down their femininity. She returned for the final rehearsals, the opening having been postponed until April 1993. Building work was still going on, and as the theatre was freezing cold she came wrapped in two shawls, while Lassalle arranged a flask of hot tea for her and drove her home when rehearsals ran late into the evening.[27]

After a further delay the Vieux-Colombier finally opened on 7 April for a five-week run with Nathalie's double bill. The resurrection of the theatre under the auspices of the Comédie française was a major cultural event, and the plays were widely and mostly very positively reviewed. The comment in the *Canard enchaîné* to which Françoise d'Eaubonne objected on Nathalie's behalf was an exception, and the critics singled out both the comedy and the incisive intelligence which had been brought out in the production.[28] Nathalie's theatrical career was crowned in 1996 when she was awarded the Grand Prix by the Society for Writers and Composers for the Stage.[29]

In the meantime, moves were afoot for a volume of *Complete Works* in Gallimard's prestigious Pléiade series. This was a form of consecration, and perhaps an ultimate compensation (at least in Nathalie's eyes) for Gallimard's rejections at the start of her career. Consecration in the form of "complete works" meant that, almost by definition, Pléiade volumes were posthumous. Beginning with the publication of Gide's diaries in 1939, there had been just eleven exceptions to this retrospective rule, and Nathalie's volume was the twelfth. She was an exception, too, by virtue of her sex. The only other women writers in a series representing some two hundred men were (predictably) George Sand, Mme de Sévigné, and Colette, with the addition of Marguerite Yourcenar in 1982. Nathalie had long cherished the ambition of publication in the Pléiade, and before his death Raymond had prepared a selection of her unpublished lectures for eventual inclusion. She was delighted when Jean-Yves Tadié, who had recently overseen the four-volume re-edition of Proust's *Remembrance of Things Past* for the Pléiade, agreed to act as general editor. As she wrote to Antoine Gallimard, "I think it would be impossible to find anyone better suited."[30]

She was, however, concerned that "pléiadification" would result in academic overload and that her writing would be mummified by footnotes and scholarly apparatus, in a version of the fate that befalls the sculpture in *Do You Hear Them?* when it is moved to a museum. She was assured that the volume would appear with the lightest of editorial touches, and she herself vetted and assisted the editorial contributors—Valerie Minogue, Arnaud Rykner, and me. She made herself available to answer any queries we might have, and I recall several visits where, over whisky and cigarettes, and having urged me to take off my shoes, she would alternate expressions of pity at the editorial task facing me with anxiety that excessive erudition would detract from the literary concerns of her writing. The essential purpose of the publication was, as she said in an interview, "for all the texts to be brought together and properly presented." And, she added, "I am very pleased about it."[31]

Nevertheless, the title *Complete Works* implied that there would be no more writing, and this was inconceivable. As she explained in 1992, "If I had to stop writing now, I would feel I had stopped living."[32] What followed, then, was a process whereby the *Complete Works* would be rendered incomplete by the appearance of further work. In the event, delays in preparation of the volume meant that there was time for *Here*, published in September 1995, to be included—only for the process of incompletion to be resumed thereafter.

Here maintains the formula adopted with *The Use of Speech* and consists of twenty short texts headed by Roman numerals. With an increased sense of precariousness, the book explores various moments where language fails. When a name eludes memory, this opens up a breach through which can be felt "the exhalation, the breath of the irreparable absence, of extinction . . . ," and following a break in conversation, "a patch of nothingness opens up and something escapes through it . . . like the harbinger of the definitive disappearance, of annihilation."[33] Nathalie had never been quite so explicit about such existential menace. She also allows the spotlight of her explorations to encroach much more visibly on her own life than in the rest of her fiction.

Thanks to the daily encounters with friends and visitors, she was familiar with the pitfalls that can derail even the most anodyne conversation. One text examines the way a character responds after accidentally using the word "dead" with another character who is evidently bereaved, a situation in which Nathalie can all too easily be imagined. Another text recalls the performance of *Cindy* she saw in Harlem with its chants of U.G.L.Y., and another comments on Nathalie's own stylistic tics, such as her habit of using the masculine form of adjectives for women, or her use of a collective "they" where the singular is the norm. The collection ends with a meditation on a sentence from Pascal's *Pensées*, "The eternal silence of those infinite spaces terrifies me." The threat of annihilation is palpable, and at the age of ninety-five Nathalie had good reason to be aware of it. But, as ever, there's nothing confessional or autobiographical about the writing, and "here" is a deliberate substitute for the word "I," since, as she explained to an interviewer, "Inside us, there's neither an 'I,' nor a 'you'; there's just a 'here' where things happen."[34]

Writing remained a lifeline. Although she now stayed at home and no longer went to the café to write, she kept to the old routine of working for two hours each morning—even after the publication of the *Complete Works* in November 1996. She continued to give interviews and took part in TV programmes, including a fine film for the series A Century of Writers made by Jacques Doillon in which Isabelle Huppert, who knew and liked Nathalie's work, read extracts. It was screened in September 1995.

At some point she decided to leave her papers to the Bibliothèque nationale. She had kept all her manuscripts, much of her correspondence, a number of engagement diaries, and various other documents, but there was no question of simply handing them over lock, stock, and barrel. From May 1993, just after the reopening of Le Vieux-Colombier, she began to sort through all her papers, assisted by Annie Angremy from the Department of Manuscripts, assembling an archive to be housed alongside those of Flaubert, Proust, and Sartre in France's national library. (Nathalie's 1935 reader's card had long since lapsed.) It was a slow process, which took her back over the nine decades of her life. In parallel with the *Complete Works*, she was preparing a posthumous legacy for herself, subjecting a life lived in the present to the anticipated retrospect of future scholars—and biographers. She also collaborated in the preparation of the exhibition mounted by Annie Angremy at the Bibliothèque nationale in May 1995, providing photographs and authorising the display of selected manuscript pages. Some sense of her ambivalence about the event may be inferred from the fact that she didn't attend the opening, claiming that she was tired and that, in any case, she had received enough honours already.[35]

In private, she was becoming more preoccupied with issues arising from this return to a distant past. She told Jacques Lassalle that she felt more Russian and more Jewish than she ever had. She kept a bottle of Russian vodka under her bed for the nights when she couldn't sleep, and began reading the Old Testament—Ecclesiastes and the books of the Maccabees, Daniel, and Jonah, to which her friend Géralde Nakam suggested she add the books of Judith and Esther as well as the Song of Songs.

She also became curious about the Jewish prehistory of her family, and Nakam, with whom she would discuss Judaism, reported that enquiries of her own had established that the Jews of northern and western Ukraine and Belarus (who included the Tcherniaks) had come from Poland in the sixteenth and seventeenth centuries, while Jews from southern Ukraine (who may have included the Shatunovskys) were Sephardis who had arrived via Turkey following their expulsion from Spain.[36] Nathalie was now willing to accept that Jewishness was more than the product of anti-Semitism, and to consider that there existed an irreducible, positive Jewish identity based in the history and religion of the Jewish people.[37] In her diary for December 1998, she notes—without comment—a Russian saying she had come across: "A thief unpunished / A horse cured / A yid converted / Are all the same."

By the time *Here* was published in September 1995, she had already embarked on a new project. Idleness was not an option, and *Ouvrez* (Open up) appeared two years later in September 1997. It was her last book, but it was nonetheless a new departure. Written entirely in dialogue, like *You Don't Love Yourself*, the speakers are words themselves, giving literal reality to comments that Nathalie had previously made when in 1978 she said to Lucette Finas, "My real characters, my only characters are words. But charged, freighted. They're not words for the sake of words." In a similar vein, she had told Viviane Forrester, "For me, words are living things."[38] Her old preoccupation with exclusion is played out here with words, as the unacceptable ones are corralled behind a glass partition, calling to the acceptable ones to "Open up." The intimations of definitive disappearance and annihilation in the previous book are nowhere to be seen, and despite a passing reference to "that Race" (the Jews) or the forgetfulness of old age, the constant discussion that the words have with and about each other is a source of almost untranslatable verbal comedy. (It's the only one of her books that has never appeared in English.) Consisting once again of a series of numbered prose texts (fifteen in all), the writing succeeded in combining prose with a theatrical dimension that Nathalie herself saw as having potential for realisation on stage or—at least—on radio. Published one year after the *Complete Works*, *Ouvrez* finally succeeded in destroying the Pléiade's ambition of exhaustiveness.[39]

Visits from family and friends continued as before, and there was almost always someone with whom Nathalie could share an evening meal, often at one of the nearby restaurants, Sous l'olivier or the Lebanese Noura. But physical decline was making itself felt. The diaries provide a record of medical appointments and physical ailments, largely minor and temporary, along with notations of time spent walking (as recommended by her doctor), the occasional day in bed, and in 1991 and 1992 there are poignant entries that read "Very difficult night" or "Terrible night." Towards the end of the decade, depression alternates with anxiety, and there are notes of medication for both.

In conversation Nathalie would often refer to the imminence of death, urging her visitors not to delay returning because she soon wouldn't be there. She would ask Werner Spies for health reports on Ernst Jünger, five years her senior, and anyone from England would be quizzed for the latest news about the dancing exploits and gin consumption of the Queen Mother, who was almost exactly the same age as Nathalie. In conversation with Claude Régy in 1989 she spoke quite frankly about her fear of death. What she dreaded was "the awareness of death, ... sensing it come."[40] She read Montaigne,

Dante, and Pascal, and returned to Strindberg's theatre. *The Dance of Death* became bedside reading. In addition to providing meditations on death and the afterlife in which Nathalie did not believe, these books—Strindberg in particular—were also a stimulus for more writing.

Almost two decades after her last play, *For No Good Reason*, the theatrical element of *Ouvrez* had revived Nathalie's interest in the theatre. In a letter of June 1998, Françoise d'Eaubonne, with whom she was once again in regular contact, wrote to say, "You must be on holiday in Normandy or somewhere else, if there is such a thing as holidays for you who never stop working, much to the benefit of us ever eager readers."[41] The existence of a potential audience was reason to keep writing. Nathalie may also have been encouraged in a return to the theatre by two current performances of *For No Good Reason*, one in a revival of Benmussa's production at the Théâtre des Champs-Elysées, and a new production by Jacques Lassalle at the Théâtre de la Colline, a performance of which Nathalie attended in October 1998.[42] Lassalle recalled her urging him to stage *Ouvrez*, when she said, "You'll find a solution, I'm sure." And then, as he was leaving, she added, "Come back soon. I'll read you the beginning of the new play."[43] This was the last time he ever saw her. He never heard the play, and there is now no trace of the manuscript.

The diary for 1999 provides a record of continuing visits. In June—the last month for which there are entries—a note about direct flights to the Balearic Islands, where for the previous four years Nathalie had spent the month of August, suggests that she was planning to keep her old holiday routine going. However, a drop in blood pressure confined her to bed, and thereafter her health declined. She was treated at home while her daughters maintained an assiduous presence, and visitors—of whom Werner Spies was the last—were eventually turned away. By October she had pulmonary congestion, difficulty breathing, and pains in the chest. The symptoms from which she had suffered with TB returned at the end, and she refused both food and sedatives. Nor in her dying moments was she spared the awareness of the approach of death that she had so dreaded, and which she had so vividly imagined and attributed to Chekhov in *Ich sterbe*. When the final moment came on a Tuesday morning, 19 October 1999, she raised herself from her pillow and announced, "It's finished." Claude, who was standing at the foot of the bed, was unable to determine whether these words expressed relief that all was finally over or angst at the imminence of extinction.[44] It was ninety-nine years and almost exactly three months since her long life had begun on Wednesday, 18 July 1900 in Ivanovo. Just short of a century.

The funeral took place the following Saturday in Chérence, under a grey sky with a blustery wind and intermittent rain showers. The ceremony was minimal, and there were no speeches. Some eighty people came to pay their respects, and the last to arrive, after proceedings had begun, was Catherine Trautmann, the minister of culture. Aside from Nathalie's three daughters, her grandchildren, and her son-in-law Jean-François Revel, there was Maurice Nadeau, who was now Anne Sarraute's unofficial partner, Antoine Gallimard, Jean-Yves Tadié, Betsy Jolas, Claude Régy, Isabelle Huppert, Werner Spies and his wife Monique, Roland Husson, Rolande Causse, Arnaud Rykner, and many others of whom there is no official record. The master of ceremonies knew nothing about the woman whose body he was burying alongside that of her husband, and referred to her throughout as "Madame Serraute." No one else spoke and there was some confusion over the distribution of the roses for mourners to throw into the grave. Once the proceedings were over, they were left to climb back into their cars and return to Paris on the roads that had become so familiar to Nathalie over the course of the previous half a century.[45]

Within a few weeks, the apartment in Avenue Pierre 1e de Serbie had been cleared. The books from Nathalie's study were passed to a bookseller who disposed of them without prior cataloguing; her furniture went to auction; and only some of the remaining documents promised to Annie Angremy found their way to the Bibliothèque nationale. Decorators arrived to prepare for new tenants at the address that had been Nathalie's Paris home for more than sixty years. The house in Chérence, with its plaque marking her occupancy, remained in the family for several more years, preserved more or less exactly as it had been during her lifetime until, when the upkeep became too much, it was sold. And then? A newly constructed esplanade in the eighteenth arrondissement, with which Nathalie had had no connections in her lifetime, was opened in December 2013 and named after her. The windswept development, laid out along-side railway lines running up from the Gare de l'Est, houses the Václav Havel Library and the Rosa-Luxemburg Gardens, where, whether by accident or design, Nathalie finds herself memorialised in the company of a dissident and a revolutionary from Eastern Europe. A strand from her early life had come full circle.

Preface

1. "Biographie: Nathalie Sarraute," interview with Viviane Forrester, France Culture, 4 February 1977; Olivier Soufflot de Magny, "Entretiens avec Nathalie Sarraute Archives du XXe siècle," 10–11 April 1973, INA (Institut national de l'audiovisuel), Paris; Arnaud Rykner, "Entretien avec Nathalie Sarraute," in *Nathalie Sarraute*, 2nd ed. (Paris: Le Seuil, 2002), 169–99 (177).

2. Magny, "Entretiens avec Nathalie Sarraute," in reply to the question, "Can you imagine someone writing your biography one day?"

3. Ibid. See Marcel Proust, *Against Sainte-Beuve and Other Essays*, trans. John Sturrock (London: Penguin, 1988).

4. Sonia Rykiel, "Nathalie Sarraute: Quand j'écris, je ne suis ni homme ni femme ni chien," *Les Nouvelles*, 9–15 February 1984, 39–41 (41).

5. Simone Benmussa, *Nathalie Sarraute: Qui êtes-vous? Conversations avec Simone Benmussa* (Lyon: La Manufacture, 1987), 155.

6. Carmen Licari, "'Qu'est-ce qu'il y a, qu'est-ce qui s'est passé? Mais rien.' Entretiens avec Nathalie Sarraute," *Francofonia* 9 (1985): 3–16 (10); and Isabelle Huppert, "Nathalie Sarraute," *Les Cahiers du cinéma* 477 (1994): 8–14 (14).

7. Viviane Forrester, "Portrait de Nathalie," *Magazine littéraire* 196 (1983): 18–21 (18); interview with Isabelle de Vigan, *Nathalie Sarraute, écrivain des mouvements intérieurs, portrait-interview*, Collection Témoins, Vidéo VHS, 1984.

8. Huppert, "Nathalie Sarraute," 12.

9. Quoted in NS, "From Dostoievski to Kafka," in *Tropisms, and The Age of Suspicion*, 71.

10. Rykner, "Entretien avec Nathalie Sarraute," 171–72.

11. Interview with François-Marie Banier, "Un anti-portrait de la romancière," *Le Monde des livres*, 11 April 1983, 13, 16 (13) and letter from NS to Maurice Blanchot, 16 July 1963, in *Maurice Blanchot*, ed. Éric Hoppenot and Dominique Rabaté (Paris: L'Herne, 2014), 153.

12. Magny, "Entretiens avec Nathalie Sarraute." She is almost certainly referring to D. D. Akhcharoumov et al., *Dostoïevski vivant. Témoignages*, trans. Raïssa Tarr (Paris: Gallimard, 1972).

Chapter 1. Russian Childhoods, 1900–05

1. NS, *Childhood*, 33.

2. V. S. Byakovsky, *Doma i liudi. Po dostoprimechatelnym mestam goroda Ivanova* (Ivanovo, 1998), 159–77.

3. Olga Zakharova, "Snachala eyo zvali Emmoi," *Rabochiy Krai*, 15 October 1993, 3. Zakharova was the senior archivist at the Regional State Archive of Ivanovo. She published a series of articles about the Tcherniak family in *Rabochiy Krai* (The Workers' Region).

4. K. E. Baldin, "Natsionalnye diaspory v Ivanovo-Voznesenk v nachale XX veka," *Granitsy*, Almanakh tzentra etnicheskikh i natsionalnikh issledovannii Ivanovskovo Gosudartsvennovo Universiteta 1 (2007): 12–24.

5. Byakovsky, *Doma i liudi*, 174.

6. See Ilya's application for French nationality, Archives Nationales, Paris, BB/11/5547 dossier 11079 X 12.

7. Ibid. and Annie Angremy, ed., *Nathalie Sarraute. Portrait d'un écrivain* (Paris: Bibliothèque nationale de France, 1995), 7.

8. "Chronologie," in *Œuvres complètes*, xxix; Registres d'inscriptions aux cours, CH UNIGE/aap/30/1984/31/3 and CH UNIGE aap/414A2.

9. Registres d'inscriptions aux cours, CH UNIGE/aap/30/1984/31/5.

10. Claude Sarraute, *Avant que t'oublies tout!* (Paris: Plon, 2009), 23.

11. www.encyclopedia.com/science/dictionaries-thesauruses-pictures-and-press -releases/shatunovsky-samuil-osipovich. I have used the English transliteration of Samuil's name and kept the French for Polina in conformity with her student record at the University of Geneva.

12. Transcript of interview with NS by James Knowlson, Museum of English Rural Life and Special Collections, University of Reading, JEK A/7/89.

13. See Benjamin Pinkus, *The Jews of the Soviet Union: The History of a National Minority* (Cambridge: Cambridge University Press, 1988).

14. See Ilya's application for French nationality, Archives Nationales, BB/11/5547 dossier 11079 X 12.

15. Manfred Hildermeier, *The Russian Socialist Revolutionary Party before the First World War* (New York: St. Martin's, 2000).

16. For the presumed dates of Liolia's death, see Byakovsky, *Doma i liudi*, 166.

17. www.jewishgen.org/databases/jgdetail_2.php.

18. Baldin, "Natsionalnye diaspory v Ivanovo-Voznesenk," 20–21.

19. Cited in Zakharova, "Snachala eyo zvali Emmoi."

20. See Byakovsky, *Doma i liudi* and Zakharova, "Snachala eyo zvali Emmoi."

21. Zakharova, "Snachala eyo zvali Emmoi."

22. Joseph Conrad, *Under Western Eyes* (Oxford: Oxford University Press, 1983), 357.

23. Zoya Boguslavskaya, "U Natalie Sarraute gody spustya," *Literaturnaya Gazeta*, 17 December 1986, 15.

24. Ilya Ehrenburg, *People and Life: Memoirs of 1891–1917*, trans. Anna Bostock and Yvonne Kapp (London: McGibbon & Kee, 1961), passim.

25. Marie Darrieussecq, *Être ici est une splendeur. Vie de Paula M. Becker* (Paris: P.O.L., 2016); Ehrenburg, *People and Life*, passim; Rainer Maria Rilke, *The Notebook of Malte Laurids Brigge*, trans. John Linton (Oxford: Oxford University Press, 1984).

26. NS, *Childhood*, 17.

27. Alain Norvez, *De la naissance à l'école: santé, modes de garde et préscolarité dans la France contemporaine* (Paris: PUF, 1990), 20.

28. NS, *Childhood*, 22.

29. NS, *Childhood*, 34–44.

30. Rilke, "Das Karrussell," translated as "The Merry-Go-Round" by Stephen Cohn in Rainer Maria Rilke, *New Poems: A Bilingual Edition* (Evanston, Ill.: Northwestern University Press, 1992), 101.

31. "What Birds See," in *The Age of Suspicion*, 135.

Chapter 2. Between Petersburg and Paris, 1905–11

1. Baldin, "Natsionalnye diaspory v Ivanovo-Voznesenk."

2. Reported by NS in interview with Mariusia Klimova, *Mitin Zhurnal*, 17 September 1997.

3. D. S. Mirsky, *A History of Russian Literature* (London: RKP, 1964), 341–43.

4. See records in RGALI, Russian State Archive of Literature and Art, Moscow, where entries for Polina feature under her married names of Boretzkaya and Boretzkaya-Bergfeld.

5. Quoted in extracts from Korolenko's correspondence with various interlocutors about *Russkoe Bogatstvo*, http://az.lib.ru/k/korolenko_w_g/text_1920_korolenko .shtml.

6. Benmussa, *Nathalie Sarraute*, 159.

7. For these accounts of Polina's novels, I am indebted to the unpublished summaries by Leo Shtutin.

8. Typescript of interview with Nina Cassian (later published in the Rumanian journal *La Roumanie littéraire*) in letter from Cassian to NS, December 1968, Fonds Nathalie Sarraute, Bibliothèque nationale de France, NAF 28088(184). All further citations to the Nathalie Sarraute archive are indicated by catalogue number.

9. NS, *Childhood*, 63–64*.

10. See interview with Pierre Démeron, "Nathalie Sarraute ou littérature sans cabotinage," *Arts*, 3–9 June 1959, 2.

11. Lev Lourié, "Eks na Fonarnom," *Sobaka* 23 (November 2004), http://kn.sobaka .ru/n23/04.html.

12. P. Kochel, *Istoria syska v Rossiy*, www.gumer.info/bibliotek_Buks/History /koshel/11.php.

13. Reported by Claude Mauriac in his diary entry for June 1958, *Le Rire des pères dans les yeux des enfants* (Paris: Éditions Grasset et Fasquelle, 1981), 111.

14. Vladimir Nabokov, *Speak, Memory* (Harmondsworth: Penguin, 1969), 111–15.

15. Information in Ilya's application for French nationality, Archives Nationales, BB/11/5547, dossier 11079 X 12.

16. See also the photocopy of a letter from Ilya Tcherniak, presumably to Branting, sent from Geneva, 20 February 1908, NAF 28088(198), where Ilya also refers to his "wife."

17. Isaac Deutscher, *The Prophet Armed. Trotsky: 1879–1921* (London: Oxford University Press, 1954), 223.

18. NS, *Childhood*, 173*.

19. Forrester, "Portrait de Nathalie."

20. NS, *Childhood*, 54–55. See also Charles-Ferdinand Ramuz, *Paris, notes d'un Vaudois*, in *Œuvres complètes*, vol. 17, ed. Gustave Roud and Daniel Simond (Lausanne: Éditions Rencontre, 1968), 295.

21. NS, *Childhood*, 115.

22. Photo in Sarraute Family Collection.

23. NS, *Childhood*, 229.

24. Postcards in Sarraute Family Papers.

Chapter 3. Schooldays, 1912–18

1. Forrester, "Portrait de Nathalie."

2. Magny, "Entretiens avec Nathalie Sarraute."

3. Letter to NS from Mme J. Villey-Desmeserets (formerly Jeannette Buvat), 22 February 1984, Sarraute Family Papers.

4. Archives de Paris, PEROTIN/704/73/1, 55.

5. Lucette Finas, "Comment j'ai écrit certains de mes livres," *Etudes littéraires* 12, no. 3 (1979): 393–401 (394). With the exception of one item which is in the Fonds Nathalie Sarraute at the BnF (Bibliothèque nationale de France), the French compositions are in private papers belonging to the Sarraute family.

6. Simone de Beauvoir, *La Céremonie des adieux* (Paris: Gallimard, coll. folio, 1988), 184; Forrester, "Portrait de Nathalie."

7. NS, *Childhood*, 192.

8. Sarraute Family Papers.

9. Marc Saporta, "Portrait d'une inconnue, conversation biographique," *L'Arc* 95 (1984): 5 23 (10).

10. NS, philosophy assignment dated 30 October 1917, Documents biographiques, NAF 28088.

11. "Foreword," in *The Age of Suspicion*, 7–8*.

12. Quoted in Serge Nicolas, *Théodule Ribot (1839–1917): Philosophe breton, fondateur de la psychologie française* (Paris: L'Harmattan, 2005), 61.

13. NS, *Childhood*, 230.

14. This composition is in the Sarraute Family Papers.

15. Draft of Chronology for *Complete Works*, Sarraute Family Papers.

16. As recalled by Marguerite Châtelain, a pupil at the school, 1912–20, in *Livre d'or du centenaire de l'Association amicale des anciennes et anciens élèves du Lycée Fénelon 1896–1996* (Paris: Lycée Fénelon, 1996), 20–21.

17. Letter to NS from Ilouche Minor, 20 January 1916[?], Sarraute Family Papers.

18. Draft of Chronology for the *Complete Works*, Sarraute Family Papers.

19. Letters in Sarraute Family Papers.

20. Interview with Nicole Minor, daughter of Choura Minor.

21. Letter from Léon Minor to NS, 23 March 1919, Sarraute Family Papers.

22. With the exception of one letter from Léon Minor to Nathalie, NAF 28088(208), all these letters are in the Sarraute Family Papers.

Chapter 4. England, 1919–21

1. Hélène Pézard, "Témoignage," in *Livre d'or du centenaire de l'Association.*

2. NS, *Childhood*, 233*.

3. "Nathalie Sarraute Talks about Her Life and Works: Extracts from a Conversation Recorded in Swansea," *Romance Studies* 4 (1984): 8–16 (11).

4. www.sorbonne.fr/la-sorbonne/histoire-de-la-sorbonne/.

5. NS, "Nathalie Sarraute," in *Three Decades of the French New Novel*, ed. Lois Oppenheim, (Urbana: University of Illinois Press, 1986), 119–31 (120).

6. Emile Legouis and L. Cazamian, *A History of English Literature*, vol. 2: *Modern Times (1660–1914)*, trans. W. D. MacInness and L. Cazamian (London; Toronto: J. M. Dent, 1927), 391.

7. Benmussa, *Nathalie Sarraute*, 49.

8. Degree certificates from the Sorbonne, Archives nationales, AJ/16/4800.

9. Unpublished interview with NS by Edith McMorran and Ann Jefferson, 24 March 1997.

10. No. 19 in the 1939 edition. *Tropisms, and The Age of Suspicion*, 46.

11. Sergei Vladimirovich Volkov, Baza Dannykh No. 2, "Uchastniki Belovo dvizheniya v Rossii" (1995–2014), http://swolkov.org/index.htm.

12. R. F. Butler and M. H. Pritchard, eds., *The Society of Oxford Home-Students: Retrospects and Recollections* (Oxford: Oxonian Press, 1930).

13. College Register, St Anne's College Archives, and unpublished interview with NS by Edith McMorran and Ann Jefferson, 24 March 1997.

14. Paul Vinogradoff, *Self-Government in Russia* (New York: E.P. Dutton, 1915), 3.

15. *Dictionary of National Biography*, www.oxforddnb.com/view/article/36664, and copy of letter from NS to Robert Gibson, 5 June 1979, NAF 28088(211).

16. Katherine B. Scott, quoted in Butler and Pritchard, *Society of Oxford Home-Students*, 118–19.

17. "Nathalie Sarraute Talks about Her Life and Works," 10.

18. Interview with Ann Jefferson and Edith McMorran.

19. Both in Sarraute Family Papers.

20. The essay on the Vikings is the Documents Biographiques, NAF 28088. The other two are in the Sarraute Family Papers.

21. Saporta, "Portrait d'une inconnue," 10.

Chapter 5. Berlin, 1921–22

1. Banier, "Un anti-portrait de la romancière," 16.

2. Documents biographiques, NAF 28088.

3. Sarraute Family Papers.

4. See Robert C. Williams, *Culture in Exile: Russian Émigrés in Germany, 1881–1941* (Ithaca, N.Y.: Cornell University Press, 1972).

5. The preface dates from 1962. Vladimir Nabokov, *The Gift*, trans. Michael Scammell with the collaboration of the author (London: Panther, 1966), 8.

6. Brian Boyd, *Nabokov: The Russian Years* (London: Chatto & Windus, 1990), 184.

7. Nabokov, preface to *The Gift*, 8; Nina Berberova, *The Italics Are Mine*, trans. Philippe Radley (London: Chatto & Windus, 1991), 151–54.

8. Ilya Ehrenburg, *Truce: 1921–33*, vol. 3 of *Men, Years—Life*, trans. Tatania Shebunina with Yvonne Kapp (London: MacGibbon & Kee, 1963), 10 and passim.

9. Introduction to *Economic Life in the Modern Age: Werner Sombart*, ed. Nico Stehr and Reiner Grundmann (New Brunswick, N.J.: Transaction, 2001), xiii.

10. Quoted in Herman Lebovics, *Social Conservatism and the Middle Class in Germany, 1914–1933* (Princeton, N.J.: Princeton University Press, 1969), 52.

11. Françoise Asso, "Nathalie Sarraute," *La Quinzaine littéraire*, 1–15 August 1992, 29, and draft replies for an interview with Diana Mihajlova (Zagreb),1987, NAF 28088 (Interviews, Conférences).

12. Banier, "Un anti-portrait de la romancière," 16.

13. Thomas Mann, *Tonio Kröger and Other Stories*, trans. David Luke (New York: Bantam Books, 1970), 159, 217, 177. Choura's letter is undated, but he begins by saying he hopes it will reach her in Berlin before she returns to Paris. See chapter 3.

14. Mann, *Tonio Kröger*, 169.

15. Interview with Diana Mihajlova.

16. Asso, "Nathalie Sarraute," 29.

Chapter 6. Pierre Janet's Patient, 1922

1. *Portrait of a Man Unknown*, 139.

2. Pierre Janet, *La Médicine psychologique* (1923; Paris: L'Harmattan, 2005), 125–29.

3. Henri F. Ellenberger, *The Discovery of the Unconscious: The History and Evolution of Dynamic Psychiatry* (1970; London: Fontana, 1994), 344.

4. "Nathalie Sarraute Talks about Her Life and Works," 14.

5. Madeleine Guérin-Wright, "Entretien avec Nathalie Sarraute," in "Nathalie Sarraute: 'Entre la vie et la mort': une interprétation linguistique" (PhD thesis, University of Wisconsin–Madison, 1973), 197–214 (202).

6. Léon Chertok, *Mémoires: les résistances d'un psy*, ed. Isabelle Stengers and Didier Gille (Paris: Éditions La Découverte, 1990), 14.

7. Guérin-Wright, "Entretien avec Nathalie Sarraute," 203.

8. "Nathalie Sarraute Talks about Her Life and Works," 13.

9. Raymond Roussel, *Comment j'ai écrit certains de mes livres*, "Les caractères psychologiques de l'extase," 175–83, from Pierre Janet, *De l'angoisse à l'extase*, 2 vols. (Paris: Librairie Félix Alcan, 1926–28), 1:132–37.

10. *Portrait of a Man Unknown*, 28.

11. *Tropisms, and The Age of Suspicion*, 36.

12. Recalled by J.-B. Barrère, *La Cure d'amaigrissement du roman* (Paris: Albin Michel, 1964), 93–94.

13. Pierre Janet, *La Médecine psychologique* (1923; Paris: L'Harmattan, 2005), 93, 146.

14. Francine Mallet, *Nathalie Sarraute: portrait d'une inconnue*, France 2, 31 May 1976.

15. Pierre Janet, *Psychologie expérimentale et comparée. La Pensée intérieure et ses troubles. Compte rendu intégral du cours professé par M. Pierre Janet au Collège de France. 1926–1927*, Fascicules 1–6, 1927. The copy was in NS's library in Chérence.

16. Mallet, *Nathalie Sarraute*.

17. Jean-Louis de Rambures, "Nathalie Sarraute: une table dans un coin de bistro," *Le Monde*, 14 January 1972, 16.

Chapter 7. Independence, 1922–25

1. Finas, "Comment j'ai écrit certains de mes livres," 393.

2. Saporta, "Portrait d'une inconnue," 9.

3. NS, "Nathalie Sarraute," 120.

4. Archives nationales, AJ/16/1735.

5. Natalia Tikhonov Sigrist, "Les femmes et l'université en France, 1860–1914," *Histoire de l'éducation* 122 (2009): 53–70.

6. Françoise Vitry, "L'heure de la femme," La Renaissance politique, littéraire, artistique, 27 August 1921, quoted in Christen-Lécuyer Carole, "Les premières étudiantes de l'Université de Paris," *Travail, genre et sociétés* 2, no. 4 (2000): 35–50, www.cairn.info /revue-travail-genre-et-societes-2000-2-page-35.htm.

7. Victor Martinez, *André du Bouchet: Poésie, langue, événement* (Amsterdam: Rodopi, 2013), 169; letter to NS from Fernande Elosu, 25 April 1985, NAF 28088, Lettres reçues à l'occasion du décès de Raymond Sarraute.

8. "Nathalie Sarraute," in *Beckett Remembering, Remembering Beckett: Uncollected Interviews with Samuel Beckett and Memories of Those who Knew Him*, ed. Elizabeth Knowlson and James Knowlson (London: Bloomsbury, 2007), 81–84 (82).

9. Jacques Boulenger, "La femme moderne: devant le feu," *Illustration*, 6 December 1924, quoted in Mary Louise Roberts, *Civilization without Sexes: Reconstructing Gender in Postwar France, 1917–1927* (Chicago: University of Chicago Press, 1994), 19. Roberts also quotes Drieu, 2.

10. *Revue des deux mondes*, 15 October 1923, quoted in Roberts, *Civilization without Sexes*, 179.

11. NS, "Nathalie Sarraute," 120.

12. Archives Nationales, BB/11/8566 dossier 33509 X 24.

13. Finas, "Comment j'ai écrit certains de mes livres," 393.

14. Saporta, "Portrait d'une inconnue," 11.

15. NS, "Nathalie Sarraute," 120.

16. Interview with Dominique Sarraute.

17. Finas, "Comment j'ai écrit certains de mes livres," 393–94. A entrance slip for the Conférence du stage session dated 17 January 1930 bears the signature Natalie [*sic*] Sarraute, Sarraute Family Papers.

18. Robert Badinter, *Un antisémitisme ordinaire. Vichy et les avocats juifs (1940-1944)* (Paris: Fayard, 1997), chap. 1.

19. Mimica Cranaki and Yvon Belaval, *Nathalie Sarraute* (Paris: Gallimard, 1965).

20. *Golden Fruits*, 527–28, and 609; see also *For No Good Reason*, n.p.

21. Postcard from Raymond Sarraute to NS, 21 July 1924, Sarraute Family Papers.

Chapter 8. Raymond

1. Interview with Dominique Sarraute.

2. Benmussa, *Nathalie Sarraute*, 151–52.

3. Jean Blot, *En amitié* (Paris: La Bibliothèque, 2015), 143–44.

4. Huppert, "Nathalie Sarraute," 14.

5. Benmussa, *Nathalie Sarraute*, 156.

6. Claude Sarraute, *Avant que t'oublies tout!*, 21.

7. Leslie Derfler, *Alexandre Millerand: The Socialist Years* (The Hague: Mouton, 1977), 166, and Charles Rappoport, *Une vie révolutionnaire, 1883–1941: les mémoires de Charles Rappoport*, ed. Marc Langana (Paris: Les Éditions de la MSH, 1991), 214.

8. Saporta, "Portrait d'une inconnue," 13.

9. *Notice extraite de Fichiers de Pierre Moulinier: Corpus des étudiants étrangers et des femmes reçus docteurs en médecine à Paris entre 1807 et 1907*, www.biusante.parisdescartes.fr/histoire/biographies/?cle=27001.

10. Claude Sarraute, *Avant que t'oublies tout!*, 20.

11. Rappoport, *Une vie révolutionnaire*, 214–15.

12. The Passy address is on Joseph's rail card for 1906–7, Sarraute Family Papers.

Chapter 9. Coming of Age with Modernism, 1923–27

1. Grant Kaiser, "Interview de Nathalie Sarraute," *Romans 20/50* 4 (1987): 117–27 (122) and NS, "À propos d'André Gide," *La Quinzaine littéraire*, 1–15 November 1969, 20.

2. Kaiser, "Interview de Nathalie Sarraute," 122.

3. Asso, "Nathalie Sarraute," 29.

4. Claude Mauriac, *Le Rire des pères*, 112–13.

5. Asso, "Nathalie Sarraute," 29.

6. Benmussa, *Nathalie Sarraute*, 65.

7. Virginia Woolf, "Modern Fiction," in *Collected Essays*, vol. 2, ed. Leonard Woolf (London: Chattto & Windus, 1967), 103–10 (108). First published in *The Common Reader*, 1925. See NS, "Conversation and Sub-conversation."

8. Sylvia Beach Papers, Princeton University Library, Shakespeare & Company Lending Library, Borrowers Cards, 1922–61, box 43.

9. NS, replies to questionnaire, 1963, Interviews, conférences, NAF 28088.

10. NS, "Nathalie Sarraute," 121.

11. Rolande Causse, *Conversations avec Nathalie Sarraute* (Paris: Le Seuil, 2016), 26.

12. Benmussa, *Nathalie Sarraute*, 66, 158, 153.

13. Undated letters from Raymond to NS, probably written in early 1928, Sarraute Family Papers.

14. Interview with Marie Darrieussecq.

Chapter 10. Marriage and Motherhood, 1925–33

1. Marriage certificate, Sarraute and Tcherniak, Mairie du 6e arrondissement, Archives de Paris.

2. Letter to NS from Bibliographisches Institut, Mannheim, 17 October 1966, and draft of reply from NS, NAF 28088(182).

3. Blot, *En amitié*, 144.

4. Interview with Dominique Sarraute; Claude Sarraute, *Avant que t'oublies tout!*, 27.

5. David Garnett, *Lady into Fox* (1922; Minneola, N.Y.: Dover, 2013), 63.

6. Letter from Raymond to NS, Thursday 13 [February] 1928, Sarraute Family Papers.

7. Benmussa, *Nathalie Sarraute*, 157, 159.

8. See Elinor A. Accampo, "The Gendered Nature of Contraception in France: Neo-Malthusianism, 1900–1920," *Journal of Interdisciplinary History* 34, no. 2 (2003): 235–62, and Anne-Claire Rebreyend, "Sexualités vécues. France 1920–1970," *Clio. Histoire, femmes et sociétés* 18 (2003): 209–22.

9. An envelope in Raymond's handwriting posted from Vincennes on 23 June 1927 is addressed to Madame Sarraute at 58 boulevard Raspail, Sarraute Family Papers.

10. Undated letters to NS from Raymond in Sarraute Family Papers.

11. Letter from NS to Raymond, "Monday, 2," no date, Sarraute Family Papers. I have translated *il* as "it" rather than "he."

12. www.cliniquevalmont.ch/site/assets/files/68379/laventure_valmont.pdf. Unfortunately, the clinic has kept no record of Nathalie's stay.

13. Undated letter to NS from Ilya Tcherniak, NAF 28088(208).

14. Letters to NS mostly undated from Raymond, Lena, and Nadia; letter to NS headed Val-Mont, Glion, and dated 21 March 1928 from Dr [illegible]; prescription from Dr Louis Ramond dated 22 April 1928, Sarraute Family Papers.

15. Skype interview with Hélène Comay (née du Bouchet).

16. Rykiel, "Nathalie Sarraute," 41; Claude Sarraute, *Avant que t'oublies tout!*, 26.

17. Interview with Claude Sarraute.

18. Claude Sarraute, *Avant que t'oublies tout!*, 26; letter from Anna Haag to NS, 1 August 1990, NAF 28088(189).

19. Benmussa, *Nathalie Sarraute*, 80.

Chapter 11. The First Tropism, 1932–34

1. Kaye Mortley, "With Nathalie Sarraute," interview in NS, *Just for Nothing*, trans. Kaye Mortley (Newton, NSW: Barberism & Monograph Press, 1997), n.p.

2. Ibid.

3. Interview with Dominique Sarraute.

4. Jean Larnac, *Histoire de la littérature féminine en France* (Paris: Éditions KRA, 1929), 257.

5. Archives du Commissariat général aux questions juives, Archives Nationales, AJ/38, 3404–5.

6. NS, "Nathalie Sarraute," 122.

7. Rykiel, "Nathalie Sarraute," 40.

8. Interview with Claude Sarraute.

9. NS, *Tropisms, and The Age of Suspicion*, 18*.

10. Rambures, "Nathalie Sarraute," 16.

11. Licari, "Entretiens avec Nathalie Sarraute," 9.

Chapter 12. A Pause, 1935–37

1. Saporta, "Portrait d'une inconnue," 13; interview with Dominique Sarraute.

2. Gretchen Besser, "Colloque avec Nathalie Sarraute," *French Review* 50, no. 2 (1986): 284–89 (286)

3. Ibid.

4. NS, *Tropisms*, 32.

5. Letter from NS to Raymond Sarraute, envelope postmarked 8 May 1935, Sarraute Family Papers. This recently discovered letter makes it clear that NS visited Moscow in 1935 rather than 1936. The dates she herself provided vary between the two years.

6. André Gide, *Return from the U.S.S.R.*, trans. Dorothy Bussy (New York: Knopf, 1937), 16.

7. Bernard Pares, *Moscow Admits a Critic* (London: Nelson, 1936), 34, 55.

8. Gide, *Return*, xiii.

9. Pares, *Moscow Admits*, 88.

10. NS, "Chronologie," in *Œuvres complètes*, xxxvi.

11. Saporta, "Portrait d'une inconnue," 13.

12. Photocopy sent by Alexis de Morlanges to NS of her handwritten letter to Sartre, 11 November 1956, NAF 28088(194). Morlanges asked for permission to include the letter in an edition of Sartre's political writings, but NS refused. The interview with Sartre to which she is responding was published in *L'Express*, 9 November 1956, where at one point he says, "the Russian people are innocent, as of course are all peoples, as

long as keeping silent does not make them complicit with any concentration-camp system established inside their country. In the U.R.S.S., the astonishment on the part of the population after the return of the detainees demonstrates pretty clearly that they knew nothing. Speaking for myself, my feelings for the brave and hard-working Russian people have not been altered by the crimes committed by their government." www.lexpress.fr/informations/apres-budapest-sartre-parle_590852.html.

13. Gide, *Return*, 51.

14. Mary Ann Caws, ed., *Maria Jolas, Woman of Action. A Memoir and Other Writings* (Columbia: University of South Carolina Press, 2004), 101 and 103.

15. Interview with Dominique Sarraute.

16. *transition*, 16–17 June 1929.

17. The 1937 number was in NS's library at Chérence. The record of the borrowings is in the Sylvia Beach archive.

18. Unpublished letter from Maria Jolas to *Le Monde*, 1982, quoted in Vincent Giroud, "Transition to Vichy: The Case of Georges Pelorson," *Modernism/modernity* 7, no. 2 (2000): 221–48 (223).

19. Engagement de location, 19 October 1936, Sarraute Family Papers.

20. Mallet, *Nathalie Sarraute*.

Chapter 13. Publication, 1938–39

1. Hector Bianciotti, "Nathalie Sarraute," *Digraphe* 32 (1984): 66–68 (67).

2. Undated letter to NS from Félicien Marceau, [Autumn 1965?], NAF 28088(191).

3. François Poirié, "Nathalie Sarraute à la source des sensations," *Art Press*, July–August 1983, 29.

4. Paul Valéry, *Cahiers*, ed. Judith Robinson, vol. 2 (Paris: Gallimard, Bibl. de la Pléiade, 1974), 387.

5. Draft of letter from NS to various publishers, NAF 28088(203).

6. Letter from Jean Paulhan to NS, 23 August 1938, NAF 28088(203).

7. Letter from Raymond to NS, July 1938, NAF 28088, Documents biographiques.

8. Ibid.

9. Letter from Gaston Gallimard to NS, 14 October 1938, NAF 28088(203).

10. Letter from Henry Muller to NS, 3 November 1938, NAF 28088(203).

11. Louis-Ferdinand Céline in *Castle to Castle* (1957), quoted in A. Louise Staman, *With the Stroke of a Pen: A Story of Ambition, Greed, Infidelity, and the Murder of French Publisher Robert Denoël* (New York: St. Martin's, 2002), 306.

12. NS, "Nathalie Sarraute," 123.

13. Denoël contract, NAF 28008.

14. Undated draft of letter from NS to André Gide, NAF 28088(203).

15. Personal conversation with NS.

16. Letter from NS to Gide, 6 May 1939, found inside copy of *Tropismes*, Archives Catherine Gide, quoted in Alain Goulet, "Échos gidiens dans la représentation sarrautienne," in *Nathalie Sarraute et la représentation*, ed. Monique Gosselin-Noat and Arnaud Rykner, *Roman 20–50* (2005): 67–79 (73).

17. Victor Moremans, "Ce qu'on lit," *Gazette de Liège*, 3 March 1939, reproduced in NS, *Œuvres complètes*, 1726.

18. Henri Hertz, *Europe*, 15 August 1939, and Joë Bousquet, *Cahiers du Sud*, January 1940.

19. Undated letter from Max Jacob to NS, NAF 28088(203), reproduced in NS, *Œuvres complètes*, 1724-25.

20. Letter from Charles Mauron to NS, 28 January 1939, NS, *Œuvres complètes*, 1725.

21. Undated letter from Jean-Paul Sartre to NS, NAF 28088(203), reproduced in NS, *Œuvres complètes*, 1725.

22. Letter to NS from Georges Pelorson, 3 March 1939, NAF 28088(203), reproduced in NS, *Œuvres complètes*, 1725.

23. Letter to NS from Jean Paulhan, 2 July 1939, NAF 28088(203).

24. Magny, "Entretiens avec Nathalie Sarraute."

25. Maurice Imbert and Raphaël Sorin, eds., *Adrienne Monnier et la Maison des amis des livres, 1915-1951* (Paris: IMEC éditions, 1991), 40.

26. Letter from Raymond to NS, Saturday [1939], NAF 28088, Documents biographiques.

27. Letter from Georges Pelorson to NS, 3 March 1939, NAF 28088(203).

28. Postcard from Georges Pelorson to NS, 12 August 1939, NAF 28088(203).

29. Letter from NS to Raymond, "Wednesday," Sarraute Family Papers.

Chapter 14. Jewish by Decree, 1939-42

1. Letter from RS to NS [July 1938], NAF 28088, Documents biographiques.

2. Annie Daubenton, "Les faits divers de la parole," and interview with Nathalie Sarraute by Claude Régy, *Les Nouvelles littéraires*, 10-17 January 1980, 28-29 (28). Letters from NS to Raymond, dated September 1939, describe her stay in Bayonne, Sarraute Family Papers.

3. Letter from RS to NS, "Thursday evening" [1939], NAF 28088, Documents biographiques.

4. Letter from NS to RS, 6 July [1940], NAF 28088, Documents biographiques.

5. *Golden Fruits*, 30; interview with Dominique Sarraute. See chapter 23.

6. German-language document issued to NS, 3 August 1940, Sarraute Family Papers.

7. Claude Sarraute, *Avant que t'oublies tout!*, 32-33.

8. NS, "Pourquoi Céline?," *Arts*, 22 December, 1965, 12; Giraudoux quoted in Michael R. Marrus and Robert O. Paxton, *Vichy France and the Jews* (New York: Basic Books, 1981), 53.

9. Badinter, *Un antisémitisme ordinaire*, 61-63.

10. Raymond Sarraute and Paul Tager, "Introduction," *Les Juifs sous l'Occupation. Recueil des textes français et allemands 1940-1944* (Paris: Centre de documentation juive contemporaine, 1945), 2.

11. NS conversation with me. See Françoise Dekeuwer-Défossez, *La Séparation dans tous ses états—divorce, désunion* (Paris: Lamy, 2010).

12. The divorce is recorded on Raymond Sarraute's birth certificate. There is a typed transcription of the court proceedings in the Sarraute Family Papers.

13. File on the Établissements Tcherniak, Archives du Commissariat général aux questions juives et du Service des biens des victimes des lois et mesures de spoliation, Archives nationales, AJ38/5402, dossier 26041.

14. Letter to Bernard Rumeau, administrateur provisoire, 24 December 1942, incl. Estimation de la valeur actuelle de l'action Tcherniak, Archives nationales, AJ38/5402, dossier 26041/3280–82.

15. See Claude Sarraute, *Avant que t'oublies tout!*, 39; Charles de Gaulle, *Discours et messages I. Pendant la guerre juin 1940–janvier 1946* (Paris: Plon, 1970), 3–4.

16. Magny, "Entretiens avec Nathalie Sarraute."

17. http://museedelaresistanceenligne.org/media5593-Plaque-en-hommage-A.

18. *Avocats inscrits au tableau*, 1938, and List of lawyers at the Paris bar arrested on 21 August, Archives nationales, AJ 38/7.

19. Badinter, *Un antisémitisme ordinaire*, 133–39, 145.

20. *Paris-soir*, 12 September 1941, 1, 3.

21. Quoted in Badinter, *Un antisémitisme ordinaire*, 137.

22. Claude Sarraute, *Avant que t'oublies tout!*, 37.

23. Interview with Dominique Sarraute.

24. Raymond Sarraute file, Paris Préfecture de police archives (77W1680-87814*).

25. Undated and unsigned handwritten note, Sarraute Family Papers.

Chapter 15. In Hiding, 1942–44

1. Sarraute and Tager, "Introduction," 2.

2. Saporta, "Portrait d'une inconnue," 18.

3. NS, in *Beckett Remembering, Remembering Beckett*, 82.

4. Interview with Dominique Sarraute; Magny, "Entretiens avec Nathalie Sarraute."

5. See letter from Liselotte Wolff to NS from New York, 1 November 1945, where she asks for news of the family after "those terrible years," NAF 28088(201).

6. Draft of letter from NS to James Knowlson, 22 April 1991, NAF 28088(190).

7. Claude Sarraute, *Avant que t'oublies tout!*, 34–35.

8. NS, in *Beckett Remembering, Remembering Beckett*, 83.

9. See chapter 20.

10. Letters of 17 October 1959 and 29 December 1962, *The Letters of Samuel Beckett 1957–1965*, ed. George Craig et al. (Cambridge: Cambridge University Press, 2014), 247, 521.

11. Magny, "Entretiens avec Nathalie Sarraute." The entire episode is recounted by NS in this interview.

12. Darquier de Pellepoix, public pronouncement December 1942, quoted in Marrus and Paxton, *Vichy France*, 299.

13. Saporta, "Portrait d'une inconnue," 17.

14. Ibid.

15. Letter to NS from Joseph Grebelsky, 31 December 1968, NAF 28088(188).

16. All information provided by Fernande Elosu in a recorded interview with Alain Bancaud and Henry Rousso, 30 May 1995, http://purl.org/poi/crdo.vjf.cnrs.fr/crdo -ihtp_a19871753_B, and an extract from a manuscript by Fernande Elosu, "Chronique du siècle écrite à l'intention de mes petits-enfants et pour usage familial," Institut d'histoire du temps présent (IHTP), Paris, ref. ARC 109.

17. Elosu, "Chronique du siècle," IHTP, ARC 109.

18. Ibid.

19. Interview with Dominique Sarraute.

20. Magny, "Entretiens avec Nathalie Sarraute."

21. Ibid.

22. Ibid.

23. Personal conversation with NS, and interview with Dominique Sarraute.

24. On this, see Jacques Semelin, *The Survival of the Jews in France, 1940–44*, trans. Cynthia Schoch and Natasha Lehrer (New York: Oxford University Press, 2019).

25. Interview with Dominique Sarraute.

26. "From Dostoievski to Kafka," in *Tropisms, and The Age of Suspicion*, 82.

27. NS, *The Planetarium*, 220.

28. Raymond Sarraute and Jacques Rabinovitch, *Examen succinct de la situation actuelle juridique des juifs* (Paris: Éditions du Centre de documentation des déportés et spoliés juifs, 1945).

29. Raymond Sarraute, *De la Libération à la répression. Étude sur la situation des immigrés en France* (Paris: Éditions du Comité français pour la défense des immigrés, 1953).

30. Comité français pour la défense des immigrés.

31. Interview with Dominique Sarraute.

32. Letter from Jacques Tcherniak, 28 March 1946, Archives Nationales, AJ38, dossier 26041/ 5213.

Chapter 16. Saint-Germain-des-Prés, 1944–47

1. Quoted in Annie Cohen-Solal, *Sartre. A Life* (London: Heinemann, 1988), 212.

2. Jean-Paul Sartre, "Les écrivains en personne," in *Situations IX* (Paris: Gallimard, 1972), 9–39 (18).

3. "The Art of Fiction. Nathalie Sarraute Interview with Shusha Guppy and Jason Weiss," *Paris Review* 115 (1990): 152–84 (160).

4. Magny, "Entretiens avec Nathalie Sarraute."

5. Simone de Beauvoir, *Force of Circumstance*, trans. Richard Howard (London: André Deutsch, 1965), 19*.

6. Butor, *Obliques* (1981), quoted in Cohen-Solal, *Sartre*, 222*.

7. Jean-Paul Sartre, *Anti-Semite and Jew*, trans. George J. Becker (New York: Schocken Books, 1976), 76.

8. Ibid., 69.

9. Letter to Sartre from NS, 11 November 1956, photocopy sent to NS by Alexis de Morlanges, NAF 28088(194).

10. Pseudonym of Janine Héron de Villefosse.

11. Magny, "Entretiens avec Nathalie Sarraute."

12. Françoise d'Eaubonne, "Beauvoir et Sarraute: un conflit," *Simone de Beauvoir Studies* 19 (2002–3): 126–28.

13. Colette Audry interview with Jansiti, 1987, quoted in Carlo Jansiti, *Violette Leduc* (Paris: Grasset, 1999), 166.

14. Quoted in Jansiti, *Violette Leduc*, 123.

15. Séverine Liatard, *Colette Audry (1906–1990). Engagements et identités d'une intellectuelle* (Rennes: Presses universitaires de Rennes, 2011).

16. Letter from Colette Audry to Carlo Jansiti, 18 November 1987, in Jansiti, *Violette Leduc*, 167.

17. Letter from NS to Leduc, 7 June 1945, Leduc Archive (LDC), IMEC (Institut Mémoires de l'édition contemporaine), L'Abbaye d'Ardenne, Caen.

18. Violette Leduc, *Correspondance 1945–1972*, ed. Carlo Jansiti (Paris: Gallimard, 2007), 43–44.

19. Undated letter from NS to Leduc, Leduc Archive, IMEC.

20. Letter to NS from Leduc, 11 September 1947, NAF 28088(191).

21. René de Ceccatty, "Entretien avec Nathalie Sarraute," *Le Serpent à plumes* 28 (1995): 17–22 (20).

22. Letter to NS from Leduc, "Wednesday evening," quoted in Olivier Wagner, "La correspondance entre Violette Leduc et Nathalie Sarraute," in *Lire Violette Leduc aujourd'hui*, ed. Mireille Broude, Anaïs Frantz, and Alison Péron (Lyon: Presses Universitaires de Lyon, 2017), 71–83 (73–74).

23. Violette Leduc, *Mad in Pursuit*, trans. Derek Coltman (1970; London: Rupert Hart-Davis, 1971), 48*, 54.

24. Ibid., 78*, 47.

25. Pages from unpublished MS of Leduc's *L'Affamée* [The Starving Woman] in the Sarraute Archive, NAF 28088(191), quoted in Wagner, "La correspondance," 80.

26. Ibid., 80–81.

27. Letter from Leduc to NS, "Friday morning," probably written ca. 1952, quoted in ibid., 78.

28. Colette Audry, quoted in Jansiti, *Violette Leduc*, 169.

29. Jansiti, *Violette Leduc*, 171–72.

30. Undated pencilled note, NAF 28088(191).

31. Ceccatty, "Entretien avec Nathalie Sarraute," 20.

Chapter 17. The Elephant's Child, 1947–49

1. Undated letter from NS to Leduc, Leduc archive, IMEC.

2. Beauvoir, *Force of Circumstance*, 79.

3. Huppert, "Nathalie Sarraute," 10.

4. Contract with Nagel for *Portrait d'un inconnu*, NAF 28088.

5. "Je ne peux pas passer pour un modèle," interview with Maurice Nadeau, *L'édition littéraire aujourd'hui*, ed. Olivier Bessard-Banquy (Bordeaux: Presses universitaires de Bordeaux, 2006), 67–74.

6. Laure Adler, *Françoise* (Paris: Éditions Grasset & Fasquelle, 2011), chap. 24.

7. Letter from François Emmanuel [Erval] to NS, "Tuesday" [21 September 1948], NAF 28088.

8. Undated draft of letter to Éditions Denoël in Raymond's handwriting, NAF 28088.

9. Letter of 18 May 1949 from Leduc to Beauvoir, Leduc, *Correspondance 1945–1972*, 112.

10. Letter of 29 May 1949 from André Hartemann to NS, NAF 28088(189).

11. Letter from Leduc to Simone de Beauvoir, 11 August 1949 in Leduc, *Correspondance 1945–1972*, 121.

12. *Combat*, 11 August 1949, 4.

13. *Gazette des lettres*, 14 May 1949, 4.

14. Letters from André Spire to NS, 1 July 1947 and 14 May 1949, NAF 28088(199).

15. Carbon copy of letter from NS to Éditions Denoël, 5 December 1949, NAF 28088.

16. Benmussa, *Nathalie Sarraute*, 41.

17. In NS's personal library, Chérence.

18. NS, interview with Gabriel d'Aubarède, "Nathalie Sarraute," *Les Nouvelles littéraires*, 30 July 1953, 4.

19. Marianne Alphant, "Intérieur Sarraute," *Libération*, 28 September 1989, 21–23 (23).

20. Unpublished extract from *La Folie en tête*, BnF, Archives et manuscrits, NAF 28892.

21. Beauvoir, *Force of Circumstance*, 80.

22. NS, "Paul Valéry et l'enfant d'éléphant," in *Œuvres complètes*, 1528. The essay was first published in *Les Temps modernes*, January 1947. There is no English translation.

23. NS et Arturo Carmassi, "La communication difficile," *Culture et média*, actes du colloque de juillet 1981, ed. Gilbert Gadoffre, Institut collégial européen, 1981, 34–45 (39).

24. Magny, "Entretiens avec Nathalie Sarraute."

25. Beauvoir, *Force of Circumstance*, 80*.

26. Magny, "Entretiens avec Nathalie Sarraute."

27. All anecdotes are from ibid.

Chapter 18. New Horizons, 1949–53

1. Françoise Benassis, "Le lien Sarraute" (unpublished manuscript).

2. Interview with Dominique Sarraute.

3. Interview with Dominique Sarraute.

4. From Ilya's copy of *Portrait* now owned by Olivier Tcherniak, the son of Nathalie's brother Jacques.

5. Benmussa, *Nathalie Sarraute*, 159.

6. NS, "From Dostoievski to Kafka," in *The Age of Suspicion*, 71. Letters from NS to Raymond between September 1947 and January 1948 trace the ups and downs of NS's recovery, Sarraute Family Papers.

7. Licari, "Entretiens avec Nathalie Sarraute," 9; Huppert, "Nathalie Sarraute," 14.

8. Stanley Karnow, *Paris in the Fifties* (New York: Times Books, 1997), 26.

9. Interview with Betsy Jolas.

10. Letter from Betsy Jolas to Rainier Rocchi, 6 October 2009, Rainier Rocchi, *L'intertextualité dans l'écriture de Nathalie Sarraute* (Paris: Classiques Garnier, 2018), 769 n.248.

11. Mallet, *Nathalie Sarraute*; Patrick Glâtre, *Balade en Val-d'Oise: sur les pas des écrivains*, ed. Marie-Noëlle Craissati (Paris: Éditions Alexandrines, 1999), 181.

12. Interview with Nathalie Vierny.

13. Undated letter from Monique Wittig to NS, probably ca. 1983, Sarraute Family Papers.

14. Nathalie Sarraute, "The Age of Suspicion," *Envoy* 15 (1951): 45–56.

15. Foreword to the first number of *Envoy*, December 1949.

16. Letter from Harry Levin to Maria Jolas, 16 May 1951, NAF 28088(192).

17. Letter to NS from André Spire, 9 February 1951, NAF 28088(199).

18. *Gilbert Gadoffre, un humaniste révolutionnaire: entretiens avec Alice Gadoffre-Staath* (Paris: Créaphis, 2002), 14.

19. Ibid., 65.

20. Interview with Michel Butor.

21. Mimica Cranaki, "Journal d'exil," *Les Temps modernes* 58 (1950): 327–40 (340).

22. Interview with Dominique Sarraute.

23. Letter from Mimica Cranaki to NS, 27 September 1950, NAF 28088(184).

24. Interview with Dominique Sarraute.

25. Mauriac, *Le Rire des pères*, 109–10.

26. Letter from Agnès Varda to NS, 20 April 1955, NAF 28088(201).

27. Letter from Agnès Varda to NS, 5 January 1992, NAF 28088(201).

28. Francis Ponge, *Album amicorum*, ed. Armande Ponge (Paris: Gallimard, 2009).

29. Letter from Francis Ponge to NS, 15 May 1963, NAF 28088(203), copyright Armande Ponge.

30. Letter from NS to Francis Ponge in response to *Le grand receuil*, 17 May 1963, NAF 28666.

31. Mauriac, *Le Rire des pères*, entry for 30 June 1958, 110.

Chapter 19. A Gallimard Author, 1953–56

1. Engagement diary, 1952, NAF 28088(41).

2. Ibid.

3. Pierre Assouline, *Gaston Gallimard. Un demi-siècle d'édition française* (1984; Paris: Gallimard, 2006), 578.

4. Colette Audry, "Nathalie Sarraute: communication et reconnaissance," *Critique* 80 (1954): 14–19; Gabriel d'Aubarède, "Instantané," *Les Nouvelles littéraires*, 30 July 1953, 4.

5. Letter to NS from Gerda Zeltner, 8 April 1954, NAF 28088(202).

6. Interview with Michel Butor.

7. Letter from Jean Paulhan to NS, 28 December 1954, NAF 28088(196).

8. Letter from Clarisse Francillon to NS, 23 July [1960?], NAF 28088(186).

9. Letter from NS to René Micha, 14 January 1963, NS, "Lettres à René Micha, 1959–1976," NAF 28194.

10. Anne Simonin, *Les Éditions de Minuit 1942–1955. Le Devoir d'insoumission* (Paris: IMEC Éditions, 1994), 424.

11. Dominique Aury, *Vocation: clandestine. Entretiens avec Nicole Grenier* (Paris: Gallimard, 1999), 52, and Assouline, *Gaston Gallimard*, 158.

12. Interview with Jean-Yves Tadié.

13. Mauriac, *Le Rire des pères*, 100–101. He refers to Aury as "T."

14. Undated draft of letter from NS to Butor 1964 or 1965, NAF 28088(183).

15. As reported by NS to Mauriac, *Le Rire des pères*, 107.

16. Letter to NS from Gaston Gallimard, 26 May 1961, NAF 28088(187).

17. Draft of letter from NS to Claude Gallimard, 15 June 1966 (some deletions removed), and reply from Gallimard to NS, 16 June 1966, NAF 28088(187).

18. Interview with Nathalie Vierny; email from Éric Legendre, Responsable des archives, Éditions Gallimard, 3 October 2017.

Chapter 20. The Nouveau Roman, 1956–59

1. NS, "Le cercle," *Monde nouveau* 95 (1955): 51–56.

2. Alain Robbe-Grillet, *Les derniers jours de Corinthe* (Paris: Éditions de Minuit, 1994), 83–84.

3. Alain and Catherine Robbe-Grillet, *Correspondance 1951–1990*, ed. Emmanuelle Lambert (Paris: Fayard, 2012), 146.

4. Letter from NS to Raymond and her children, "Sunday," Sarraute Family Papers.

5. *Gilbert Gadoffre, un humaniste révolutionnaire*, 91–92.

6. Typed copy of extract from the *Observer*, 5 August 1956, in the Fonds Gilbert Gadoffre, Université Paris-Est Marne-la-Vallée.

7. Robbe-Grillet, "Le réalisme, la psychologie et l'avenir du roman," *Critique* 111–12 (August–September 1956): 695–701 (701).

8. Magny, "Entretiens avec Nathalie Sarraute"; draft of letter from NS to Claude Simon, 30 December 1960, NAF 28088(196); Mauriac, *Le Rire des pères*, 135.

9. Denise Bourdet, "Nathalie Sarraute," *Revue de Paris* 45 (June 1958): 127–30 (128).

10. Letter from Jérôme Lindon to NS, 13 September [1956], NAF 28088(192).

11. Draft of letter from NS to Lindon, 6 May [1964], NAF 28088(192).

12. Émile Henriot, "Le nouveau roman," *Le Monde*, 22 May 1957, 8–9; Maurice Nadeau, "Nouvelles formules pour le roman," *Critique* 123–24 (August–September 1957): 707–22; *Esprit* 7–8 (July–August 1958).

13. Letter from Lindon to NS, 14 February 1957, NAF 28088(192).

14. Alain Robbe-Grillet, *Préface à une vie d'écrivain* (Paris: France Culture/Le Seuil, 2005), 119.

15. Undated draft [1958?] of letter from NS, presumably to Gaston Gallimard, NAF 28088(192).

16. Anne Simonin, "La photo du Nouveau Roman. Tentative d'interprétation d'un instantané," *Politix. Revue des sciences sociales du politique* 3, nos. 10–11 (1990): 45–52.

17. E.g., Rykner, *Nathalie Sarraute*, 206, and Angremy, *Nathalie Sarraute*, 31.

18. Letter from Pingaud to NS, "Tuesday 19th" [1965], NAF 28088(196).

19. Letters from NS to Gala Barbizan, 30 January 1959, and from Barbizan to NS, 4 May 1964, NAF 28088(207).

20. Letter from Robbe-Grillet to the Médicis jury, 30 November 1962, and from Jean-Pierre Giraudoux to Robbe-Grillet, 5 December 1962, Correspondance Prix Médicis, NAF 28008(202).

21. Letter from NS to Robbe-Grillet, 23 November 1960, Fonds Robbe-Grillet, IMEC, ARG 533 211873.

22. Carbon copy dated April 1962 of NS's replies to Artur Portela in reply to his questions for publication in *Jornal de Letras et Artes*, NAF 28088(196).

23. Draft of letter from NS to editor of *Akzente*, 23 May 1958; carbon copy of letter from Maria Jolas to Barney Rosset, 26 May 1958; and letter from Robbe-Grillet to NS dated "Friday," NAF 28088(197).

24. See note from Polina with receipt for payment of rent, 1 January 1951, NAF 28088(207).

25. Boris Kreis, *Résistance et survivance du bacille tuberculeux aux médications antibacillaires* (Paris: Masson et cie., 1966).

26. Interview with Dominique Sarraute. The B.K.s. refer to Koch's bacilla.

27. Mauriac, *Le Rire des pères*, 104.

28. Letter from NS to Claude Sarraute, 2 August 1958, Documents biographiques, NAF 28088.

Chapter 21. *"One of the Great Novelists of Our Time," 1959–62*

1. Bourdet, "Nathalie Sarraute," 127–28.

2. Clarisse Francillon, "Le roman aujourd'hui. Un entretien avec Nathalie Sarraute," *Gazette de Lausanne*, 29 November 1958; "Nathalie Sarraute nous parle du *Planétarium*," interview with Geneviève Serreau, *Les Lettres nouvelles*, 19 April 1959, 28–30.

3. See manuscript page reproduced in Angremy, *Nathalie Sarraute*, 25.

4. NS, "Traduction d'une conversation de NS avec François Bondy" [1963], in Cranaki and Belaval, *Nathalie Sarraute*, 211–22 (216).

5. NS, *The Planetarium*, 33.

6. Simone de Beauvoir, *Beloved Chicago Man: Letters to Nelson Algren 1947-64* (London: Victor Gollancz, 1998), 573; Françoise d'Eaubonne, *Une femme nommée Castor, mon amie Simone de Beauvoir* (Paris: SOFINEM, 1986), 22–24.

7. Beauvoir, *Force of Circumstance*, 271; Mauriac, *Le Rire des pères*, 106.

8. Simone de Beauvoir, *The Mandarins*, trans. Leonard M. Friedman (London: Collins, 1957), 485–86, 602; and see Jorge Calderon, "Simone de Beauvoir et Nathalie Sarraute: analyse d'un différend," *Simone de Beauvoir Studies* 1 (2000–2001): 162–72.

9. Beauvoir, *Force of Circumstance*, 468*.

10. *Tel Quel* 1 (1960): 42.

11. Mauriac, *Le Rire des pères*, 102.

12. Démeron, "Nathalie Sarraute ou littérature sans cabotinage," 2. The American publication referred to was probably the March 1959 number of *Harper's Bazaar*, which contains an extract from Maria Jolas's translation of *The Planetarium* under the title "The Doorhandle" and carries an unflattering photograph of NS by Richard Avedon (pp. 160–61, 178–79, 182). The comment about the happy Eskimo would seem to be more than justified.

13. François Mauriac, "30 mai," *L'Express*, 4 June 1959.

14. François Mauriac, *Le Nouveau Bloc-notes 1958-1960* (Paris: Flammarion, 1961), 210.

15. Draft of letter from NS to Gaëtan Picon, 20 June 1960, NAF 28088(196).

16. *Le Procès du réseau Jeanson*, ed. Marcel Péju, *Cahiers libres* 17–18 (Paris: François Maspéro, 1961), 132.

17. NS's contribution to "Les signataires s'expliquent," in *Le Droit à l'insoumission* "le dossier des 121," ed. François Maspéro (Paris: François Maspéro, 1961), 93–94.

18. Jacques Mosel, "Les 'aveux spontanés' de Nathalie Sarraute," *L'Arche*, December 1959, 43–45 (44).

19. Letter from NS to Maria Jolas, from Rabat, Morocco, 18 August 1952, Jolas Archive, box 36, folder 768.

20. "Retour de Cuba. Nathalie Sarraute s'entretient avec Jeanine Parot," *Les Lettres françaises*, 28 September 1961, 1, 5.

21. Draft of letter from NS to Fidel Castro, 21 December 1964, NAF 28088(184).

Chapter 22. Nathalie Abroad, 1959–64

1. Letters from Renée Spodheim to Maria Jolas, 5 and 21 November 1957, Jolas Archive, box 47, folder 1041.

2. Letter from Maria Jolas to Abraham Rothberg at Braziller, 25 September 1959 and from Rothberg to Jolas, 28 September 1959, Jolas Archive, box 47, folder 1041.

3. Genêt [Janet Flanner], "Letter from Paris," *New Yorker*, 25 July 1959, 56–64, 58.

4. See letters to NS from Zofia Jaremko-Pytowska, 7 November 1958, NAF

28088(190), Živojin Živojnovič, 1 February 1960, NAF 28088(202), and Ljerka Radovic, 12 July 1960, NAF 28088(197).

5. The unpublished lecture is reproduced in Angremy, *Nathalie Sarraute*, 19–24.

6. Letter from NS to Jean Blot, 18 February 1960, NAF 28088(209).

7. Undated draft of letter from NS to Niels Egebak, NAF 28088 (209).

8. Draft of letter from NS to Ingrid Mesterton, 11 January 1961, NAF 28988(193). The booklet was published by Chelius & Co., Stockholm, 1907.

9. Anon. [Rayner Heppenstall], "A Pronoun Too Few," *Times Literary Supplement*, and "A Continuing Present," in *The Fourfold Tradition* (London: Barrie and Rockcliff, 1961), 249–71.

10. Undated draft of letter from NS to Rayner Heppenstall, NAF 28088(189).

11. NS, "Rebels in a World of Platitudes," in *The Writer's Dilemma*, ed. Stephen Spender (Oxford: Oxford University Press, 1961), 35–41.

12. Letter to NS from Owen Leeming, 7 April 1960, NAF 28088(191).

13. John Calder, *Pursuit: The Uncensored Memoirs of John Calder* (London: Calder Publications, 2001), 180. See 178–85 for his account of the tour.

14. "New Movements in French Literature: Nathalie Sarraute Explains Tropisms," *The Listener*, 9 March 1961, 428–29.

15. Calder, *Pursuit*, 183.

16. Interview with Jean-Pierre Faye.

17. Draft of letter in English from NS to Hope Wright, 1 July [1961], NAF 28088(201).

18. Undated draft of letter in English from NS to Hilary Spurling, Sarraute Family Papers. See also Hilary Spurling, *Ivy: The Life of I. Compton-Burnett* (London: R. Cohen Books, 1995), 489.

19. See letter to NS from Henri Peyre, 21 June 1960, NAF 28088(196); letter to NS from André Berne-Joffroy, 24 July 1960, NAF 28088(182).

20. Letter dated 7 August 1960 from NS to Maria Jolas, Jolas Archive, box 36, folder 768. Heppenstall's first name was Rayner and not Richard, Howard is Robbe-Grillet's translator Richard Howard, Arthur Crook was the editor of the *TLS*, and Henri Peyre and Harry Levin were professors at Yale and Harvard, respectively.

21. Letter from Germaine Brée to NS, 6 August 1967, NAF 28088(183).

22. Nathalie's letters to Raymond are in the Fonds Nathalie Sarraute (NAF 28088) now published as Nathalie Sarraute, *Lettres d'Amérique*, ed. Carrie Landfried and Olivier Wagner (Paris: Galllimard, 2017). All references are to this edition, 47–48, 61, 49.

23. Ibid., 93, 76.

24. Ibid., 76, 89, 88, 124.

25. Ibid., 106–7; Beauvoir, *Beloved Chicago Man*, 573.

26. NS, *Lettres d'Amérique*, 87, 84.

27. Ibid., 120–21, English original in italics.

28. Benmussa, *Nathalie Sarraute*, 93.

29. NS, Engagement Diary, January–March 1964, NAF 28088(62).

30. Letter from Arendt to Karl Jaspers, 14 May 1964, in Hannah Arendt and Karl

Jaspers, *Correspondence 1926–1969*, ed. Lotte Kohler and Hans Saner, trans. Robert and Rita Kimber (San Diego, Calif.: Harcourt Brace, 1993), 557*.

31. Letters from Hannah Arendt to Mary McCarthy, 18 May 1960 and 8 August 1969, in *Between Friends: The Correspondence of Hannah Arendt and Mary McCarthy 1949–1975*, ed. Carol Brightman (New York: Harcourt Brace, 1995), 76, 241.

32. Letter from Hannah Arendt to Mary McCarthy, 13 February 1971, in *Between Friends*, 282.

Chapter 23. A Reading Public, 1963–66

1. Quoted in Edwin Williamson, *Borges: A Life* (New York: Viking Press, 2004), 345.

2. See Jacqueline Piatier, "Nathalie Sarraute remporte le Prix international des éditeurs," *Le Monde*, 7 May 1964, and "Le congrès de Salzbourg a dressé son palmarès de la littérature mondiale," *Le Monde*, 9 May 1964.

3. Matthieu Galey, "Trois romans: des appels dans la nuit," *Arts*, 24 April 1963, 4.

4. Letter from Leduc to Beauvoir, 4 May 1963, Leduc, *Correspondance 1945–1972*, 382.

5. Bernard Pivot, "Nathalie Sarraute gagne la coupe pour ses 'Fruits d'or,'" *Le Figaro littéraire*, 7 May 1964.

6. Germaine Brée, "Interviews with two French Novelists," *Contemporary Literature* 14, no. 2 (1973): 137–46 (143).

7. "What Birds See," 122*.

8. *Golden Fruits*, 88, 35, 59*.

9. A remark made to me by Alain Robbe-Grillet in informal conversation at a conference in London in 1994.

10. Letter from NS to Blanchot, 16 July 1963, in Hoppenot and Rabaté, *Maurice Blanchot*, 153. See also undated draft of the letter NAF 28088(182). Blanchot's review was "A Rose Is a Rose . . . ," *NRF* 127 (July 1963): 86–93.

11. *Golden Fruits*, 52*.

12. Huppert, "Nathalie Sarraute," 12. Butor's essay was published in 1961. NS's "*Histoire extraordinaire* de Michel Butor" appeared in the *Bulletin de la N.R.F.* 21 (February 1961): 2.

13. NAF 28088, passim.

14. Letter to NS from Sabine Raffy, 12 February 1995, NAF 28088(197). Raffy also published a critical study of NS, *Sarraute romancière: espaces intimes* (New York: Peter Lang, 1988). She died in 2000.

15. Huppert, "Nathalie Sarraute," 10.

16. Draft of letter from NS to Olivier de Magny, 22 July 1958, NAF 28088(193).

17. Undated draft of letter from NS to Gaëtan Picon, NAF 28088(196).

18. Draft of letter from NS to Matthieu Galey, 19 October 1975, NAF 28088(203).

19. Letter from Alain Bosquet to NS, 20 November 1961 and undated draft of reply from NS, NAF 28088(183).

20. Letter from NS to Alain Bosquet, 16 May 1968, Bibliothèque Jacques Doucet, Paris, Ms 47262 (2).

21. Béatrix Beck, *Noli* (1978; Paris: Chemin de fer, 2017), 45. See François Grosso, "Postface," in Beck, *Noli*, 107–8.

22. Interview with Georges Raillard.

23. Yvon Belaval, review of *Tropismes*, *NNRF* 62 (1958): 335–37.

24. Letters to NS from Yvon Belaval, 14 and 23 July 1964, NAF 28088(182).

25. Letter to NS from Marcel Arland, 14 February 1960, NAF 28088(181); reply from NS, 16 December 1960, Fonds Marcel Arland, Bibliothèque Jacques Doucet; letter from NS to René Micha, 16 December 1960, NAF 28194.

26. Letter from NS to René Micha, 12 February 1962, NAF 28194.

27. See NS, "Lettres à René Micha, 1959–1976," NAF 28194; René Micha, *Nathalie Sarraute* (Paris: Éditions universitaires, 1966). See also Guillaume Fau, "'Loin dans la percée poétique . . .'. Deux lettres de Nathalie Sarraute à René Micha, présentées par Guillaume Fau," *Revue de la Bibliothèque nationale de France* 30 (2008): 81–87.

28. Letter from NS to Micha, 19 October 1965, NAF 28194.

Chapter 24. Friendships

1. Letter to NS from Geneviève Serreau, 12 April 1961, NAF 28088(198).

2. "Nathalie Sarraute. Biographie," France Culture, 4 February 1977.

3. NS, *Lettres d'Amérique*, 47.

4. Undated letter from André du Bouchet to NS, NAF 28088(185).

5. "Nathalie Sarraute, 'Lettre à André du Bouchet'," 3 August 1999, *L'étrangère* 16–18 (2007): 495.

6. Letter from Mimica Cranaki to NS, 25 August [1953?/1958?], NAF 28088(184).

7. Information from Assia's son, Serge Gavronsky, email, 16 October 2013, and extracts from Assia's unpublished memoir, kindly copied by Serge Gavronsky.

8. Letter to NS from Assia Minor, 15 May [1961?], NAF 28088(194).

9. NS, *Lettres d'Amérique*, 54.

10. Françoise d'Eaubonne, *Mémoires irréductibles: de l'entre-deux guerres à l'an 2000* (Paris: Dagorno, 2001), 606, 1017. It's not clear how restrictively d'Eaubonne is using the feminine gender of the noun.

11. Letter from Françoise d'Eaubonne to NS, ca. 1969 [date illegible], and copy of letter from d'Eaubonne to Bernard Thomas, 17 May 1993, NAF 28088(186).

12. Geneviève Bollème, *Parler d'écrire* (Paris: Le Seuil, 1993), 19–20. The letter from NS to Geneviève Bollème has been lost, but Nora Scott saw it and conveyed its contents in a personal conversation.

13. Letter from Mary McCarthy to Hannah Arendt, 1 June 1962, in *Between Friends*, 134.

14. Carol Brightman, *Writing Dangerously: Mary McCarthy and Her World* (London: Lime Tree, 1993), 521.

15. Letter from McCarthy to Arendt, 9 June 1964, in *Between Friends*, 165.

16. Letter from Mary McCarthy to Arendt, 18 January 1965; Arendt's reply, 2 April 1965; McCarthy to Arendt, 22 June 1965, in *Between Friends*, 174, 176, 186.

17. Brightman, *Writing Dangerously*, 522.

18. See letters from McCarthy to NS, July 1969 and 6 October 1969, Sarraute Family Papers.

19. Undated draft of letter from NS to Robert Silvers, in reply to his, 21 December 1983, Sarraute Family Papers.

20. Quoted in Brightman, *Writing Dangerously*, 518–19.

21. In Frances Kiernan, *Seeing Mary Plain: A Life of Mary McCarthy* (New York: Norton, 2000), 736.

22. Letter from Brooke-Rose to NS, 17 February 1964, NAF 28088(183).

23. Letter from Christine Brooke-Rose to NS, 19 May 1966, and Christmas card, December 1966, NAF 28088(183).

24. Letters from Lucette Finas to NS, 5 May [1980], NAF 28088(203) and 30 June 1963, NAF 28088(186).

25. Letter to NS from Monique Wittig, 6 December [1982?], NAF 28088(201).

26. Letter to NS from Monique Wittig, 8 August [1971?], NAF 28088(201).

27. Letter from NS to Monique Wittig, 15 November 1965, in private papers belonging to belonging to the Literary Estate of Monique Wittig.

28. Ibid.

29. Ceccatty, "Entretien avec Nathalie Sarraute," 19; see chapter 18.

30. Interview with Jean Blot (whose original name was Alexandr Blokh).

31. Draft of letter from NS to Gaëtan Picon, 6 February 1963, NAF 28088(196).

32. Letters from Tina Jolas to NS, 2 July 1987 and 1 May 1993, NAF 28088(190).

33. Interview with Paule du Bouchet.

Chapter 25. *"The Heroine of Post-Stalin Russia," 1960–67*

1. See letters to NS from Berta Tcherniak, Grigory Moiseevich Kaplunov, and Leonid Zernov, NAF 28088(208).

2. Michèle Pardina, "Un entretien avec Nathalie Sarraute," *Le Monde des livres*, 26 February 1993, 25, 29 (25). NS mentions having attended a conference during this visit, but there is no record of her having done so, and she was almost certainly thinking of later visits to the Soviet Union. In an article in the *Literaturnaya Gazeta* in January 1962, she mentions visiting as a tourist in August 1956.

3. Copy of letter from NS to Sartre, 11 November 1956, NAF 28088(194). See chapter 12.

4. Mauriac, *Le Rire des pères*, 105. The diary entry is dated 24 June 1958.

5. "Nathalie Sarraute, la mémoire. Entretien avec E. Morin, *et al*" (1960), France Culture, 5 February 1988; Bourdet, "Nathalie Sarraute," 129–30.

6. Engagement diaries, NAF 28088(43, 44, 46, 51, 52).

7. NS, "Tolstoï," *Les Lettres françaises*, 22 September 1960, 1, 5,

8. Letters to NS from Olga Kraevskaya, 1959–65, NAF 28088(208).

9. Letter to NS from Boris Nikolaevich Agapov, 12 January 1961, NAF 28088(207).

10. NS, "Vstrecha s Moskvoy" [Meeting with Moscow], *Literaturnaya Gazeta*, 11 January 1962.

11. Ibid.

12. Interview with Jean Blot.

13. NS, "Vstrecha s Moskvoy."

14. Interview with Jean-Pierre Faye. The comment about Nathalie's Russian comes from Yevgeny Yevtushenko, *Zavtrashniy Veter* (Moscow: Izd-vo "Pravda," 1987), 262.

15. Interview with John Calder.

16. Reported by Werner Spies, *Les Chances de ma vie. Mémoires*, trans. Bernard Lortholary (Paris: Gallimard, 2014), 376.

17. Drafts of letters from NS to Claude Gallimard, undated and 22 June 1966, NAF 28088(187), and letter to NS from Lydia Delt, 1 March 1969, NAF 28088(207).

18. The expression "decade of euphoria" comes from Maurice Friedberg, *A Decade of Euphoria. Western Literature in Post-Stalin Russia, 1954–64* (Bloomington: Indiana University Press, 1977). The conference is described by Bernard Pingaud in "L'année dernière à Léningrad," *Esprit* 329 (1964): 14–21.

19. "Nathalie Sarraute, la mémoire," Radio programme with Edgar Morin, et al., 1960, rebroadcast on France Culture, 5 February 1988.

20. Reported in V. I. Badelin, "Vozvrashchenie v fabrichnoe detstvo," *Zemle Ivanov*, Ivanovo (2001): 468–75 (471).

21. Ilya Ehrenburg, "Entre Klebnikov et Joyce: différences et convergences," *Esprit* 329 (1964): 56–62.

22. NS, "Nathalie Sarraute," in "Roman, chelovek, obshchestvo. Na vrstreche pisatelei Evropy v Leningrade," *Inostrannaya Literatura*, November 1963, 237–38; "Le romancier cherche une réalité inconnue," *Le Monde*, 21 September 1963; and "Les deux réalités," *Esprit* 329 (1964): 72–75.

23. Efim Etkind, "Préface" to Ewa Bérard, *La Vie tumultueuse d'Ilya Ehrenbourg, juif, russe et soviétique* (Paris: Ramsay, 1991), 8.

24. Letter from NS to Roland Husson, 26 February 1984, Sarraute Family Papers.

25. NS, Documents biographiques, NAF 28088.

26. Letter from NS to Rita Raït, 26 December 1967, Rita Raït-Kovaleva personal archive; letters from Raït to NS, 28 January 1967 and 12 August 1968, NAF 28088 (208).

27. Carbon copy of letter from NS to Prof. Dr. Wilfried Floeck, 16 May 1982, NAF 28088(186).

28. Letter from Rita Raït to NS, 27 July 1969, Sarraute Family Papers.

29. Letter to NS from Margarita Aliger, 28 March 1973, Sarraute Family Papers.

30. Transcription of interview with Marusya Klimova in letter to NS from Tatiana Kondratovich (real name of Marusya Klimova), 29 August 1997, NAF 28088(208).

Chapter 26. Radio Plays, 1962–72

1. Spies, *Les Chances de ma vie*, 372.

2. André Bourin, "Techniciens du roman," *Les Nouvelles littéraires*, 25 June 1959, 1, 7; Letter to NS from Lily Siou, 20 April 1960[?], NAF 28088.

3. "Nathalie Sarraute Talks about Her Life and Works," 14.

4. NS, in *Werden wir richtig informiert? Massenmedien und Publikum*, ed. Leonhard Reinisch (Munich: Ehrenwirth, s.d.), 29–47.

5. Engagement diary, 1963, NAF 28088(58) and letter to NS from Dr. Margrit Engelke, Bochum Deutsches Vortragsamt, Bochum, 22 January 1963, NAF 28088(209).

6. On NS's proficiency in German, see Catherine Bézard, "Nathalie Sarraute: je ne relis jamais mes livres . . . ," *L'événement du jeudi*, 17 July 1986, 67–68 (68).

7. Bourin, "Techniciens du roman."

8. Interview with Fernando Arrabal.

9. Engagement Diaries, October–December 1958, NAF 28088(43); Geneviève Serreau, *Histoire du nouveau théâtre* (Paris: Gallimard, 1966).

10. "Conversation and Sub-conversation," in *Tropisms, and The Age of Suspicion*, 109.

11. Letter from Schale to NS, 20 September 1963, quoted by Joëlle Chambon, "Nathalie Sarraute du roman au théâtre en passant par la radio," *Sken&graphie* 15 (2015): 87–104 (98), from correspondence between Schale and NS held in the Archives of Südwestrundfunk in Stuttgart.

12. Letter from Schale to NS, 22 May 1964, NAF 28008.

13. Engagement diary, 11 December 1963, NAF 28088(61).

14. Letter from Marcel Arland to NS, 20 April 1966, NAF 28088(181).

15. Letter from NS to Marcel Arland, 30 June 1965, Fonds Marcel Arland, Bibliothèque Jacques Doucet, ARL C.

16. Interview with Jean-Louis Barrault, 10 January 1967, www.ina.fr/video/CAF89022979.

17. NS, "The Inside of the Glove: Nathalie Sarraute Talks about Her Plays," trans. Valerie Minogue, *Romance Studies* 2, no. 2 (1984): 1–7 (6).

18. Bettina L. Knapp, "Interview avec Nathalie Sarraute," *Kentucky Romance Quarterly* 4, no. 3 (1967): 283–95 (291–92).

19. Simone Bemussa, "Nathalie Sarraute au Petit Odéon," *La Quinzaine littéraire*, 1 February 1967.

Chapter 27. The Writing Life, 1964–68

1. Rykner, "Entretien avec Nathalie Sarraute," 169.

2. Rambures, "Nathalie Sarraute," 16.

3. Poirié, "Nathalie Sarraute," 28, and Licari, "Entretiens avec Nathalie Sarraute," 8.

4. Mauriac, *Le Rire des pères*, 105.

5. Draft of letter to Jill Krementz, 22 February 1973, Sarraute Family Papers.

6. Benmussa, *Nathalie Sarraute*, 98.

7. Licari, "Entretiens avec Nathalie Sarraute," 15.

8. Letter from John Calder to NS, 15 July 1966, NAF 28088.

9. Matthieu Galey, *Journal intégral, 1953–1986* (Paris: Robert Laffont, 2017), 639.

10. Geneviève Serreau, "Nathalie Sarraute et les secrets de la création," *La Quinzaine littéraire*, 1–15 May 1968, 4.

Chapter 28. Revolution and May 68

1. Nathalie Sarraute, "Speaking of Books: The Novel for Its Own Sake," *New York Times Book Review*, 24 April 1966, 2, 43.

2. Cecil Woolf and John Bagguley, eds., *Authors Take Sides on Vietnam* (London: Owen, 1967), 45.

3. Sarraute Family Papers.

4. Interview with Jean-Pierre Faye.

5. Published in *Le Monde*, 10 May 1968.

6. Interview with Jean-Pierre Faye.

7. Quoted in Patrick Combes, *La Littérature & le mouvement de mai 68* (Paris: Seghers, 1984), 50.

8. Appel aux intellectuels en vue d'un boycott de l'O.R.T.F., in "Mai–juin 1968: tracts du comité d'action étudiants-écrivains," *Lignes* 33 (1991): 113.

9. Interview with Michel Butor.

10. Boris Gobille, *Le Mai 68 des écrivains: crise politique et avant-gardes littéraires* (Paris: CNRS éditions, 2018), 99.

11. "Le Comité d'action étudiants-écrivains: nous sommes tous la pègre," *Le Monde*, 28 May 1968.

12. Maurice Blanchot, "Par le pouvoir de refus . . . ," *Lignes* 33 (1991), 122.

13. Huppert, "Nathalie Sarraute," 14.

14. Letter from Dominique Rolin to Philippe Sollers, 12 July 1968, in Dominique Rolin, *Lettres à Philippe Sollers 1958–1980*, ed. Jean-Luc Outers (Paris: Gallimard, 2018), 296.

15. Simone Benmussa, "Nathalie Sarraute. Regards sur l'écriture," Bibliothèque Publique d'Information and Éditions Gallimard, 1978.

16. Guy Le Clec'h, "Drames microscopiques," *Les Nouvelles littéraires*, 28 February 1972, 4–5 (4).

Chapter 29. Israel, 1969

1. Copy of letter from NS to deans of faculties of letters in universities of Jerusalem, Tel-Aviv and Haifa, January 1969, NAF 28088(209).

2. Charles de Gaulle, *Discours et messages V. Vers le terme, janvier 1966–avril 1969* (Paris: Plon, 1970), 232.

3. Mosel, "Les 'aveux spontanés' de Nathalie Sarraute," 44–45.

4. Engagement diary, 27 October 1964, NAF 28088(65).

5. Erwin Spatz, "Nathalie Sarraute au kibboutz," *La Quinzaine littéraire*, 16 October 1969, 12–13.

6. Reported in letters to NS from Jacob Tsur, 26 December 1969, NAF 28088(200) and from Erwin Spatz, 12 December 1969, Sarraute Family Papers; Denise Goitein, "The Reality Beneath and Beyond," *Jerusalem Post Magazine*, 14 November 1969, 10.

7. Letter from Mary McCarthy to Hannah Arendt, 23 September 1969, in *Between Friends*, 245–46.

8. Letter from Hector de Galard to NS, 24 October 1969, Sarraute Family Papers.

9. NS, "Deux poids et deux mesures," *Le Monde*, 11 November 1969, 4.

10. Letter to NS from Bouma Yassour, 27 November 1969, Sarraute Family Papers.

11. Letter to NS from A. Pozniak, 10 November 1969, Sarraute Family Papers.

12. Undated letter to NS from Hélène Cixous, Sarraute Family Papers.

13. Copy of letter from NS to Jean-Pierre Lavergne, 21 November 1969; letters to NS from Jérôme Lindon 13 and 18 November 1969, copy of replies from NS, 17 and 20 November 1969, Sarraute Family Papers.

14. Letter from Hannah Arendt to Mary McCarthy, 17 October 1969, in *Between Friends*, 248–49.

15. Letter from Monique Wittig to NS, 8 August [1971], NAF 28088(201).

Chapter 30. The End and Afterlife of the Nouveau Roman, 1971–82

1. Quoted in Philippe Forest, *Histoire de Tel Quel 1960–1982* (Paris: Seuil, 1995), 52.

2. *"Tel Quel* raconté par Jean-Edern Hallier (inédits)," *Le Journal de la culture* 17 (2005): 26–42 (38).

3. Interview with Philippe Sollers.

4. NS, "Flaubert le précurseur," *Preuves* 168 (1965): 3–11.

5. Jean Ricardou, *Problèmes du nouveau roman* (Paris: Le Seuil, 1967), 111.

6. NS, "Ce que je cherche à faire," in *Nouveau roman: hier, aujourd'hui*, vol. 2 (Paris: UGE, 1972), 25–40 (25).

7. Letter to NS from Anna Otten, 10 August 1971, Sarraute Family Papers.

8. NS, "Ce que je cherche à faire," 37.

9. "Nathalie Sarraute. Biographie," France Culture, 4 February 1977.

10. Interview with Françoise Guyon.

11. Letter from Anne Heurgon-Desjardins to NS, 30 March 1973, Sarraute Family Papers.

12. NS, "Proust est-il actuel? Témoignage de Nathalie Sarraute," in *Rencontres proustiennes de l'été 1971*, ed. Gilbert Gadoffre, Actes ronéotypés de l'Institut collégial européen (Loches), Bulletin 1971, 13; discussion, 13–18.

13. Letter to NS from David Saint-Amour, 20 October 1975, and drafts of NS's reply, NAF 28088(198); letter from NS to Shulamith Weissman, 9 January 1977, in Frida S. Weissman, *Du monologue intérieur à la sous-conversation* (Paris: Nizet, 1978), 9–11.

14. NS, "Lettre," in *Narrative Voices in Modern French Fiction: Studies in Honour of Valerie Minogue on the Occasion of Her Retirement*, ed. Michael Cardy, George Evans, and Gabriel Jacobs (Cardiff: University of Wales Press, 1997), 6.

15. B. P., "Nathalie Sarraute a réponse à tous," *Figaro littéraire*, 4 February 1972, 13.

16. See letter from NS to Marion Boyars, 18 September 1964, Calder & Boyars Archive, Lilly Library, Bloomington, Ind., LMC 2196, Series I, box 17, folder 1964, September 17–22.

17. Pardina, "Un entretien avec Nathalie Sarraute," 29. Nathalie has misremembered the date of her visit, which was in 1969.

18. Rykiel, "Nathalie Sarraute," 41.

19. Letter to NS from Karel Ptáčník, Vice-President of the Czech Writers' Union, 19 March 1970, NAF 28088(209), and "Conférences de Nathalie Sarraute," in Benmussa, *Nathalie Sarraute*, 205.

20. "Le bonheur de l'homme" was subsequently published in *Digraphe* 12 (1984): 58–62.

21. Benmussa, *Nathalie Sarraute*, 70, 75.

22. Draft of letter from NS to Gérard Abensour, cultural attaché at French Embassy, New York, [date?] 1973, NAF 28088(210).

23. Rykner, "Entretien avec Nathalie Sarraute," 173.

24. Roger Shattuck, "The Voice of Nathalie Sarraute," *French Review* 68, no. 6 (1995): 955–63 (955).

25. Nathalie Sarraute, *L'usage de la parole* [Enregistrement sonore] (Des Femmes, 2002).

26. Letter to NS from Roger Shattuck, 18 October 1966, NAF 28088(198).

27. Shattuck, "Voice of Nathalie Sarraute."

28. Beck, *Noli*, 45. See chapter 23.

29. Letter to NS from Pat Bothfeld, 10 September 1966, NAF 28088(183).

30. Interview with Olivier Tcherniak.

31. NS, "Nathalie Sarraute," and Monique Wittig, "The Place of the Action," in Oppenheim, *Three Decades of the French New Novel*, 119–31.

32. Tom Bishop, "Opening Remarks," in Oppenheim, *Three Decades of the French New Novel*, 13–19 (13).

Chapter 31. Plays on Stage, 1972–88

1. Quoted by Chantal Guinebault-Szlamowicz, "À la recherche de l'espace mental," in *Claude Régy*, ed. Marie-Madeleine Mervant-Roux (Paris: CNRS éditions, 2008), 24–51 (37).

2. NS unpublished interview with Saïd Ben-Slimane, 1985, included in his doctoral thesis "Les tropismes dans le théâtre de Nathalie Sarraute, ou la 'la communication, tu parles!'" (Université de Lyon II, 1987), 178.

3. Rykner, *Nathalie Sarraute*, 198.

4. NS, "The Inside of the Glove," 7.

5. Matthieu Galey in *Combat*, 7 February 1973, quoted in *Isma*, ed. Arnaud Rykner (Paris: Gallimard, coll. folio-théâtre, 2007), 117.

6. NS, "The Inside of the Glove," 3.

7. Ben-Slimane, unpublished interview, 178.

8. Claude Régy, "*C'est beau*, théâtre de violence," *Cahiers Renaud Barrault* 89 (1975): 80–89 (87).

9. See chapter 23.

10. NS, "La communication difficile," in *Culture et média*, 41.

11. Jean-Patrice Courtois, "L'autre espace du sonore. Essai sur la mise en scène radiophonique d'*Elle est là* de Nathalie Sarraute (1980)," in Mervant-Roux, *Claude Régy*, 66–77 (70).

12. *Les Nouvelles littéraires*, 14–21 February 1980, quoted in NS, *C'est beau*, ed. Arnaud Rykner (Paris: Gallimard, 2000), 73.

13. Galey, *Journal intégral*, 761.

14. Interview with Françoise Asso.

15. Spies, *Les Chances de ma vie*, 380.

16. Ceccatty, "Entretien avec Nathalie Sarraute," p. 21.

17. Letter from Wittig to NS, 6 December [1982?], NAF 28088(199).

18. Letter from Duras to NS 19 December 1968, NAF 28088(185); Jacques Lassalle, "Nathalie Sarraute ou l'obscur commencement," in *Trois conférences* (Paris: Éditions de la Bibliothèque nationale de France, 2002), 43–65 (23).

19. Personal information from Arnaud Rykner, former theatrical assistant to Régy.

20. Jean-Damien Barbin, interview.

21. "Écouter voir," NS interview with Bernard Babkine, *Acte 1 Magazine*, January 1986, 16.

22. Michel Cournot, *Le Monde*, 28 February 1986, quoted in NS, *Pour un oui ou pour un non* [*For No Good Reason*], ed. Arnaud Rykner (Paris: Gallimard, 1999), 68.

23. Unpublished interview with Jacques Doillon by Françoise Dumas, 2006, in *Nathalie Sarraute* (Arte vidéo, 2006).

Chapter 32. A Life and a Death, 1983–89

1. See chapter 30.

2. NS, *Childhood*, 3.

3. Interview with Michel Bufor; Werner Spies, *Un inventarie du regard*, ed. Thomas W. Gaehtgens (Paris: Crallimard, 2011), 218; Mallet, *Nathalie Sarraute*, referring to Démeron, "Nathalie Sarraute ou littérature sans cabotinage."

4. Quoted from the manuscript of *Childhood* in Sheila Bell, *Sarraute. Childhood* (Glasgow: University of Glasgow French and German Publications, 2007), 35.

5. Philippe Lejeune, "Aussi liquide qu'une soupe," in *Les Brouillons de soi* (Paris: Le Seuil, 1998), 277–313, and Bell, *Sarraute*, 81.

6. Jacqueline Piatier, "Le défi de Nathalie Sarraute," *Le Monde des Livres*, 15 April 1983; *Le Nouvel Observateur*, 16 August 1983.

7. NS, "Entretien avec Roger Vrigny," France Culture, 23 June 1983, and "Entretien avec Roger Colas," France Culture, 25 April 1983.

8. Interview with Arno Mayer.

9. Lejeune, "Aussi liquide," 277.

10. Described in a letter from NS to Monique Wittig, 4 November 1977, Wittig personal archive. There are frequent references in the engagement diaries to Insadol and Imudon, medications for mouth infections.

11. Interviews with Dominique Sarraute and Michel Butor.

12. Galey, *Journal intégral*, 760.

13. Vigan, *Nathalie Sarraute, écrivain des mouvements intérieurs*.

14. NS letter to Monique Wittig, 22 January 1984, Wittig personal archive.

15. NS letter to Monique Wittig, 20 May 1984, Wittig personal archive.

16. Lettres reçues à l'occasion du décès de Raymond Sarraute, NAF 28088 (203–5), passim.

17. Huppert, "Nathalie Sarraute," 13.

18. Benmussa, *Nathalie Sarraute*.

19. Ibid., 82.

20. *You Don't Love Yourself*, 89.

21. Ibid., 74.

22. Ibid., 125.

23. Interview with Betsy Jolas. The word *difficile* is used by Théodore Louis in his review in *La Libre Belgique*, 21 December 1989.

Chapter 33. The Last Decade, 1990–99

1. V. S. Byakovsky later included the article in his *Doma i liudi*.

2. Forrester, "Portrait de Nathalie," 21.

3. Interview with Marie Darrieussecq.

4. See chapter 24.

5. Benassis, "Le lien Sarraute."

6. Recorded in the diaries for the decade.

7. Vigan, *Nathalie Sarraute, écrivain des mouvements intérieurs*.

8. Interview with Arno Mayer; Forrester, "Portrait de Nathalie," 21.

9. Engagement diary, August 1991, NAF 28088(132).

10. Marianne Alphant, "Intérieur Sarraute," 22.

11. Causse, *Conversations*, 148–56.

12. Mallet, *Nathalie Sarraute*.

13. Pardina, "Un entretien avec Nathalie Sarraute," 29.

14. Danièle Sallenave, "Nathalie Sarraute: à voix nue," France Culture, 23–27 March 1992.

15. "Traduction d'une conversation de Nathalie Sarraute avec François Bondy," 220.

16. "Un discours autour: Entretien avec Pierre Soulages," *Digraphe* 32 (1984): 111–23 (115).

17. Spies, *Les Chances de ma vie*, 368; two letters to NS from Pierre Soulages, 4 October 1995 and undated, and undated draft of reply from NS, NAF 28088(205).

18. Monique Wittig, *The Straight Mind and Other Essays* (Boston: Beacon, 1992), 12.

19. Viviane Forrester, "Nathalie Sarraute," in *Mes passions de toujours: Van Gogh, Proust, Woolf, etc.* (Paris: Fayard, 2006), 157–80 (158).

20. *Autour de Nathalie Sarraute*, ed. Valerie Minogue and Sabine Raffy (Paris: Les Belles lettres, 1995).

21. Letters to NS from Véronique Pagès, 24 May 1992, and Véronique Montémont, 16 May 1992, NAF 28088(196 and 194).

22. Wittig cancelled publication when Nathalie died in October 1999. The book appeared posthumously as *Le Chantier littéraire*, ed. Benoît Auclerc et al. (Lyon: Presses universitaires de Lyon, 2010).

23. Letter from Jacques Lassalle to NS, 24 May 1991, NAF 28088.

24. Drafts of documents by NS, 20 January 1989 and March 1991, NAF 28088.

25. Letter to NS from Michel Dumoulin, 2 July 1991, NAF 28088.

26. Photocopy of letter from Jacques Lassalle to Michel Dumoulin, 23 September 1991, NAF 28088.

27. Lassalle, "Nathalie Sarraute, ou l'obscur commencement" 43–65.

28. See chapter 24.

29. Grand Prix de la Société des auteurs et compositeurs dramatiques.

30. Photocopy of handwritten letter from NS to Antoine Gallimard, 19 December 1989, NAF 28088.

31. Ceccatty, "Entretien avec Nathalie Sarraute," 19.

32. Sallenave, "Nathalie Sarraute."

33. NS, *Here*, 25, 90. The text was edited by Viviane Forrester for the Pléiade volume.

34. Isabelle Rüf, interview with Nathalie Sarraute, "En art, il n'y a pas de progrès," *Le Temps*, 20 October 1999, www.letemps.ch/opinions/nathalie-sarraute-art-ny-progres.

35. Causse, *Conversations*, 141–42.

36. Letters to NS from Géralde Nakam, 28 March 1994, ff., NAF 28088(195).

37. Interview with Géralde Nakam.

38. "Nathalie Sarraute, 'Mon théâtre continue mes romans,'" interview with Lucette Finas, *La Quinzaine littéraire*, 16–31 December 1978, 4–5 (4); Forrester, "Portrait de Nathalie," 19.

39. It was included in a revised edition of the *Œuvres complètes* in 2011, edited by Valerie Minogue. For reasons of space, its inclusion unfortunately entailed the removal of the accounts of the critical reception of each of the texts.

40. "Nathalie Sarraute: Conversations avec Claude Régy," TV, La Sept, 29 September 1989.

41. Letter to NS from Françoise d'Eaubonne, 21 June 1998, NAF 28088(186).

42. Interview with Jean-Damien Barbin who acted the part of H 1 in Lassalle's production.

43. Lassalle, "Nathalie Sarraute," 26.

44. Interview with Claude Sarraute.

45. Spies, *Les Chances de ma vie*, 362, Causse, *Conversations*, 182–85, and interview with Jean-Yves Tadié.

BIBLIOGRAPHY

Nathalie Sarraute's main books and publications, listed chronologically in order of publication in French, followed by details of English publications.

For a more detailed bibliography, see Sheila Bell, *Nathalie Sarraute: A Bibliography* (London: Grant & Cutler, 1982), and Rainier Rocchi, *L'intertextualité dans l'écriture de Nathalie Sarraute* (Paris: Classiques Garnier, 2018), 841–52.

1939
Tropismes (Paris: Denoël).

1947
"Paul Valéry et l'Enfant d'Éléphant," *Les Temps modernes* 16.

"De Dostoïevski à Kafka," *Les Temps modernes* 25; "From Dostoïevski to Kafka," trans. Maria Jolas, in *Tropisms, and The Age of Suspicion* (London: John Calder, 1963).

1948
Portrait d'un inconnu, preface by Jean-Paul Sartre (Paris: Robert Marin).

1950
"L'ère du soupçon," *Les Temps modernes* 52; "The Age of Suspicion," trans. Maria Jolas, in *Tropisms, and The Age of Suspicion*.

1953
Martereau (Paris: Gallimard); *Martereau*, trans. Maria Jolas (London: Calder, 1964).

1956
"Conversation et sous-conversation," *N.N.R.F.*; "Conversation and Sub-conversation," trans. Maria Jolas, in *Tropisms, and The Age of Suspicion*.

L'ère du soupçon (Paris: Gallimard), including "Ce que voient les oiseaux" ["What Birds See"]; in *Tropisms, and The Age of Suspicion*, trans. Maria Jolas (London: John Calder, 1963).

1957
Portrait d'un inconnu, 2nd ed. (Paris: Gallimard); *Portrait of a Man Unknown*, trans. Maria Jolas (London: John Calder, 1959).

Tropismes, 2nd enlarged ed. (Paris: Éditions de Minuit); in *Tropisms, and The Age of Suspicion*, trans. Maria Jolas (London: John Calder, 1963).

1959
Le Planétarium (Paris: Gallimard); *The Planetarium*, trans. Maria Jolas (London: John Calder, 1961).

1960
"Rebels in a World of Platitudes," *Times Literary Supplement*, repr. in *The Writer's Dilemma*, ed. Stephen Spender (London: Oxford University Press, 1961).

1963

Les Fruits d'or (Paris: Gallimard); *The Golden Fruits*, trans. Maria Jolas (London: John Calder, 1965).

1964

L'ère du soupçon (Paris: Gallimard), rev. ed. with added preface.

Le Silence, Le Mercure de France 1204; *Silence*, trans. Maria Jolas, in *Collected Plays* (New York: George Braziller, 1981).

1965

"Flaubert le précurseur," *Preuves* 168.

1966

Le Mensonge, Cahiers Renaud-Barrault 54; *The Lie*, trans. Maria Jolas, in *Collected Plays* (New York: George Braziller, 1981).

1968

Entre la vie et la mort (Paris: Gallimard); *Between Life and Death*, trans. Maria Jolas (London: Calder & Boyars, 1970).

1970

Isma, ou ce qui s'appelle rien, in *Isma, suivi de Le Silence et Le Mensonge* (Paris: Gallimard); *Izzum*, trans. Maris Jolas, in *Collected Plays* (New York: George Braziller, 1981).

1972

Vous les entendez? (Paris: Gallimard); *Do You Hear Them?*, trans. Maria Jolas (London: Calder and Boyars, 1975).

"Ce que je cherche à faire," *Nouveau Roman, hier, aujourd'hui*, vol. 2, ed. Jean Ricardou and Françoise van Rossum Guyon (Paris: UGE, 1972).

1975

C'est beau, Cahiers Renaud-Barrault 89; *It's Beautiful*, trans. Maria Jolas, in *Collected Plays* (New York: George Braziller, 1981).

"Le gant retourné," *Cahiers Renaud-Barrault* 89; "The Inside of the Glove: Nathalie Sarraute Talks about Her Plays," trans. Valerie Minogue, *Romance Studies* 2, no. 2 (1984), slightly modified from original.

1976

"disent les imbéciles" (Paris: Gallimard); *"Fools Say,"* trans. Maria Jolas (London: John Calder, 1977).

1978

Elle est là, in *Théâtre* (Paris: Gallimard), also including *C'est beau, Isma, Le Mensonge, Le Silence*, trans. Maria Jolas; *It Is There*, trans. Barbara Wright, in *Collected Plays* (New York: George Braziller, 1981).

1980

L'usage de la parole (Paris: Gallimard); *The Use of Speech*, trans. Barbara Wright (London: Calder, 1983).

1982

Pour un oui ou pour un non (Paris: Gallimard); *Just for Nothing*, trans. Kaye Mortley (Newtown, NSW: Barberism & Monograph Press, 1997).

1983

Enfance (Paris: Gallimard); *Childhood*, trans. Barbara Wright, with a new foreword by Alice Kaplan (1984; Chicago: University of Chicago Press, 2013).

1986

Paul Valéry et l'Enfant d'Éléphant. Flaubert le précurseur (Paris: Gallimard), repr. of articles first published in 1947 and 1965.

1989

Tu ne t'aimes pas (Paris: Gallimard); *You Don't Love Yourself*, trans. Barbara Wright (New York: George Braziller, 1990).

1995

Ici (Paris: Gallimard); *Here*, trans. Barbara Wright (New York: George Braziller, 1997).

1996

Œuvres complètes, ed. Jean-Yves Tadié et al., Bibliothèque de la Pléiade (Paris: Gallimard), expanded ed., 2011.

1997

Ouvrez (Paris: Gallimard).

INDEX

Abetz, Otto, 167
Agafonoff, Valerian N., 27
Agapov, Boris, 285, 286, 287, 292,
Albérès, Pierre, 247
Alexander II, 8
Alexander III, 8
Algren, Nelson, 237, 255–56, 257
Aliger, Margarita, 294–95, 363
Aliger, Masha, 295
Allen, Woody, 366
Angremy, Annie, 375–76, 379
Antelme, Robert, 187
Apollinaire, Guillaume, 97
Aragon, Louis, 134, 136, 243, 288
Arban, Dominique, 220
Arendt, Hannah, 257–58, 273, 274–75,
    321, 324, 340, 365
Arland, Marcel, 204, 21, 213–14, 215, 267,
    301
Aron, Jean-Paul, 349
Arrabal, Fernando, 299
Artaud, Antonin, 133, 299
Asso, Françoise, 273, 336, 356, 366
Audiberti, Jacques, 297
Audry, Colette, 177, 178–79, 181, 183, 185,
    191, 194, 207, 212, 227,
Aury, Dominique, 214–16, 226, 260
Austen, Jane, 47
Avedon, Richard, 238, 239, 400
Aksyonov, Vasily, 288, 291, 294–95

Bajan, Mikola, 287
Bazhan, Nina, 287
Baker, Josephine, 101
Baker, Ida, 198
Balzac, Honoré de, 57, 176, 366
Balmer, Jean-François, 350, 359
Banier, François-Marie, 355, 365–66
Barbizan, Gala, 226, 227
Barbisan, Lucciano, 226, 227

Barrault, Jean-Louis, 301–02, 345, 347,
    349, 350
Barthes, Roland, xi, 223, 226, 238
Bataille, Georges, 69, 101, 226
Baudelaire, Charles, 97, 117, 263
Beach, Sylvia, 98–99, 191
Beaumarchais, Pierre-Augustin Caron de,
    360–61
Beauvoir, Hélène de, 208
Beauvoir, Simone de, 33, 130, 151–52, 173–
    74, 177–83, 185, 186, 188–89, 190–95,
    204, 208, 213, 222, 237–38, 242, 243,
    244, 255–56, 260, 263, 266, 269, 272,
    274, 279, 289, 293, 312, 314, 357
Beck, Béatrix, 266, 273, 276, 341
Beckett, Samuel, 127, 128, 159–60, 211,
    225, 259, 276, 299, 308, 371
Beecher Stowe, Harriet, 30
Belaval, Yvon, 206, 266–67, 268, 270, 287,
    310, 339
Bell, Angelica, 103
Bell, Sheila, 354, 356
Belmont, Georges (see also Pelorson), 129
Benmussa, Simone, 301–03, 307, 237,
    349–51, 355–56, 357, 359, 360, 369, 378
Bense, Max, 296
Berberova, Nina, 61, 62, 134
Bergson, Henri, 36
Berne-Joffroy, André, 252
Béthou, Monsieur (French teacher),
    35–36
Bettencourt, Liliane, 365
Bianciotti, Hector, 131, 366
Bely, Andrei, 61, 62
Billard, Claire, 34
Bishop, Tom, 341–42, 350, 359
Blanchot, Maurice, 226, 262, 312, 315, 330
Blanzat, Jean, 189
Blot, Jean (Aleksandr Blokh), 102, 247,
    280, 286, 356, 365

Blot, Nadia, 280, 356, 365
Blum, Léon, 16
Bœuf, Monsieur (student), 46
Bollème, Geneviève, 272–73
Bondy, François, 260, 296, 298, 331
Borel, Adrien, 69
Boretzky-Bergfeld, Nikolai Petrovich
     (Kolya) step-father, 11–12, 13, 14, 17, 18,
     20–21, 22, 27, 31, 38, 51, 59, 60, 63, 80,
     90, 98, 107
Borges, Jorge Luis, 259, 336–37
Bosquet, Alain, 265–66, 277–78
Boucher, François, 367
Bouchet, André du, 109, 128, 189, 270
Bouchet, Hélène du (Comay), 109
Bouchet, Nadia (Wilter), 101, 108, 109,
     128, 143, 149, 201, 229, 269, 271, 280,
     364
Bouchet, Paule du, 282
Bouchet, Victor du, 109
Bouissounouse, Janine, 177
Bourdet, Denise, 226, 227, 235–36
Burtsev, Vladimir Lvovich, 27
Bousquet, Joë, 136, 306
Boylesve, René, 31, 34
Branting, Karl, 24, 25
Brasillach, Robert, 147
Brauner, Victor, 228
Braziller, George, 245–46
Brébant, demoiselles, 30
Brée, Germaine, 253–54, 261
Brezhnev, Léonid, 291, 333
Breton, André, 69, 99, 100, 187
Brik, Lily, 62
Brik, Osip, 62
Brontë, Charlotte, 191
Brontë, Emily, xiv, 47, 191, 198, 338
Brooke-Rose, Christine, 273, 276–77, 280
Browning, Robert, xii, 47
Bubu-les-yeux-tatoués, 84
Burroughs, William, 308
Butor, Marie-Jo, 208
Butor, Michel, 175, 205, 208, 211, 213, 214,
     216, 222, 225, 252, 260, 263, 288, 297,
     313, 329, 330, 353, 356

Calder, John, 245, 248, 249–50, 276, 287,
     308

Camus, Albert, 85, 181, 183, 185, 213
Capone, Al, 256
Casarès, Maria, 351
Castro, Fidel, 243–44
Causse, Rolande, 365, 367, 379
Cavaillès, Jean, 171
Cazamian, Louis, 46–47, 48
Céline, (Louis-Ferdinand Destouches),
     133, 134, 147, 175
Césaire, Aimé, 129
Chaliapin, Feodor, 157
Chaplin, Charlie, 101, 104
Chapsal, Madeleine, 241
Charcot, Jean-Martin, 107
Chardin, Jean-Baptiste-Siméon, 367
Charlemagne, 55
Chatounovskaïa, Khina Perl, also known
     as Polina Ossipovna (mother), 3–4,
     7–8, 9–14, 17–22, 27–31, 38–39, 42, 51–
     52, 60, 62, 65, 67, 80, 90, 98, 107, 113,
     114, 144, 146, 157, 159, 160, 177, 196–97,
     229, 247, 274, 283, 287, 353
Chekhov, Anton, 10, 20, 100, 103, 198,
     298, 340, 343, 378
Chernack, Edgar Abel, 150
Chertok, Léon, 70, 207
Chevalier, Ania, 363–64
Shklovsky, Viktor, 62
Choiseul, Étienne-François, duc de, 34
Church, Henry, 138
Churchill, Winston, 142
Cixous, Hélène, 277, 323
Close, Glenn, 350
Cocteau, Jean, 100
Colette, Sidonie-Gabrielle, 114–15, 136,
     373
Collin, Françoise, 365
Compton-Burnett, Ivy, 249, 250–52, 277
Conrad, Joseph, 11, 99
Corneille, Pierre, 34
Cramaussel, Edmond, 40
Cranaki, Mimica, 205–06, 266–67, 268,
     270–71, 280, 287
Crook, Arthur, 253

Dali, Salvador, 255
Daniel, Yuli, 291
Dante Alighieri, 378

Darrieussecq, Marie, 364
Darsonval, Lycette, 193
Degas, Edgar, 108
Delbo, Charlotte, 179
Demarteau, Edgar, 150, 169, 196, 212
Démeron, Pierre, 239, 410 (note 3)
Denoël, Robert, 132–34, 136, 142, 186–87, 222
Depardieu, Gérard, 344-45, 347
Deschevaux-Dumesnil, Suzanne, 159
Desjardins, Paul, 329
Detaille, Édouard, 39
Díaz Parado, Flora, 244
Dickens, Charles, 50, 191
Diderot, Denis, 360
Dieudonné, Madeleine (Tatoune), 161, 162–63, 165
Dieudonné, Robert, 161, 165
Dobkovitch, Sonia, 81, 160, 229
Doillon, Jacques, 351, 365, 375
Doisneau, Robert, 164
Dondero, Mario, 224–25
Dostoevsky, Fyodor, xiv, xv, 17, 39, 66, 68, 74, 95, 96, 99, 103, 117, 134, 193, 198, 204, 234, 253, 285, 367
Dreyfus, Alfred, 91, 241-42
Drieu la Rochelle, Pierre, 81, 212
Dulud, Maître (lawyer), 84
Dumayet, Pierre, 189
Dumoulin, Michel, 351, 359, 372
Duras, Marguerite (Donnadieu), 222, 226, 248-50, 278, 297, 312, 314, 347-48, 366
Dussollier, André, 351
Duthuit, Georges, 128

Eaubonne, Françoise d', 272, 280, 373, 378, 403 (note 10)
Ebert, Friedrich, 60, 61
Ehrenburg, Ilya, 61–62, 255, 285, 287, 289, 290, 291, 292, 293
Eichmann, Adolf, 257
Einaudi, Guido, 259
Eisenstein, Sergei, 284
Eliot, George, 47, 191
Elosu, Fernande, 81, 142, 161
Elosu, Suzanne, 142
Elsner, Gisela, 260

Enzensberger, Hans Magnus, 295
Errera, Roger, 323
Erval, François (Emmanuel), 186–88, 189, 203, 260, 264

Fadeyev, Alexander, 294
Faguet, Émile, 96
Faulkner, William, 178, 181, 191
Faye, Jean-Pierre, 250, 287, 312, 313, 316
Fellini, Federico, 366
Feue de La Martinière, Charles, 27
Finas, Lucette, 273, 277, 377
Flaubert, Gustave, 10, 254, 273, 331, 338, 340, 359, 375
Forêts, Louis-René des, 226
Forrester, Viviane, 349, 364, 369, 377
Foucault, Michel, 341
Fragonard, Jean-Honoré, 367
Francillon, Clarisse, 207, 214, 235–36
Frénaud, André, 288
Freud, Sigmund, 38, 69–70
Frey, Samy, 350, 359
Friedan, Betty, 179

Gasha (maid), 17
Gadda, Carlo Emilio, 259
Gadoffre, Alice, 208, 365
Gadoffre, Gilbert, 203–04, 208, 219, 220, 240, 248, 275, 299, 334–35, 338, 346, 365
Galey, Matthieu, 264, 308, 344, 346, 347, 357
Gallimard, Antoine, 217, 374, 379
Gallimard, Claude, 216–17
Gallimard, Gaston, 133, 134, 187, 211, 213, 216, 224
Garnett, Constance, 103
Garnett, David, 103
Gary, Romain, 191
Gascar, Pierre, 227
Gaskell, Elizabeth, 47, 55
Gatti, Armand, 299–300
Gaulle, Charles de, 150–51, 318,
Gauthier-Villars, Gilles, 365
Gauthier-Villars, Henry, 115
Gauthier-Villars, Hervé, 115
Gautier, Théophile, 38
Gavronsky, Assia (and see Minor), 359,

Genet, Jean, 175, 195
Genette, Gérard, 371
Georgin, Monsieur (Latin teacher), 35
Giacometti, Alberto, 195
Gibbon, Edward, 55
Gide, André, 69, 95–96, 97, 112, 117, 122–
    23, 128, 131, 133, 135, 138, 152, 175, 181,
    373
Gilot, Françoise, 208
Giono, Jean, 297
Giraudoux, Jean, 100, 133, 147, 226
Giraudoux, Jean-Pierre, 226, 227
Glanville, Maxwell, 257
Gogol, Nicolas, 17
Goitein, Denise, 321
Golding, William, 249
Goldsmith, Oliver, 191
Golovanov, Leonid, 157
Golovanov, Madame, 157, 160
Goncharova, Natalia, 173, 207, 368
Gorbachev, Mikhail, 363
Gornfeld, Arkady, 19
Gosselin, Monique, 365
Gourfinkel, Nina, 207, 257
Grande Mademoiselle, Anne-Marie-
    Louise d'Orléans, la, 220
Grebelsky, Joseph, 160–61
Green, Henry, 250
Gregory, Brian O'Terrall, 49
Gregory, Constance, 48, 52
Gregory, Joseph, 48, 49
Gregory, Sheelah, 48, 50
Grindea, Miron, 203
Gros, Antoine-Jean, 39, 88
Guillaumin, Armand, 34
Guillaumin, Marguerite, 34–35, 39
Guyotat, Pierre, 313

Hadjilazaros, Matsie, 205, 280, 359
Hallier, Jean-Edern, 330–31
Hartemann, André, 188–89
Heidegger, Martin, 189
Henriot, Émile, 223
Heppenstall, Rayner, 248–49, 253, 276
Hertès, Denise, 181
Hertz, Henri, 136
Heurgon, Édith, 334
Heurgon-Desjardins, Anne, 334

Hitler, Adolf, 63, 142, 143, 167, 257, 315
Hoffmann, Dr Heinrich, 60
Hugo, Victor, 13, 36
Huppert, Isabelle, 90, 263, 375, 379
Husson, Roland, 291, 294, 379

Ionesco, Eugène, 204, 299, 300, 308, 349
Ivanova, Tamara, 292

Jacob, Max, 100, 136, 137
Jakub, M. M., 8
James, Henry, 134
Janet, Paul, 36, 68, 74
Janet, Pierre, 36, 68–75, 96, 98, 116, 117,
    334
Jarry, Alfred, 96
Jaspers, Karl, 257
Jaujard, Jacques, 163
Jaurès, Jean, 24, 25, 91, 119
Jean, Raymond, 335
Johnson, Lyndon, 255, 256
Johnson, Mrs Bertha, 53, 54
Johnson, Uwe, 259
Jolas, Betsy, 128, 201, 362, 379
Jolas, Eugene, 127–28, 201, 360
Jolas, Maria, 127, 128, 129, 149, 201, 202,
    203, 206, 228, 243, 245, 246, 252–53,
    271, 280, 293, 311, 360, 362, 365
Jolas, Tina, 128, 270, 281–82, 365
Jordis, Christine, 265
Jouhandeau, Marcel, 180, 297
Joyce, James, 95, 99, 127, 203
Jünger, Ernst, 377

Kafka, Franz, 68, 74, 85, 167, 178, 181, 193,
    194, 198, 214, 258, 308,
Karnow, Stanley, 198–99
Kermadec, Eugène de, 209, 368
Kermadec, Lucette de, 209, 368
Kessel, Joseph, 51, 113
Khodasevich, Vladislav, 61
Khrushchev, Nikita, 283, 289, 291
Kipling, Rudyard, 45, 193
Kirov, Sergei, 123
Knutson, Greta, 208, 368
Koestler, Arthur, 195
Korolenko, Vladimir, 18–19, 22
Kosakiewicz, Olga, 173

Kosakiewicz, Wanda, 173
Kraevskaya, Olga, 285, 292
Kralik, Erika, 359
Kreis, Boris, 229–30
Krementz, Jill, 307
Krupskaya, Nadezhda, 27, 92

La Bardonnie, Mathilde, 365
Lacan, Jacques, 70, 207
Lafayette, Comtesse de, 36,
La Fontaine, Jean de, 36
Lagrolet, Jean, 331
Lamartine, Alphonse de, 36
Lambrichs, Georges, 211, 218, 365
Lambrichs, Gilberte, 365
Lang, Fritz, 101
Larbaud, Valery, 99
Larionov, Mikhail, 173
La Rochefoucauld, François, Duc de, 36
Lassalle, Jacques, 371–73, 376, 378
Lataste, Marie, 102
Leclerc de Hauteclocque, Philippe,
    Maréchal, 166
Leduc, Violette, 177–84, 185, 188, 189, 191,
    193, 195, 205, 260, 306
Lees, Mrs (history tutor), 55
Legouis, Émile, 46, 48
Leiris, Michel, 69, 101
Lejeune, Philippe, 354, 356
Lenin, Vladimir Ilyich Ulyanov, 8, 27, 92,
    122, 123, 293, 312, 316
Levin, Harry, 203, 253
Lévy, Suzanne, 151
Lézine, Mania (see also Péron), 81, 151,
    159, 166, 207
Liber, Lena, (also Gauthier-Villars), 53–
    54, 56, 72, 80, 81, 82, 86–87, 97, 105,
    108–09, 115, 119, 144, 157, 160, 207,
    229, 269, 271, 280, 365
Liber, Moses, 53
Liber, Nadine, 157, 158
Liber, Nahum (Nonia), 160
Liber, Sonia, 160
Liebknecht, Karl, 60
Lindon, Jérôme, 211, 222, 223, 224, 225,
    323
Lobel, Eli, 322
Lonsdale, Michael, 344, 347

Loti, Pierre, 31, 34
Louis XIV, 204, 220
Louis XV, 34
Lowry, Malcolm, 207
Lucas, Mme (café proprietor), 160
Luxemburg, Rosa, 60, 92, 380

Maar, Dora, 208, 368
Magny, Olivier de, 264,
Mayakovsky, Vladimir, 62
Mallarmé, Stéphane, 97, 337
Mallet, Francine, 72–73, 75, 226, 353
Malot, Hector, 22, 30
Malraux, André, 152, 240
Manet, Eduardo, 244
Mann, Thomas, 59, 64–66, 96, 112, 117,
    175, 298
Mansfield, Katherine, xii, 198
Mansour, Joyce, 349
Marceau, Félicien, 227, 297
Margueritte, Victor, 81
Marin, Robert, 186–88, 190, 210
Mary of Teck, Queen consort, 55, 57, 371
Mauriac, Claude, 207, 208, 209–10, 216,
    221, 222, 225, 227, 230, 239, 265, 284,
    297, 306
Mauriac, François, 96, 175, 207, 239–40
Mauriac, Marie-Claude (Mante), 208
Maurois, André, 289
Mauron, Charles, 136–37
Mayer, Arno, 201, 366
McCarthy, Mary, 179, 201, 257–58, 260,
    273–76, 277, 278, 280, 311, 321–22,
    324
Melville, Herman, 191
Merleau-Ponty, Maurice, 151, 194
Micha, René, 214, 267–68
Michelet, Jules, 340
Middleton, Christopher, 340
Miller, Henry, 128
Millerand, Alexandre, 91, 153
Minogue, Valerie, 336, 374
Minor, Assia (also Gavronsky), 33, 34, 40,
    41–42, 79, 80, 82, 90, 95, 122, 149, 252,
    269, 271, 280, 359, 364
Minor, Choura (Alexandre), 41–42, 84,
Minor, Ilouche, 41–42
Minor, Léon, 41–42, 43, 126

Minor, Osip, 40, 41–42
Mishima, Yukio, 260
Modersohn-Becker, Paula, 13, 64
Mokeev, Vasily Lavrentievich, 5
Molière, Jean-Baptiste Poquelin, 34, 35–36, 192
Monet, Claude, 201
Monnier, Adrienne, 135, 138
Montaigne, Michel de, 36, 377
Moore, Virginia, xiv, 191
Moravia, Alberto, 260
Moremans, Victor, 136
Mortley, Kaye, 350, 365

Nabokov, Vladimir, 25, 60–61, 62
Nadeau, Maurice, 187, 223, 226, 235, 299, 312, 314, 360, 379
Nakam, Géralde, 365, 376
Napoleon I, 39
Nekrasov, Viktor, 267, 287, 289, 294
Némirovsky, Irène, 51, 113, 133, 167
Noailles, Anna de, 114

Obaldia, René de, 204
Ocampo, Victoria, 337
Oguse, Sophie, 93
Ollier, Claude, 222, 225, 227, 297, 329
Orwell, George, 250
Orwell, Sonia, 249, 250, 251
Owen, Peter, 245

Painter, George, xiv
Paustovsky, Konstantin, 288, 291, 292
Parain, Brice, 288
Pascal, Blaise, 375, 378
Pasternak, Boris, 62, 247, 288
Paulhan, Jean, 132–33, 134, 138, 139, 141, 185–86, 194, 213, 214–15, 218
Péguy, Charles, 39,
Pelorson, Georges, (see also Belmont), 128–29, 137–38, 140–41
Pereverzev, Micha, 80
Péréverzev, Madame, 80
Péron, Alfred, 151, 159, 166
Péron, Mania, see Lézine, Mania
Peyre, Henri, 253, 401 (note 20)
Philips, Miss (nanny), 44
Picasso, Pablo, 13, 205, 208, 367

Picon, Gaëtan, 204, 240, 264, 273, 281, 301
Pingaud, Bernard, 226, 228
Pinget, Robert, 222, 227, 260, 297, 329, 342
Pirandello, Luigi, 100, 298, 343
Pitoëff, Georges, 100, 371
Pivot, Bernard, 260, 336, 352
Plievier, Theodor, 187, 188
Pogodin, Nikolai, 285, 287
Poiret, Paul, 116
Ponge, Francis, 117, 204, 208–09, 280, 330
Ponge, Odette, 208
Ponson du Terrail, Pierre Alexis de, 31
Pontalis, Jean-Bertrand, 151
Portela, Artur, 228,
Pushkin, Alexander, 123
Proust, Marcel, xi, xiv, xv, 66, 75, 79, 95, 97, 99, 108, 117, 133, 175, 251, 266, 289, 297, 308, 335, 367, 374, 375
Provost, Cécile, 32

Queen Elizabeth the Queen Mother, 57, 377
Queneau, Raymond, 128–29, 134, 140, 141, 187

Rabinovitch, Jacques, 153, 168
Raffy, Sabine, 263
Raillard, Georges, 266, 356, 365
Raït, Rita, 292–93
Rappoport, Charles, 91, 93
Rathenau, Walter, 62
Régy, Claude, 343, 344–46, 347, 348, 350, 377, 379
Remizov, Aleksei, 62
Renaud, Madeleine, 302, 347
Renoir, Auguste, 108
Resnais, Alain, 219, 249
Revel, Jean-François, 274, 275, 379
Revel, Nicolas, 33, 359
Ribot, Théodule, 38, 70
Ricardou, Jean, 329, 331–32, 333, 334
Rilke, Rainer Maria, 13, 16, 64, 98, 99, 108, 117, 135, 175, 258, 298
Rimbaud, Arthur, xi, 75, 117
Riva, Emmanuelle, 342, 345, 347
Robbe-Grillet, Alain, xiii, 211, 216, 219–

23, 225, 226–29, 239, 245, 248–50, 252, 262, 276, 288, 308, 329–31, 338, 342, 347, 349

Robbe-Grillet, Catherine, 219, 334

Robert, Marthe, 228

Roche, Maurice, 313

Rogers, Miss, 40, 45, 48

Roland, Mme, 241

Rolin, Dominique, 138, 315, 331, 366

Rol-Tanguy, Henri, 158

Rolland, Romain, 128, 289

Rosset, Barney, 229

Roubaud, Jacques, 313

Rousseau, Jean-Jacques, 235, 248, 267, 360

Roussel, Raymond, 71, 334

Roy, Claude, 227

Ruebner, Tuviah, 320, 321

Rykiel, Sonia, 110, 116, 337, 350

Rykner, Arnaud, 374, 379

Saillet, Maurice, 135, 138

Saint-Étienne, Madame de (German teacher), 44, 60

Saint-Exupéry, Antoine de, 289

Saint-Simon, Louis de Rouvroy, Duc de, 204, 235, 340, 360

Salinger, J. D., 253, 256, 292

Sallenave, Danielle, 368

Sand, George, 36, 373

Sarotte, Maître (lawyer), 152

Sarraute, Anne (daughter), 109, 110, 127, 128, 154, 158, 160, 162, 163, 165, 166, 202, 208, 359, 360, 379

Sarraute, Claude (daughter), 91, 92, 203, 104, 105, 106, 110, 111, 116, 127, 128, 142, 146–47, 153, 158, 159, 163, 166, 197, 198, 272, 274, 359, 379

Sarraute, Dominique (daughter), 110, 127, 145, 154, 157, 158, 160, 162–64, 165, 166, 230, 319, 360, 364

Sarraute, Gabriel (cousin of Raymond), 306

Sarraute, Joseph (father of Raymond), 90–92, 93, 104, 119, 143, 152, 153, 154–55, 190

Sarraute, Livcha Lourié (mother of Raymond), 90–93, 153

Sarraute, Raymond (husband), 83, 85, 87, 88–94, 95–97, 99, 100–01, 102–09, 112, 115, 117, 120, 121, 129, 132–34, 138–40, 141, 142–46, 148–49, 150–51, 152–55, 156–66, 168, 179, 186, 196, 197, 199–200, 203, 205, 206, 207, 229–30, 254–55, 257–58, 273, 280, 291, 298, 299, 305, 306, 308, 320, 337–38, 341, 356–58, 359, 360, 362, 367, 373

Sarraute, Véra (sister of Raymond), 92, 306

Sartre, Jean-Paul, xiii, 35, 44, 124, 137–38, 151–52, 164, 173–79, 181, 186, 188–89, 190–95, 197, 204, 207, 222, 243, 254, 258, 260, 284, 289, 293, 312, 314, 330, 357, 375, 390–91 (note 12)

Schale, Jochen, 300

Schleiermacher, Friedrich, 40

Schloezer, Boris de, 204, 220

Schweitzer, Karl, 44

Scott, Walter, 191

Scriabin, Alexander, 220

Scriabin, Marina, 220

Sée, Camille, 32

Segalen, Victor, 97

Ségur, Sophie Rostopchine, Comtesse de, 21–22

Sened, Alexander, 320

Sened, Yonat, 320–21

Serreau, Geneviève, 238, 299, 300, 310, 314

Serreau, Jean-Marie, 299

Sévigné, Marie de Rabutin-Chantal, Marquise de, 373

Shahar, Gad, 320

Shakespeare, William, 50

Shatunovskaya, Lola (cousin), 283, 363

Shatunovsky, Grigory "Grisha" (uncle), 8, 16, 124, 283

Shatunovsky, Samuil Osipovich (uncle), 7, 42,

Shattuck, Roger, 339, 340

Sheinin, Lev, 285, 287

Silvers, Robert, 275

Simenon, Georges, 289

Simon, Claude, 221, 222, 225, 227, 260, 278, 297, 329, 330, 342

Sinyavsky, Andrei, 285, 286, 291, 294

Siou, Lily, 297, 301

Smolenskin, Peretz, 8

Sokolnicka, Eugénie, 69

Sollers, Philippe, 297, 330–31

Solzhenitsyn, Alexandr, 260, 290, 291

Soulages, Pierre, 368–69

Sombart, Werner, 59, 63–64

Sorokine, Natacha (Nathalie Moffat), 173, 177

Spatz, Erwin, 321

Spender, Stephen, 249

Spies, Werner, 296–98, 353, 356, 377, 378, 379

Spire, André, 189, 203

Spodheim, Renée, 245

Staël, Germaine de, 182

Stalin, Joseph, 3, 121–22, 123–24, 125–26, 283–84, 285, 294, 315

Starobinski, Jean, 204, 247

Steele, Bernard, 134

Stendhal (Henri Beyle), 193, 266

Sternberg, Josef von, 101

Stolypin, Piotr, 24

Strindberg, August, 164, 297, 299, 343, 378

Szenes, Árpád, 358

Tadié, Jean-Yves, 374, 379

Tager, Paul, 148, 156

Talbot, Miss (Principal of Cherwell Hall), 53, 56

Tchelpanova, Nathalie, 288

Tcherniak, Berta Petrovna (cousin), 283

Tcherniak, Elena, Liolia (sister), 8, 9, 28

Tcherniak, Grigory, "Grisha" (uncle), 8, 16, 124, 283

Tcherniak, Israël Evseïevitch, Ilya (father), 3–11, 14–15, 17–19, 22, 23–30, 39–40, 43, 45, 51, 52–53, 55, 57, 65, 67–68, 71, 72, 79, 83–84, 92, 94, 96, 101, 102, 107–08, 115, 122, 124, 145, 146–47, 148, 149–50, 157, 160, 168–69, 177, 196–98, 229, 247, 287, 318, 323, 341, 358, 363

Tcherniak, Yakov, "Yasha" (uncle), 23–25, 27, 40, 91, 242, 248, 341

Tcherniak, Hélène, "Lili" (half-sister),

Mme Berenstein, 28, 29, 31, 35, 40, 44, 67, 83, 115, 150, 169, 198, 247

Tcherniak, Jacques (half-brother), 40, 67, 83, 115, 145, 150, 169, 197, 198, 341

Tcherniak, Olivier (son of Jacques), 341

Tcherniak, Piotr, "Pierre" (uncle), 124

Tcherniak, Vera Cheremetievskaïa, (stepmother), 26–28, 44–45, 72, 80, 81, 83, 111, 121, 123–24, 177, 196, 198

Tejera, Nivaria, 243

Tennyson, Alfred Lord, 349

Thackeray, William Makepeace, 51

Thévenin, Paule, 299

Thomas, Chantal, 365

Thomas, Henri, 227

Tiepolo, Giambattista, 367

Tison-Braun, Micheline, 334

Tolstoï, Aleksei, 62

Tolstoy, Leo, 16, 20, 39, 103, 197, 253, 285, 289

Tophoven, Elmar, 246, 293, 296, 298, 359, 365

Tophoven, Erika, 365

Toynbee, Philip, 220

Trautmann, Catherine, 379

Trintignant, Jean-Louis, 351

Triolet, Elsa, 62, 114, 134, 136, 191, 288

Trollope, Anthony, 366

Trotsky, Leo, 27, 124

Tsingos, Christine, 205

Tsingos, Thanos, 183, 205, 368

Tsvetayeva, Marina, 62

Tsur, Jacob, 321

Twain, Mark, 31

Tzara, Christophe, 208

Tzara, Tristan, 133, 208

Ungaretti, Giuseppe, 247

Valéry, Paul, 131–32, 190, 192–93, 359

Van Gogh, Vincent, 116, 306

Van Rossum-Guyon, Françoise, 335

Van Velde, Bram, 208

Varda, Agnès, 208, 369

Vérone, Maria, 119–20

Vian, Boris, 300

Vierny, Antoine (grandson), 202, 359

Vierny, Nathalie (granddaughter), 202, 217, 359, 360, 366

Vigan, Isabelle de, 357, 366

Vilato, Javier, 205, 368

Vilar, Jean, 164, 299

Vinaver, Eugène, 57, 204, 250, 372

Vinaver, Michel, 372

Vinogradoff, Pavel Gavrilovich, 52, 55

Vischniac (engineer), 150

Vittorini, Elio, 187, 247

Vogt, Carl, 6

Wahl, Jean, 204–05

Wallace, George, 256

Watteau, Antoine, 367

Weber, Max, 63

Weightman, John, 275

Weil, Simone, 33

Weissman, Frida Shulamith, 336

Westhoff, Clara, 13

Widmer, Henri Auguste, 107–08

Wilter, Nadia, see Bouchet, Nadia du

Wilter, Nora, 81

Wittig, Monique, 202–03, 273, 278–80, 324, 342, 348, 357, 359, 361, 366–67, 369, 371, 412 (note 22)

Wolff, Lieselotte, "Lilo,", 143, 144, 153, 158

Wolk, Germaine, 208

Woog (engineer), 150

Woolf, Cecil, 311

Woolf, Virginia, 47, 50, 66, 98–99, 115, 117, 129, 136, 178, 187, 248–49, 311, 330, 349

Wright, Barbara, 365

Yacine, Kateb, 299

Yassour, Avraham, 320–21

Yesenin, Sergei, 62

Yevtushhenko, Yevgeny, 287, 289, 291, 294

Yourcenar, Marguerite, 138, 352, 373

Zeig, Sande, 359, 366

Zeltner, Gerda, 213, 296

Zonina, Lena, 293–94, 360

Zonina, Maria, "Masha", 294, 360

A NOTE ON THE TYPE

THIS BOOK has been composed in Miller, a Scotch Roman typeface designed by Matthew Carter and first released by Font Bureau in 1997. It resembles Monticello, the typeface developed for The Papers of Thomas Jefferson in the 1940s by C. H. Griffith and P. J. Conkwright and reinterpreted in digital form by Carter in 2003.

Pleasant Jefferson ("P. J.") Conkwright (1905–1986) was Typographer at Princeton University Press from 1939 to 1970. He was an acclaimed book designer and AIGA Medalist.

The ornament used throughout this book was designed by Pierre Simon Fournier (1712–1768) and was a favorite of Conkwright's, used in his design of the *Princeton University Library Chronicle.*